Global Governance

Global Governance

Feminist Perspectives

Edited by

Shirin M. Rai

and

Georgina Waylen

palgrave
macmillan

First published 2008 by
PALGRAVE MACMILLAN
Houndmills, Basingstoke, Hampshire RG21 6XS and
175 Fifth Avenue, New York, N.Y. 10010
Companies and representatives throughout the world

PALGRAVE MACMILLAN is the global academic imprint of the Palgrave Macmillan division of St. Martin's Press, LLC and of Palgrave Macmillan Ltd. Macmillan® is a registered trademark in the United States, United Kingdom and other countries. Palgrave is a registered trademark in the European Union and other countries.

ISBN-13: 978–0–230–53704–0 hardback
ISBN-10: 0–230–53704–9 hardback
ISBN-13: 978–0–230–53705–7 paperback
ISBN-10: 0–230–53705–7 paperback

This book is printed on paper suitable for recycling and made from fully managed and sustained forest sources. Logging, pulping and manufacturing processes are expected to conform to the environmental regulations of the country of origin.

A catalogue record for this book is available from the British Library.

A catalog record for this book is available from the Library of Congress.

10   9   8   7   6   5   4   3   2   1
17   16   15   14   13   12   11   10   09   08

Printed and bound in Great Britain by
CPI Antony Rowe, Chippenham and Eastbourne

Contents

Acknowledgements

This book is the result of several years of collaborative work and as such there are a number of people and institutions that deserve our thanks. The seeds of this project on global governance grew out of an ESRC seminar series on gender, globalization and governance that took place in the Political Economy Research Centre (PERC) at the University of Sheffield and the Centre for the Study of Globalization and Regionalization (CSGR) at the University of Warwick between June 2002 and July 2003. Further workshops and roundtables on this theme were held at BISA conference in Birmingham in 2003 and ISA Conventions in Montreal in 2004. These generated critical and wide-ranging discussions as a result of which we decided to focus more directly on issues of global governance. CSGR generously funded an international workshop on gender and global governance in September 2004 that provided the jumping-off point for this book. Some of the chapters in this book were presented at the ISA, Chicago in 2007 and it was clear from the discussions that this book will be filling an important gap in the literature. All those who participated in all the different seminars and workshops provided us with inspiration as well as critical insights that have contributed to this later work. In particular we would to thank Diane Elson, Eleonore Kofman, Gillian Youngs, Sumi Madhok, Diane Perrons, ThanDam Truong and Maxine Molyneux. Ruth Pearson, who was the co-convenor of the original ESRC seminar series and contributor to the subsequent special issue of *International Feminist Journal of Politics* that came out of it, also deserves special thanks for the key role she has played in the development of our ideas. Thanks are also due to Laura Mcleod for editing the bibliography and to Ted Svensson for making the list of acronyms. Finally, we would like to express our thanks to the contributors to this book who have all worked with us with patience, good cheer and solidarity to make this an exciting project.

Shirin M. Rai
Georgina Waylen

List of Contributors

Kate Bedford is a Research Fellow at the Kent Law School, University of Kent, UK. She was the 2005–2007 Mellon Post-Doctoral Fellow in Women's Studies at Barnard College, Columbia University. She received a Ph.D. in Political Science from Rutgers in 2005. She has also worked on various development projects in Asia, Europe and Latin America. Her current research focuses on the interactions between heteronormativity, international development and gender policy in the World Bank.

Louise Chappell teaches and researchers in the area of gender, politics and rights in Government and International Relations, University of Sydney, Australia. In 2003 her book *Gendering Government* (UBC Press) was awarded the American Political Science Association's Victoria Schuck Award for the best book in the field of Women and Politics. Her recent publications include *The Politics of Women's Interests* (Routledge) co-edited with Lisa Hill as well as articles in *Politics and Gender* and *Global Society*.

Carol Cohn is the Director of the Boston Consortium on Gender, Security and Human Rights. Her research interests are in the fields of Gender and Armed Conflict, Gender and Peacekeeping, Gender Mainstreaming, Feminist Security Studies and Weapons of Mass Destruction. She has written widely on these topics. Her recent publications include, "The Relevance of Gender for Eliminating Weapons of Mass Destruction", co-authored with Felicity Hill and Sara Ruddick, *Disarmament Diplomacy*, 80 (Autumn 2005), 39–48 and "Women, Peace and Security: Resolution 1325", co-authored with Helen Kinsella and Sheri Gibbings, *International Feminist Journal of Politics*, vol. 6, no. 1 (March 2004): 130–140.

Catherine Hoskyns is Emeritus Professor in European Studies at Coventry University and a visiting fellow at the Centre for the Study of Globalization and Regionalization at the University of Warwick. Her main area of study is the implementation of gender equality policies and she is the author of *Integrating Gender – Women, Law and Politics in the European Union* (Verso 1996). She currently holds a grant from the British Academy to study the application of gender mainstreaming in the macroeconomic policy of the EU.

Debra J. Liebowitz is Associate Professor of Political Science and Women's Studies at Drew University in New Jersey, USA. Dr Liebowitz has worked for the past five years doing gender and human rights-related training and research at the United Nations. Her research interests are in the areas of gender and transnational political organizing, with particular attention to human rights, international economic issues, the United Nations and Latin American Politics. She is currently working on a book focused on gender and United Nations human rights agreements. She guest-edited a special issue of the *International Feminist Journal of Politics* (IFJP) and has published articles in journal like *Women's Studies Quarterly* and *IFJP* as well as in many edited volumes.

Elisabeth Prügl is Associate Professor in the Department of International Relations and Geography at Florida International University, the public university in Miami. Her research focuses on international organizations, the European Union and women's labour; current projects involve gender construction in European agriculture and gender mainstreaming in international organizations. In addition to articles in International Relations and Women's Studies journals, she has published *The Global Construction of Gender: Home-based Work in the Political Economy of the 20th Century* (Columbia 1999), and is the co-editor of *Gender Politics in Global Governance* (Rowman and Littlefield 1999).

Shirin M. Rai is Professor in the Department of Politics and International Studies, University Of Warwick. Her research interests are in the area of feminist politics, democratization and development studies. She has written extensively on issues of gender, governance and democratization. Her most recent publications are *Gender and Political Economy of Development: From Nationalism to Globalisation*, Polity Press, 2002, *Rethinking Empowerment: Gender and Development in a Global/Local World* (co-edited with Jane Parpart and Kathleen Staudt) Routledge, 2002, *Mainstreaming Gender, Democratising the State? Institutional Mechanisms for the advancement of women*, 2003, published for and on behalf of the United Nations, Manchester University Press. She is currently working on a manuscript *"The Gender Politics of Development"* for Zed Books. She is the co-editor of the Series "Perspectives on Democratic Practice".

Kathleen (Kathy) Staudt (Ph.D. University of Wisconsin 1976) is Professor of Political Science and Director, Center for Civic Engagement, at the University of Texas at El Paso. She teaches courses on borders, leadership, public policy and women/gender. Kathy has published twelve books, four of which focus on the US–Mexico Border, the latest being

Fronteras No Mas with Irasema Coronado 2002; *Pledging Allegiance*...with Susan Rippberger 2002. Her forthcoming book is titled *Violence and Activism at the Border: Gender, Fear and Everyday Life in CD. Juarez*. Kathy is a community activist and nonprofit board member; she co-chaired Border Interfaith for three years, a coalition of faith-based organizations affiliated with the Industrial Areas Foundation, organizing around social justice.

Jacqui True is a senior lecturer in the Department of Political Studies, University of Auckland, New Zealand, where she teaches courses on international political economy, international relations theory and global civil society. She is the author of *Gender, Globalization and Postsocialism* (Columbia University Press 2003), a co-author of *Theories of International Relations* (third edition, Palgrave 2005) and a co-editor of *Feminist Methodologies for International Relations* (Cambridge University Press 2006).

Georgina Waylen is Reader in the Department of Politics at the University of Sheffield. Her research focuses on gender and transitions to democracy, governance and political economy. In addition to publishing articles in large number of journals including *Comparative Political Studies, World Politics, International Feminist Journal of Politics* and *Review of International Studies*, she is the author of *Gender in Third World Politics* (Lynne Rienner 1996) and *Engendering Transitions* (Oxford University Press 2007) and the co-editor of *Gender, Politics and the State* (Routledge 1998) and *Towards a Gendered Political Economy* (Palgrave 2000).

Stefanie Woehl is Assistant Lecturer at the political science department at the University of Vienna, Austria. She received her Ph.D. "Gender Mainstreaming in the European Union. A State-theoretical Approach" from the University of Marburg, Germany. Main subjects of interest are Gender and State theory, European Integration and social transformation. Latest publications include: "Staatlichkeit und Geschlechterverhältnisse im Anschluss an Antonio Gramsci, in: Buckel, Sonja/ Fischer-Lescano, Andreas (eds) 2007: Hegemonie gepanzert mit Zwang. Zivilgesellschaft und Politik im Staatsverständnis Antonio Gramscis, Baden-Baden: Nomos. Email: stefanie.woehl@univie.ac.at

List of Acronyms

ABAC	APEC Business Advisory Council
AGGI	SOM Ad Hoc Advisory Group on Gender Integration
AOA	Agreement on Agriculture
APEC	Asia-Pacific Economic Cooperation Forum
ASEAN	Association of Southeast Asian Nations
AWID	Association for Women's Rights in Development
BEPG	Broad Economic Policy Guidelines
BIA	Bilateral immunity agreement
BMC	Budget and Management Committee
BPA	Beijing Platform for Action
CAH	Crime against Humanity
CAP	Common Agricultural Policy
CAS	Country Assistance Strategies
CEDAW	Convention on the Elimination of All Forms of Discrimination against Women
CEO	Chief Executive Officer
CICC	Coalition for the International Criminal Court
CIDA	Canadian International Development Agency
CGA	Country Gender Assessment
CHR	Commission on Human Rights
CONAMU	Consejo Nacional de las Mujeres (The Ecuadorian State's Women council)
CSD	Civil Society Dialogue
CSW	United Nations Commission on the Status of Women
CTI	Committee on Trade and Investment
CWHRCS	Coalition for Women's Human Rights in Conflict Situations
DAW	United Nations Division for the Advancement of Women
DAWN	Development Alternative with Women for a New Era
DC	District of Columbia
DDR	Doha Development Round
DG	Directorate-General
DNA	Deoxyribonucleic Acid
DRC	Democratic Republic of the Congo
EAGGF	European Agricultural Guarantee and Guidance Fund

EC	European Community
ECA	Elements of Crime Annex
ECOFIN	Economic and Financial Affairs
ECOSOC	Commissions of the Economic and Social Council
EES	European Employment Strategy
EGGE	European Union Expert Group on Gender and Employment
EMU	Economic and Monetary Union
EOU	European Commission's Equal Opportunities Unit
EP	European Parliament
EPZ	Export Processing Zone
EU	European Union
FAO	United Nations Food and Agriculture Organization
FBI	Federal Bureau of Investigation
FTA	Free Trade Agreement
FTAA	Free Trade Area of the Americas
FTE	Full Time Equivalent
FY2005	Fiscal Year 2005
G-21	Group of 21
G98	Group of 98
GA	General Assembly
GAD	Gender and Development
GATS	General Agreement on Trade and Services
GATT	General Agreement on Tariffs and Trade
GDP	Gross Domestic Product
GDR	German Democratic Republic
GFPN	Gender Focal Points Network
GIF	Gender Integration Framework
HC	Office of the High Commissioner for Human Rights
HSA	Hemispheric Social Alliance
IAP	Individual Action Plans
ICC	International Criminal Court
ICHIMU	Instituto Chihuahuense de la Mujer
ICTR	International Criminal Tribunal for Rwanda
ICTY	International Criminal Tribunal for Former Yugoslavia
IDB	Inter-American Development Bank
IGTN	International Gender and Trade Network
ILO	International Labour Organization
IMF	International Monetary Fund
INGO	International Non-Governmental Organization

INMUJER	Instituto Nacional de la Mujer
IO	International Organization
IPE	International Political Economy
IR	International Relations
IWHR	International Women's Human Right Clinic
MAI	Multilateral Agreement on Investment
MERCOSUR	Mercado Comun del Cono Sur (Southern Cone Common Market)
MGJ	Movement for Global Justice
NAFTA	North American Free Trade Agreement
NAP	National Action Plan
NGO	Non-Governmental Organization
NY	New York
OAS	Organization for American States
OECD	Organization for Economic Cooperation and Development
OMC	Open Method of Coordination
OSCE	Organization for Security and Co-operation in Europe
PAN	Partido Acción Nacional (National Action Party)
PRD	Partido de la Revolución Democrática (Democratic Revolutionary Party)
PREM	Poverty Reduction and Economic Management
PRI	Partido Revolucionario Institucional (Institutional Revolutionary Party)
PRODEPINE	Proyecto de Desarrollo de los Pueblos Indígenas y Negros del Ecuador (Development project for indigenous and Afro-Ecuadorian peoples)
PRSP	Poverty Reduction Strategy Paper
RPE	Rules of Procedure and Evidence
SC	Security Council
SME	Small and Medium Enterprises
SOM	Senior Officials Meeting
SWW	Second World War
TAN	Transnational Advocacy Network
TAXUD	Taxation and Customs Union
TNC	Trans-National Corporation
TRIPs	Trade Related International Property Rights
UCLA	University of California Los Angeles
UK	United Kingdom
UMIST	University of Manchester Institute of Science and Technology
UN	United Nations

UNCTAD	United Nations Conference on Trade and Development
UNDP	United Nations Development Programme
UNESCO	United Nations Educational, Scientific and Cultural Organization
UNIFEM	United Nations Development Fund for Women
US	United States
USA	United States of America
USD	United States Dollar
VAT	Value Added Tax
WCGJ	Women's Caucus for Gender Justice
WEDO	Women's Environment and Development Organization
WICEJ	Women's International Coalition for Economic Justice
WID	Women in Development
WIDE	Women in Development Europe
WIGJ	Women's Initiatives for Gender Justice
WILPF	Women's International League for Peace and Freedom
WHO	World Health Organization
WLN	Women Leader's Network
WPS	Women, Peace and Security
WSSD	World Summit on Sustainable Development
WTO	World Trade Organization

Introduction: Feminist Perspectives on Analysing and Transforming Global Governance

Shirin M. Rai and Georgina Waylen

This book brings feminist perspectives to bear on the analysis of global governance. It seeks not only to understand how global governance is gendered, but also to investigate the ways in which global governance can be transformed. The recent changes in global governance have pre-occupied many scholars as well as activists and policymakers. Since Rosenau's (1992, 1995) path-breaking work on this theme, a plethora of writing has been produced analysing different aspects of the problem of the globality of governance in contemporary world politics. A huge range of questions and issues as well as a variety of different methodologies and approaches can be accommodated under the broad umbrella term 'global governance'. So much so that some commentators even question the utility of the term.

A number of themes predominate. The key shift underlying the emergence of this literature has, of course, been defined as the shift from state-based studies of government to the supranational understanding of the regulation of both the economy and the polity. The increased importance of international organizations (which are often, though perhaps erroneously, referred to as global) has therefore engaged the interest of international relations scholars especially as the reach of these organizations, their institutional profile, their relations with individual states as well as with non-state organizations have changed (Shaw 1997). However, the changing nature and roles of non-state organizations and actors in shaping regulatory systems within and from outside increasingly important global institutions have also become important. The literature on governance covers both the increasingly global language in which epistemic communities influence our political vocabulary and even imagination, as well as their input into framing and legitimizing policy at

the global level (Clark *et al.* 1998). At the same time, new social movements have emerged and become global players – their interaction with
international organizations such as the UN, the World Bank and even
the IMF is evidence of this (O'Brien *et al.* 2000). They lobby, challenge
and support specific causes and also shape what we think about those
causes. The environmental and ethical trade and indeed the women's
movements have been particularly visible at that level (Bretherton 1998;
Liebowitz 2002).

Scholars have put forward a number of arguments in favour of addressing the conceptual and institutional framework of global governance.
Two of these approaches have been particularly influential: instrumental
approaches that suggest that global economic activity needs regulation
at a global level, and normative concerns, which argue that the democratization of national level institutions needs to be matched by that
of international institutions and underpinned by common norms of
human rights as well as of common public good such as health and
food security. Some instrumental approaches have been criticized for
being overly technocratic and managerial in ways that attempt to turn
governance into a depoliticized policy framework. As such 'global governance' often attracts disapprobation as ideology – 'a realignment of
elite thinking to the needs of the world market' (Murphy 2000) dressed
up as a normative framework for analysing world institutions. A third
approach that has recently grown in influence is that of the critical
International Political Economy (IPE). It addresses the key relationship
between states and markets in the context of the processes of globalization (Murphy 1994; Gill 1995; Brodie 2005). Linked to all these
approaches is the analysis of the state, which remains at the heart of the
international system but which can often become obfuscated when we
speak of global governance. Despite this range of issues and approaches,
much of the mainstream work on global governance has been largely
associated with policy studies, political science and international relations and thus has missed the complexity of many of the processes under
consideration.

Indeed, in all this growing body of literature marking out the field
of global governance, there is little attention paid to the way in which
both the processes and the institutions of governance are gendered and
result in an institutional, discursive and structural bias in favour of men
that leads global governance to take particular forms, which affect different sections of society unequally. It is then not surprising that feminist
scholars have begun to challenge this mainstream literature and demonstrate the importance of gendered analyses of global governance, even if

the body of scholarship produced to date is small in comparison to the gendered analyses of globalization (Bell 2001).

Feminism itself has always been characterized by diversity – indeed it is probably more appropriate to talk of feminisms and, as such, a range of feminist perspectives exist. Feminism has been understood as a political movement, as an ideology as well as the basis for scholarship. The emergence of feminism as a significant force within the academy was closely related to the development of second wave feminism as an important political movement in many parts of the world. Many scholars have also been practitioners and activists. Feminists would concur that women are subordinated. Feminist scholars therefore attempt not only to understand that subordination but also to change it even if the analyses and the solutions advocated vary. In the period since the emergence of second wave feminism, a variety of different feminisms have been identified including liberal, socialist, radical, post-colonial, working class, black and lesbian. But for all feminists, gender as a social construct is ontologically central. However, the category of woman is itself problematic. It has been increasingly recognized that intersectionality is crucially important. Other factors such as race, class and sexuality interact with gender differences and cannot be ignored, as relations of power and domination are multi-faceted and linked together in complex ways. All feminists therefore recognize a range of inequalities, including gender inequalities, even if they have different ways of understanding those inequalities. Analyses informed by feminism are therefore concerned with asking what possibilities there are for change in the dominant gender order. Some feminist analyses have focused on the actions of non state actors in civil society, focusing particularly on the oppositional roles played by women's movements in their efforts to change their situation from the outside. Others have focused more directly on strategies that engage with institutions and attempt to effect change from the inside (Waylen 2006a).

Reflecting this diversity, feminist scholarship has long prided itself on pluralism and interdisciplinarity. Within this heterogeneous corpus of work, there are a range of feminist perspectives that use different theoretical and methodological approaches. Many feminist analyses of global governance and related fields such as globalization have been undertaken by scholars with varied backgrounds in international relations, IPE/feminist economics and development studies. Although it is important not to over-emphasize them, there are differences in the intellectual origins and the methodologies and epistemologies that scholars use, as they are still tied perhaps inevitably to their disciplinary origins. Some work, predominantly from an International Relations (IR) background, has been more influenced by many of the humanities debates about postmodernism, language and identity and has often been positioned as post-positivist within the paradigm debate within IR. It is more likely to stress the importance of the cultural and ideational as well as the material, focusing on subjectivity and human agency (often of women activists). Much of the feminist work influenced by IPE/feminist economics and development has tended to give greater emphasis to structures and the material often from a more empiricist position. As a result it has also been more concerned with affecting policy-outcomes and intervening into policy debates and policymaking processes and therefore with engaging with institutions on the inside (Waylen 2006a).

The feminist writing on global governance, frequently coming from an international relations/political science perspective, has already addressed a number of important themes. Its initial focus was on the ways in which women's activism has engaged institutions of governance and attempted to shift their policy parameters as well as opened them to women's membership. The role that women's movements have played in this process, especially through lobbying the UN, international institutions and conferences, has also been highlighted (O'Brien *et al.* 2000; Stienstra, 1994; Friedman 2003). One early contribution in this area that took this approach was the collection edited by Meyer and Prügl (1999), *Gender Politics in Global Governance*. In their introduction the editors outline three key themes in the analysis of global governance: the spaces women have carved for themselves inside the institutions of global governance; the interchange between intergovernmental organizations and states including international women's movements; and contestation of both formal and informal rules and discursive practices that have global reach (Prügl and Meyer 1999). In recent years, another separate – and more institutionally based – strand has emerged to complement the early concentration on women actors outside of the institutions of global governance in some of the feminist literature. In particular, this has examined the struggles around gender mainstreaming both within institutions and policy processes (Hafner-Burton and Pollack 2002; True 2003; Walby 2005a). Issues of political participation and representation as well as the outcome of institutional deliberations have also been highlighted in this growing literature.

But a number of significant gaps remain. As Waylen and Rai (2004) point out in a special issue on globalization, governance and gender in

International Feminist Journal of Politics, it is necessary to integrate the gendered analyses of governance and globalization because if we believe that globalization is not an immutable and irresistible force, our analyses of globalization can only be improved by a greater understanding of the gendered ways in which these processes are constructed and regulated, thereby increasing our capacity to challenge and modify them. Therefore, in contrast to the mainstream work, the feminist literature on global governance also needs to be fully interdisciplinary, incorporating the insights of gendered political economy. In addition, it is clear from the work already produced that feminist scholarship needs to give greater attention to institutions and institutional practices beyond that of the state – a multi-level analysis of the gendered nature of institutions is critical. And to take our understanding forward, this analysis of a range of institutions needs to be brought together with the study of the relationship between social movements and the state. This book attempts to fulfil this agenda by integrating the analysis of institutions and the strategies that can be employed to change them from both inside and outside, thereby investigating both the ways in which global governance is gendered and how it can be transformed.

To undertake this task, *Global Governance: Feminist Perspectives* draws on both the mainstream and feminist literatures to bring together an interdisciplinary and multi-level analysis of global governance within a coherent theoretical framework that can integrate the study of structures and actors to a much greater degree than has happened to date. But there are a number of things this book does not attempt to do. It does not undertake an extensive critique of the existing gender-blind literature on global governance, nor does it explore all the possible areas that could be examined in relation to global governance. For example, although they are important themes that have been investigated by other scholars, it does not consider resistance to different governance regimes or the role of masculinity in any detail because they do not fall directly within the remit of this book (Amoore 2005; Eschle and Maiguashca 2005).

The purpose of this book is therefore to show how a gendered perspective on the key issues of global governance can, through a rigorous analysis, transform both our understanding of these processes and also transform the field of study itself. The chapters advance further the feminist arguments at theoretical, as well as analytical, empirical as well as discursive levels. Underlying this ambitious agenda is a coherent understanding of globalization and governance underpinning all the chapters, an engagement with mainstream arguments while at the same time a grasp of alternative modes of thinking that feminists have brought to challenge these arguments, and most importantly, an endeavour to push further the boundaries within which both mainstream and feminist debates on global governance have taken place thus far.

Underlying themes of the book

A number of theoretical and analytical premises are therefore fundamental to this book. Despite a range of disciplinary backgrounds, geographical locations and writing styles, the contributors to this collection share key assumptions around three important themes regarding global governance. All the contributors believe in the utility of the concept of governance, while being critical of many of its current usages. They agree that the concept is preferable to a number of other approaches, such as regulation theory, which are more specific in their focus and identified more closely with a particular literature and set of ideas. However, there is consensus on the need for a more focused definition of governance than many that are commonly used in much of the literature. It reflects our belief that non-gendered and somewhat de-politicized nature of governance theorization can lead us into political *cul-de-sacs* that detract from the ability to achieve meaningful change. The definition used in this book is one that re-politicizes the concept and recognizes the continued centrality of the state. It moves away from technocratic and managerial discourses of governance towards those which highlight that the state signifies not government or institutions but a set of gendered social relations reflecting but also constitutive of capital/labour/market interaction. To refine this concept of governance, the book also takes seriously the role played by institutions. These institutions might be state legitimated but could also be seen as mediating between state and capital at an international level (such as a supra-state organization like the WTO that regulates in the interests of global instead of national capital regimes for instance).

This collection therefore reflects these common working assumptions regarding the meanings of (global) governance at the same time as individual contributors analyse governance from their own standpoint. These shared understandings include the following:

(i) The political shift from government to governance reflects a need for regulating a gendered global capitalist economy. Here, capitalism is not simply an economic framework, but a set of gendered social relations, which is reflected in and structures the way we produce and exchange goods and services as well ideas and ideologies. The effects of globalization are uneven and fragmentary and set up profound contradictions and counter movements which create possibilities for resistance.

(ii) In line with the above, that governance can be seen as a gendered system of rules and regulatory norms and mechanisms that translate these through the discourses of law as well as policy and thus secures the realignment of the current economic regimes within the neo-liberal framework.

(iii) And finally, that rules and norms of global governance are shaped not only by dominant global economic actors, but also through the mediations of the state between global and national/local capital as well as by struggles, both discursive and material, against the unfolding consequences of capitalist globalization.

Thus underlying this book is a shared belief in the need to histor-icize the contemporary situation as the state has been reconfigured under globalization/neo liberalism. Political shifts have led to the polit-ical narrative of leaking sovereignty of the state, the emergence of the competition state, which formed the background of the discursive move from government to governance; the shift in focus from the state to non-state actors; and a confusion between the importance of relations between structures of power and transformative agency. Finally, the role of international organizations has also been transformed with the move from the Bretton Woods system to a system of global governance, which reveals the consolidation of rules and regulations securing neo-liberal policies, discourses and frameworks essential for the functioning of global capitalism. Also fundamental to this book is a recognition of the importance of gendered links between different international regimes/organizations/institutions, for example, of trade, finance and production; state and non-state actors, the interplay between them and ways in which these are related to the state, materially and discursively. Gender concerns are therefore 'up front' rather than having feminist perspectives as an addendum to an ungendered conceptualization of particular issues or frameworks.

With these shared themes in common, the contributors to this book use a range of different feminist perspectives informed by different dis-ciplinary and methodological approaches. But perhaps inevitably these are primarily influenced by the burgeoning feminist scholarship in fields of IR and IPE. And in common with feminist scholarship in other areas that emphasizes that one purpose of analysis is to help to effect change, the focus of the collection is both on analysing and understanding how global governance is gendered and on how it can be made more gender-friendly. Transformation is therefore a key part of any feminist agenda regarding global governance. The book uses these more sophisticated analyses that combine insights from the mainstream and feminist work to inform the goals and strategies that are/can be used in attempts to transform global governance. And although there is a danger of dichotomizing process and outcome, this division between analysis and transformation is a useful heuristic device. Some contributions consider the range of possible goals/outcomes – from prefigurative ones at one (more strategic) end of the spectrum to more specific (practical) goals at the other. Other contributions discuss the strategies and processes that can be used to achieve these goals and outcomes. Some are more concerned with 'insider' strategies working within institutions and others with the strategies adopted by actors outside institutions as well as alliances that can be developed between those inside and outside institutions. For example, they consider the nature of different entry points and the potentially different roles of advocacy and knowledge networks in achieving change but without dichotomizing the differences between the two. The book addresses the complexity of the processes involved in governance and highlights the links, for example between structural/systemic factors and contingency/agency, at the global, regional and local levels.

The organization of the book

Informed by the themes outlined above, the chapters in the book address three key areas: the theoretical and conceptual issues in analysing global governance; the issues of transformation of global governance from within institutions; and an assessment of the challenges to global governance institutions from the outside through the work of civil society organizations and women's movements. Using a range of feminist perspectives all the contributions deal with both the analysis and the transformation of global governance although the extent to which they examine each of these themes varies between chapters. The chapters at the beginning of the book set up the analytical terrain and the later chapters use the themes outlined early in the book to inform their analyses. The early chapters focus more on the concept of governance as well as its various processes (Rai, Prügl and Woehl). Beginning with a critical analysis of the literature in the field of global governance and how this might be re-conceptualized in the first chapter (Rai), the two subsequent chapters (Woehl and Prügl) engage with different theoretical approaches to global governance in order to make visible the gendered regimes that frame governance. The focus is somewhat different in the next five chapters, as these concentrate more on transforming governance processes and institutions from the inside (True, Hoskyns, Bedford, Chappell and Cohn). These chapters examine the strategies used for opening up new discursive and policy spaces within institutions and reflect upon their effectiveness. The next two chapters (Liebowitz and Staudt) shift the analysis to consider the strategies of transforming governance processes and institutions from the outside through social movements that either resist policy outcomes or try and reform policies and institutions. These chapters are also concerned with the strategic and practical challenges that women's movements pose for global governance, and how in turn those movements may face issues of co-optation and disciplining and their response to these. However, the links between all the pieces are considerable and in the final chapter, Waylen examines the overall possibilities for transforming global governance in the light of the preceding contributions.

Together, the book provides a range of feminist approaches to the analysis of global governance. For example, some take a broadly critical IPE approach (Rai) others use predominantly institutionalist perspectives (Prügl, True and Waylen) while still others are more influenced by Foucauldian conceptualization of governmentality (Woehl). The chapters also focus on different levels of analysis. Some examine the international (Cohn, Chappell and Liebowitz), some the regional (True, Hoskyns and Woehl) and others the national/local (Prügl, Bedford and Staudt) as well as the interactions between different levels (Bedford). In many of the contributions 'gender mainstreaming' emerges as the main strategy that has been used to attempt to transform governance from the inside to date. Cohn and Chappell examine its implementation at the international level, while True and Hoskyns focus on the regional level. They all take a different area of policy in a range of institutional settings: Cohn looks at security in the context of the UN; Chappell looks at international law and the International Criminal Court (ICC); True looks at trade in Asia-Pacific Economic Cooperation Forum (APEC); and Hoskyns looks at macroeconomic policy in the EU. In all four contributions both the potential and the limitations of gender mainstreaming as a transformatory strategy emerge as a central issue. Bedford takes a slightly different focus examining how World Bank gender policy elaborated at the international level is translated into implementation at the local and household level. The chapters (Liebowitz and Staudt) that examine strategies that come from the 'outside' focus primarily on women's activism and its role in the transformation of global governance in two different arenas: trade and the regulation of borders. As the chapters deal with a range of global institutions and policy frameworks, the book as a whole spans the spectrum of the trade, human rights, security, economic and financial regimes that characterize contemporary global governance. This spread allows the book to redress some of the gaps in the existing literature and demonstrate the specificity of the interaction between actors and institutions in constructing and changing different governance regimes as well as drawing out any common themes.

The major arguments and issues

In the first substantive chapter, Shirin Rai introduces the thematic and definitional issues of global governance in 'Analysing Global Governance'. She assesses the competing definitions of global governance and addresses the ungendered nature of these. She outlines the importance of deconstructing existing definitions to show how engendering concepts needs to be part of the transformative impulse of feminist analysis. She does this by outlining the existing literature in three different political arenas: markets, institutions and ideology and argues that we need to add a fourth arena to our analysis in order to better understand the interplay between the three. This is the arena of political spectacle which is used to both discipline and challenge dominant modes of thinking about governance. In doing so, Rai then examines whether the central questions posed in the mainstream literature would be different if feminist concerns were taken as central to these four arenas. The chapter moves from analysing competing mainstream definitions to examining the different feminist analytical approaches to global governance. In doing so, the chapter shows how these approaches, while building on different theoretical traditions, do centre a gendered perspective on governance that allows us to move the debate forward in not only examining the consequences of global governance for women and men but also in challenging the gendered premise of the concept itself. Rai argues that this is important if strategies attempting to achieve a transformation of global governance through, for example, critical gender mainstreaming or women networking across borders are to succeed and to have an impact on different policy areas and institutions.

Elisabeth Prügl in her chapter, 'Gender and the making of Global Markets: An Exploration of the Agricultural Sector', seeks to contribute to the feminist project of dismantling neoliberalism's hegemony from a self-consciously institutionalist perspective, using the case of European agricultural politics to illustrate the ways in which institutions in the European agricultural sector make markets. Prügl's analysis focuses on three institutions: the agricultural exchange regime, the agricultural welfare regime and the rural development regime. Each consists of identifiable rules, some of which have changed with the push to create a global free market in agriculture, the struggle for women's rights and the struggle of environmentalists to counteract the adverse impacts of productivist farming methods. She argues that these regimes are gendered: they produce gendered market agents and gendered behaviour in markets that account for differential outcomes for women and men in terms of wealth, power, and well-being. The paper conceptualizes agricultural markets as gendered institutions and develops the notions of agricultural, exchange and rural development regimes. It probes the way in which gender has informed the rules that make up these regimes in the European multi-level system of governance.

Using a rather different theoretical approach, in her chapter on 'Global Governance as Neoliberal Governmentality: Gender Mainstreaming in the European Employment strategy', Stefanie Woehl discusses forms of global governance from a governmentality approach. She aims to set up a theoretical framework to explain the material effects of governance processes from a discursive gender perspective by drawing on the theoretical background of Foucault's studies on governmentality and a deconstructive gender approach. To illustrate this theoretical approach, Woehl concentrates on changes in national welfare state restructuring in the employment sector within the supranational governance framework of the European Union and its effects on the living conditions of different women. Processes of governance can then be understood as a configuration of social forces that transform state policies and their institutional setting and by doing so alter the workings of the nation state. Within the governmentality framework, power is not only focused on the level of institutions but also on the micro-level of subjects and this increases the possibilities for a gendered analysis of global governance on multiple levels.

Building on the conceptual discussions about the gendered nature of global governance, the five subsequent chapters examine how far attempts to change governance institutions from the inside have resulted in transformations of discourse and policy frameworks. The chapters also assess the weaknesses and failures of particular modes of engagements that have, for the most part, been labelled as some form of 'gender mainstreaming'. In her chapter, 'Governing Intimacy in the World Bank', Kate Bedford charts the policymaking efforts of gender staff in the World Bank – the world's largest and most influential development institution. She analyses those efforts through the lens of governance, attempting to make strange accepted, expert-supported truths of gender policy in order to demonstrate the Bank's involvement in micro-level adjustments of human intimacy. Specifically, she explores the efforts of staff to resolve a core neo-liberal tension emerging in gender lending, regarding paid and unpaid labour, by restructuring loving relations between men and women. Exploring the activities of Bank gender staff in Ecuador (a key site of feminist policy entrepreneurship in the institution), Bedford argues that policymakers attempt to resolve dilemmas between paid and unpaid work by restructuring normative heterosexuality to encourage a two-partner model of love and labour, wherein women work more and men care better. The chapter elucidates the deployment of gender policy expertise on which this attempted governance of intimacy rests, before examining the common-sense assumptions about sexuality and masculinity embedded therein. This discussion is in part intended to re-scale governance discussions, to link the macroeconomic concerns of multilateral institutions to subjectivities, caring practices and expressions of love. It is also intended to track the common-sense assumptions about partnership, love, gender and savagery upon which this policy option rests, and to demonstrate how those assumptions result in governance practices that require feminist contestation.

The next two chapters examine the way in which regimes of governance create as well as mediate gender inequalities, how these regimes are challenged and with what levels of success. Catherine Hoskyns also examines governance regimes at the regional level. In her chapter, 'Governing the European Union: Gender and Macroeconomics', she notes that the European Union has had an overt commitment to gender mainstreaming in all of its policies since 1996. However, despite some successes, the policy has overall been weakly articulated especially in the key areas of macroeconomic policy, which form the centre of the EU's remit and competence. She argues that there are both conceptual and institutional reasons why this should be so and that these throw light on the forms of governance which have developed within the EU framework in the context of globalization and their implications for gender equality. The chapter looks in detail at four aspects of macroeconomic policy in the EU context: employment strategy, broad economic planning, direct taxation and international trade negotiation. These four areas, while they all fall within the general rubric of macroeconomics, differ in the degree of Community competence, the extent to which the case for gender relevance has been articulated, and the characteristics of non-governmental organization (NGO) activity. These different scenarios set up complex interactions between politicians, officials, academics and activists. They illustrate the extent to which economic activity is distanced from its social context, a distancing that is enhanced at EU level by global pressures and competition. So, while on issues of taxation the member states retain veto powers, in international trade negotiation the European Commission has sole competence. On employment the gender case is well articulated and set out in numerous studies and papers, whereas on taxation and broad economic planning the gender case has hardly been made. On issues to do with trade there is an active international campaign within which women's organizations are active; on tax there is a growing campaign but so far women's organizations have been very little involved. These different scenarios set up complex interactions between the leading players. Hoskyns concludes that what stands out is a reluctance to take gender seriously in these areas; a reluctance compounded by the way in which economic concerns are formulated and understood and by the hierarchical and non-transparent nature of EU decision making.

In her chapter 'Gender Mainstreaming and Regional Trade Governance in Asia-Pacific Co-operation (APEC)', Jacqui True examines how through various forms of direct action, civil society actors have challenged the elitist, technocratic decision-making power of trade organizations and held them responsible for the global inequities, including the gender inequities that have apparently increased as a result of trade liberalization. At the same time, regional trade organizations, keen to harness the potential of women's entrepreneurship to expand global trade, have begun devising means for integrating gender perspectives into their economic policies and programmes. In this chapter, True examines the efforts by APEC to integrate gender equality issues within its trade policymaking work. She addresses three main questions: (1) What gender mainstreaming initiatives have been advanced by APEC and why? (2) How do the political, discursive and institutional contexts of this regional organization explain its capacities to promote gender equality in economic relations? (3) How are APEC member states responding to APEC's gender mainstreaming framework and what are the implications (if any) for women's participation in trade policymaking, entrepreneurship and export trade as well as for women's organizing at the regional level? Finally, the chapter assesses the APEC mode of gendered trade governance alongside that of the EU and Americas regions, suggesting a framework for feminist comparative institutional analysis.

The focus of the next two chapters is the different aspects of global security that often fall under the umbrella of the global human rights regime and its regulation. Louise Chappell extends the analysis of global security in her chapter, 'The International Criminal Court: A new arena for justice', by analysing the creation of the International Criminal Court (ICC) as a recognition of the need to develop international responses to inter- and intra-state conflict and for the protection of human security. At the same time, she suggests that it has provided an opportunity to contest the gendered assumptions upon which international law has been based that conceive of women narrowly as vulnerable victims and the dependants of men. This chapter asks, to what extent this new institution for governing international justice reflects its promise, particularly from the perspective of gender justice advocates? It first outlines the conflicts that gender advocates have had with conservative and religious state representatives in their efforts to transform the gendered nature of international law through the ICC as well as the limitations of the court, including the unwillingness of the United States to become a signatory to the Rome Statute. The chapter then assesses the extent to which the ICC statute reflects demands of gender activists in terms of expanding the nature of crimes under international law to better reflect women's experiences of war and conflict as well as ensuring women's representation in the governance aspects of the court. Chappell argues that compared to efforts by women's activists in other international settings, particularly within the UN human rights arena, these activists have achieved a significant measure of success in achieving their goals. She proposes three explanations for their success: first, the 'newness' of the court has helped in opening opportunities for gender advocates. Second, that gender advocates have pursued both inside and outside strategies in attempting to influence the court, reinforcing each others' efforts to ensure that women's access to justice has been placed (and remained) on the agenda. Finally, and most speculatively, that the nature of legal institutions make them more amenable than others, especially government bureaucracies, to the acceptance of new norms, such as those concerning gender justice.

In her chapter, 'Mainstreaming Gender in UN Security Policy: A Path to Political Transformation?', Carol Cohn examines attempts at gender mainstreaming within security seen as a particularly masculinist area of global governance. Drawing on her experiences as a participant observer, she focuses on how in the past five years an expanding group of advocates in and around the United Nations have sought to ensure women's protection in armed conflict, and women's participation in peace processes and post conflict reconstruction. The policy vehicle they have relied upon to move the so-called 'women, peace and security agenda' forward is gender mainstreaming. The transposition of a feminist activist agenda into a bureaucratic policy fix has in many ways been costly, even while it has also produced some significant gains. Using the case study of Security Council Resolution 1325, she explores some of the severe limits of gender mainstreaming as a strategy for political transformation, and for operationalizing policy change. Cohn delineates two analytically separable realms of concern: first, she analyses the ways in which the bureaucratic organization and political dynamics of the UN itself militate against successful gender mainstreaming in security. And second, she situates the conceptual boundaries of gender mainstreaming within a wider, more radical terrain of anti-war feminism, and explores some of the consequences of discursively operating within the narrower, but more politically acceptable frame of mainstreaming. The next two chapters then focus more directly on reforming governance institutions through struggles from outside governance institutions.

In 'Governing Globalization: Feminist Engagements with International Trade Policy', Debra Liebowitz explores the important and often invisible role gender analysis and women's rights advocates play in the governance of globalization. She argues that most mainstream accounts of globalization paint all protestors with one sweeping stroke where their ideas and concerns are under-examined and overly homogenized. Such over-generalized and simplistic depictions of activists contesting the discourses and rules of global governance mean that only certain critiques and critics are noticed (even if they are, in reality only occasionally heard). For example, the concerns of labour union activists, those working on agricultural issues, and consumer advocates are more likely to be noticed than those issues raised by advocates of indigenous, immigrant, and women's rights or racial, ethnic and religious minorities. This chapter examines the efforts of feminist activists struggling to influence the governance of globalization – particularly those efforts targeting the governance international trade policy. She argues that while these efforts have become more numerous, they confront a host of significant obstacles. While the logic behind feminist activist efforts to influence the governance of globalization shares many themes and concerns with the broader oppositional movement, feminist activism is clearly distinct from it. Indeed, the rationale propelling feminist activists to engage the governance of globalization as well as the challenges they face in so doing are different from those of the broader global economic justice movement. Both feminist activism and the larger movement emanate from a critique of neo-liberal economic policy, yet gender-based concerns are often overlooked or marginalized when women's organizations are not at the table. She concludes that since the broader movement is not generally attentive to feminist concerns and, indeed, in some cases, the inclusion of women is token, feminist activists bring a critical analysis to this sphere.

But global governance is also about reading and regulating different borders differently. In her chapter 'Gender, Governance, and Globalization at Borders: Femicide at the US-Mexico Border', Kathleen Staudt argues that globalization, free-trade ideologies, and relatively open borders raise questions about the extent to which the nation-state can or should be the primary accountability institution for citizens and residents. Indeed it is often argued that we can no longer take state borders to be the only recognizable demarcation of sovereignty. While borders have always been permeable the regulatory force of new economic and political regimes makes the poor more vulnerable as they try and cross these old/new borders. The focus of Staudt's chapter is the metropolitan region of El Paso-Juarez, a densely settled population of two million people, and is a case in point, particularly in the high levels of domestic violence and the decade-long murders of girls and women. The chapter is devoted to cross-border organizing around the murders in Ciudad Juarez affecting approximately 370 girls and women, a third of them raped and mutilated. Governmental responses have been limited, for reasons outlined in the body of the paper. Activists have raised awareness with high-visibility, media-dependent events; cultural imagery, colours, and icons; reports and resolutions, though at some costs, including division and co-optation. Staudt examines people's common interests that span national borders, whether borderlands are densely or sparsely populated. She finds that male privilege and peculiar national and cultural patriarchies also transcend borders, manifested in many injustices, including a tolerance for violence against women, from domestic battering to serial mutilation murders. Staudt argues that International Non-Governmental Organizations (INGOs) address gender issues but operate in a space of privileged access and resources that remove them from local accountabilities and grounded understandings of borderland conditions. This chapter discusses the various types of borderlands, in both concrete and metaphoric forms. It then outlines the peculiarity of local governance at borderlands and grounds its analysis in the United States – Mexico borderlands, to assess what factors facilitate and impede cross-border organizing. In conclusion, the chapter raises questions about the extent to which cross-border activists have success-fully challenged (patriarchal) policy paradigms and/or gained powerful voices in governance coalitions.

In the final chapter of this book, 'Transforming Global Governance: Challenges and Opportunities', Georgina Waylen examines the possibil-ities for transforming global governance in the light of the preceding contributions. After discussing what transformation actually means, she argues that it is a complex undertaking involving more than the incorporation of previously excluded actors into structures of global governance. Different sites of global governance offer very different chal-lenges and possibilities for transformation. Because it has emerged in many of the chapters as a the strategy that has become central to many attempts to transform institutions from the inside and has been adopted as a policy goal by many feminists and institutions alike, Waylen goes on to assess the opportunities and limitations of gender mainstreaming. Using the contrasting examples of attempts to mainstream gender into human rights regimes and economic governance, she argues that the political opportunity structure, the ways in which issues are framed as well as the actions of key actors, both inside and outside institutions, are crucial. She also reflects on the opportunities that can be offered by the creation of new institutions. She concludes that transforming global gov-ernance is a multi-faceted task. It needs a sophisticated understanding of different institutions and their opportunity structures. No one strategy can therefore be sufficient to change all institutions and their cultures, making them transparent, accountable and open to previously excluded groups.

This book therefore uses a range of feminist approaches to interrog-ate different facets of global governance. The book demonstrates that a gendered analysis of global governance can enhance our understand-ing of both the key concepts and frameworks as well as institutions and strategies of transformation. The book also explores exactly what is meant by transformation – what are the potentialities and the limits to the transformation of global governance? This complex analysis needs to take place at multiple levels. We must be aware of the diversity within and between various regimes and institutions of global governance as well as the multiple intersections of a whole range of factors such as class, race and sexuality with gender. As a result simplistic answers are not pos-sible. And in order to transform global governance, we need to examine strategies that involve both insiders and outsiders. Feminists need more comprehensive and sophisticated understandings of the various aspects of contemporary global governance to inform their broad repertoire of goals and strategies, particularly of the nature and workings of different international institutions. This book attempts to inform these ongoing analyses and debates and to make a contribution to the growing literature on gender and global governance.

1
Analysing Global Governance

Shirin M. Rai

Introduction

This chapter addresses some analytical issues that are important to the debate on global governance. Reviewing the literature on global governance and the feminist research presented in this and other books, we find that the gender-blindness in mainstream literature skews the analysis towards certain issues, modalities and methodologies rather than others, which are therefore unable to see alternative modes of thinking about and 'doing' governance. This chapter examines the current debates on global governance in order to demonstrate this contention and then suggests how, if global governance was 'engendered', might alternative paradigms emerge. Gendered perspectives on governance allow us to move the debate forward not only in examining the consequences of global governance for women and men but also in challenging the gendered premise of the concept itself. It argues that this is important if strategies attempting to achieve a transformation of global governance through, for example, critical gender mainstreaming or women networking across borders are to succeed and to have an impact on different policy areas and institutions.

Framing the global governance literature

Approaching the concept of governance from a critical gender and international political economy (GIPE) perspective, central to which is not only the engendering of global political economy analyses but also a close attention to issues of South/North inequalities, this chapter outlines, analyses and critiques the frameworks within which global governance is understood as a system of rules for public life. From this perspective, global governance is viewed as a conceptualization of the need for regulation of contemporary gendered capitalism, which is primarily defined as a historically embedded system of production of 'means of existence' such as food, shelter and tools of production as well as social reproduction,[1] of life itself. And that the contradictions fundamental to global capitalism shape the discursive move from government to governance, through struggle between the dominant and the subaltern.

While there are discrepancies between different mainstream frameworks seeking to explain and use this term, some elements remain constant. The global governance literature has largely analysed the governance of polities as encompassing three different political arenas:

1. Markets. The argument is that global markets are now too big, the volume of exchange of goods and services is too high and the complexity of interactions especially in the sphere of finance is too great to be able to be regulated by the state. The linking of local, national, regional and international markets has created multiple sites of both production and exchange, which per force mean that the state is unable to exercise its authority over market processes. At the same time, the primacy of markets has the effect of leaching market norms into political institutions until they become institutional norms.

2. Institutions. Here the argument is that institutions participating in the regulation of the global economy are increasingly of a wide range – from the national state to private agencies. This reflects the complexity of market interactions on the one hand and changing patterns of political actors and their behaviour on the other. Transnational companies as well as transnational movements operate both globally and locally, using increasingly sophisticated media for their work making it difficult for states to always be able to mediate between them or to exercise its authority over them. At the same time state institutions also participate in refashioning the interaction between institutions and regulation of the economy at different levels – local, national, regional and international.

3. Ideology. This has included analyses of how certain ideas attain the status of 'common sense', how the normativity of particular discourses becomes entrenched as self-evident. It suggests the hegemonic dominance of certain epistemic communities – experts, policy-analysts, policy-makers and intellectuals. The literature also takes into account how the ontologies of governance are promoted

through networks of influence and authority as well as how these are normalized through being embedded institutionally through international policies, conventions, treaties and so on.

While noting the ahistorical gender-blindness of these frameworks, which I will discuss below, I would add another dimension to these three in order to understand the interplay between markets, institutions and ideologies and to arrive at a more comprehensive picture of how governance is being used in our political vocabulary. This is the arena of the spectacle.

4. Spectacle. Spectacle of governance refers to the modes of production of meanings through a display of political power such that transgression and disciplining of the other are seen as the exercise of legitimate power. Some cultural norms then become human rights and other human wrongs, consent to and legitimacy of dominant relations of power is then produced for us through performance – international summits, military success of 'shock and awe', participatory modes of politics both violent and peaceful at both local and global levels. The capturing of these spectacles and their distribution is carried through both traditional and new means of communication – the print and electronic media, who circulate images of these spectacles that support the ideologies of power.

Defining global governance

Hewson and Sinclair (1999) have outlined three shifts that have occurred in international relations theory in response to global post-Cold War change: first, in the work of Rosenau, the shift of authority from the state to multiple arenas of governance. The second shift, seen in the work of the UN Commission on Global Governance (1995), Falk (2000) and the cosmopolitan theorists like Held (2002), is the emergence of a global, rather than previously national, civil society. Finally, in the work of Cox they see a review of the work of transnational economic and political elites and coalitions of social forces (1999: 5–8). This body of work is a rich tapestry of analysis of the changing contours of the international system and takes us out of the more narrowly focused, issue-based analyses of regime theory of the 1980s. As such, this shift is to be welcomed.

The various interventions made in the global governance debate predictably cover the entire spectrum – from realism to Marxism to feminism, from converts to sceptics. In this section, I reflect upon some of these debates and the questions that they pose for us. I then examine whether these questions would be different questions, and answers different answers, if feminist concerns were taken as central to these discourses rather than marginal or even neglected entirely.

Brought into political currency by the Report of the Commission on Global Governance (1995), the concept of governance came to be identified with 'global values', 'common rights' rather than the rights and sovereignty of the state in the international arena. The Report addresses the role and potential of a transformative politics of civil society organizations and the non-governmental organizations (1995: 56–57). Its view of security is broader than the security of individual state borders, and encompasses people's human rights, and the need for de-militarization as part of the security agenda (pp. 71–74). It also points out that globalization of the market is confined to the movement of 'capital (but not labour) flows...' suggesting that attention to labour movement might allow us to review inter-state relations as well as create new agendas for global governance.[2] The Commission's approach falls within the liberal-internationalist school which is concerned primarily with illuminating the rational (efficiency) calculus of international co-operation while failing to acknowledge the inequalities of power that tend to undermine democracy' (McGrew 2002: 9).

In his book, *Governance Without Government*, James Rosenau uses the term global governance to emphasize 'rule systems' through which 'we can trace and assess the processes of governance wherever they may occur... the way in which authority is created, dispersed, consolidated and otherwise employed to exercise control with respect to the numerous issues and processes that states are unable or unwilling to address' (Rosenau, 2000: 188). Upon this view, governance thus has been cut loose from the nation-state. Building on the Commission's dethroning of the state, Rosenau's focus shifts to what Held and McGrew call a 'multilayered... structural enmeshment of several principal infrastructures of governance: the suprastate (such as the UN system), the regional [EU, Mercado Comun del Cono Sur (Southern Cone Common Market – MERCOSUR), Association of Southeast Asian Nations (ASEAN) and so on] the transnational (civil society, business networks and so on) and the substate (community associations and city governments)' (2002:9). Thus, this understanding of global governance filters the debates on the changing nature of the state into a broader thematic ordering of the global political economy.

Marxist scholars have shied away from the term 'governance' but have had to engage with the concept. Marxists have looked to the earlier debates on imperialist competition to understand the current political economy. The crisis-ridden capitalist system is the arena where advanced capitalist states compete for markets and resources leading to the current hegemony of the United States. Gill argues, for example, that global governance discourses and institutions are engaged in normalizing US regulatory power globally (1995). Developing further this interface of hegemony and imperialism as well as of Marxist materialism and post-structuralism Hardt and Negri argue in their book *Empire* (2000): 'In contrast to imperialism, Empire establishes no territorial centre of power and does not rely on fixed boundaries or barriers. It is a *decentred* and *deterritorialised* apparatus of power that progressively incorporates the entire global realm within its open, expanding frontiers' (pp. xi–xii; emphasis in the original). Others have noted that a convergence of institutional political discourses of governance embedded in global organizations such as the UN and the World Bank and IMF secures the hegemonic position of the United States and provide the framework for the further expansion of the processes of capital accumulation worldwide (see Panich and Gindin 2005).

One critical, post-structuralist thinker whose work is increasingly making an impact on governance debates is Michel Foucault. His lectures on what he calls governmentality are being used to understand how the institutional form of the state, 'governing' and the 'mentality' that that form both creates and is itself stabilized through, mesh together. Governmentality thus allows us to reflect upon the effects of domination generated by the everyday governance of the state: 'It plays a decisive role in his analytics of power in several regards: it offers a view on power beyond a perspective that centers either on consensus or on violence; it links technologies of the self with technologies of domination, the constitution of the subject to the formation of the state; finally, it helps to differentiate between power and domination' (Lemeke 2000). However, critics have also pointed out that governmentality, with its emphasis on individual subjectivity and technologies of dominations, dilutes the place of the state in the theorization of governance (Hunt and Wickham 1994).

While these major strands of governance theory bring a great deal of sophisticated analysis to bear upon the changing nature of state and governance, all are predominantly 'gender blind' as well as 'race blind' or at best addressed the issues of gender and race in the context of the impact of the various political economic shifts on the lives of women and people of colour. And further, that all focus on the governance of polities rather than of communities, which means that the relational link between the private and the public, the civic and the intimate, at the heart of feminist analyses remains unrecognized.

Different feminist approaches to global governance have addressed this gap by engendering these debates. As pointed out in the *Introduction*, feminist work is diverse in its approach to issues of governance, ranging as in this book, from political economy to institutionalist, to post-structuralist perspectives. However, all feminist work is aware of differences among women – on grounds of race, class and sexuality – as well as between men and women, and brings this key insight to bear on the analyses of global governance. First, feminists have focused on institutional structures and processes: gender in global governance is seen as 'involving institutional structures in which women have found or carved out niches for themselves and their interests as women' and therefore 'introduce into global governance women-centred ways of framing issues...' (Meyer and Prügl 1999: 4–5), however contested these might be on grounds of differences of interests among women. Second, feminists approach global governance through critical gender politics 'exploring the purposive, goal-oriented... social-movement strategies to influence the United Nations...' and Bretton Woods institutions (p. 5; also see O'Brien *et al.* 2000). Finally, feminists have approached gender politics in the context of global governance as 'contestations of rules and discursive practices in different issue areas' (Meyer and Prügl 1999: 5). If these insights of feminist and critical scholars and activists are taken into account, it becomes possible to assess the nature of gendered global institutions as based on market principles, promoting market-based solutions to social and political problems and stabilizing these solutions with the support of dominant epistemic elites (Taylor 2000). Thus, in analysing the constitutive parts of governance, as noted above, a feminist analysis can deepen, historicize and engender the debates on the governance of markets, the changing role of the state, the ideologies of governance and governance as spectacle.

Governance of markets

Markets lie at the heart of capitalist social relations. These are the arenas of exchange of goods and services, and it is the globalization of these arenas that have posed challenges to regulatory systems, states and governance institutions. While mainstream critical IPE theorists have focused on the unevenness of the market arena in the context of global capitalist social relations by examining the relative positions of states, extending production chains and the role of transnational corporations, feminists have argued that markets are socially embedded institutions and roles 'within market systems are structured by non-market criteria' (Harriss-White 1998: 201).

These non-market, though clearly not non-economic, criteria lead to specific gender-based distortions in the markets (see Palmer 1992; Elson 1995; van Staveren 2001). In the market system, participants come to specific markets with unequal capabilities and bargaining capacities and resources as a result of and which inhere in unequal market structures, regulated and stabilized by gendered state formations, and characterized by more or less unequal power – class, race and gender are three bases for unequal power relations operating in the market. Evans argues that 'the power to threaten or disrupt economic relationships beyond the para- meters of principal-agent relations is the kind of extra-economic coercion or influence that the neo-classical model fails to make explicit' (Evans 1993: 25). It thus fails to take into account the embedded nature of the markets. It does not query that individuals can pursue their economic self-interests in ways that has nothing to do with the 'best price'. Neither do they question the 'degree to which self-interest places economic goals ahead of friendship, family ties, spiritual considerations, or morality' (Block 1990: 54). Nor, indeed how reproductive roles might change in the playing out of market roles (Harriss-White 1998). Finally, there is an assumption that instrumentality in decision-making goes hand in hand with obedience to rules, and with maximizing interests, rather than a set of signals that can lead to conflictual economic and social behaviour in different groups of populations. The social embeddedness of markets is therefore not considered, other than as a distortion, by neo-classical economists. Together this brings into question the assumed neutrality on the basis of class, race as well as gender and other cleav- ages of inequality of markets in terms of access, competitiveness and efficiency.

Markets, however, are stabilized and institutionalized not only in the functioning of global capitalism but also through the institutions of global governance. This, through the processes of 'new constitutional- ism' – in contrast to traditional constitutionalism that is associated with the state – which 'can be defined as the political project of attempt- ing to make transnational liberalism, and if possible liberal democratic capitalism the sole model for future development' (Gill 1995: 412). It is in this project that institutions of global governance – the IMF, the World Bank and the WTO – become stronger vis-à-vis the state, that are presented as neutral players seeking maximum economic efficiency for all through attempting to ensure 'fair dealing' in the markets.[3] These institutions also symbolize the separation of the economic from the political, thus taking the heat out of macroeconomic policy-making. Within the framework of neo-liberalism 'good governance' is then associated with the qualities deemed by global governance institutions to emphasize the discipline of the market, and those that enhance that discipline through increasing transparency and accountability of the state. Law is an important framework for institutionalizing market neo-liberalism providing a set of enforceable rules known in advance, with mechanisms ensuring application of the rules. It allows conflicts arising between parties to be decided through binding decisions of an independent body and ensures that 'there are procedures for amending the rules when they no longer serve their purpose' (World Bank 1992: 30). Rules, then, are critical to 'good governance' – rules that stabilize neo-liberalism through state law, but which are disciplinary in the global sense. In the current phase of globalization, markets are seen not only as central to resource competition and allocation in the sphere of private capital, but also as central to state and governance institutions more generally. This has led critical theorists to speak of marketized institutions (Hewson and Sinclair 1999: 17).

Feminist scholars and activists have noted with alarm that even within public institutions there is a tendency towards adopting market principles of organization in the performance of their public roles. They have outlined various implications for public policy. First, without gender-sensitive indicators the allocative process cannot be an efficient one. Second, lack of gender-sensitive indicators fails to recognize the importance of the role of women in the labour market, leading to inequities which are overlooked and not addressed by policy-making (DAW 1999: 7). Third, discrepancy between the increasingly unfettered flow of capital and the highly regulated movement of labour further affects the gendered nature of inequality under global capitalism.[4] Fourth, the development discourse under globalization, with the individual market agent central to it, also requires us to take seriously the ways in which men and women of different social classes and races are able to access and play the market in order to enhance their life-chances, or standards of living. And finally, the state is an active player in restructuring not only the national gendered labour–capital relations in response to new pressures of globalization, but also reorganizing its own regulatory and political boundaries to protect its position within the globalized political economy.

Governance institutions

Mainstream global governance literature starts with the assumption that the state is no longer capable of addressing the issues arising from the global reach of capitalism whether these are related to competition in and regulation of the market, or to maintaining rules within its borders in order to resolve the collective problems of its citizens. From the argument outlining the 'leaking sovereignty' (Strange 1995) of the state to its 'lost' sovereignty (Cable 1995) the state is seen to be incapable of addressing the needs of global capitalist economy. The diffusion of trade and finance is also diminishing the erstwhile centralized authority of the state.

This analysis of the 'leaking sovereignty' of the state is reflected in the discourse of the dysfunctional state in another context. One of the early interventions in the global governance debate was indeed made by one of the primary institutions involved in the 'governance' of global economic rules – the World Bank. In its 1990–1992 World Development Report, the Bank set out the case against the state. The state was, in line with the rhetoric of resurgent liberalism, the problem not the solution; the state hindered the expansion and functioning of markets that was a key to the stabilization of the world economy. Too much government was stifling the energies of entrepreneurs waiting to take advantage of expanding markets. 'Weak institutions – tangled laws, corrupt courts, deeply biased credit systems, and elaborate business registration requirements – hurt poor people and hinder development…' according to the World Development Report on Building Institutions for Markets (World Bank 2002: http://econ.worldbank.org/wdr/WDR2002). This does not seem like a weak state, but a dysfunctional one. The question then was whether the state could respond to the new pressures of global political economy and if so, what should be the parameters of its functioning? While the state continues to suffer within hegemonic discourse of governance under globalization, both realist and Marxist scholars challenge this position.

The realists emphasize the continued centrality of the state by asserting 'the absence of a legitimate authority to which states are subordinate and give allegiance' (Gilpin 2002: 237). Upon this rather well-rehearsed position, the state and its interests – security and independence – continue to hold supreme and determine national behaviour. Therefore, the attempts by theorists of governance to disentangle (state) government from (supra-state) governance are misguided and do not reflect the power that states continue to wield. They also point the 'democratic deficit' that will inevitably arise if such disentanglement is allowed especially in the context of 'the increasing mismatch between the distribution of authority within and among existing institutions and the changing distribution of power in the international system' (Gilpin 2002: 242). The 'new medievalism' (Hedley Bull 1977) which argues that national sovereignty is at an end is also rejected. While networks of policy-making bodies might challenge the monopoly over information that the states used to hold, realists argue that the role of NGOs and other policy-making bodies is so recent that the 300-year-old state cannot be effectively challenged, even though some of its functions might be supplemented by these new organizations (pp. 243–244). For the realists, the clearest rejection of the governance discourse comes from asking question of power: '... governance for what? What are the social, political and economic purposes that governance is to serve? Unless these issues can be resolved, proposals for international governance must be greeted with considerable scepticism' (Gilpin 2002: 246).

A similar question is asked by the Marxists and neo-Marxists but from within a very different theoretical framework. They emphasize that class-based production and appropriation of value produced need regulation by the state. Such a starting point does allow the possibility of the state to be displaced by governance institutions so long as they can play the same role in the global political economy as the state. Marxists do not find this a possibility: 'National states exist as political "nodes" or "moments" in the global flow of capital' and that their development is part of the crisis-ridden development of capitalist society (Burnham 1999: 8). Upon this view then, the recent changes in the global political economy are analysed as being predominantly about reorganizing states rather than by-passing them, with 'state managers' actively attempting to restructure, and respond to, 'a crisis of labour/capital relations' (p. 8). One of the most innovative analyses of the national state from a neo-Marxist position is that of Robert Cox who argues that what we are witnessing is not the demise of the nation-state but its 'internationalization'; not its destruction but its transformation. In brief, Cox argues that from being bulwarks against the global intrusions into national economies, today's states are becoming mediators, adapters and negotiators with the global political economy. To perform this changed role they have to reconfigure the power structures of government, giving far more emphasis to the role of finance and trade in economic regulation rather than industry and labour, for example. The state's role, therefore, becomes one of helping to adjust the domestic economy to the requirements of the world economy (1996). In a sympathetic critique of this position, Burnham points out that Cox's analysis 'underplays the extent to which "globalization" may be authored by states and regarded by state agents (both liberal market and social democrat) as one of the most efficient means of restructuring labour/capital relations to manage crisis in capitalist society' (1999: 5) In this context, the nostalgia for a benign or at the very least powerless, nation-state is clearly misplaced. And furthermore, that this aspect of the internationalization of the state points to the current contradictions in globalization as to extract surplus globally, capital depends on national and global public goods provision while at the same time reducing the capacity of states to generate tax revenue, and by putting them under the discipline of neo-liberalism through structural adjustment policies, to provide those 'public goods'. Thus, Panich and Gindin argue, 'It is in these terms that we should conceptualize the "relative autonomy" of the capitalist state: not as being autonomous from capitalist classes or the economy, but rather in having capacities to act on behalf of the system as a whole (autonomy), while their dependence on the success of overall accumulation for their own legitimacy and reproduction nevertheless leaves those capacities bounded (relative).' (2005: 102) If the state is a participant in the reconstitution of its own relations with the global political economy, then it continues to be a focus for the struggles against this changing relation – whether it is from (dis)organized labour in the urban or the rural context or whether it is from other social movements.[5]

Engaging with deconstructing the concept of the state in the light of political engagements both with and against the state, feminist theorists have brought many insights to bear on the 'state debate'. One of the most important insights is that gendered social relations are constitutive of the state while at the same time, the state is crucial to the continued dominance of patriarchal relations of social production and reproduction (Pringle and Watson 1990; Rai 1996; Randall and Waylen 1997). It has been argued that 'group interests do not pre-exist, fully formed, to be simply "represented" in the state ... they have to be continuously constructed and reproduced. It is through discursive strategies, that is, through creating a framework of meanings, that interests come to be constructed and represented in certain ways' (Pringle and Watson, 1990: 229–230). In this context, Polanyi's concept of embeddedness[6] becomes useful to analyse not only the market, his original concern, but also the state. In this context of embeddedness, an examination of how different state fractions relate differently to each other, and to other civil and economic groups in post-colonial states and diverse cultural milieus becomes important (Rai 1996). Post-colonial feminist theorists working in the broad field of international relations have further complicated our understanding of states, globalization and governance both by critiquing the discipline as well as proposing radically alternative ways of approaching a more inclusive 'worldism' (Agathangelou and Ling 2004).

Women's movements have been grappling with this changing role of the state. As the sites of production and reproduction shift within states, as new regimes of production make for different forms of work – part-time, flexible, concentrated in Export Processing Zones (EPZs), migratory – women have to organize differently. As global capital's presence is felt directly, less mediated through the state, and as local spaces are opened up to the forces of market, the challenges to global economic forces and organizations are also posing issues of political discourse and mobilization for women. While the state continues to be a central focus of women's mobilization on various issues, supra-territorial strategies are being increasingly employed in order to either counter the state, to delegitimize its position, or to mobilize global discursive regimes in their interests. This is because the relationship between a modernizing state and a civil society, within which it is configured, is a complex one. In this context, to view the state as a unitary entity becomes paralysing, and regarding civil society as 'a space of uncoerced human association' perilous (Rai 1996: 17–18).

The analysis of the changing role of the state also gave impetus to the discourse of democratization of the state. As part of the liberal convergence of post-Cold War politics, democratization came to be linked to economic development. It built on a return to the classical liberal theoretical traditions where markets were central and the free-contracting individual the preferred economic actor on the one hand and the resurgence of neo-liberal economic panacea of opening up economies to international trade on the other. However, this literature did pay attention to the multi-level analysis of the international system on the one hand and the state and civil society relations on the other, which was to become a hallmark of the governance debate (Rueschemeyer *et al.* 1992). For Marxist scholars democratization is the form that the capitalist state takes under the current regime of globalization – a distancing or depoliticization of the state through law of property and liberal democracy (Burnham 1999; Panich and Gindin 2005).

Feminist studies of transitional and democratizing states focused on the impact of liberalising economies and the marketisation of the state on women's lives (Einhorn 2000) as well as considered how women can engage the state in a globalizing context where the state is coming under multiple pressures and is repositioning itself in different ways in different contexts (Jaquette and Wolchik 1998; Eschle 2000; Rai 2000, 2002;

Blacklock and Macdonald 2002; Waylen 2007). If the state is a participant in the reconstitution of its own relations with the global political
economy, then it continues to be a focus for the struggles against this
changing relationship – whether it is from unorganized labour in the
urban or the rural context, or whether it is from other social movements. The nation-state as the focus of developmental struggles allows
historical knowledges of traditions, cultures and political contexts to
be mobilized with greater facility than the amorphous 'international
economic institutions' peopled by shadowy figures not visible to the
local oppositional struggles. Thus, state accountability and the space
for political participation for both men and women form an important part of the understanding of governance for many women's groups
(Tambiah 2002). Taking political institutions seriously has meant that
feminist scholars and activists have taken seriously the participation in
political institutions. They have insisted upon the importance on representation of women in these institutions from different standpoints –
that women do politics differently/better, or that it is just that historically excluded groups be allowed a say in the 'governing' that affects their
lives. Strategizing for this, feminists have argued for quotas for women in
political institutions in order to make women more visible and audible
in political processes. They have also engaged with political institutions
by participating in bureaucracies, policy-making bodies and representative organizations under the broad principles of gender mainstreaming
(Razavi and Miller 1995; McBride Stetson and Mazur 1999; Rai 2003).

If the realists, the Marxists and the feminists hold on to the state as
a centre piece in the international system and of global capitalism, the
liberal internationalists do not shy away from cutting loose from the
state or at least from envisioning a post-statist world order. McGrew
notes four presumptions of liberal internationalism: first, that reason
and rationality are necessary and sufficient requirements for the effective
conduct of international affairs. Second, the growing interdependence
of states promote international regulation. Third, international institutions promote peace by creating international norms to which both the
powerful and the less-powerful countries accede and by creating new
mechanisms for managing inter-state conflict. And finally, liberal internationalism has aspirations towards 'the improvement of the human
and global condition' (2002: 268).

The liberal institutionalist literature addresses some of these concerns
by examining the consequences of the rise of global institutions. On the
one hand, the various interventions focus on the need for conceptu-
alizing alternatives to state institutions of government in the context

of the global political economy. On the other hand, the literature focuses on addressing the democratic deficit of the global institutions themselves. How can these institutions be made more accountable in a context where they seem to be usurping the power of the state (Woods 2002)? The effectiveness of global institutions, especially the UN system and the Bretton Woods institutions, are evaluated and found wanting leading to prescriptions of reform. New governance institutions are recommended to regulate actors and issues emerging as key in a globalized world, such as mechanisms of consultation, surveillance and co-ordination of macroeconomic policies, an 'international financial architecture' stabilized through global institutions and the regulation of capital [Trans-National Corporation (TNCs)] and labour (migration) (Nayyar and Court 2002: vii–xi). Democratic deficit of old international institutions is identified as a reason for attempting to reform the global governance regime.

While engaging with important issues and providing some useful insights, the mainstream literature both from the liberal and the Marxist positions remains predominantly 'gender blind'. At best it addresses gender issues in the context of the impact of the various political economic shifts on the lives of women. There is no systematic analysis for example of the ways in which different women's labour is crucial to capital accumulation under the pressures of globalization. The questions that feminists have asked in challenging the discipline of international relations and its subjects of study are fundamentally different – of inter-subjectivity rather than sovereignty; of agency grounded in both understandings of identity and structural power, of critical syncretic engagement rather than dominant notions of legitimacy – because in asking different questions about governance they also allow us different visions of alternative modes of governing (Agathangelou and Ling 2004: 44).

Governance as ideology

The stabilization of markets, and also of marketised institutions, requires this third form of governance. Governance as ideology is produced and circulated through hegemonic discourses, educational institutions and media, both traditional and digital. Critical scholars have pointed to the ways in which epistemic authority secures the neo-liberal discourse by evoking images of knowledge-based manegerialism, which if allowed access to governance channels, results in efficiency gains based on objective problem-solving approaches to the challenges of globalization (Gill 1995; McMichael 2000; Baxi 2002; Rai 2002). The hegemonic dominance of certain professional communities – experts, policy-analysts and policy-makers, intellectuals – at multiple levels of governance can be assessed by focusing on the construction of epistemic authority. Such authority then reinforces the ideological message through research, dissemination of that research through seminars, publications and policy networks (Rai 2004).

Governance as ideology is mapped out early in the 1980s in key texts articulating liberal triumphalism in the discourse of convergence after the 'fall of the Wall'. In these sketches of the world system in late twentieth century, liberal values triumph over others; aspects of western civilization over other cultures and modernity's concerns are resolved through these triumphs. Struggles within the parameters of other cultures, religions and ideologies, upon this envisioning, are doomed to failure unless they recognize the impossibility of reform from within. The logical conclusion then is that a liberal world is the only future that we can 'rationally' look forward to if we wish to live civilized, non-violent and democratic lives (Fukuyama 1991; Barber 1996; Huntington 1996). The 'clash of civilisations' scenario takes on tremendous force in the context of the September 11 attacks upon the World Trade Centre, and the idea of governance faces its first major challenge. The 'war on terror' has become a part of the governance discourse – Afghanistan and Iraq both become examples of an active engagement with the politics of convergence. Non-liberal regimes, especially those that defy rather than work with western 'civilization' become legitimate targets of attack and reconfiguration. This western civilization is also a 'market civilisation' (Gill 1995: 399) where the individual competes for resources in the market and where the market civilization 'tends to generate a perspective on the world that is ahistorical, economistic, materialistic, "me-oriented" short-termist, and ecologically myopic"' (ibid.). Democratic regimes, while being the only acceptable face of governance, are finding space to enact 'anti-terrorist legislation', which undermines the principles of democratic rights for individual citizens. At the same time, the image of the 'woman' behind the veil is constantly invoked to suggest the trope of rescue.

Three different strands become visible when we examine the context in which 'governance' emerged as discourse. First was the collapse of the Soviet Union and the beginning of the post-Cold War period in the international system, and building on this was the convergence of economic policies under globalization within the liberal and neo-liberal framework. Second, as a consequence of the collapse of 'communism' and the rise and dominance of the neo-liberal framework in the global economy, was a re-examination of the role of the state in the context of the post-Cold War globalization. And third, the emergence of the discourse of democratization as the most appropriate framework within which both political and economic transitions could be accomplished – democracy became the bulwark against both forms of totalitarianism as well as the return to state-managed economies. The concept, indeed ideology, of global governance has come to take account of all these three strands.

For most critical governance theorists, such as the contributors to this book, neo-liberal economic theory is the ascendant framework for policy-making today. Building on classical liberal economic theory and challenging what Ruggie has called 'embedded liberalism' or Keynesian welfare economics of the 1930s, which were the bases of the European welfare state models, the neo-liberals posit the centrality of the markets in the economy. The discourse of neo-liberalism, then emphasizes, and indeed normalizes, the 'efficiency, welfare and the freedom of the market, and self-actualisation through the process of consumption' (Gill 1995: 401) even though the outcomes of these policies are contradictory, hierarchical and inefficient to protect human life and the world in which we live. This discourse of the market also has another message – if market-based competition is the most efficient way of allocating resources in society, then any attempts to interfere in its functioning would be per se inimical to the 'greater good'. As we have seen above, any attempts by the state to regulate markets then become scrutinized through the concerns of the economic actors that occupy the dominant positions within the market. In his critique of the work of the Commission on Global Governance, Baxi comments on the discrepancy between the assumptions of globality by the Commission and the 'central facts of contemporary world disorder' (1996: 530). Violence and poverty in particular are growing apace, and both affect women in particular ways. The feminisation of poverty and violence against women in creating and policing new and old inter-state borders has made this co-operative development a fraught discourse for women. In this context, Baxi rightly comments that 'If governance is to be conceived as a process, it is well to recall that process is permeated by structures-in-dominance, both in states and civil societies.' (p. 532)

Governance as ideology requires the validation by epistemic communities – researchers, academics, policy-advisers – as gatekeepers of disciplines as well as of the possible. What is deemed feasible as an alternative runs the gauntlet of academic scrutiny, research developments and peer-reviewed publications as well as of policy-makers whose presumptions of the 'normal', the self-evident trump alternative visions (Bedford, this book). Feminists have long critiqued the parameters drawn around and by epistemic authority by challenging the definitions and recognized processes of knowledge production (Woehl, this book). Feminist critics have focused on how epistemological frameworks have been constitutive of the binaries of rational/emotional, universal/particular and objectivity/subjectivity. As Hartsock has pointed out, 'the vision of the ruling class (or gender) structures the material relations in which all parties are forced to participate, and therefore cannot be dismissed as simply false' (1997: 153). However, feminist work has also been done on a more assertive project. This has meant rethinking the relationships between these binaries so that the historical identification of emotions, particularity and subjectivity with the subordinate or the subaltern is challenged by suggesting the mutually constitutive nature of these binaries (Jaggar 1997). So, for example, in terms of the central concerns of regulatory regimes of global capitalism, and the role of global governance institutions in securing these regimes through Trade Related International Property Rights (TRIPs), for example, feminist interventions in theorizing knowledge production can have a radical impact on our understanding of the roles that institutions play in stabilizing structures-in-dominance and therefore can lead us to ask different and important questions about the nature of privatized knowledge and the application of this framework to global regulatory regimes. For example, some have argued that perhaps these insights should lead us towards exploring the merits of 'social patents', thus broadening the acknowledgement of knowledge creation. Thus regard to the gendered dimensions of knowledge production can provide insights into the nature of epistemic authority, practical policy shifts as well as critical evaluation of how 'disciplinary neo-liberalism' works to entrench dominant social relations through legal provisions, such as TRIPs, regulated by institutions of global governance such as the WTO.

Feminist concerns with the politics of convergence have reflected the multi-layered nature of the global economy, processes of democratic transition as well as the changing nature of governance.

Governance as spectacle

The dominance of certain states and ideologies within international relations literature has led to an increasing acceptance of the term 'governance' despite some unease about its political foundations. I would suggest that this dominance is embedded in the popular imagination about governance through the casting of political spectacles. Therefore on the one hand, we need to understand the importance of these spectacles and dissect these to lay bare their politics. On the other, we can understand spectacle *as* politics in contemporary times where it stands for 'the colonization of social life by capitalism: it is the submission of ever more facets of human sociality to the "deadly solicitations" of the market' (Stallabrass 2006: 92–93). Such analysis cannot replace the critical materialist analysis of governance presented above and in much of this book, but adds another dimension to our understanding of the concept of governance. This dimension is particularly important to understand as increasingly the media – traditional and virtual – is becoming a battleground of ideas and spaces where ideologies of governance converge and contend. This arena was first opened up for scholarly scrutiny by Guy Debord who in his book *The Society of the Spectacle* argued that modern spectacle was 'the autocratic reign of the market economy which had acceded to an irresponsible sovereignty, and the totality of new techniques of government which accompanied this reign' (1998: 2). The spectacular power was, he suggested, concentrated (totalitarian state power such as the Soviet Union) as well as diffuse (democratic systems such as the United States). In his 1988 *Comments on the Society of the Spectacle*, he expanded this to include integrated power of the spectacle through which spectacle has gone global: 'the globalization of the false was also the falsification of the globe' (1988: 10). Further expanding this discussion of the political economy of the imagery of power, Michel Foucault argued in his book *Discipline and Punish* (1991b) that the spectacle of corporeal punishment is disciplining of not only the one being punished, but also of those who witness the punishment being meted out. Foucault saw the exercise of power as not limited within the boundaries of sovereign states, through the enforcement of law but also as the development and exercise of the 'techniques and tactics' of domination (1991b: 102). The state thus enacts (as well as the exercises) disciplinary power.

Engendering this analysis of power, Judith Butler in her book *Gender Trouble* (1990) argued that gendered power is a fiction that needs to be sustained in the domain of political economy through social performitivity. Through the enactment of dominant gender roles we recognize, circulate and reproduce the meanings of masculinity and femininity and thus perpetuate gendered social hierarchies. Though neither Debord nor Foucault bring a gendered perspective to bear on their work, the focus on the performitivity of power opens up an important analytical seam for the development of governance theory. We have seen above how the concept of governance has evolved, has been embraced as well as challenged. The dominance of certain states and ideologies within international relations literature has led to an increasing acceptance of the term despite some unease about its political foundations. I would suggest that this dominance is embedded in the popular imagination about governance through the casting of political spectacles.

If we examine the three arenas of market, institutions and ideology, we find that all three are consolidated through and in the space of the unfolding spectacle of governance. Whether it is 'the shock and awe' of the Iraqi war, the grey-suited men pictured at G98 Summits surrounded by security barriers, the Abu Ghraib prisoners being carted in shackles or indeed, the counter-spectacles and alternative narratives of the Battle of Seattle, the World Social Forum and Live 8 Concerts. Dominant states such as the United States put up hugely and purposefully aggressive display of military power as well as the spectacle of a 'siege' of civilization through the media's coverage of radical movements – Islamist, but also radical such as in Cuba or in the streets of Seattle and Genoa. Both sets of images create a powerful visual medium through which the dominant modes of power are captured and circulated. The co-option of journalists into militaries as embedded reporters, for example, shows us how the creation of spectacle and its distribution is organized, congealing markets, institutions and ideology into a visual manifestation power. Challenges to that power display are mounted through alternative modes of communication, largely on the web, through blogs presented to new audiences. From Lindi England in Abu Ghraib to images of burka-clad women in Afghanistan, women have both participated in and been the victims of repressive spectacles of governance. Feminist scholars and women activists have understood that gender discipline is enforced and reproduced through economic dependence, political exclusion and also through cultural markers of the subjugation. As such the challenge to patriarchal power has also been comprehensive. As Butler's work shows, feminist scholarship has ranged widely to understand the exercise of gendered power. It has always incorporated photography, theatre, poetry and art into mainstream feminist political analysis to 'display' the varied ways in which patriarchy holds sway.

Challenges by and for feminist politics

One could argue that global governance is a concept that hides as much as it reveals. On the one hand the shift from government to governance is presented as an explanatory framework seeking to account for global change, and on the other it is seen as addressing the problem of states' inability to respond to that change. In this concluding section, I look ahead to challenges that feminist scholarship and activism is placing for global governance theorizing and also at what challenges it faces also.

Feminists have built their engagements with governance institutions on some key concepts that emerged from women's struggles and scholarship:

1. a gendered analysis of the political economy and the relations between states and markets,
2. a challenge to the state reproduced division between the public and the private and
3. a commitment to transformation of gender relations that form the basis of formal and informal politics.

If we take these insights into account when assessing key areas that we have identified above – markets, institutions and ideologies together with spectacle – of global governance we stretch the boundaries of the governance debates.

One way of doing this would be to analyse, I would suggest, governance along two different axes in the different sites of governance. The first, and the one that we have focused on in this chapter, is the *governance of polities*. Governance of polities is about regulating economic and political life at different levels – markets and the state at local, national and international levels – and is also about the role that different actors play in this regulation – state and non-state (including market) actors, epistemic communities, social movements at the local, national and global levels. The second axis, which does not get much attention in the mainstream literature, does in feminist work but needs greater conceptual visibility, is the *governance of communities*. There are processes and rituals as well as discourses and spectacles of violence that are deployed in order to police community boundaries and punish transgression. The parallel sovereignties thus created both challenge and work within the state (Baxi *et al.* 2006). Feminist scholarship could make a tremendous contribution in bringing these to axes to bear upon theoretical work on global governance.

Broadly, the governance of community shows the following characteristics: first, the community's governance in this sense is aligned with the reproduction of gendered traditions. In the name of culture the languages of hatred – racism, sexism and homophobia, for example – are aired and those of alternative visions of/from the community contained. Second, the regulation and disciplining of the realm of the community takes place through both formal and informal institutions, systems and discourses – caste, religious and ethnic local governing councils, modes of communications and excommunication, and also through spectacles of violence to subdue the rebels within communities. The state is mobilized in defence of the dominant social norms through constitutional, legal and policy frameworks as well as through modes of policy implementation – police personnel, for example, are often implicated in religious riots, in participating in or at least ignoring violence perpetrated against transgressors of community norms. Third, these boundaries are also defended and policed through spectacles of violence, which while not legitimated by all state fractions, is tolerated and even participated in by others. 'Crimes of honour' and of 'passion', for example, become more than just crimes: this is violence that regulates sexuality within communities. This means that such violence is seen as a 'legitimate' means of regulating communities, securing its cultural borders and insuring against transgression of its norms. Fourth, these traditions bleed over time and space – diasporic communities everywhere take with them the burdens and the markers of community norms and rituals and diasporic 'legalities' which regulate their life away from home. They help them to make personal sense of politicized otherness in strange lands. From the local to the global, the governance of communities involves disciplinary modes of discursive as well as social power. Finally, as with governance of polities, the governance of communities is constantly challenged and reshaped by the struggles of individuals and groups both directly by crossing critical boundaries of race, caste and religion, of sexuality and of class. These challenges tap into both internal sources of strength – network of sympathizers, as well as networks of support from outside. Circulation of political vocabulary allows them access to alternative political languages, visions of society and of other imagined communities. What I want to emphasize here is that it is in the interplay of the two axes of governance – of polities and communities – that the concept is best be understood.

Feminist scholarship and activism also faces some other challenges (Cohn, this book). While feminists have posited a powerful critique to mainstream global governance literature, they also need to present an alternative articulation of what governance means (Pearson, 2004). If they do not like marketised institutions, they need to be able to sketch the outline of governance institutions that they would like to see. Catherine Hoskyns and I (1998) have argued that '[f]or both strategic as well as practical reasons women have had to organize separately as women. ... [However, the] feminist challenge is limited by a current lack of focus on the importance of redistributive policies that are rooted in the structural inequalities of capitalist production and exchange' (p. 362). We posed the question: can gender recover class? Following Spivak, I would argue that a recognition of the importance of redistribution allows us '[b]oth in the economic area (capitalist) and in the political (world-historical agent)...to construct models of a divided and dislocated subject whose parts are not continuous or coherent with each other' (ibid. 276). And these dislocations and discontinuities are where women seeking transformation within political economy as well as the discursive circuits of power can find agency. This is particularly relevant now when marketization and the retrenchment of welfare provision under globalization is creating tremendous pressures and inequalities across different social and spatial boundaries. We see, however, that feminists are engaging with institutions within the convergent ideological framework of neo-liberal governance because the space for alternatives has scaled down even as the recognition of gender-based inequalities has increased. This is not to suggest that these engagements are not important. Indeed the solid ground of embedded liberalism has fractured so much under the neo-liberal onslaught that the protection of the welfare state seems a radical project well worth participating in. However, a recognition of the limits of the strategies of engagement with 'constitutional neo-liberalism' also need to be taken seriously if we are to be effective in developing political strategies of empowerment for both poor women and men.

Feminists too are engaged in this debate as they see a 'general broadening of the field of international reorganisation from a preoccupation with describing the output of intergovernmental organisations, their formal attributes and processes of decision-making to a concern with structures of governance' (Meyer and Prügl 1999: 4). These structures include organizations such as the UN, and NGOs as well as social and political movements in a 'global civil society'. A concern with issues of governance also helps explode the myth of consent that is a feature of the earlier globalization literature – a consent that is often juxtaposed with the inevitability of globalization and therefore conceals the power relations within which the process is developing. One could argue as Palan does, that 'the language of global governance, with its attendant rather unflattering insinuations about the functions, legitimacy, and aptitude of the state (and society)...makes sense only once an agreement is reached about some prior, if normally undeclared, common human goals, political functions and so on' (1999: 67). These *a priori* notions are themselves markers of closures – not the same as operated under nationalist regimes, but new closures which make for new winners and losers – in both the public and the private spheres, and take both national and local/global forms.

In this chapter, I have argued that issues of gender have particular salience in the debates on governance. Unless we use the insights that have emerged from feminist theory and practice we will not be able to encompass the needs of the future in the conversations about the global present. To reiterate, feminist contributions to these conversations lie in ways in which political activism and theoretical insights have been methodologically imbricated to develop insights on governance. These insights have examined the discursive as well as the material power wielded in embedding certain dominant explanations of governance in the mainstream literature which have then shaped the agendas for 'governing' (Kooiman 2003) and paradigms of governance. Specifically, feminist interventions in the areas of knowledge creation, recognition and institutionalization have particular salience for the processes of embedding neo-liberal marketised discourses of globalization and governance. Feminist debates on the state and democracy have relevance for the way in which political activism as well as the relational understanding between the state and global institutions of governance might be viewed. Gendered critiques of markets as not only uneven spaces of exchange, but as inefficient and distorted mechanisms that build upon unequal gendered social relations subject the normalization of rationality of the market to rigorous scrutiny. The global governance debate needs to make a conceptual shift to embed these insights, developed through everyday struggle at local, state and global levels, as well as through engagements with and critiques of mainstream literature if theories of critical governance are to fundamentally challenge the structures-in-dominance within this field.

Notes

1. Feminist economists have defined social reproduction as activities including biological reproduction, unpaid production in the home (both goods and services), social provisioning (by this we mean voluntary work directed at meeting needs in the community), the reproduction of culture and ideology, the provision of sexual, emotional and affective services (such as are required to maintain family and intimate relationships).
2. The debate on the provisions and rules of General Agreement on Trade and Services (GATS) is extremely relevant here. See Gill (2002), who argues that GATS negotiations have three main elements: (1) expanding market access commitments; (2) placing new constraints on state regulation of the domestic sphere and (3) expanding GATS rules and disciplinary framework to include emergency safeguards, subsidies and government procurement.

3. One could argue that this disciplinary neo-liberalism is clearly evident in the increasing convergence between the economic policy frameworks of the World Bank and the United Nations Development Programme (UNDP), especially in addressing the anti-poverty agenda as well as in initiatives for the management of capital–labour relations through the Global Social Compact, which builds on the idea of 'corporate social responsibility' – one way of privatizing social governance.

4. The impact of globalization of labour markets in this particular way has, of course, enormous implications for women's work and migration.

5. It is fascinating to note how global economic institutions such as the World Bank are clearly recognizing this participating state in particular political ways. Thus, the 2000 World Development Report clearly states, 'Poverty is an outcome not only of economic processes – it is an outcome of inter-acting economic, social and political forces. In particular, it is an outcome of the accountability and responsiveness of state institutions.' (p. 99) The economic forces then get depoliticized, while the state becomes associated with mal-administration (non-accountability) as well as with politics (lack of responsiveness to its 'clients' interests).

6. Polanyi, of course, sets up a dichotomy between pre-capitalist embedded markets and that of a capitalist unembedded price setting market of a 'modern society' (1957). However, the idea of the embedded market is now widely used to understand the different ways in which different sectors and regions experience the market, and how markets are 'distorted' by or enmeshed in cultural and historical spaces.

2
Gender and the Making of Global Markets: An Exploration of the Agricultural Sector

Elisabeth Prügl

The globalization of markets in the late twentieth century has entailed a significant restructuring of gender relations. Women have become workers in export-oriented manufacturing, they have moved into the informal sector and home-based work, and they have left farms and homes to work as maids, nannies, and in the global sex industry. In the agricultural sector, as in industry, restructuring in many places has furthermore entailed a feminization of labour.[1] The outcomes for women's status have been ambiguous: scholars have described highly exploitative situations, but sometimes also more gender equality (see Benería 2003: 83, 120–129). New opportunities to participate in markets have affected women, as has the gendered structure of these markets. While it is clear that there is a relationship between the globalization of markets and gender relations, it is less clear how this relationship operates. What are the mechanisms by which the globalization of markets (the construction of a seemingly unitary space of economic exchange) has affected gender relations (typically imagined as embedded in local cultural and historical contexts)?

Feminists have argued that the globalization of markets is socially and politically produced, the outcome of rules, regulations, ideologies, and discourses that the editors of this collection propose to subsume under the label "governance" (Rai and Waylen, this book). In this chapter, I suggest a focus on market-making institutions or regimes (I use the terms interchangeably) as a conceptual bridge between the globalization of markets and gender relations. Contemporary market-making institutions proliferate neo-liberal and patriarchal ideologies and discourses that globalize markets while constructing gender. I conceptualize such institutions as elements of the capitalist state, "a set of gendered social relations reflecting but also constitutive of capital/labor/market interaction" (ibid.) that operate across local, national, regional, and international scales. I seek to shed light on the way in which the re-regulation of markets along neo-liberal ideals produces new understandings of femininity and masculinity. I suggest that the institutions that globalize markets remake gender relations by re-specifying property rights, rules of exchange and welfare, and by proposing new visions of an ideal economy. These rights, rules, and visions are part of a system of governance that constructs gendered identities and empowers gendered agents in new ways.

The agricultural sector provides an interesting case study of the way in which the making of global markets re-constructs gender. Agriculture is fiercely contested in contemporary international trade negotiations. The stated purpose of the Doha round is to "establish a fair and market-oriented trading system" in agricultural commodities.[2] While the negotiating parties are disputing the relative importance of trade liberalization, rural welfare, food security, justice for Third World producers, and environmental sustainability in such a system, they have paid no attention to issues of gender equity. They largely have ignored the UN mandate to mainstream gender into all policy areas and make "the concerns and experiences of women as well as of men an integral part of the design, implementation, monitoring and evaluation of policies" (quoted in UNIFEM 2000: 34). By focusing on market-making institutions in the agricultural sector, I hope to illustrate how gender constructions are infused into liberalized markets and provide an argument for the need to mainstream gender into agricultural trade negotiations.

The internationalization of the state leads me to explore market-making regimes that bridge the international scale of the WTO, the regional scale of the EU, the national and sub-national scales of the German and Bavarian governments, and the local scale of the *landkreis* (county) of Freyung-Grafenau, a structurally disadvantaged region in South-East Germany. People have long eked out a marginal existence from farming in the region and have long combined farming with other sources of income-earning. The liberalization of markets, the restructuring of the agricultural welfare state, and new visions of rural development all have entailed new rules and rights for women farmers in the region, partly reproducing patriarchal divisions of labour and power, partly enabling new subjectivities and forms of agency.

Agricultural markets, the international state, and gendered institutions

One of the premises of this book project is that states continue to be central to legitimating and enabling both capitalism and patriarchy. Yet, states have changed with the globalization of markets. They have internationalized, i.e., they no longer are bulwarks against international forces, but "mediators, adapters and negotiators with the global economy" (Rai 2004: 585). In addition, new forms of governance have emerged in parallel with the transformation of states, including changed multilateral institutions (Ruggie 1993), transgovernmental networks (Slaughter 2004), private forms of authority (Hall and Biersteker 2002), global civil society, and transnational advocacy networks (Keck and Sikkink 1998; Keane 2003; Tarrow 2005). These new forms of governance have contributed to a dispersal of state authority, creating what Caporaso has called "post-modern states" (Caporaso 1996; Ruggie 1998).

How is one to conceptualize the role of these postmodern states in the reproduction of capitalism and patriarchy? The early feminist engagement with the patriarchal state often started from Marxist state theory and focused on unveiling ideologies and divisions of labour effecting women's oppression (e.g., Barrett 1980; Sargent 1981; Delphy 1984). These approaches ran afoul of postmodern and Third World feminist critiques for their unitary projection of white Western women's experiences as universal. In the wake of these critiques, many feminists abandoned theorizing "the patriarchal state" and turned to studying power relations in local contexts and gendered discourses. The state was seen as "a category of abstraction that is too aggregative, too unitary and too unspecific to be of much use in addressing the disaggregated, diverse, and specific (or local) sites that must be of most pressing concern to feminists" (Allen 1990: 22). The reproduction of gender inequality was no longer seen to be located in the state but in cultural politics (Brown 1995).

But the accumulating overwhelming evidence of the detrimental effects of neoliberal economic policies on women around the world has led feminists working on international political economy to recall state theory and argue that it could contribute to a better, i.e., a more political, understanding of processes of "global governance" that arguably are at the center of economic liberalization (Randall and Waylen 1998; Rai 2004; Waylen 2004). Such a recalling of state theory cannot step back to the theorizations of patriarchy of the 1980s, but needs to take into account the developments in feminist theory since then, in particular the rejection of unitary logics of oppression. Indeed, there seems to be a family resemblance between suggestions that state authority has dispersed with globalization and the feminist understanding of gender politics as operating in dispersed sites. A non-unitary understanding of the state could perhaps help bring the state back into feminist research.

The contemporary state is dispersed in two ways: First, there has been an unbundling of state authority so that national states share authority with local, regional, and international organizations. Second, as suggested in neo-Gramscian conceptualizations, states are not merely political institutions but "state-society complexes" (Cox 1983) engaged in the reproduction of gender and class hegemonies. These processes do not have to follow a unitary class or masculinist interest, but can be conceptualized as the institutionalization of discourses, including those operating at the international level (compare Whitworth 1994; Prügl 1999). The institutions of re-articulated international state-society complexes continue to regulate production, reproduction, and sexuality; they continue to monopolize the means of violence and the technologies of security; and they continue to deploy a masculinist bureaucracy as an apparatus of governance. These are the modalities of state power identified in feminist state literature (as summarized in Brown 1995). It is appropriate to probe the ways in which these modalities operate in the contemporary postmodern state to reproduce gender difference and subordination.

In this chapter, I interrogate only one modality of state power, i.e., the capitalist state. When feminists have talked about the capitalist dimension of state power, they have focused on the way in which the state guarantees property rights and on the way in which it organizes production, distribution, consumption, and legitimation. The capitalist state reproduces patriarchy by creating, through the rules of the welfare state and through the legal regulation of marriage, a gender division of labour that makes women available for free reproductive work and maintains them as a reserve army of low-wage labour.[3] Beyond these functional effects of capitalist rule-making identified in the feminist state literature, researchers have probed the identity (and associated distributional) effects of the state's rule-making and found considerable diversity depending on cultural and political contexts. For example, in Europe, the Americas, and in international organizations, they have identified constructions of men as breadwinners, of women as maternal and in need of social protection, as equal but supplementary and home-bound workers, and as flexible labourers. In the colonial Caribbean, on the other hand, black women were identified as exploitable field workers, and in colonial India as non-workers that nevertheless produced for the world market.[4] These gendered identities empowered unequal forms of agency and yielded unequal entitlements.

Thus, whereas functional arguments predict uniform outcomes of capitalist state rule-making for a unitary category called women, arguments probing identity effects direct the attention to diverse outcomes and processes of construction in particular contexts. Combining insights from postmodern feminism and feminist political economy, I seek to develop arguments about the gendered identity outcomes of global governance by introducing the notion of regimes, sets of rules that cut across levels of governance and that institutionalize global markets. Such regimes are created in the interaction of the postmodern state (including national states, regional organizations, international organizations) with civil society (including capitalists, labour, advocacy networks, and social movements). They define the shape of economic exchange, circumscribe the welfare of economic agents, and set the direction of economic development. In so doing, they construct gender: they empower gendered market agents, define masculinity and femininity, and allocate entitlements by employing gendered categories.

Regimes are institutions, sets of rules that make gendered agencies and structures.[5] As such, regimes are conduits of power: they produce normalized and empowered subjects, but they also routinize power, giving the effects of power permanence and structure, and in this way reproducing the constellation of *Herrschaft* that feminists have termed "patriarchy" (compare Pühl 2001). When feminists have analysed the rules of the welfare state and described patriarchal "welfare regimes," they have described a form of institutionalized authority.[6] Like them, I consider regimes as sets of rules that mediate states and societies and that constitute patriarchy in particular contexts. Unlike them, I focus not only on the way in which regimes define entitlements but also on they way in which they produce identities. In addition, rather than considering regimes "domestic" and bounded by nation-states, I attach them to functional issue areas that bridge geographical scales and produce global governance, as a constellation of market-making rules, that encompasses multiple but non-random constructions of gender.[7] Three such regimes make agricultural markets in Europe: an agricultural exchange regime, an agricultural welfare regime, and a rural development regime.

Sociologists and economists have argued that states react to the liberalization of markets by creating institutions that temper the undesirable outcomes of pure market orders (Polanyi 1944; Benería 2003). But states also actively create markets, including global markets, making possible capitalist exchange through the construction of *exchange regimes*. The most basic prerequisite for capitalist exchange is the right to property (Burch 1998). States define what counts as property, who counts as an owner, and how property gets transferred. States enable the exchange of property through a body of private law that guarantees the enforcement of contracts. States furthermore define rules of competition, levy tariffs on cross-border trades and taxes on sales or value added. They also set standards designed to overcome market failures. Together, these rules make possible the historically and culturally specific type of exchange of goods and services that makes up capitalist markets.

One of the most visible contemporary efforts to construct a new exchange regime is the European Union (Fligstein 2001); parallel efforts to construct a global exchange regime are under way in multi-lateral, private, and transgovernmental forums, such as the WTO and the Basel Committee on Banking Supervision. At both the EU and the global levels, neo-liberal principles have since the 1980s informed market-building measures; but recently these measures also have been contested in discourses of environmentalism and social welfare. Talk of a "new constitutionalism" involving neo-liberal principles has suggested new identity effects resulting from the new exchange regime. According to Stephen Gill, neo-liberalism has conferred "privileged rights of citizenship and representation to corporate capital" (Gill 2003: 132). Feminists similarly have seen gendered identity effects in the construction of a hypermasculinized techo-managerial class, or "Davos man," together with a feminized other providing "intimate labor" (Chang and Ling 2000; Hooper 2000, 2001; Benería 2003: 72).

Exchange regimes make markets possible by defining what can be exchanged, who can participate in exchange, and by specifying the rules of exchange. Property rights are one of the most central aspects of exchange regimes and land ownership specifically is one of the crucial enabling features of an agricultural market. Land rights have long been profoundly gendered, as women own only about 1 percent of all land globally (Seager 1997: 76). In a world in which almost half the population lives off agriculture this limits their ability to farm and their entitlement to exchange values generated through farming. It denies them a role as economic actors in agricultural product markets. Lacking productive capital, women farmers are excluded from factor markets as well – as non-owners they cannot sell land, lack collateral that would give them access to credit, and are thus precluded from buying land. There is an ongoing struggle in countries around the world to gain women rights to land (Agarwal 2003).

In Europe, the family farm is at the heart of patriarchal property relations. Christine Delphy and Diana Leonard have analysed European farming families as "structured hierarchical systems of social relations around the production, consumption and transmission of property" (1992: 2), describing rules that make women's unpaid labour available to male household heads (thereby alienating the property in their own labour) and rules of inheritance that systematically exclude girls from becoming farmers. Family farms employ gender to allocate labour and property, producing a strict gender division of labour and power. Within the family farm, being a wife is not only a marital status, but also a job. In Delphy and Leonard's terms, marriage to a farmer explicitly creates a relation of production.[8] Yet, the job of "spouse" is not a job like all others. It is one that is unpaid, not regulated by labour law, and devoid of social security. Despite being labourers, most governments have not accorded women farmers an occupational status. They are seen as engaged in a private family relation but not as agents on a labour market.

Markets are sustained through the creation of producers and consumers. In the Fordist model the worker mass-producing for mass consumption was constructed as male, a household head and family breadwinner, whereas the consumer (and reproducer) was constructed female, a homemaker and caretaker. Thus, from a feminist perspective, Fordism was capitalist patriarchy. National *welfare regimes,* i.e., institutions securing the welfare of the worker and "his" family, helped ensure the buying power of men and of their imagined non-working consumer housewives by institutionalizing collective bargaining, ensuring against sickness, age, and accidents. Feminists studying welfare regimes have suggested that states created different types of patriarchy through their welfare institutions. They have developed typologies of "patriarchial welfare states," reflecting the way in which European states have regulated the relationship between production and reproduction and the relative prevalence of the male-breadwinner model in national welfare policies (Lewis 1992; Schunter-Kleemann 1992; Siaroff 1994; Sainsbury 1999). Economic restructuring has been accompanied by a reconfiguration of the relationship of production and reproduction. It has entailed the end of the male breadwinner model, of women's association with reproduction, and the gendered separation of public and private on which the model was based (Young 2001b; Bakker 2003). The entry of women into the labour force has been one element of this restructuring; as women have entered the labour force, welfare regimes have increasingly abandoned the differential treatment of women and men.

Agricultural welfare regimes in industrialized countries both resemble and differ from those in industry and services. They include social insurance but, unlike in industry and services, agricultural welfare is also provided through the market, through the fixing of prices and government subsidies. Indeed, the market-based mechanisms of the EU's common agricultural policy have been conceptualized as the basis of the European agricultural welfare state (Rieger 1995). This regime has been implicated in the construction of a unique patriarchal agricultural gender order based on family farming. Here men became "farmers" – self-employed entrepreneurs, while women became "spouses." Lacking an employment status, women on family farms were constructed as non-working housewives despite their extensive participation in agricultural production and despite the difficulty of separating production from reproduction and consumption in farming households. Feminist activism has focused on gaining women farmers an employment status, and there have been some successes leading to independent access to social security benefits.

The *rural development regime* is the third market-constituting regime in the agricultural sector. It projects an ideal of how markets should be organized and gendered and supports the institutionalization of practices that realize this ideal. While taking different forms in different political contexts, rural development as promoted in international organizations (including the FAO and OECD) has long meant agricultural modernization; and the goals of such development have included a combination of achieving food security, rural welfare, and increased efficiency. Rural modernization policies have been a target of critique in the women-and-development literature, because they led to the displacement of women and to changes in women's access to income and land (Boserup 1970). In Europe, modernization similarly has had gendered effects. In Germany, it entailed a "feminization" of farming, especially on small farms (Inhetveen and Blasche 1983; Prügl 2004a), and similar effects have been reported in Italy, Portugal, and Austria (Braithwaite 1994: 63; Schunter-Kleemann 1995; Bachmann 1999: 164). But where men have stayed involved in farming, this often has meant that women lost independent sources of income (from selling eggs, jams, etc.) as the farm specialized and modernized (Kolbeck 1990). And where modernization has been successful, women apparently have turned into housewives, in charge of housework and care work, *de facto* giving up their roles as farmers (Whatmore 1991).

The global liberalization of agricultural markets has put the goals of agricultural modernization in question. It has accelerated the restructuring of European agriculture, destroying the livelihoods of small farmers while favouring the concentration of capital and the rights of agribusiness (McMichael 2003). It also has brought into focus environmental problems caused by the intensification of agricultural production under global competition.[9] Searching for new rural development strategies to keep farming viable, European policy-makers have latched on to the notion of a "European model of agriculture" that integrates concerns for the welfare of farmers, environmental preservation, and the preservation of rural traditions. Underlying the model is the suggestion that farming is "multifunctional," i.e., it not only produces private goods (food), but also public goods (a unique rural landscape; environmental preservation; recreational values). European policymakers have argued in the WTO that agriculture deserves continued government subsidies so that it can provide these public goods. Unlike the old modernization policy, which was held responsible for large-scale pollution, the European model of agriculture now celebrates (at least in rhetoric) the notion of environmental sustainability and the farmer as a steward of the environment. It puts new emphasis on strengthening small farms with diversified sources of income and extensive production patterns in tune with natural cycles. Finally, it also has begun to recall women farmers as diversifiers of income, seeking to revive the market role of these women, converting them from "non-working housewives" to "rural entrepreneurs."

In what follows, I illustrate changes in the agricultural exchange regime, the agricultural welfare regime, and the rural development regime in a particular context, i.e., the *landkreis* of Freyung-Grafenau, a site within the European multi-level system of governance and within the emerging international free-trade regime in agricultural commodities. The local perspective allows me to illustrate the way in which gender identities and patriarchal structures are currently being reconstructed within the three market-making regimes.

Scaling market-making regimes: agriculture in Freyung-Grafenau

Bordering the Czech Republic and Austria, the *landkreis* of Freyung-Grafenau is characterized by the mountains and woodlands of the Bavarian forest. A relatively rough climate and hilly terrain make for short growth cycles and favour animal husbandry. More than half of the farms are smaller than 10 hectares (about 25 acres) and indeed

85 percent are 30 hectares (about 74 acres) or smaller (Landkreis Freyung-Grafenau 2004). Pluriactivity, i.e., the combination of farming with other ways of income earning, is wide-spread. In 1999, 71 percent of farms were part-time (Bernhards *et al.* 2003: 6). Typically women tend to the farms while men earn off-farm income in manufacturing, in particular in the glass industry, wood-processing, and granite, or commute to nearby cities. Employment in services is comparatively low, but tourism is considered to hold potential for the future development of the region (Regionales Entwicklungskonzept: 3). Since EU enlargement the region finds itself competing with low-wage manufacturing labour in the neighboring Czech Republic. Continuing high unemployment of between 9 and 10 percent in the last few years and a series of recent bankruptcies of significant employers in the *landkreis* have brought back the importance of farming to supplement income (Bernhards *et al.* 2003: 16; Landkreis Freyung-Grafenau 2005).

By situating my analysis in the local context of Freyung-Grafenau, I take the perspective of women on small dairy farms. Sixty-eight and a half percent of all farms in the *Landkreis* hold dairy cattle (Amt für Landwirtschaft und Forsten – Regen). Such farms constitute a relatively small proportion of farming operations in Europe, but account for about 30 percent of farms in West Germany.[10] How do changes in the market-making institutions affect women farmers in this region? How do these institutions construct gendered identities and gendered conduct? How do agricultural exchange regimes, welfare regimes, and development regimes produce different gendered identities and differentially empower women and men on farms? The evidence I am presenting here is suggestive of some of the ways in which the rules of market-making institutions are gendered. I adduce almost exclusively materials available in the public domain which suffer from the fact that they rarely discuss gender or provide the perspective of women farmers. In combining discussions from different geographical scales, I hope to raise questions regarding the way in which global governance reproduces gender by constructing markets.

Agricultural exchange regimes

Gender construction in the agricultural exchange regime is best illustrated in the formation of the European common market in agriculture. Family farming has long constituted a basic building block of this market. The final resolution of the Stresa Conference of 1958, where member states developed the outlines of the CAP, asserts the "unanimous will to preserve the familial character" of European agriculture (Conférence

1958: 223). Politicians employed rhetorics of anti-communism in opposition to collective farming, romantic associations of the countryside with national health and moral fortitude, and sentiments that celebrated the traditional order for its valuing of community. The family farm continues to be the central building block of European agriculture today, and indeed, when Germany reunified in the 1990s, German politicians pledged to re-establish family farming in the East and have partially succeeded in doing so.

But with family farming has come a commitment to a particular gender order, one that employs gender to assign agency in the agricultural exchange regime. The modernization of the family farm increasingly has constructed men as the primary market agents and producers while pushing women into the role of housewives and consumers. This is reflected in European statistical practices that make a distinction between "farm managers" and "spouses," where the first is connoted as male and the second as female. According to EU statistics, only about 20 percent of farm managers in the EU were women in 1997, while they accounted for 80 percent of the spouses (Fremont 2001: 3). In Germany the picture was even starker: women accounted for only 9 percent of farm managers, but for 92 percent of all spouses (European Communities 2002: 34 and 36). And in Bavaria, where Freyung-Grafenau is located, women were reported as managing only 3.6 percent of farms in 1987, and most of the women managing farms were unmarried (Winkler 1990: 61).

But the statistical categories hide the productive role of women on Bavarian farms. Indeed, European market-making institutions may be much more patriarchal than the local family farms. Traditional patterns of property rights in Freyung-Grafenau contradict a simplistic construction of women as non-market agents or "spouses." Rights to land in Europe are customary and local, and in Lower Bavaria, including Freyung-Grafenau, farms have traditionally been co-owned by the farming couple (*Gütergemeinschaft*). As a rule, farms are passed down to a son throughout Germany, and as a result men own the vast majority of farms and the bulk of land. But co-ownership allows the wife to inherit the farm in the case of her husband's premature death and pass it on to her offspring. Furthermore, in the case of divorce, the wife is eligible to receive half of the value of the farm.

Legal experts of the Bavarian farmers' organization (*Bayerischer Bauernverband*) discourage co-ownership because it threatens the splitting up of farms. They argue that splitting up farms counteracts efforts to modernize; only large farms can take advantage of economies of scale.[11] Indeed, federal law in Germany codifies a different type of inheritance system for land, which is practiced in most parts of the country and which serves as a default in cases where no separate ownership arrangements are made at the time of marriage. Under the terms of this model, husband and wife keep separately any land they bring into marriage and only share the product jointly generated (*Zugewinngemeinschaft*). Here wives have a right to the value generated on the farm with their labour (Teipel 1996: 12), but no right to their husbands' land.[12] This is in line with EU and government policies that encourage the modernization of farming. But despite pressures to abolish egalitarian forms of ownership, 67.5 percent of all women farmers in Bavaria still co-owned according to a survey conducted in 1988 (Ziche and Wörl 1991: 671). Here modernization ran up against local customs that accord women a role as owners and thus agents of exchange in agricultural markets.

The category "spouse" also hides the role of women farmers as producers. Women contribute the bulk of agricultural labour in Lower Bavaria, accounting for 58 percent of the agricultural workforce in 1991 (Braithwaite 1994: 35). This percentage may be even higher in Freyung-Grafenau, where dairy cows and other animals are central to farming. Evidence from throughout Europe shows that on dairy farms and on farms that hold animals, women typically play a significant role and participate extensively in farm labour (European Communities 2002: 12). Indeed, a study of Freyung-Grafenau in the 1980s found that the availability of family labour was directly correlated with farm size and degree of specialization (Knickel and Seibert 1990: 158), indicating the importance of women's on-farm labour for the success of a farm.

By designating women farmers as "spouses," the rules of the European agricultural exchange regime contribute to a construction of women as non-producers and as non-market agents. Efforts to "modernize" inheritance rights further marginalize women as market agents. But regional and national market-making regimes interact with local inheritance rules. In the case of Freyung-Grafenau, egalitarian traditions of ownership seemingly contradict efforts to enlarge farms and create a globally competitive agricultural sector. But they help maintain women farmers as agents of exchange and producers, though largely invisible and marginal in a globalized agricultural market.

Agricultural welfare regimes

Where exchange regimes regulate the terms of market participation and competition, welfare regimes seek to alleviate the unequal outcomes of unfettered competition through a redistribution of resources and through social security systems, and while they create entitlements they also contribute to constructing identities. The CAP has been described as the heart of the European agricultural welfare state. Social policy considerations went into the EU's decision to establish a common market in agriculture with relatively high (compared to the world market) and guaranteed Europe-wide prices. The purpose was twofold: First, competition at the European level would force farmers to become more efficient. Second, high prices would ensure that people working in agriculture would share in the benefits of Fordist industrialization and achieve incomes comparable to those in industry.

How has the market-based welfare regime functioned to redistribute wealth and construct gender? Feminists have long criticized the abstraction of "rational economic man" as a central driving figure of markets, arguing that notions of an autonomous and independent subject reflect masculine experiences (Ferber and Nelson 1993; Cook *et al.* 2000). They also have faulted the practice of treating households as unitary entities that pool income and allocate expenditures along rational principles while ignoring power relations within households (Bruce and Dwyer 1988).[13] The effects of these biases become visible in the EU's market-making welfare regime. The target of the policy is a unitary entity (the farm) with a head (the farmer) making decisions on behalf of the farming household. Thus, under the CAP price regime, subsidies flow to the male farm manager, while women farmers benefit depending on their negotiating power inside the household.

But the effects of the CAP's price regime are not only gendered inside the household; it also accentuates differences in the market place. Because the EU's price guarantees pertain to processed foods and not to farm-gate products, benefits are paid to agri-food corporations, and farmers benefit only indirectly. Furthermore, those who produce more, i.e., industrial-style large farms, gain more subsidies than the small farms that are more likely to be managed by women.[14] Thus, the CAP's price mechanism has been a highly ineffective way of addressing rural welfare concerns, and the attacks in the WTO on the EU's market-distorting subsidies are potentially salutary from the perspective of small farmers and women farmers.

As a result of pressure in international trade negotiations, the EU increasingly has moved from providing welfare payments by setting prices to making compensatory payments directly to farmers, a practice that is (still) allowed within the WTO's "blue box." The blue box allows payments for welfare purposes based on acreage or animal numbers if they are associated with efforts to reduce production. While blue box payments decouple subsidies from production and in this way reduce incentives to produce, their gendered impact in the household remains. Direct payments go to the typically male farmer. Women have voiced concern that they have now been removed even further from claiming any entitlement to this welfare payment. Whereas in the price-based system women could cite their role in production to claim a share of the value produced, direct payments no longer are based on production and women's claim to a share in direct payments, as a result, is much more tenuous.[15] The postmodern state's shift from a price-based welfare system to direct payments thus may have weakened the negotiating power of women in European farm households.

In addition to using commodity prices and direct payments to distribute resources to farmers, European governments also have created social security systems for people working in agriculture, including retirement and health insurance. Like social security for workers outside agriculture,[16] social protection in agriculture has been gendered and in the 1980s became the focus of feminist agitation. Women farmers' lack of an occupational status precluded them from gaining equal access to pension rights. Although they often worked excessive hours, the male-breadwinner social security regime afforded them no independent rights to old age or disability pensions. If they divorced and remarried, they lost all derived rights to their former husbands' pensions. Their social security depended on their marital status, not their occupational status, and until recently their social security payments arrived via their farmer-husbands.

In the 1980s, women's organizations in agriculture began to demand that "spouses" gain a legal status as entrepreneurs, which in turn would entitle them to the same social protections as "farmers." The discussion raged at the European level.[17] In addition to separate entitlements to social security and to the recognition of their work, women farmers also demanded an income, the right to stand for office and vote in the bodies representing farmers, and equal access to training. A far-reaching directive drafted by the European Commission stumbled over the objections of Britain and Ireland.[18] The watered-down directive passed was little more than an exhortation to governments to consider the position of women farmers.

In Germany, agricultural restructuring and the need to prop up ailing welfare systems gave impetus to the demands of women farmers and led to a 1995 law to reform social insurance in the agricultural sector. The law defined women farmers as "quasi-self-employed" and required that they be included in the agricultural retirement system. For the first time they were accorded an occupational status, though in a qualified manner. The less than full employment status was necessary in order to preserve access to health insurance in the patriarchal welfare state, and activists reluctantly accepted the compromise. If women farmers on part-time farms (like those that predominate in Freyung-Grafenau) would have been redefined as self-employed, they would have lost entitlements to health insurance provided through their husbands' off-farm jobs. With the new law, about 300,000 women who had spent their lives working on farms were eligible to participate in the government-subsidized agricultural pension system (Fuhr 1995: 114). The law addressed the demand for independent pension rights while increasing the ratio of payers to payees and stabilizing the system. But it failed to address the demand for equal status as the designation "quasi-self-employed" reproduced women's unequal role in agricultural production and markets.

The changes in the agricultural welfare regime have been linked to the rapid restructuring of European farming, a process that has accelerated as a result of the progressive liberalization of agricultural markets and has threatened the livelihoods of both women and men working on farms. The decreasing number of participants in the agricultural insurance system is an immediate result of farm deaths. Similarly, the shift from the market mechanism to direct payments is justified as a cushion for the negative impacts of restructuring.[19] The corresponding changes in global welfare governance from the local perspective of Freyung-Grafenau have entailed a transformation from a hybrid market-making and compensatory regime to a purely compensatory regime with ambiguous outcomes for gender relations. While the reform of the pension system has enabled a somewhat more-equal treatment of women farmers on full-time farms, this has stopped short of defining them as entrepreneurs. Women on part-time farm continue to be defined as housewives. Similarly, direct payments privilege the household head, perpetuating an identity of women farmers as dependents and a patriarchal construct of the family farm.

Rural development regime

Unlike exchange regimes and welfare regimes, rural development regimes are forward looking, envisioning structural change. European agriculture in the twentieth century included a rural development regime which advocated an increase in the productivity of land and labour through the introduction of technologies, education, and the provision of credit. While such modernization was a shared international value, the particular form that modernization took was regulated through national policies and institutions.

In the Freyung-Grafenau area, market-oriented production only began to replace subsistence production in the mid-twentieth century, in part as a result of European agricultural policy that encouraged modernization. Some farms sought to emulate a growth-oriented strategy, but the EU's modernization programs focused mostly on large farms in favourable areas. Pluriactive households with small holdings in less favoured areas received little support. Even in the 1980s, when the growth-oriented strategy was gradually modified, only 36 percent of farms in Freyung-Grafenau received investment-related aid. This discriminatory pattern of support helped accelerate a trend toward increased disparity among farms in the *landkreis,* and it fell behind developments in agriculture for Germany as a whole (Knickel and Seibert 1990: 153). Farmers also were hampered by the EU's introduction in the mid-1980s of milk quotas to stem overproduction. Some shifted toward intensive livestock production, including beef, pigs, and poultry, that increased the stress on the rural environment. But many gave up farming. Indeed, between 1991 and 1999 the number of farms in the *landkreis* shrank by 31 percent, outpacing the general trend in Bavaria (Bernhards *et al.* 2003: 12).

In addition to production-oriented strategies, farming families coped with the stresses of agricultural modernization by diversifying their income. For the most part this took the form of men taking jobs in industry,[20] while women worked the farms with their husbands helping after hours and on weekends. Forty-two percent of "farmers" in Freyung-Grafenau engaged in off-farm employment in the late 1980s and 8 percent of "spouses" worked off the farm (Knickel and Seibert 1990: 155). Moving from dairy to livestock production is likely to have facilitated this pattern of income earning because livestock production tends to be less labour-intensive and thus frees up time for off-farm activities. Despite the prevalence of women's labour in pluriactive farming, women were rarely constructed as farmers. A farmer (*Bauer*) was male by definition, a *Bäuerin* female, and their local labour divisions incompatible with national and European understandings of what it means to be a farm manager and a spouse.

The EU's new rural development model seeks to make new markets in Freyung-Grafenau and this produces gender in old and new ways. As a designated disadvantaged area, the *landkreis* qualifies for support from European structural funds, and about 15 percent of farm profit currently derives from subsidy payments (Bernhards *et al.* 2003: 14). These payments, like most programs of the structural funds disproportionately benefit household heads and thus men. As the European Commission has recognized in a communication on gender mainstreaming in the European Agricultural Guarantee and Guidance Fund (EAGGF):

> The majority of funding [in the EAGGF] concerns the agricultural sector where women are underrepresented. Actions are primarily focused on farms and their beneficiaries are the farm owners. The fact that only one out of five farm owners is a woman reduces the possibility for women to benefit directly from these projects. Farmers' wives and female employees are ignored by this kind of funding.[21]

But there are some innovative interventions which point the way toward new gender constructions. The *landkreis* has received funding under the EU's LEADER + program to develop tourism with projects involving hiking paths, environmentally sustainable recreational opportunities, museums of local culture, and training for providers of tourism services. Paired with gender mainstreaming (which is institutionalized in the LEADER + program) this new rural development regime has created room for rural women in general and for women farmers in particular. In order to diversify on-farm income, EU policies now encourage women farmers to market the countryside to tourists, provide room and board, and teach tourists an appreciation of the natural environment. Five to 6 percent of all farming families in Bavaria already offer "farm vacations," i.e., they rent rooms to tourists, provide meals, and vacation programs. For the majority of these families income from tourism is equal to or higher than income from agriculture (Bayerisches Staatsministerium 2004: 147) and in Freyung-Grafenau household income from tourism is above the Bavarian average (Bernhards *et al.* 2003: 7).

Rural women also are encouraged to market their home economics and caring skills, to offer party services or provide care for the elderly. In Freyung-Grafenau, the *landkreis* provides counseling for women interested in reentering the job market and in starting their own businesses. For women farmers, the Bavarian government offers more specific counseling with the purpose of "increasing the entrepreneurial potential of women farmers [*Bäuerinnen*], in order to increase income opportunities on the basis of their home economics education, but also in order to increase the entrepreneurial competence of *Bäuerinnen* and thus to contribute added value to the countryside" (Bayerisches Staatsministerium 2004: 132, trans.).

In the context of the new European model of agriculture, rural development efforts are thus geared toward making women farmers into entrepreneurs – meeting precisely the demands of those who have argued for giving women farmers an occupational status. But in the new development policies equal status does not come through changes in the institutions of agriculture; it is made possible by preserving agriculture as an imagined male bastion, while using women's services to market the countryside together with female homemaking and caring skills. Women gain economic agency in fields related to on-farm production (direct marketing, farm vacations) or by establishing themselves as service providers in the rural economy. They remain spouses in the agricultural exchange regime and quasi-self-employed in the agricultural welfare regime. But they become entrepreneurial agents in the market for services, and they gain access to a portion of the ca. 22 percent of the EU's agricultural budget reserved for rural development purposes (European Commission 2007).

Conclusion

This chapter has introduced the notion of market-making regimes as components of the postmodern capitalist state and of practices of global governance. I have argued that the agricultural market that embeds women in Freyung-Grafenau can be conceptualized as ruled by three institutions: the agricultural exchange regime, the agricultural welfare regime, and the rural development regime. Each bridges geographical scales and consists of identifiable rules, some of which have changed with the push to create a global free market in agriculture. I argue that these regimes are gendered: they produce gendered market agents and identities resulting in differential outcomes for women and men in terms of wealth, power, and well-being.

A key component of the agricultural exchange regime is property rights. Local inheritance rules in Germany tend to favour men, empowering them to own farms and land and making male farmers into agents participating in product and factor markets. In Freyung-Grafenau, women may be co-owners and do most of the agricultural labour, but for the most part are not considered agents participating in these markets. The agricultural welfare regime reinforces these constructions in that it treats the male farmer as an entrepreneur with a claim to subsidies through the price mechanism and through direct payments, and with an independent claim to a pension. In contrast, the female farmer is constructed as a dependent spouse who indirectly benefits from payments distributed to the household; but recently she also has gained the status of quasi-self-employed for retirement purposes. The rural development regime has undergone a fundamental shift from promoting modernization to fostering diversification. While rules of modernization have cemented a gender order that opposes the farmer as an owner/entrepreneur to the spouse as a flexible labourer/non-worker/consumer, rules of diversification are creating the female farmer as a rural services entrepreneur outside agriculture. This re-construction potentially has far-reaching implications for gender orders on farms, although it retains agriculture as a male preserve.

How then has the globalization of markets impacted gender relations in agriculture? The picture I have painted is one of diversity and contradictions, but some general suggestions are possible. First, seemingly gender-neutral market liberalization produces unintended consequences. This includes the privileging of patriarchal property rights that encourage the agglomeration of land, thus fostering competitive structures, over more egalitarian inheritance rules. Second, the restructuring of the agricultural welfare regime from one based on the market mechanism to one based on direct payments reinforces household structures that assign men headship together with disproportionate authority and wealth. Third, feminist ideas have inserted themselves into the reformulation of market-making regimes and effected rules that empower women as agents. This includes an occupational status for women farmers in the reformed German retirement system and the creation of women as rural entrepreneurs in programs to diversify rural income. In sum, globalizing market-making regimes have perpetuated women's subordinate status on farms while opening up new markets in tourism and services with economic opportunities for women.

While gender inequalities are not on the agenda of agricultural trade negotiators, the evidence presented here suggest that they should be. Making markets is a political act producing rules that privilege some over others. Making markets is making class and gender.

Notes

1. The literature is extensive. Fernandez-Kelly (1983), Tiano (1994), Cravey (1998), Ward (1990), Boris and Prügl (1996), Mitter (1992) describe women's work in export processing and global subcontracting. Agathangelou (2004), Ehrenreich and Hochschild (2002), Chin (1998) explore the work of maids, nannies, and sex workers in the global service economy. For overviews on women in agriculture see Agarwal (2003); Inhetveen and Schmitt (2004). For the feminization thesis see Standing (1989).
2. *World Trade Organization Ministerial 2001*, Ministerial Declaration, 20 November 2001. WT/MIN(01)/DEC/1. http://www.wto.org/english/thewto_e/minist_e/min01_e/mindecl_e.htm. Accessed August 2, 2004.

3. For summaries of the literature on capitalist patriarchy see Brown (1995), Tong (1998).
4. The literature on the gendered welfare state is extensive. For a recent overview see Sainsbury (1999). For identity effects in international organizations see Prügl (1999); Whitworth (1994). For explorations on colonial constructions see Mies (1986).
5. For a development of this argument see Prügl (2004b). Note that my use of the term institutions differs from the narrow focus on political institutions in Political Science and is more akin to a sociological understanding of institutions.
6. Thus, they often use the terms "welfare state" and "welfare regime" interchangeably.
7. Here I differ from Bob Connell's suggestion that there is a "global gender order," i.e., "the structure of relationships that interconnect the gender regimes of institutions, and the gender orders of local society, on a world scale" (1998: 7). The problem with Connell's conceptualization is that it does not account for the dispersal of authority in the post-modern state. In his rather Westphalian world, local societies produce independent gender orders, which presumably emerge from the local state and other institutions contained in this society. He concedes that globalization has produced a global civil society, but apparently it has not changed the state.
8. Delphy and Leonard (1992) argue that all wives enter a production relation through marriage, but that this relation is more visible in the case of farming women.
9. These effects have spawned resistance to neoliberal institutions. In Europe farmers and consumers (often with support from governments) have developed regional networks of producers, distributors, and consumers and revived local markets (Ward and Almås 1997; for a cautionary note see Hollander 1995).
10. Farming structures in East Germany differ significantly from those in the West. While only .2 percent of dairy farms in Bavaria hold more than 100 cows, the percentage is much higher in the *Länder* of the former GDR. Sixty or close to 60 percent of farms in Brandenburg, Mecklenburg-Vorpommern, and Sachsen-Anhalt hold more than 100 cows, 35 percent do so in Thüringen, and 27 percent in Saxony (BMVEL 2003, p. 111, Table 8).
11. Virtually all farmers in Freyung-Grafenau are members of the BBV. In 2006, the *landkreis* had 1975 farms and 2080 BBV members (Amt für Landwirtschaft und Forsten – Regen).
12. The *Zugewinngemeinschaft* was established as the legal norm in 1958, replacing a law of 1900 which gave men the right to manage and profit from the farming capital their wives brought into marriage. The old law was found to contradict the equality clause of the post-World War II German constitution (Teipel 1996: 16).
13. Indeed, the internal dynamics of households have become a point of contention among economists. While Gary Becker (1981) has suggested that an altruistic family operates within a competitive market, Amartya Sen (1990) has proposed a model of "cooperative conflict."
14. In 1997, out of 100 women managing farms in EU-15, 82 were responsible for "small" holdings as compared to 68 percent of men (Fremont 2001: 4).

15. Women working on agricultural policy in Brussels told me of this concern, which they had heard expressed by organized women farmers.
16. In Germany social security has long been tied to status in the labour market, which has been particularly pernicious for women in this strong male-breadwinner state, where women's labour force participation has long been comparably low.
17. France created the distinct status of a *conjoint collaborateur* for assisting spouses in 1980 and sought to promote the status at the EU level. Feminists were highly critical of this status because it only allowed women retirement benefits if they made separate contributions, involving significant additional cost (Delphy and Leonard 1992, pp. 214–216).
18. Britain objected because it thought the directive went beyond the competence of the EU; Ireland objected because the provisions "were seen as an unjustified intervention in the affairs of the traditional rural family" (Hoskyns 1996: 150).
19. Note that blue box payments are contested in the WTO and their future seems limited.
20. The West German government subsidized rural industrialization especially along the Eastern border, where Freyung-Grafenau is located, creating manufacturing jobs mostly for men. Textile, leather, and electronics homework was wide-spread in the area and provided some of the scarce job opportunities for women.
21. Communication from the Commission to the Council, the European Parliament, the European Economic and Social Committee, and the Committee of the Regions. Implementation of gender mainstreaming in the Structural Funds programming documents 2000–2006. COM/2002/0748 final, item 3.1.3. Note that the communication fudges the distinction between farm owner and farm manager. Because co-ownership is prevalent in Freyung-Grafenau, most women are likely to be co-owners, but not the designated farm managers.

3
Global Governance as Neo-liberal Governmentality: Gender Mainstreaming in the European Employment Strategy

Stefanie Woehl

Global governance encompasses political projects that set out to extend or deepen political cooperation between state and non-state actors on multiple levels: international, national, regional and local (see Rai, this book). In addition to the International Monetary Fund (IMF), the World Bank, the World Trade Organization and the UN, nation states or regional supranational institutions such as the European Union play a major decision-making role in this process. The influence of civil society and global social movements has also increased substantially in debates on international policies such as GATTs (Meyer and Prügl 1999; O'Brien *et al.* 2000). Women's movements or organizations have been present in this process and have achieved changes for women's rights in some cases, such as implementing the Convention on the Elimination of All Forms of Discrimination against Women (CEDAW) within the United Nations, and have even gained institutional access in leading international organizations such as the World Bank. Although progress has been made in advancing equality for some women globally and placing gender issues onto the political agenda through gender mainstreaming within all policies of the European Union, the effectiveness of these policies is still debatable.

While gender issues have been mainstreamed in many international policies, global restructuring of the market has affected the working and living conditions of women and men in different regions of the world, leading to exploitation and vulnerability affecting the personal well being of poor people, especially with regard to access to welfare services, water and other global goods (Cook *et al.* 2000; Kelly *et al.* 2001). A neo-liberal capitalist-orientated market system is restructuring national and regional economies and these policies are being "locked in" through the work of international institutions such as the World Bank, the IMF and the WTO (Gill 1995; Marchand and Runyan 2000). Neo-liberal ideas such as the freedom of the market combine a discourse of personal responsibility, individualism and market-orientated rationality with the withdrawal of the state from the function of ensuring certain welfare policies. Protection of workers rights through legislation, access to public goods and services or ensuring a state financed pension system are therefore currently in transition in this neo-liberal form of deregulation (Bakker 1999; Ruppert 2000; Gill 2003). This form of deregulation has not had the consequence of a full withdrawal of nation states from welfare policies, but it has redirected their former functions towards privatization of public services to some extent and has involved other actors from civil society to implement these changes. This has not only happened in different nation states across Western Europe, but also in Latin America, certain Asian countries and the United States. This form of "governance without government" (Rosenau and Czempiel 2000), where the state is but one site of governance within a multi-level international system, has been a contested process (Commission 1995). The shifting conditions of regulating international trade, security, environment or human rights issues is described by some authors as in need of more transnational and supranational regulation (Held and McGrew 2002). But this perspective describes global governance as already somehow being the answer to the problems of government on a global scale.

In this chapter I analyse forms of global governance from a theoretical perspective following Foucault's insights on power as governmentality, which investigates the ambivalent process of governing, describes the rationality or knowledge needed to govern and in doing so creates a powerful discourse of the process of governance. While sharing the assumption that governance takes place on multiple levels at multiple sites, governmentality draws particular attention to the ambivalent effects of technologies of power needed to govern (international) space. Possible achievements as well as failures can be explained within the governmentality perspective because political and economic power can take on ambivalent forms, repressive as well as enabling and empowering. Foucault's insights on power as governmentality will provide the basis for my argument that social movements and critical civil society actors are often included in the process of global governance in the current phase of neo-liberal capitalism in ambivalent and limiting ways as part of multiple bases for restructuring global economic and political processes. I suggest that the theory of governmentality prompts us to view governance differently from the way mainstream international political economy constructs it; the focus is not on how an already existing problem can be governed globally, but how particular modes of global governance came to be the preliminary answer to certain problems of governance within a historically specific geopolitical situation. Global governance can thus be interpreted as one of the rationalities as well as programmes and techniques of contemporary governance. Governmentality explains how the governing of a population and the regulation of markets may take place within certain boundaries and spaces, through particular rationalities and specific political techniques. Using the governmentality framework allows us to problematize the way spaces between, across or beyond states are defined, which problems of governance such as trade, famine, security or unemployment occur within or across them and how these areas are constructed and regulated. Until recently, studies in governmentality have focused on the nation state as their object of analysis. Questions about the construction of the global governance and how the governmentality perspective can contribute to its analyses have only just begun (Larner and Walters 2004a). This is quite astonishing because Foucault himself "investigated the 'discourse of war'" going beyond the nation state in his own work (Larner and Walters 2004a: 6). While Foucault's earlier work concentrated on power as a disciplinary technique directed at the individual (Foucault 1994b), Foucault widened the focus of analysis from certain state institutions such as the prison or psychiatry to state actions in the late 1970s. He assumed that within a certain territory (the state) certain problems of governing such as trade, famine or security issues would need certain techniques of government to resolve. For this reason he started to analyse power as governmentality, as an art of governing and rationality of the state. While both at the state and suprastate levels this framework remains insensitive to gendered readings of governance, it does allow us to analyse historical power formations such as states or supranational institutions across international spaces both as discursively constructed and as political institutions with abilities to use multiple techniques to address key areas of governance.

The European Union is one of these modes of regional governance, where problems of security, trade, borders, identities and the market are continuously addressed across national state borders. The European integration process is a historically specific answer to the problems of governance in the post-war period. It is a contested geopolitical space where questions of governance include market competition, the construction of European citizenship and the outline and defense of its borders. The multi-level governance structures of the EU include the member states, supranational political institutions and a Single Market, which are embedded in the global political economy. As the former EU

Trade Commissioner Pascal Lamy suggested, the EU is thus a laboratory of global governance. In the first section of this chapter I briefly outline Foucault's framework on governmentality and suggest that to understand governance we need to focus on macro-political processes as well as on practices of the self to analyse neo-liberal governance. In the second section I examine the Open Method of Coordination (OMC) in the sector of employment in the EU as a new tool for gendered governance used to implement the goals of the Lisbon Strategy in the member states. I conclude that, once we engender the governmentality framework, it demonstrates that global governance is not only a contested terrain but also a political construct that offers opportunities for women and women's movements but, given the hegemonic "neo-liberal frame" (Runyan 1999) it situates them in unequal material positions within a neo-liberal consensus that is proving difficult to dismantle.

Governance as neo-liberal governmentality

Foucault's conception of governmentality can be understood as an art of governing and a way of thinking about the actions of the state or supranational state formations. The concept helps us understand the genealogy of the modern state and supranational state formations and the means of governance at their disposal. In doing so, we can grasp the micro- and macro practices of governmental actions, its neo-liberal technologies and subject formations. Foucault's term "governmentality" not only includes governance of state or state-like institutions through politics and policies, but also the scattered forms and techniques of self-guidance and leadership by others. Governmentality thus mediates between political power and subjectivity and can be understood as a certain way of problematizing political action within a geo-political boundary. This means examining specific geo-political situations, in which particular problems of governance appear and in which methodologies of governing people and things are simultaneously constructed as knowledge of the "best practices" of governing (Lemke 1997; Dean 1999). The term governmentality also differentiates between more abstract power relations and concrete relations of domination, against which resistance can be established. Finally, governmentality also allows us to examine the validated forms of knowledge/power complexes (Foucault 2000b), and to assess whether these concern the production of particular truths about the governing of the self, the avoidance of certain risks such as unemployment or diseases, or the governing of certain geopolitical economic spaces.

Thus within the governmentality framework, the state or state formations are not only institutions of repression, but also institutions of productive knowledge/power complexes in which certain problems of governance have to be solved. On a theoretical level, this means that governmentality is not only a description of macro-political technologies and technologies of the self, but also analyses the construction of norms, representations, questions of sovereignty, of law, discipline and the technologies of security as different aspects of the technologies of power (Dean 1999; Foucault 2000a; Lemke 2000b). Thus, governmentality is a "new way of thinking about and exercising power whose historical emergence Foucault dates to the eighteenth century in Europe" (Larner and Walters 2004a: 2). This form of understanding governance encourages a more differentiated understanding of sovereign power and government. While sovereignty implies the subordination to law, government was traditionally designed to govern through the exercise of "power over" the population with different technologies of political power. The political technologies to govern a population on a macro-political level were only possible through bureaucratic administrations and the police and secured the mechanisms of government for the modern state (Foucault 1994a: 86 ff; 1999: 210 ff). Foucault noted that governing with the means of scientific statistics is the key element in this context, because for state regulation economic calculations and knowledge about certain problems of governance now provided the conditions for governing. Foucault describes this type of rationality of the state as reflexive. In this sense, a certain (scientific) knowledge which was established at universities in the form of the analysis of political economy was later transferred into epistemic communities and became the condition for political actions of the state. Foucault defines governmentality as "the ensemble formed by the institutions, procedures, analyses and reflections, the calculation and tactics that allow the exercise of this very specific albeit complex form of power, which has as its target population, as its principal form of knowledge political economy and as its essential technical means apparatuses of security" (Foucault 1991a: 102).

Power is here not only focused on the level of institutions but also on the micro-level of subjects. Insofar the construction of the modern state and the rationality of government fall together with the construction of gendered subject positions, the governmentality framework provides key insights for a gendered analysis of governance. The contingent character of subjectivity and the dispersed forms of power that construct historical specific relations of domination can be retraced within the governmentality perspective. The governmentality of the state meant that the individual could now be controlled, administrated, empowered or disciplined through certain governmental techniques (police, universities, schools, welfare policies), but would be guaranteed safety within the state territory. Meanwhile, the "governmentalisation" of the state followed the (theoretical) principles of economy or economic scaling. Liberalism was the main principle for this form of governing, because it needed security technologies to proliferate its idea of freedom. But while in the time of classical liberalism the economy still needed the state to govern, neo-liberal governmentality implies that it is the economy that now becomes the regulating and main principle of the state and its form of governance (Gordon 1991; Lemke 2000b). Neo-liberalism is then not only an ideological discourse or a political reality but most of all a political project which aims to establish a social reality that it presumes as already given (Bröckling *et al.* 2000: 9). It is not individual freedom any longer, but the freedom of economy that then determines human action or political agency and establishes this new form of economic rationality as sole criteria for governance.

These insights have been used to analyse different global political phenomena in the recent past. Development discourses, as Escobar has pointed out (1995), constructed abnormalities such as "the less developed", "the illiterate", "the underfed". Important in this context is the knowledge about the constructed situation, creating a politics of "truth" through scientific acknowledgements and professionalism that reiterate these positions. The political and cultural conflicts are transformed into seemingly neutral scientific knowledge, which transfers its research back to specific institutions that are concerned with development programmes at the global level (Escobar 1995: 110; Rai 2002). Knowledge is also a key to govern "from a distance" (Rose 2000) by changing social benefit programmes into empowerment programmes, where each person is personally responsible for their loss of paid work and where the state no longer interferes. This has happened in the United States under Clinton with the Personal Responsibility and Work Opportunity Act of 1996 (Cruikshank 1999; McBride Stetson 2003) as well as in Chile, where the knowledge of grassroots movements has been used to set different agents from civil society in competition with one another and has had the effect of a retreat of the state from systems of social welfare (Parpart *et al.* 2001; Schild 2003). In this way, progressive emancipative movements have been included in this rationality of governing, using their resources and knowledge as techniques and strategies for producing gendered, rational, entrepreneurial actors who are functional for the state (Schild 2003).

These "actions on other's actions" (Gordon 1991: 10) are forms of power that do not rule with the means of direct restriction but by creating new realms of belief in the self. Certain social groups are then discursively subjected to a new form of gendered subjectivity, which conceptualizes them as actively responsible for their own well-being. It no longer draws on the norm of social coherence, solidarity and other historical assumptions of welfare states (Wöhl 2003). This discursive shift releases the state from its unifying welfare function, drawing on neo-liberal individualistic ideas, which change the norms of society such as solidarity and transform, for example, western welfare states into workfare regimes (Jessop 2003). This discursive re-articulation of the concepts of need, and entitlements and ideas of empowerment has led to severe material inequalities for certain women who now work in new informal sectors of low-wage work and has had the effect of denying former feminist demands for gender equality (Prügl 1999; Wichterich 2000). These demands are not able to be fully articulated in hegemonic public discourse and are discursively included in the hegemonic project of neo-liberal governmentality. Secondly, social identities are no longer conceptualized as in need of solidarity and as collective actors, but are rearticulated as free individuals, seemingly free of care and household work, while at the same time conservative discourses on the family and the responsibility of citizens are becoming more and more popular again in the restructuring of welfare states (Bakker and Gill 2003; Brodie 2004). This form of governance calls on the responsible citizen to take over unpaid community work or activates the unemployed to work in homes for elderly people at 1 Euro per hour as in Germany at the moment. These politics are fostering changes in the welfare state systems which do not necessarily rely on a conservative gender identity. Different gender identities seem to go along well with the individualistic idea of personal responsibility of women in this neo-liberal rationality, whether it is a single mother working in a highly qualified job or a married migrant woman working in the low paid service sector (Pühl and Wöhl 2003).

These contradictions seem to be apparent in the current phase of capitalism and lead to the question of how different categories such as class, gender and ethnicity can be conceptualized to grasp the socioeconomic changes of governance on a global scale (Brah 2002). The governmentality perspective can contribute to the analysis of global governance by highlighting the global creation of political truths and meanings perpetuated on a normative level as well analysing the material effects that these truths and means generate. Because its focus also lies on the construction and contingency of subjectivity, gender is no external category, but can always be integrated in the analysis of global governance. Governmentality can then contribute towards analysing the construction of the global as a space for institutional or non-institutional agency and to our understanding of why certain policies and different governance tools are created to solve global problems (Larner and Walters 2004b).

In the next sections I demonstrate how a gendered reading of the governmentality framework can help us analyse the ambivalent nature (disciplinary and empowering) of policy making techniques by examining the EU's OMC as a technique of governance. The employment guidelines of the Amsterdam Treaty of 1997 include gender mainstreaming goals, which are intended to ensure that gender issues need to be reflected and considered in all policies on all levels of the EU. Analysing the EU's OMC and gender mainstreaming from a governmentality perspective will allow me to explain in what ways the knowledge about governing in the sense of governmentality re-establishes gendered subjectivities in ambivalent and contradictory ways in neo-liberal political economies.

Regional governance in the EU: the open method of coordination

Economic and monetary integration have been the main political and economic projects in the integration process of the European Union (Young 2003b). Only since 1997 with the Treaty of Amsterdam have explicit gender concerns been framed in the polity of the EU and in the subsequent process of the Lisbon Strategy, which aims to make the European economy the most knowledge-based and most competitive worldwide until 2010 (Lisbon European Council 2000). Even though gender issues were considered in specific policy fields through directives in the 1980s and 1990s, a broader framework for gender equality has only been institutionalized through the implementation of gender mainstreaming and the introduction of the OMC to achieve the goals of the Lisbon Strategy: competitiveness, social cohesion and full employment.

The instrument for achieving this in the member states of the EU especially in the welfare sectors of employment and in the restructuring of pension systems is the OMC. This mode of governing is at the same time a weak mode of governance because it is not based on laws and contract but on mutual recognition and it offers framework guidelines rather than regulation by directives or uniform policies. The nature of the OMC is thus a new technology of European governance because it sets out to harmonize European space by letting the member states design and regulate their resources in welfare policy fields by themselves. Thus, the OMC is also a new rationality of government because it is not designed to regulate from the supranational level in the usual way, but to conduct policy adjustment from a greater distance. The supranational level in the form of the European Commission and European Council is designated to conduct this by installing systematic annual monitoring to report on the progress made in the different policy fields by the member states. The methods for achieving this in the different member states may vary; therefore systematic comparisons between member states are monitored by peer review, analysing the different practices across member states and finding models of "best practice". In this way the OMC is designed to encourage the member states to compete with one another by using political benchmarking. Benchmarking is an economic indicator based system of comparing achievements, formerly used by international companies, and installing a model of "best" or "good practice". Benchmarking originates from economic theory and is used to compare achievements and financial growth of companies. It is oriented according to output and filters information so that the indicators (benchmarks) that seem to bring the most financial gain are used as cornerstones for further decisions as to how a company should compete successfully. The US company Xerox is the most famous example for best benchmarking. It has become the leading company in the photo industry because Xerox best practice has become standardized globally.

Political benchmarking, as used in the OMC, is such a modus operandi of "learning by comparing". Member states of the EU which seem to have successfully raised the percentage of the work force or which have partially privatized their pension systems can be seen as examples of good practice or good governance. This "peer-pressure" is supposed to stimulate other member states to adjust their welfare systems. This form of benchmarking is used as a political decision making process based on economic results in international comparison. Performance indicators as used in the OMC have already been used in the OECD countries for a longer time to compare education and health systems. The OMC has already been in use in other fields of policy making, and elements of the method have also been employed in the macroeconomic monitoring of the monetary union.[1] Learning by comparing (economic) standards is the method of changing the welfare state systems of the national states with the OMC and employing this strategy of competitiveness at the European level. In mainstream literature, this mode of comparing is seen as stimulating new processes of reflection and creating a new knowledge-based political culture (Devetzi and Schmitt 2002;

Rodrigues 2002). Political goals at the institutional level of the European Commission have formerly often been set in cooperation with powerful actors like the European Round Table of Industrialists (Tidow 1999). Therefore, it is highly contested how a competitive strategy like the OMC can acknowledge national welfare state specifications such as the rate and cause for unemployment, while assuming the unquestioned norm of economic competitiveness for all (Ostheim and Zohlnhöfer 2002; Haahr 2004). This political goal of competitiveness is introduced and validated by scientific experts who outline the indicators for benchmarking. In Germany for example, the so-called "Hartz-Commission", named after former Volkswagen chief executor for employees Peter Hartz, was installed by the Social Democratic and Green government to restructure the whole employment sector. Scientific economic experts, managers and union members designed a policy programme called Hartz I–IV. Besides designing an activating employment sector that is based on supply-related employment policies [Angebotspolitik] and redesigning the federal employment agencies, unemployment payments were shortened to one year. After that year, if the person does not find a job within that time, the unemployment benefits are the same as the social welfare income. People who have been long term unemployed are also forced to take up jobs at 1 Euro per hour in addition to social welfare, if they do not want to loose these benefits. These methods are supposed to stimulate or activate especially the long-term unemployed to find a job. But given the high rate of unemployment, around 12 percent in Germany, finding a job is a structural problem and not just a personal responsibility.

In this sense, the OMC is much more restrictive concerning its process than the former political monitoring, which gave the member states the freedom of designing their welfare policies by themselves and did not make them compete with one another. Even though competitiveness, social cohesion and employment are supposed to be in balance with each other (Article 125 EVG), the National Action Plans reporting on the national progress in employment of the member states have now been shortened to one annual report concerning all three topics. Formerly, there was one separate report for employment in the old Lisbon Strategy. But if the new Lisbon Strategy is to succeed, it would need to do more than just implement empowering or activating strategies for employment as outlined in the European employment guidelines. At the level of subjectivities and individual identities, the new Lisbon Strategy requires a more individualistic and self-monitored comprehension of one's self; it needs individuals to take responsibility of their own welfare even as states restructure the economic landscape. In studies on governmentality this form of governing the unemployed or the poor has been analysed as governing *through* the individual subjects instead of against them (Cruikshank 1999). Empowerment strategies and knowledge originating from social movements are decontextualized and used as governmental techniques to activate and empower the unemployed. In this way the unemployed are statistically registered as a group, and the knowledge and empowerment strategies from critical civil society actors are used as powerful techniques to govern this part of the population. This form of governance does not transfer power from the macro-level of government institutions to the micro-level of individuals; rather it uses the knowledge and techniques of empowerment to secure certain mechanisms of government. As Cruikshank notes,

> (...) governmental interventions are designed to create the possibility for people to come together. To govern, then, means to first stir up the desire, the interest and the will to participate or act politically. To establish a relationship of governance, it is necessary to first re-constitute the poor and powerless as acting subjects. In short, according to the logic of empowerment, the poor have to be made to act.
>
> (1994: 48)

At the same time non-state actors such as unions are also involved as collective actors to foster these activating strategies in the employment sector at the meso-level. Because the OMC attains its competence from setting the member states in competition with one another, without calling it that explicitly, in a certain sense this new mode of governance has a lot in common with the empowerment programmes which are, at the moment, fostered at the level of individuals. If rational, self-responsible subjects can be created like this and even critical collective actors from civil society are involved in the process, then there is no need to exert pressure and to limit freedoms, because it seems plausible to act and live like this as an individual or not to participate in this form of governance as a collective actor. What can be stated for the micro-level of subjects and at the meso-level of institutional actors in this context is programmatically installed in the OMC by generating best practices between the member states' welfare policy fields. The alignment of this form of policy making is not so much seen as pressure or coercion, but certainly has these effects in the long run, while at the same time stabilizing a neo-liberal consensus of individual responsibility. The effects of these empowerment strategies are thus ambivalent: they may actually support long-term unemployed by activating their efforts to gain employment, and at the same time these techniques are an art of governing that redefines the norms and functions of welfare states into a neo-liberal framework and has the effect of a retreat of the state from ensuring welfare policies.

But restructuring a democratic process only along the lines of institutional reforms that are oriented according to market criteria also implies an undermining of democracy. Haahr notes that OMC is a form of governance that understands power "as dispersed and multifaceted and (. . .) governance as involving formalized, institutionalized and informal processes of co-coordination and will-formation" (Haahr 2004: 211). This "conduct of conduct" defines governance as a rational, calculative process to change policies. The question of how to govern and how we are being governed is thus combined with economic knowledge, which is used to govern over people and things. In this sense it is no longer individual freedom but the freedom of economy that becomes the main goal of governance. The OMC can be seen as a form of neo-liberal or advanced liberal governmentality which employs the knowledge and rational criteria of political benchmarking and does not interfere directly with state policies or actions, but steers institutional reforms and policies "from a distance" (Rose 2000). This has happened because the neo-liberal ideology of individualism has been successfully combined with empowerment strategies and has changed the norms and ideas of society. "The changing understanding of society in turn makes possible a government which is not the government of society in the welfarist sense: no longer that of securing a set of social, economic and demographic processes, the basic problem of government becomes securing governmental mechanisms." (Haahr 2004: 215)

This can be seen as a strategy of repression of individuals and disciplining national actors as well as a process of empowerment because the OMC includes critical actors such as unions, NGOs and other social partners in the process of political deliberation and economic restructuring. This mode of governance is not only a disciplinary form of neo-liberalism (Gill 1995), but it is one that enables, activates and includes different actors. Cooperation and consent are explicitly sought after and are seen as the best form of governance and will at the same time not undermine the subsidiary principle prescribed in the welfare policy field. The OMC has been explicitly installed in the welfare policies of the EU, but not in other policy fields, such as the creation of the Single Market project, where the European Commission was much more restrictive and regulating in its form of policy making. Especially in the employment sector more regulative forms of governance would be necessary though to improve the full-time employment of women and men. Although major differences exist between the Nordic and southern member states, women still represent the highest rate of low wage or part time workers across Europe (European Commission 2004). The rule of government-ality within the OMC consists of just this method of banking on the self-regulating market forces and letting the Member states regulate their resources according to the market principle in the employment sector.

> Yet, regardless of whether the situation is one of the active involve-ment of citizens in community development or of the engagement of ministerial bureaucracies or "social partners" from different states in common process of deliberation, the technologies employed share certain characteristics: the presupposition that government is the employment of techniques for the release of resources found in a domain outside government itself.
>
> (Haahr 2004: 218).

The OMC as multi-level governance technique is thus at the same time a weak mode of governance in the field of welfare policy because of the greater distance of rule from the supranational level. However, it power-fully sets economic market criteria as standards (benchmarks) to foster a competitive, neo-liberal market-oriented society on a collective and individual level. This governmental technique, which includes differ-ent actors (nation states, social partners from civil society) on different sites (European, national, local), is not only a technology of governance, but also a rationality of governance that is prescribed as the preliminary answer for solving European social problems and for governing Europe. While some of the implications of the OMC may seem to be a reas-onable form of governance within the Union, the OMC is an example of securing the mechanisms of government at the supranational level with an economic rationality that now becomes the main principle of government. William Walters and Jens Henrik Haahr see the OMC as an advanced form of liberalism in which society is mobilized not only for reasons of self responsibility, but to proliferate "various technolo-gies of power – including mechanisms of partnership, techniques of empowerment, procedures of benchmarking and methods of best prac-tice" (Haahr and Walters 2005: 119). Installing these technologies across different spaces and within different subjects makes this governmental technique more than an ideology; it opens society to become a "field of energies ... capable of generating its own "solutions" to social and ethical problems" (ibid.). The OMC employs self-agency at different levels and by different actors to optimize political performance. In this way NGOs, social partners and other critical actors are not only seen as disturbing the political process of governance, but as resources for reaching the overall goal of a competitive knowledge-based economy in the European Union. Having this framework in mind, we can now look at how gender aspects are integrated into this form of multi-level governance at the European level.

The OMC and gender mainstreaming in the European employment guidelines

Taking into account that the dominant projects in the European integration process were configuring the Single Market and the economic and monetary union in the governance structures of the European Union in the 1990s (Bieling and Steinhilber 2001; Bieling and Deppe 2003), women organizations' lobbying for gender mainstreaming had to make a strong case against dominant actors and their interventions to implement gender pillars and guidelines were only taken up in the supranational institutional contract of the Amsterdam Treaty in 1997 after a very long process of political bargaining (Young 2001; Hoskyns 2004 and this book). This shows how, in this field of structural and strategic selectivity, powerful actors select and modify their interests to their advantage. Gender mainstreaming was then finally anchored in the employment guidelines of the Amsterdam Treaty. At the same time Article 105, in Chapter 2 of the Amsterdam Treaty still gives price stability the highest priority in the political goals of the union. Even though several binding legal directives have been installed during the 1980s and 1990s to foster gender equality in employment and to secure working conditions for women, these cannot be seen as a coordinated social policy (Ostner and Lewis 1995). With the OMC as an instrument to implement the employment guidelines, gender mainstreaming is now supported only by soft law, making it dependent on the willingness of the member states to further gender equality in the employment sector. The coordination in the employment guidelines is based on the national action plans of the member states. These were quite vague and focused largely on preventive measures against unemployment and enabling policies (employability) for individuals formulated in the first part of the employment chapter. The second goal of the employment chapter, which seeks to foster self-entrepreneurship and the creation of new jobs focused mainly on the service sector and how to cut the costs of entrepreneurs (Ostheim and Zollnhofer 2002). The flexibility of work contracts and working hours is part of the third goal and has already had consequences for workers in Germany: collective wage agreements [Flächentarifverträge] are being allowed to expire and working hours are increased in the service sector and community hospitals, all sectors in which women represent a high percentage of the workforce. All in all, most member states have been able to neglect the recommendations of the Commission or to weaken them in the employment sector. This shows that European social policy is still underdeveloped and weak in comparison to other policy fields.

With the advent of the OMC in the employment sector, European social policy has been extended by a political process of benchmarking that fits into the market rationality of the integration process. Problems of installing the European employment strategy can be recognized in this context: results and achievements of the member states' national action plans have mainly focused on the first part of the employment guidelines (employability) and results in the sector of entrepreneurship (Jacobsson and Schmid 2004). In most countries employability has been the main focus in restructuring the employment sector, while gender mainstreaming goals to foster gender equality have mainly been neglected (Bothfeld *et al.* 2002). The implementation deficit of the third (adjustment) and fourth goal (gender equality) is also due to the neglect of the relevance of macroeconomic indicators concerning employment (see Hoskyns in this book). Since the macroeconomic goals of the integration process are very restrictive, the effects on national budgets are not considered in a way that would foster employment or shift more of the national budget to employment policy. Thus, the national action plans reflect more the already existing employment policies of the member states rather than follow the recommendations of the European Commission. In Denmark for example, where best practice in employment policies has been fostering employability since 1994, local and individual action plans seem to follow a bottom-up process rather than being influenced by the European employment guidelines.

"The degree of correspondence between the national action plan guidelines and the local planning documents is rather a matter of coincidence. Local priorities coincide with the European Employment Strategy." (Jacobsson and Schmid 2004: 81) This shows that the national action plans for employment are dependent on the political will of the responsible ministers at the national and local level and that the implementation is mainly dependent on the power of the social partners to negotiate. The power of unions as negotiating actors plays a central role in this process, but especially women working in the service sector are often not adequately represented in this procedure. For the implementation of the fourth goal – gender equality – of the European employment strategy, a working group was installed in the women's ministry in Germany in 1999, which meant that the weakest ministry was now considered responsible for monitoring gender mainstreaming in the employment sector. At the same time a main bureaucratic reform to modernize the state was started in order to optimize performance, which had the effect that gender mainstreaming was delegated to the women's unit of the specific bureaucratic sectors and led to the fact that gender mainstreaming was not employed at all levels of bureaucracy. The idea and project of gender mainstreaming was thus not realized. Gender issues were mainly just shifted back to women's advocacy.

The advisory character of gender mainstreaming makes it a weak instrument in the employment sector. It cannot intervene directly on specific policies and has been too unspecific to change the gendered segregation of work in specific sectors until now. Insofar it is dependent on the political will of the different institutional actors to actually implement gender training measures, gender budgets or to realize gender sensitive statistics. The Hartz reforms in Germany have meanwhile had different material effects for different women: most new jobs for women were created in the low-paid service sector. These so called "mini-jobs" at 400 Euro per month allow women who formerly worked illegally in private households to receive social security for their services; women who became entrepreneurs profited the most from the reforms and the subsidies supplied by the federal employment agencies in this case. But the percentage of women who actually do become entrepreneurs is relatively small; for other women, who are not entrepreneurs, the dependency on their husbands or partners is increased because if these women become dependent on social welfare, the income of the partner is deducted from the social benefits. Even though gender mainstreaming has had a discursive effect in some state institutions in Germany by devoting attention to the needs of women, its implementation in the employment sector is minimal and in most sectors not a direct consequence of gender mainstreaming (Bothefeld *et al.* 2002). As a top-down model, gender mainstreaming was designed to create employment for women by eliminating unequal pay and unequal working conditions as well as to eliminate the gendered segregation of work. But the new paths to employment that are concentrated on employability have not led to equality between women and men. The neo-liberal idea of "human resources" rather promotes the construction of difference between women and men and this construction is then used to employ those who are considered to be more efficient as workers (those who do not need maternity cover, for example) and to generate employability and an enabling employment policy (Schunter-Kleeman 2003). This has not led to the empowering of women in an emancipative sense, or to make them more economically independent. Rather it helps to limit the social welfare expenditure and the need for an active job-creating policy of the state. It also creates a market-based rationality of individual responsibility in the employment sector. While having some positive effects in the member states, gender mainstreaming is too vaguely designed to counteract against the enabling, supply-side policies in the employment sector. While progress can be seen especially in the southern European countries such as Greece, Italy and Spain where the rate of women's employment has increased, the strategies remain ambivalent: in Great Britain women workers' rights were strengthened in flexible and part time work, while directives on economic gender equality from the EU were blocked by the government in the past (Cook 1998; Rubery *et al.* 1998). These examples demonstrate how gender mainstreaming can be implemented within a neo-liberal market economy, which is based on deflationary politics resulting from the Maastricht criteria without actually changing the gender regime of states.

From a governmentality perspective, gender mainstreaming can be seen as a framework, which may bring advantages for highly qualified women and men by opening paths to higher employment or creating a market for "gender experts". But the evidence provided here also underlines the fact that gender mainstreaming can be compatible with neo-liberal market criteria and with a bureaucratic reform in Germany that is oriented towards economic efficiency. While knowledge about gender has increased in the field of gender studies at universities, this knowledge is now used as a governmental technique and as expertise in an ambivalent way: gender mainstreaming is generated from the same governmental techniques that it actually seeks to transform. This may be seen as a process of empowerment, but at the same time it has lost its former emancipative meaning. What has been described as "governing at a distance" in the studies on governmentality has now found its way to govern the knowledge about gender including the formerly emancipative meanings and technologies of empowerment by grassroots and women's movements into multi-level governance structures. In this sense the critical intention of gender mainstreaming formulated by women's movements at the Women's World Conference in Beijing in 1995 has to show its effectiveness within neo-liberal market criteria to be compatible with the broader goals of the European Union. This does not imply that gender mainstreaming will not have any positive effects at all, but that the hegemonic neo-liberal frame and the main policy outline of the Lisbon strategy weaken its critical emancipative intention to change existing forms of domination. The transformative potential of gender mainstreaming will depend on the actors engaged in implementing it, on the power of different social forces at the local level and finally on how much of the budget is spent for gender sensitive analysis. As a top-down model, gender mainstreaming will be dependent on men in higher positions in bureaucratic institutions to promote a change not only in policy but institutional mentality towards gender equality. This will only happen, as examples of femocrats in institutions have shown in the past, if non-institutional activists support the implementation process at the local level. The problem of gender mainstreaming as a concept lies not only in local predicaments, but also in the very different welfare state arrangements of the member states and the different gender regimes that go along with them. Thus, gender mainstreaming will have to be translated into the different gender regimes of the member states to actually focus the specific forms of the gendered segregation of work and the gendered political culture of the member states.

Conclusions

Global governance within the neo-liberal framework in the sense of neo-liberal governmentality does not only offer many opportunities for women's lobby groups, but settles them in a terrain of power relations, in which they can also actively redefine policies but in a contested hegemonic space of action (see Waylen, this book). Global governance is then not only a space for the permanent democratic inclusion of civil society actors and global social movements as other authors have argued (Weiss 2000), but an ambivalent field of power on different levels: international, regional and local. Governance itself involves knowledge and other technologies of power to stabilize the global forms of rule. Global governance also reflects political arrangements, which may favour the ideas and strategies of powerful civil society groups, powerful states or supranational state actors, such as the European Round Table of Industrialists in the EU while at the same time involving and using the knowledge and actions of other political actors (NGOs, trade unions and grassroots movements). The European Union is for sure one of the most aggregated forms of cooperation in international politics, but as such not necessarily the best example for good governance and for democratic inclusion of civil society. The inclusion and cooperation with civil society actors and NGOs does not necessarily imply a democratic modus operandi of (global) governance or more accountability in global governance (Keohane 2005), but reflects the ambivalence of global governance as a technology of power: the technologies employed can empower individual and collective actors, relying on their own energies and resources to restructure the state, society or international space *while* establishing a neo-liberal consensus.

In this hegemonic arena of discourse, different interest groups articulate their ideas of the global, society, and how the public and private should be (re-)organized. This struggle over meaning in global governance is the performative discursive aspect, in which women's "interests" are produced and accounted for in institutional settings and where their personal responsibility, dependency or difference can be constructed, modernized or be maintained. These identities can then be actively involved for the stabilization of certain capitalist modes of production and for assuring mechanisms of governance on a global scale. The governmentality perspective can focus more accurately on this combination of power and knowledge as a governmental technique, and as a discourse and strategy of power in and of global governance than approaches previously engaged in analysing global governance.[2] As we have noted above, empowering the individual, specific groups or projects is then a gendered governmental technique, which governs "at a distance", but employs neo-liberal rationality of free markets on the individual gendered subject, institutions from civil society and welfare state institutions. On the European level this knowledge-based rationality of governing is now creating a space of economic action that makes its neo-liberal rationality difficult to circumscribe and difficult to injure. In conclusion, therefore, it is necessary to take a closer look at the hegemonic projects fostered in the European Union and at the global level of institutions at the moment to study in what way they are able to stabilize consent in multi-level global governance and can discursively and materially reproduce different forms of inequality along the axes of gender, class and ethnicity. When these subtle mechanisms of power become visible, the struggle for equality can respond to the challenges posed by neo-liberal capitalism today.

Notes

1. But while the European Commission was much more restrictive regarding the economic and monetary union because the deficit spending of the member states should not exceed 3 percent of the GDP, the OMC has no such restrictions right from the outset.
2. International Political Economy scholars who have focused on hegemony usually also do not include the construction of gendered subjects in their analysis (exceptions are Bakker and Gill 2003 as well as Young 2003).

4
Governing Intimacy in the World Bank

Kate Bedford

Introduction

This chapter charts the policymaking efforts of gender staff in the World Bank – the world's largest and most influential development institution.[1] It attempts to analyse those efforts through the lens of governance, a process that draws on four particularly important insights:

(1) That governance, as "a system of rules for public life," involves multiple sites and actors employing heterogeneous strategies oriented to numerous – and sometimes conflicting – ends (Waylen and Rai, this book; Rose 1999: 21; Mosse and Lewis 2005). The state is only one actor among many here, and multilateral institutions have become increasingly central players in global governance debates (Larner and Walters 2004a).

(2) That the deployment of expertise is a key mechanism of governance (Valverde 1998; Terry 1999).

(3) That there are crucial links between micro and macro governance projects. Using Nikolas Rose's formulation, government refers to the processes through which individuals are urged and educated to bridle their own passions and control their own instincts (Valverde 1998; Rose 1999: 3). The governance perspective thus presupposes the freedom of the governed (Rose 1999: 4), but it considers how apparent exercises of free will are connected, in complex and uneven ways, to larger social, economic, and political processes (Cruikshank 1999). For example the family has often been a target of state management efforts, and many attempts to achieve national and imperial prosperity have relied on expert interventions into individual lives, using notions of hygiene, education, health, and so on (Rose

1999: 6; Levine 2003). This insight provides space to consider how multilateral institutions oriented to economic development, trade, and finance, are involved in governance of micro level concerns.

(4) That analysis of governance involves tracking the common-sense nature, or normativity, of discourses entrenched as self-evident (Rai, Chapter 1, this book). Specifically, the governance lens requires a disturbance of what forms the "groundwork of the present," to make the given seem strange and to question what is taken as natural (Rose 1999: 58).

In this chapter I apply these four insights to analysis of the Bank, attempting to make strange accepted, expert-supported truths of gender policy in order to demonstrate the institution's involvement in micro-level governance projects that would otherwise be overlooked. Specifically, I trace the efforts of Bank gender staff to resolve an oft-cited tension in neo-liberal development regarding paid and unpaid labour by restructuring intimate attachments between men and women. This discussion is in part intended to re-scale governance discussions, to link the macroeconomic concerns of multilateral institutions to subjectivities, caring practices, and expressions of love. It is also intended to identify the common-sense assumptions about sexuality and masculinity upon which these interventions rest, in order to facilitate their feminist contestation.

The World Bank, gender, and governance debates: the social reproduction dilemma revisited

A focus on the Bank is particularly important for feminists interested in global governance. It remains the "flagship" (Yunus 1994: ix) and "pace-setter" (Hancock 1989: 57) of international development policy, employing nearly 10,000 people and lending more money to more countries than any other development body – the Board approved US$22.3 billion in loans and grants for 278 projects in FY2005 (World Bank 2006). The institution's growing research role also ensures that its staff remain entrenched as *the* development experts. As Arturo Escobar puts it the prevailing wisdom in the policy field is that "if 'the Bank' does not have clear answers, nobody else does" (1995: 160; see also Birdsall and Kapur 2005: 4).

This primacy is of particular relevance to feminists due to the Bank's recent shift in mission to embrace social concerns. During the 1980s the Bank was a key advocate of the neo-liberal Washington Consensus, aiming to cut back the state, open trade, reduce social spending, dereg-ulate, and privatize. However, the institution was transformed after the appointment of James Wolfensohn as President in 1995 (Fox and Brown 1998; Gilbert and Vines 2000; O'Brien *et al.* 2000; Pincus and Winters 2002; Mallaby 2004). Wolfensohn met with Bank critics, he launched partnership initiatives with civil society groups, and he spoke of holistic development frameworks that re-centered poverty. He also made gender more central to Bank lending. He led the Bank's delegation to the UN's 1995 Beijing Conference on Women, for example, and between 1995 and 2001 the proportion of projects that included some consideration of gender issues in their design almost doubled, to nearly 40 per cent (Long 2003: 7). By 2001 the Bank was positioning itself as the disseminator of "good practice" on gender in the development community (World Bank 2001: 273).

I am interested in the impact of this mission-shift on the Bank's response to a key dilemma outlined by feminist political economists regarding tensions between paid and unpaid work. Overall, the Bank has prioritized efforts to get women into paid work as the "cure all" for gender inequality.[2] Yet this prioritization of employment leaves the Bank with a remaining policy problem, since it must deal with the work women already do – the unpaid labours of caring, socialization, and human needs fulfilment known in feminist literature as social reproduc-tion work. This includes childcare, housework, subsistence agriculture, cooking, voluntary work to sustain community organizations, and so on – activities that are rarely counted in official statistics as work because they are seen as non-productive. Feminists have long argued that dom-inant models of growth overlook the economic value of these activities, disproportionately done by women (Waring 1988; Folbre 1994; Elson 1996; Peterson 2003; Benería and Feldman 1992). Many have criticized the Bank specifically for assuming what I call an exhaustion solution to the social reproduction dilemma, wherein it does nothing to resolve tensions between renumerated employment and unpaid caring labour such that women are overburdened when they are forced, through eco-nomic necessity, to enter paid work (O'Brien *et al.* 2000; Long 2003; Wood 2003; Zuckerman and Qing 2003; Kuiper and Barker 2006). To reiterate, however, the Bank has changed. Space now exists for fem-inist policy entrepreneurs to seize hold of the Bank's discovery of the "social," to argue that markets are socially embedded institutions to which gendered processes are central (Rai, Chapter 1, this book). How is the social reproduction dilemma being resolved in this space, and how are feminist interventions reshaping the governance of development?

To explore these issues I focused on World Bank gender activities undertaken in Ecuador since Wolfensohn took over as President in 1995. Using interviews with Gender And Development (GAD) staff and consultants conducted in 2003 and 2004, analysis of relevant documents put out by the Bank's resident mission in Quito, and fieldwork on Bank gender lending, I considered how Bank GAD policy entrepreneurs were attempting to resolve the social reproduction dilemma. Ecuador is an excellent site for research into Bank gender policy. The Latin American and Caribbean region is regarded as having the most advanced gender unit in the Bank (Hafner-Burton and Pollack 2002: 368; Long 2003: 9; Zuckerman and Qing 2003: 27). In turn the Bank's resident mission in Quito put out one of the most comprehensive gender reviews of all countries in the region, mentioned in a recent worldwide Bank report on gender progress within the institution (World Bank 2000a: 27). Bank gender staff in Ecuador also have close links to domestic feminists,[3] funding national events for women's day, and collaborating with academic institutions, the state's women council (CONAMU), and Afro-Ecuadorian and indigenous women's groups. Finally, the Bank has put out several important documents on gender in Ecuador, including most notably Caroline Moser's research into gender and household coping strategies under structural adjustment (1993, 1996, 1997; World Bank 1996). Moser is particularly well known for a pioneering study in the 1980s on gender and poverty in a low-income housing settlement in Guayaquil (Ecuador's largest city). This was subsequently extended into a larger project on household vulnerability to economic change, funded and published by the Bank as *Confronting Crisis*. More recently, the Bank funded an important study on gender and time use focused on the Ecuadorian flower industry (Newman 2001), used to inform the aforementioned *Ecuador Gender Review*. In short Ecuador is a good site for investigating Bank gender policy because feminists are active policy entrepreneurs in this resident mission, attempting to intervene in the governance of the global economy to promote gender equity. Exploring their experiences is thus helpful in ascertaining how they grapple (if at all) with the social reproduction problem.

Feminist recognition of the social reproduction dilemma

Getting women into paid employment was a clear priority for Bank gender staff in Ecuador, expressed in both interviews and policy documents. Work was framed as a way to increase productivity and growth, to achieve poverty reduction, and to empower women.[4] Policy success was thus identified based on work-related criteria. For example the abstract of the *Ecuador Gender Review* used women's increased labour force participation as proof that "Ecuador has made considerable strides in addressing gender issues" (Correia 2000: v). Moreover work was marked as a continued policy priority, given remaining problems of unequal wages, unequal training opportunities, higher female unemployment, and occupational segregation. This led to a persistent emphasis on work-related solutions to gender concerns. For example the gender chapter of a 2002a Bank report on dollarization in Ecuador identified getting women into work as part of a broader empowerment initiative, concluding that increasing women's labour force participation "enhanc(es) their economic independence and reduc(es) their vulnerability" (Correia 2002: 205). Increased employment was also framed as part of an effort to "break the culture of dependency" (206) affecting poor communities, whereby women were targeted as potential employees in order to increase self-reliance and thereby achieve empowerment.

That said, however, gender policymakers were also fully aware of the social reproduction dilemma. Gender staff on one loan frequently expressed concern about women being overburdened through projects that failed to take into account their multiple responsibilities, for example, and one consultant told me that most people considered un- or underemployed by the Bank were wrongly classified since they were engaged in productive subsistence activities. Similarly when teaching staff and organizations how to "do" gender in Bank-funded projects attention was devoted to Caroline Moser's triple role framework, a planning tool that highlights the importance of non-market activities (see P.R.O.D.E.P.I.N.E. 2001: n.p.). Time use surveys, which record social reproduction labour as work, were also used in case studies of gender and ethnicity conducted for a prominent rural development loan (see Bedford 2005b for a more in-depth discussion).

Bank gender texts on Ecuador replicated this recognition of unpaid labour. For example Moser's *Confronting Crisis* study repeatedly noted the blurred boundaries between productive and unproductive work, and it urged the Bank to value women's reproductive and community managing roles as crucial to household and community survival. The first line to the section on "balancing productive work with domestic responsibilities" argued that "although labor is understood to be the poor's most valuable asset, the invisibility of domestic labour means that demands on women to perform unpaid domestic labour remain unrecognized" (Moser 1997: 68). Women's need to take on extra work to pick up the slack of economic restructuring was also seen to have generated unmet care needs for children and the sick (Moser 1996: 68; 1997: 12), and to have caused depression, anxiety, and burn-out (Moser in World Bank 1996: 129). Likewise, recognition of social reproduction concerns was evident in the *Ecuador Gender Review*, the Bank's flagship gender document on the country. The report asserted unambiguously that women's employment opportunities were restricted because they "continue to bear the burden of care giving and domestic tasks" (Correia 2000: 35), and it noted that increased female labour force participation caused by macro-economic crisis could lead to "greater pressures on (women's) time" (50). Thus one of the "lessons learnt" from a recent attempt to integrate gender into a rural development loan was "the need to address women's reproductive and domestic time constraints in conjunction with supporting their productive activities" (76). Similar arguments were made in the gender chapter of the Bank's 2002a report on Ecuador's dollarization (Correia 2002: 178).

Crucially, awareness of the social reproduction dilemma also made its way into more mainstream Bank discussions. For example the 1996 *Ecuador Poverty Report* contained several references to the issue, outside of Moser's chapter on gender which repeated the claims made above. The introduction noted that household and childcare duties "are the major reason why women do not participate in the workforce, and these are more pressing the poorer they are" (World Bank 1996: 39). The Bank's 2003 report on *Ecuador: An Economic and Social Agenda in the New Millennium* also included multiple references to social reproduction. These were particularly evident in Alexandra Ortiz's chapter on urban development, which used Moser's research to argue that during economic crisis "mothers are forced to increase their participation in the working world and decrease the amount of time they spend taking care of their children" (Ortiz 2003: 259). The prioritization of these findings reflected an awareness that unpaid work was important, and that "trade offs" between market and non-market labour could overburden women.

In short, then, gender staff at the Bank in Ecuador recognized that unpaid caring labour must be dealt with in policy if efforts to get women into work were to be effective – they expressed this in interviews and gender texts, and were relatively successful at getting the recognition into the Bank's mainstream documents. Staff did not endorse an exhaustion solution to the social reproduction dilemma, and they did not assume women's time to be "infinitely elastic" (Elson 1996: 71). It remains to examine the solutions designed in response, and to explore how they relate to governance concerns.

Governing intimacy to resolve the social reproduction dilemma

The most prominent policy solution[5] endorsed by Bank gender staff to the tension between paid work and social reproduction was the restructuring of normative heterosexuality to encourage a two-partner model of love and labour, wherein women work more and men care better. This sharing approach attempted to (re)privatize responsibility for social reproduction by adjusting the way in which love was expressed in the family. It stemmed from the Bank's framing of gender policy as involving complementary attention to men and women, and from the promotion of loving partnerships as empowering. Indeed Bank gender efforts hinge on assumptions about the normative desirability of complementary relations between men and women at the personal level.[6] In its formally cleared, D.C.-level documents the Bank has defined gender policy as requiring male inclusion, and thus attention to men and to encouraging men and women to share development benefits and responsibilities is a key contemporary characteristic of GAD work. Policies and projects that are seen to ignore men are designated failures, and pressure is put on gender staff at the country level to include men in their activities.

This approach to gender was clearly evident in Ecuador. As defined by one consultant, the official policy was that "we don't believe that there should be projects for women and projects for men; there should be projects with a focus on equity for men and women." Likewise, in policy texts attention to men and organizing in mixed groups were identified as key elements distinguishing an "ideological women in development approach over a true gender perspective" (Correia 2000: 76). Gender analysis itself was thus defined as involving complementary attention to men and women. Hence the *Ecuador Gender Review* criticized Ecuador's state feminist organization CONAMU for failing to include men in its gender work, and it recommended the inclusion of men and the organizing of men's groups as one of the "lessons learnt" from a failed rural development loan (Correia 2000: 80). Similarly the chapter on gender in the Bank's 2002a report on Ecuador's dollarization lamented that literature on gender and macroeconomic crisis "focuses almost solely on women to the exclusion of men" (Correia 2002: 178).

Given that the Bank's gender efforts required inclusion of men and rested on a celebratory approach to sharing couplehood, the solutions to the social reproduction dilemma that were preferred by staff focused on keeping men around and making them more reliable partners. Specifically, the Bank's gender specialists sought to teach poor Ecuadorian men how to be responsible family members, particularly in order that they could help pick up the slack of unmet care needs as their wives moved into paid employment. Getting poor women into work and getting poor men into parenting classes were thus considered complementary strategies, persistently framed as mutually supportive and equally necessary priorities, and as empowering to both parties. Consider, for example, the priority areas mentioned by the *Ecuador Gender Review*:

> First, both female and male gender issues need to be considered when designing and implementing social safety nets and emergency assistance programs, so that, inter alia, programs strengthen the role of fathers and provide income generating opportunities for women
> (Correia 2000: xii).[7]

Specific suggested interventions included "programs to promote men as fathers" which although "still very new in the Region and elsewhere... could be piloted in Ecuador" given models that exist elsewhere (xi). For example the *Gender Review* mentioned the need for reproductive health programs that include men "to develop services for men in line with their needs, and to promote more active male participation in childcare and parenthood" (54). It also noted approvingly that "increasingly adolescent men are the targets of safe sex, family planning and responsible parenthood programs" (16). Later the report recommended teaching parenting skills to boys and girls as part of its health sector reform (57). Elsewhere, in a discussion of how to help female farmers overcome obstacles to participation in rural development, the report mentioned "working with male farmers so that they understand that supporting women's participation does not mean they are "mandarinas" (wimps/softies/unmanly) *and training men to share domestic chores and childcare*" (59 emphasis added). Another report recommended using the United States as a guide:

> "one possible model is that of Family Resource Centers that have been established in poor latino communities in the United States to target mothers, fathers, adolescent boys, and adolescent girls in dealing with issues such as responsible fathering, male alcoholism, women's economic opportunities and empowerment, pregnancy among teenage girls, and gang violence and drug abuse among male adolescents. *In particular, these centers have played an important role for men by broadening their roles as fathers*" (Correia 2002: 206 emphasis added).

In some respects these policies were understood to empower all people, since "broadening male gender roles could benefit men as well as women and their families, given that substance abuse, violence and depression among men have been linked to gender roles and the limited ways men have to affirm their identity" (Correia 2000: xi). That said, however, the effort to liberate men from restrictive masculinity did not apply equally. It was intended to "promote men's roles as fathers and caregivers, *particularly among unemployed men*" (xi, emphasis added), because:

> "Men are often underemployed or off work during economic down-turns and therefore could share the burden of household responsibilities. In contrast, women often enter the workforce to compensate for household income losses during periods of economic crisis and have less time to engage in domestic chores" (xiv).

Global economic shifts were hereby understood to have generated an abundance of poor men sitting around with time on their hands, the perfect candidates for an apparently easy and universally empowering resolution of tensions between unpaid care and renumerated labour.

Gender expertise and policy formulation

Knowledge from gender experts was crucial in these initiatives. Indeed this policy preference is a nice case study of the ways in which epistemic authority gets deployed in debates about gender, to enhance what Rai (Chapter 1, this book) calls the "knowledge-based managerialism" of multilateral institutions in reference to the social reproduction dilemma. The expert voices privileged in such a process were those advocating a privatized solution to tensions between paid and unpaid work resting on re-distribution of caring labour within loving couples. For example, asserting that the "the problem of the gender division of labour in the household is universal and is not limited to Latin America or to Ecuador" (Correia 2000: 36), the *Ecuador Gender Review* discussed the research of US social psychologist Francine Deutsch, claiming that her findings would be relevant to the country.[8] Arguing that "equality in parenting is achieved in the details of everyday life" (Deutsch 1999: 3), Deutsch's research sought out "equal sharers . . . ordinary people simply inventing and reinventing solutions to the dilemmas of modern family life" (11). Her policy advice centred on encouraging complementary sharing among mothers and fathers such that they could "buffer each other" (228) and better serve their children's needs. This is precisely the solution to the domestic labour burden being advocated by the Bank. Thus the *Ecuador Gender Review* closed a discussion headed "domestic work and childcare" with the following policy argument:

> "According to Deutsch's seminal research on how shared parenting works in the United States, three conditions need to be in place if gender equality in the household is to be achieved: (a) men need to learn new skills; (b) women need to give up the control they have had over the household; and (c) men and women need to have flexible work schedules. Short-term efforts in Ecuador should focus on the first two conditions, which can be promoted by civil society organizations working at the local level, for example, through youth programs, community water programs, adult education programs etc. The last condition – which involves the reorganization of work – would be a long-term objective given the pressing nature of unemployment in Ecuador today"
>
> (Correia 2000: 58/9).

There was no mention of childcare provision whatsoever in this section; the issue of "domestic work and childcare" was framed as one about shared parenting, men learning caring skills, and women giving up caring monopolies. Thus the Bank's own gender policymakers ended up endorsing a completely privatizing solution to the social reproduction dilemma and erasing childcare provision as a priority, using U.S. gender experts advocating similar policies.

Questioning the mainstreamed common sense about sexuality

As noted above, a key insight of the governance perspective is that power can operate very effectively when deployed in arguments about common sense and "the natural order of things," allowing the production of alliances based on shared worldviews that do not seem, to their advocates, to involve explicit political claims. In addition to tracing the deployment of expertise evident in this policy site, then, it is also helpful to explore the common sense assumptions at work, particularly as they relate to sexuality. As Foucault notes, "[S]exuality is not the most intractable element in power relations, but rather one of those endowed with the greatest instrumentality, useful for the greatest number of manoeuvres and capable of serving as a point of support, as a linchpin, for the most varied strategies" (1990 [1978]: 103). Most obviously, of course, the policy solution rests on appeals to apparently universal common-sense truths about normative (hetero) sexuality, or heteronormativity. Heteronormativity refers to practices that help normalize specific forms of heterosexuality and make them hegemonic (Berlant and Warner 1998: 548). It is different from heterosexuality (which can also refer to multiple behaviours and desires), since it refers less to sex and more to norms, institutions, and structures that help naturalize dominant forms of heterosexuality as universal and morally righteous. Proponents of heteronormativity as an analytic concept thus recognize that normative forms of heterosexuality change across time and space, and rely for their success on profoundly political interventions.

These interventions have normally been explored on the state level.[9] However multilateral institutions are also involved in the production, reproduction, and alteration of forms of heterosexuality considered normative. Indeed, to pick up on Foucault, it appears that adjusted heterosexuality is a linchpin of the Bank's current attempts to secure the continued provision of caring labour in a neo-liberal context. Two claims about normative (hetero) sexuality appear particularly important in this respect: that sharing coupling is natural, and that it is empowering to men and women. The caring couplehood promoted by the Bank as a solution to the social reproduction dilemma is common-sensical because, in many respects, it is naturalized and seen as driven by biological impulse. For example when Bank staff had to explain gender analysis in workshops for P.R.O.D.E.P.I.N.E. (a rural development loan oriented to Afro-Ecuadorian and indigenous communities) they did so in part by making biological claims about how evolution compels "opposite sexes" to couple up. Gender relations were framed as flexible, and always-already changing, ensuring that the project's attempts to change them in specific caring directions were not marked as political interventions. Biological sex, conversely, was presented as static and natural, and it was hereby cast into the prediscursive domain – a central mechanism through which hegemonic heterosexuality is currently forged (Butler 1990; Terry 1999; Delphy 2000; Fausto-Sterling 2000; Ingraham 2005). Thus the *Basic Document and Guide to the Theme of Gender* prepared for P.R.O.D.E.P.I.N.E. opened by citing a Bank text which defined sex as biological and gender as social (P.R.O.D.E.P.I.N.E. 2001: n.p.). These definitions were repeated in the loan's case studies on gender and ethnicity (Eguiguren *et al.* 2002: 7), and in training workshops for local organizations. A booklet on sex education for indigenous adolescents produced by P.R.O.D.E.P.I.N.E. also taught a biological two-sex model, with the cover photograph showing a diagram of male and female bodies. Pairing up between opposite bodies was presented as natural, with the text defining adolescence as involving "the stage of attraction for the other sex" (Conejo 2002–3: 15). Moreover monogamous love was rendered timeless, universal, and natural, "one of the most powerful forces that exists, stronger than time, death, or law...found identically in all places and all times" (46). Such definitions foregrounded a binarized, but complementary, vision of gender in the projects activities, in which normative forms of coupling up between men and women were presented as functional and driven by timeless, biological impulse.

In addition, the vision of loving, sharing, heteronormative balance embedded in the Bank's gender policies was also promoted as common-sensically empowering. In one of the first gender workshops organized by P.R.O.D.E.P.I.N.E. in 2000 the head of the Bank's gender initiatives in Ecuador stated that while men and women had different roles, each was of equal value and complemented the other (Velasquez 2000: n.p.; also see P.R.O.D.E.P.I.N.E. n.d.). A gender workshop in the Amazon framed gender roles as impeding both men and women from expressing liberty as human beings: "from men (they) tak(e) the right to cry, and from women the right to participate in public life" (Aulestia and Quintero-Andrade 2001: 7). "Understanding of the unity of the genders" was needed to overcome such limitations. Men would hereby be empowered through opportunities to explore their caring side – their right to cry – while women would gain through employment and participation in the public sphere. While these policy arguments were in part grounded in naturalized claims about "opposite" sexes partnering up due to functional imperative, they also involved normative claims about the desirability and empowering nature of loving couplehood.

Such claims appear to have succeeded in making the policy seem non-controversial and *not* about sexuality. As Davina Cooper notes in relation to state policies, interventions dealing with normative expressions of intimacy are often "naturalized into invisibility" (1995: 63), or seen as simply common-sensical – a key reason why the Bank's current attempts to promote loving partnership generate so little comment or criticism. It is worth reflecting upon the Bank's definition of successful mainstreaming in this respect. As Bank gender policymakers understand it:

> Something is said to be mainstreamed when it is so routine that it provokes neither conflict nor comment. Computerization of office

work, the numbering of streets, and sending six-year-olds to school are all illustrative of the concept of mainstreaming (World Bank 2000b: 2).

Hence "success often renders the issues less visible" (2). In this sense the promotion of adjusted partnerships in which women work more and men love better has become a piece of GAD common sense – it has been mainstreamed into invisibility as a policy intervention such that it is ignored by the institution's critics, in part because the assumptions about sexuality on which it rests are left unquestioned.

Questioning the common-sense about semi-savage masculinity

The common-sense assumptions on which the privatized policy solution to the social reproduction dilemma rests are also crucially linked to certain claims about masculinity. Indeed men were often understood to be the major problem to which the Bank's gender efforts were directed, in another example of the need to focus on masculinity in development studies (Cleaver 2002; Jackson 2001). A gender consultant for P.R.O.D.E.P.I.N.E. stated this directly, claiming that gender activities needed to be focused on men because:

> We're not working with women here, right? We're working more with men, because the problem is the men (laughing). The problem isn't the women, the problem is the men. You have to be working with them.

Specifically, men were a problem when they were perceived as lazy and unreliable, as failing to adhere to a complementary model of good partnership. As I have explored in detail elsewhere (Bedford 2005b), such behaviour was understood by Bank staff as linked to ethnicity in the P.R.O.D.E.P.I.N.E. rural development loan oriented to indigenous and Afro-Ecuadorian communities. Gender relations in all communities were assessed based on their approximation to an idealized norm of loving partnership, and non-monogamy was framed as a marker of ethnic identity. Amazonian men (identified as polygamous) and Afro-Ecuadorian men (identified as serially unfaithful) were regarded as particularly oppressive, and women in those communities were considered disempowered. Conversely Andean communities in the Sierran highlands – long framed in Ecuador's nationalist imaginary as more progressive, respectable, and civilizable than Amazonian indigenous groups or Afro-Ecuadorian communities (Crain 1996; Rahier 2003; Kyle 2000;

Colloreado-Mansfeld 1999) – were understood to already practice the sharing approach endorsed by the Bank. They were thus seen by gender staff as offering a culturally authentic model of empowering love and male monogamy for others to emulate.

The expertise invoked to support these claims warrants attention. Some scholars argue that gender relations in some Andean communities are characterized by harmony and equity. For example Sarah Hamilton's research on an Andean community shows an "extraordinary degree of economic, social, and political gender-egalitarianism" (Hamilton 1998: 8, see also Meisch 2002: 9) though she is cautious about over-generalizing her findings. However not all academics (or activists) share this perspective. Gioconda Herrera (2001) argues that dichotomous arguments which posit inequality as absent or which ignore variation in gender roles are largely unhelpful, and that more nuanced approaches would seem merited, while Marisol de la Cadena (1995) challenges recent ethnographic work claiming relations of complementarity between Andean men and women (see also Barrig 2005 and Prieto *et al.* 2005). These discourses are sites for struggle, and they certainly do not represent fixed authentic "truths" about ethnic groups. Nonetheless the Bank's *Ecuador Gender Review* cited Hamilton's claim that the Sierra is characterized by gender equality without further discussion (Correia 2000: 40), and a later text repeated as a fact that Andean groups were more sharing in their gender roles than other communities (Correia 2002). Loan staff hereby intervened to shore up models of partnership marked as culturally authentic while designating communities seen to have alternative arrangements of sexuality as disempowered. This process reinforced a racialized hierarchy in which Afro-Ecuadorian and Amazonian men were framed as more oppressive to women.

The common-sense claims about masculinity evident in this policy site were also crucially classed, as evident in gender activities targeted on poor communities in general. These claims could be indirect and perhaps unintentional, and often stemmed from the attention to poor men's irresponsibility given by Ecuadorian women themselves.[10] For example, Moser's gender chapter in the Bank's 1996 Poverty Report on Ecuador – based on her Cisne Dos research – included several text boxes which highlighted personal stories of community members. These overwhelmingly featured women who had been deserted, abused, financially exploited, or mistreated by men (World Bank 1996: 126, 127). One text box focused on a man who had to abandon his dental studies due to cost and whose family remained below the poverty line despite the fact that both he and his son had several jobs (Moser 1997: 44). However this was one of the only positive representations of poor men in the report – a pattern that was repeated in more recent Bank texts (Correia 2002: 186).

More significant than this disproportionate focus on poor male irresponsibility are the direct claims made elsewhere that poor men were more oppressive to women than their better-off counterparts. Many of the Bank's recent texts argued that gender role stress leads poor men, and particularly unemployed men, to be violent, and to have reduced capacities for caring. For example increased male violence was proof of the gendered impact of economic restructuring for the *Ecuador Gender Review*, since "for men, unemployment threatens their role of family provider and creates problems of self esteem and depression – which may have other possible negative effects such as violence" (Correia 2000: 50). Although subsequently violence was linked to alcohol abuse, leading to suggestions that drunk men should be detained by the police as a violence prevention strategy, both violence and alcoholism were understood to be caused by wounded masculinity. Thus the report argued that:

> Causes of male violence – including street violence and sexual and domestic aggression – have been linked to masculinity and gender roles. According to Barker (1998), to be a man in Latin America is equated with working hard, earning well, being responsible, and providing financially for the family. When these goals become difficult to achieve, men regularly assert their masculinity through violence (ibid.).
>
> (22)

The Bank's chapter on gender in its recent dollarization report went even further than the *Ecuador Gender Review* in this negative portrayal of poor masculinity, mentioning not only violence but also stunted emotional development and "destructive behavior" which are "probably the result of socialization processes, which inhibit men from expressing their feelings" (Correia 2002: 201). Again poor men were particularly stunted in this regard, since "aggression among men has been associated with male gender roles and expectations, and in particular the inability of men earning low incomes to live up to societal and familial expectations of being full income earners" (189). Unemployed men were thus again framed as a violent threat, at risk "of alcoholism, violence, delinquency, or depression" if unable to fulfil their breadwinner role (188), while working women were considered less likely to be victimized because participation in economic activities increased their negotiating power in the household.

These claims of working women's liberation and poor men's irresponsibility and violence are endemic to Bank texts, inside and outside of Ecuador (Bedford 2005a). Again, the expertise being invoked to support them warrants critique. While the citation to Barker 1998 in the above quotation is to a conference paper, better known literature on Latin American or Ecuadorian masculinity, which questions pathologizing portrayals of poor men as hyper-violent, addicted, or irresponsible was ignored (see Melhaus and Stolen 1996; de la Torre 2000; Ferrándiz 2003; Gutman 2003;Uzendoski 2003). I note this not to denigrate the conference paper, but rather to draw attention to the politics of citation evident in the Bank's referencing practices, whereby certain work on masculinity is visible because it in turn makes certain men visible in particular ways.

Moreover, these claims about hyper-oppressive unemployed poor men and empowered working women persist despite contradictory evidence, some of which is cited in these same Bank texts. For example, as the *Ecuador Gender Review* notes, Deutsch's work in the United States – used to support the sharing couple as the solution to the social reproduction dilemma – found that working class families actually shared household labour more equally than middle class families (Correia 2000: 36). There was no attempt to interrogate how these findings related to claims that poor men were particularly uncaring, particularly in need of attention to ensure they could fulfil new roles in the two-earner, two-lover family model. Claims about poor men's laziness also persisted despite the recognition by the Bank's macroeconomists that poor men in Ecuador start work earlier than non-poor men (Hrenstschel Lanjouw in World Bank 1996: 74); that poor boys drop out of school to work at faster rates than any other group (Correia 2000: 5); and that many regions of the country suffer from gender imbalances caused by poor men's migration for work (11). Similarly, one study on domestic violence in Ecuador, cited in the *Ecuador Gender Review*, found *no* significant relationship between socio-economic class and domestic violence, or between women's employment status and their vulnerability to abuse. Moreover unemployed men were *less* dangerous than employed men (Correia 2000: 22). While all of these findings challenge the portrayal of poor men as uncaring, none received elaboration.

To clarify, by drawing attention to these trends in the Bank's recognition of Ecuadorian men I seek neither to romanticize anyone's masculinity, nor to deny very real problems of irresponsibility and violence. I seek simply to demonstrate the common-sense claims being made in these policy texts about masculinity – race- and class-inflected claims that persist despite empirical evidence to the contrary. I raise this issue in part to counteract the continued reluctance, in scholarship and practice, to critically assess the troubling ways in which poor men have been framed in GAD conversations. Moreover, I am concerned that feminist policymakers are using such common-sense claims about certain men to generate bad policy. The Bank's efforts to resolve the social reproduction dilemma seek to include men in extremely limited terms that pathologize already marginalized masculinities and that render individual poor men culpable for a range of development outcomes that are better explained – and resolved – at the suprahousehold level. Through these policies, those lacking access to or opting to remain outside of normative partnership models are made even more vulnerable to poverty, and many efforts to enhance women's autonomy through enabling them to break attachments to irresponsible men are rendered unspeakable. Marriage is recommended as the ultimate anti-poverty strategy (Mink 1998), and the strategy best placed to resolve tensions between paid and unpaid labour, leaving aside a whole range of possibilities less focused on privatized loving. While the Bank's new interventions to resolve the social reproduction dilemma are thus an important step in the recognition of unpaid labour as economically relevant, then, they are far from trouble-free.

Tensions in governance

So far, this chapter has traced the efforts of Bank gender staff to resolve an oft-cited tension in neo-liberal development regarding paid and unpaid labour by restructuring intimate attachments between men and women, paying particular attention to the deployment of both gender expertise and common sense in the process. To close, I wish to briefly mention some of the unresolved tensions evident in the Bank's advocacy of adjusted partnerships to resolve the social reproduction dilemma. This is necessary to ensure that analysis remains attentive to the contradictions evident in governance procedures, lest they be attributed a coherence or an inherent system-stabilizing impact that their diverse, unexpected, and sometimes conflicting effects deny.

Firstly, in practice, the definition of gender analysis as hinging on complementary attention to men and women caused serious conceptual problems for the Bank, confusing staff and the projects with which they worked. One Bank policymaker stated that the institution's gender efforts had been less than successful in part because it was hard to maintain the position that gender refers to men and women when "I was always focusing more on women ... Really, it was a little bit of a clash." Also, pressure was put on Ecuador's state feminist agency, CONAMU, by the Bank to shift its approach in order to achieve the goal of male inclusion, causing conflict with domestic feminists who were less than enthusiastic about a concentration on men and sharing partnerships. Consider this account from a former Bank consultant about Bank-CONAMU interactions in a project to increase gender analysis in Bank lending:

> For CONAMU although they speak of gender, (they have) a strong focus on women. In contrast the World Bank, as you may have seen, makes an effort towards gender because gender takes into account the theme of men, perhaps not in the line of masculinities... but more in the more technical line, that takes into account social inequalities that affect men. And CONAMU refused very firmly to work like this... They don't want to work towards (the benefit of) men, so this provoked a very strong disagreement... The relationship turned very *very* bad, very bad, and this affected all types of personal relations. But it was very ugly, this polemic – very ugly.

This consultant clearly sympathized with the position of the state women's council, and felt that gender staff had been pressured into a complementary focus on men by the Bank.[11] These pressures significantly damaged personal relations between feminist colleagues, such that some were moved to tears when relaying the fights they caused. I mention this tension to suggest that Bank alliances with liberal feminist organizations like CONAMU (organizations grounded in the notion that women suffer discrimination and need equality in the public sphere) can be dramatically unsettled by the focus on sharing couples so central to the Bank's current gender policy.

Secondly, this tension over the focus of gender efforts is related to an unresolved debate over the nature of empowerment in the new, post-Wolfensohn World Bank.[12] In some respects, as its critics are well aware, the Bank invokes a limited notion of empowerment as individual autonomy, with frequent references to neo-classical household models which consider how individuals bargain within families. With discussion papers using game theory to model dowry murder as a bargaining tool (Bloch and Rao 2000), one can certainly see the Bank-specific manifestations of Rose's claim that "all aspects of social behaviour are now reconceptualized along economic lines – as calculative actions undertaken through the universal human faculty of choice" (Rose 1999: 141).

However in other respects, Bank gender staff understand sharing partnerships, rather than autonomous individuals, as emblematic of empowerment. "Autonomy" is hereby imagined within a couple. Moreover the attachments required in this framing are *not* freely chosen to the extent that they are regarded as natural and prescribed as empowering, especially for the poor. To reiterate, the emphasis on sharing partnerships stems from, and attempts to resolve, macroeconomic concerns. It is thus targeted on poor people, since partnership-based empowerment is required for the poor to cope with neo-liberal capitalism through privately absorbing the costs of care.[13] Poor women's economic empowerment through work requires their necessary attachment to men, and poor men's liberation through love requires interventions to deal with their perceived irresponsibility to their families – their lack of what a gender consultant in the Amazon called "family love." There is thus a core, and unresolved, tension in Bank work on empowerment, reflecting a clash between the radical individualism and calculative assumptions embedded in neo-classical economics, and heightened reliance on new policy formulations involving love, care, and adjusted heteronormativity to pick up the slack of social reproduction. Both options are circulating, in conflict, in the contemporary institution.

Finally, tensions emerge among Bank staff over the redeemability of men. On occasion, men are positioned as relentlessly irresponsible, and thus they are targeted for coercive, repressive governance strategies. This is evident when publications recommend arresting drunk men, or when staff comment on how women are empowered through off-farm rural employment because they get money that their husbands would otherwise drink. Such men are hereby positioned as outside of appeals to reason and unable to regulate themselves – a framing with disturbing resonances. As many scholars have noted, the disciplinary "despotism of the self" (Rose 1999: 43) demanded of certain civilized subjects in standard liberal modes of governance relied on the pathological framing of uncivilized others located outside the realm of the responsible – those whose freedom to self-govern was denied, and who were thus deemed in need of coercion and domination by others (see espec. Rose 1999: 47; Zein-Elabdin 2003). "Primitive" men of colour were typically the epitomes of such lack of self-control, the unredeemable savages against whom the civilized subject's capacity for self-governance was measured. Although often eschewing the normalizing, disciplinary tendencies of liberalism in favour of notions of individual empowerment and self-actualization through the market, neo-liberal governance models also mark key boundaries between included and excluded populations – boundaries in which poor men of colour are often targeted for repressive state and non-state practices. One can certainly see traces of this boundary-marking process in the Bank's framing of poor drunk men.

That said, however, more typically gender policymakers recommend teaching men to behave differently, understanding them to have potential for self-actualization through caring. Indeed the poor men of interest to the Bank are seen as especially in need of such corrective interventions, given their emasculating poverty and perceived sexual excesses. Hence the fatherhood programmes and gender workshops endorsed by Bank staff. These are in fact classic examples of *inclusion* in neo-liberal governance, fulfilling vital social and economic functions. In his discussion of neo-liberalism, Rose notes that ideally contemporary citizens will govern themselves in a context of reduced social services – but first they have to be "responsibilized and entrepreneurialized" (Rose 1999: 139). With women targeted for the entrepreneurialism, understood to gain empowerment through employment, men are increasingly targeted for responsibilization. Indeed poor men's autonomy is clearly being re-imagined in global social policy conversations that seek to cultivate particular attachments in order to resolve neo-liberal economic crises. These conversations rest on male redeemability, and on policymakers' willingness to include marginalized men in non-repressive governance practices.

Exploring the tensions between these two approaches to marginalized masculinity requires considerably more space than is available here. Suffice it to say that it is extremely significant that the poor, racially marked men discussed as policy problems by Bank gender staff so often become targets for classically (neo)liberal governance initiatives, rather than more obviously coercive efforts. Certainly, as noted above, this targeting falls unevenly, and valorizes men from some indigenous groups as hyper-responsible. Yet so far, in keeping with the Bank's new emphasis on inclusion of the marginalized, I have found that all groups are being incorporated into the process. No communities are abjected, none are so vile or degraded, no ways of being or forms of existence so shameful, that they are "rendered beyond the limits of the liveable, denied the warrant of tolerability, accorded purely a negative value" (Rose 1999: 253; for contrast see Povinelli 2002). Policymakers imagine no ethically marked "savage spaces" on the margins entirely peopled by non-citizens (Rose 1999: 259), and the inclusion strategies being put in place are not unilaterally repressive. Men who were the radical uncivilized "other" have thus been partially incorporated into governance frameworks – an important shift requiring careful consideration.

Conclusion: tools and languages of governing

Through a focus on the Bank, this chapter has attempted to show how macroeconomic concerns are being linked to expressions of intimacy, and to elucidate the assumptions about sexuality and masculinity upon which the Bank's current GAD approach rests. The tensions embedded in this approach warrant further examination, if only to enable better identification of the spaces within which we can critically intervene. The policies to which I draw attention are sites for struggle within the Bank – they should at the very least be subjects for debate among feminist development scholars.

To close with this issue in mind, it is helpful to revisit an enduring question about feminist policymaking and its relationship to global governance institutions posed by Kathleen Staudt. In a recent essay on feminist policymaking, she asked "to 'speak truth to power' has long been the goal of policy analysts, but just how similar must the speech be to the master's language?" (2002: 52). Contesting Audre Lorde's claim that activists cannot use the master's tools to dismantle the master's house, Staudt insists that "master-free houses are few and far between" (2002: 57), and hence that "engagement in the master's house is one among many valid political strategies in contemporary development enterprises" (58). On this basis effective engagement rests, at least in part, on knowing when the languages we are using should not be ours. As I have argued elsewhere, this is relatively straightforward when feminists are discussing Bank efficiency rhetoric, grounded in claims that integration of gender concerns will increase productivity and growth (Bedford 2007). Feminists both inside and outside the Bank have been relatively confident in their ability to distinguish "the master's language" from "ours" here, especially given that economics-based efficiency talk sounds foreign to many of us.

However since 1995 the Bank has opened up to other languages, including those that sound far less foreign to feminist policymakers. The distinction between "them" and "us" is far harder to draw when we talk about empowerment as balanced complementary sharing, when we use promises of happy loving couples to get support, when we frame certain men as pathologically violent and irresponsible and seek to include them through domestication. To know how to fully answer Staudt's question, then, we must first know what the master's language is, in order that we can know what concessions we are making; how "his" language influences "our" policymaking, and when "we" are actually generating that language ourselves. In this sense I suggest that the Bank's current solution to the social reproduction dilemma relies on, and reinforces, common sense languages about sexuality and masculinity that should not be ours. If we are to help generate policies that promise an alternative vision of empowering freedom, and that forge different, more politically progressive connections between macroeconomic tensions and individual subjectivities, we might start by revisiting our policy languages and the common sense assumptions on which they are based.

Notes

1. The "World Bank Group" includes five organizations. It is customary to refer to the two most prominent agencies – the International Bank for Reconstruction and Development and the International Development Association – as "the Bank."
2. I trace the emergence of this policy preference, and the institutional factors that explain it, in Bedford 2005a.
3. See Lind 2004; Herrera 2001; Prieto 2005 for an introduction to the Ecuadorian women's movement.
4. These arguments are also central to the Bank's prioritization of women's employment outside of Ecuador; I trace this process in the Bank's broader D.C.-produced, formally cleared gender policy texts in Bedford 2005a.
5. It was not the only response – infrastructural provision was also an important priority. See Bedford 2005a.
6. I explore this in far greater detail, and connect it to sexuality studies literature on functional heteronormativity in Bedford 2005a and 2005b.
7. This "priority" to make women into workers and men into responsible loving family members was repeated word for word in the summary to the report (53). Institutionally sensitive reading methods should direct particular attention to opening and closing pages of Bank documents, given that they are often the only parts of a text read by busy staff – see Bedford 2005a for more on reading methodology as it relates to Bank texts.
8. Interestingly Deutsch expresses doubt about whether her findings are broadly applicable in the US; her sample was 96 per cent white and 100 per cent English speaking, and in half of her couples both husbands and wives had graduate degrees (1999: 240).
9. See for example Cohen 1997; Smith 2001; Cooper 1995; Carabine 2000; Ingraham 2005. For exceptions to the tendency of sexuality studies to focus on state actors, see Alexander 1994; Wilson 2004; Adams and Prigg 2005.
10. I recognize that the emphasis accorded poor men's misbehaviour in this publication stems from the complaints of women in the sample. Yet this raises methodological issues of crucial importance to feminist development researchers. Given the difficulty of ascertaining causality when discussing macroeconomic issues, and given the tendency to blame proximate factors for one's own life crises, how does one develop analyses that remain attentive to people's lived experiences when informants persistently blame poor men, migrants, sex workers, and so on for their own poverty?

11. I examine the consequences of this institutionally conditioned pressure to include men in far greater detail in Bedford 2007.
12. Evidence of an unresolved tension between empowerment as individual autonomy and empowerment as sharing partnership is prominent in all D.C. formally cleared Bank policy texts on gender – see Bedford 2005a.
13. I thank Shirin Rai for help in clarifying this argument.

5
Governing the EU: Gender and Macroeconomics

Catherine Hoskyns

Introduction

The European Union (EU) predates and prefigures debates about global governance. The post-war decision to create an economic union between previously warring states, strong enough both to restrain hostile intent and build prosperity, involved innovative macroeconomic thinking. The resulting union has developed many of the features at regional level, which are now seen as characterizing global governance. In particular, it operates through a widespread and diffuse interstate bureaucracy interacting with highly specialized professional networks, the so-called 'epistemic communities'. The effect of this is to produce, particularly in the commercial and business field, a broad spread of regulation enforced through European law. These developments have involved new roles for the state, the functions of which have become fragmented in the economic sphere while remaining central in the social sphere and in the harnessing of public loyalty. Up to now, this has allowed a neo-liberal thrust in external policy to co-exist with more welfare-oriented social policies. This combination has proved sufficiently powerful for the union gradually to absorb states in the northern and southern peripheries and towards the east.

In the EU, as with global governance more generally, concerns about accountability and democracy surface but are rarely confronted head on or dealt with effectively. The underlying rationalization (though not always articulated in these terms) remains that the member states have democratic political systems and that they can therefore be trusted to act for the general good at the European level. An additional argument is that the bureaucratic/interest group form of politics is the most efficient way to handle macroeconomic policy making at the global

107

level. Thus, democracy at member state level is seen as a guarantee of democracy further up despite the marked loss of national sovereignty, particularly in economic matters, which EU membership entails and globalization intensifies. The political structures which have grown up alongside the EUs regulatory system, while robust compared with others at international level, have been unable so far to establish political legitimacy or develop an idea of European identity which is acceptable to the majority of the people. In the context of greater globalization, these contradictions are becoming more pronounced, as demonstrated in May 2005 by the defeat in referendums in France and the Netherlands of the proposed new EU constitution. What European economic integration, undeniably successful in its own terms, rests on and has produced is a fragmented, anxious and largely nationally defined public opinion.

The EUs policy on women's rights/gender equality, which has been developing since the 1970s, needs to be seen in this context. Despite the limitations of the policy, it has created an awareness and a base for challenging some of the above developments and for inserting greater gender sensitivity into EU programmes and actions. In the early stages at least, there was a sense that creating a floor of rights for workers (including improving the situation of women workers) would help to create the common market and further trade. Currently such measures are more likely to be seen as trade distorting. So while there have been important gains for women, particularly in employment rights, further progress is in danger of being undermined by changing economic and political circumstances. The current programme of gender mainstreaming rests on a fragile base.

The core of the EU project involves the co-ordination of macroeconomic policy to create a common economic space and to operate more effectively in an increasingly interdependent world. It is therefore the sphere of macroeconomics, as it exists at EU level, which is the focus of this chapter. The aim is to assess to what extent gender issues have been or could be taken on board in these areas and what governance strategies favour or inhibit such inclusion.

In talking about macroeconomic policy in this way, I am referring in particular to:

General economic policy (creating, maintaining and regulating the market, and maintaining balance between the different sectors)
Trade policy (trade liberalisation and protection; priorities in the negotiation of external commercial relations)

Fiscal and monetary policy (money supply and currency, interest rates and tax)
Labour market policy (the supply of labour and its regulation).

In pursuing the theme of gender mainstreaming as a governance strategy in these areas, the chapter begins with some general comments on macroeconomics, gendered economic analysis and gender mainstreaming. It continues by looking in more detail at four areas where attempts have been made, or could be made, to introduce a gender dimension into the EU policy: employment, broad economic policy, taxation and trade. As such this chapter takes an institutionalist approach informed by much of the feminist scholarship within gendered political economy and feminist economics (Cook *et al.* 2000; Cagatay 2001; Elson 2004). This kind of approach may begin to give some answers to the always disputed question as to whether opening up and liberalizing as is now being carried through at global level, provides greater or fewer opportunities for gender empowerment.

Macroeconomics and gender analysis

Macroeconomics is generally seen as being concerned with the aggregate performance of the economy and its measurement. This involves examining broad aggregates in the fields set out above and their interrelationship over time. Such measurements give important information about the 'success' or otherwise of an economy, depending upon the criteria being used. They also, again depending upon the criteria, suggest what the direction of policy should be. While economics depicts itself as a technocratic and neutral science, the assumptions and orthodoxy which lie behind these measurements and their interpretation, in fields which by their very nature are not always easy to quantify, are extremely influential.

Microeconomics, which in contrast to the abstraction of the macro, focuses on the decision-making of individuals (consumers, workers and firms); and mesoeconomics, which deals with intermediate public and private infrastructures, are influenced by the macro and at the same time underlie its assumptions. The nature of these influences is complex and unclear and results in a debate within macroeconomics as to whether the aggregates should be seen as resulting entirely from the decisions of individuals or whether the macroeconomy itself has a distinct presence, 'a life of its own' (Evers 2003: 7). Though gendering might be easier if the first conceptualization is adopted, I would agree with Evers in preferring the second. The task is then to see how gender relations can be identified and made visible using this more structural approach, and taken account of in the complex institutionalization of the macroeconomy. Far from being neutral, these formal and informal processes and practices are, in Diane Elson's words, themselves 'the bearer of gender' (Elson 2000).

On the whole then, macroeconomic policy is not concerned with and is distanced from social reality and the social consequences of policies being pursued. The degree of regulation at macroeconomic level, and its direction, as well as who decides what policy options should be pursued, are important factors, whether at European or national level. Recently, the orthodoxy has been to let the market 'regulate itself' and to 'interfere' as little as possible. Key decisions on interest rates and money supply have been distanced from politics by giving autonomy to the Bank of England and the European Central Bank. However, a great deal of regulation of the market is still needed and still takes place. Globalization requires that much of this is negotiated externally in organizations such as the World Trade Organisation (WTO) and the International Monetary Fund (IMF). It is appropriate and efficient (and in the case of trade, a requirement) for the EU to act in a co-ordinated way in such negotiations.

Within the EU there is a growing tension between what is done at the national and the European level. There is also considerable debate and experimentation about exactly how and through what procedures policy at EU level can be devised and applied now that there are 25 member states. The net result, as already discussed, is that democratic control and transparency are often lacking and this applies particularly to macroeconomic policy. As a result of all these factors, EU macroeconomic policy displays a somewhat different set of competences, concerns and restraints from that which is usual at national level. The development of convincing and appropriate macroeconomic policies remains, however, central to the success of the EU and to the economies of its member states.

Gender analysis

A great deal of work has been done by feminists over the last twenty years to challenge conventional economic theory and take on the macroeconomic level of analysis and policy making.[1] There have been two main aspects to this: in development studies where concern about the North/South divide and the way underdevelopment affects women has led to an increasing critique of international policy and its ethos (Rai 2002); and international political economy where both mainstream and critical International Political Economy (IPE) have been seen as failing to take on a sufficiently gender-sensitive view of the current dynamics of the international economy and global macroeconomics (Cook 2000). In both of these strands there is a conceptual aspect, with challenges being made to paradigms and assumptions and the level of theorizing. There is also an activist element involving grass-roots research and campaigning, which has had the effect of raising awareness and generating policy proposals. Where the conceptual and the activist combine and feed into each other the impact is greatest.

Central to all these studies and activities is the demand that 'social reproduction' is taken seriously in economic analysis and is seen as a component in market functioning. Social reproduction means not only biological reproduction but also the 'social provisioning' needed to maintain individuals, groups and communities and underpin economic and other activity. Social reproduction above all rests on women's unpaid labour which makes an important and largely unrecognized subsidy to the economy as a whole (Picchio 1992). It also acts as a safety net in times of crisis. Taking social reproduction as a central part of economic modelling at macro, meso and microlevels would constitute a transformation in the assumptions which underlie economics. This possibility comes a little nearer with the substantial entry of women into the labour force. The characteristics of this part of the labour force and the constraints/benefits implied by the social reproductive role are beginning to become a serious concern for economic planning and management. However, this takes place at a time when the social contract, the social wage and what John Ruggie described as 'embedded liberalism'[2] (all ways in which in the past economies took account, even if inadequately, of social reproduction) have disappeared or are crumbling. It is this that persuades people to talk about a crisis in social reproduction (Katz 2003).

The argument for giving a central place to social reproduction has been set out most cogently by Isabella Bakker and Stephen Gill, who see the expansion and restructuring of capital on a global scale (and the introduction of the market into new areas including social provisioning) as creating confrontation over basic human needs and security. This, they argue, can only be resolved by transforming the conceptualization of the market, to take account of the social reproduction upon which it rests and of power relations more broadly (2003). Similar arguments using a development frame and giving more substance to the gender aspects are made by a variety of authors in *Macro-Economics – Making Gender Matter* (Gutierrez 2003) Finally, Spike Peterson, writing from a critical international relations and post-modern perspective, calls for a re-conceptualization of the global economy giving equal weight to reproductive, productive and virtual aspects (2003). The publication of all of these books, around a common theme even if the approach and theorization is different, suggests a convergence of analysis appropriate to the time.

At the policy and campaigning level, striking material and evidence is being produced about the situation of women and the role they play in the global economy. So Than Dam Truong links sex trafficking and prostitution to the Asian financial crisis, and work on the position of women within production chains illuminates aspects not revealed by the usual business view (Truong 2000; Barrientos *et al.* 2003). In the north, attention has been paid to the role of multinationals and the degree to which their profits are based on low-paid, largely female labour in the third world (Ross 1997). Campaigns springing from this, for example, for the application of core labour standards in the south, have roused controversy and debate (Kabeer 2004). In these debates, the situation and role of women is central.

It remains an anomaly that so little of this research and activity is recognized in EU macroeconomic planning and analysis – although some inroads are beginning to be made. The next sections of this chapter look first at how gender mainstreaming is positioned overall in EU policy and then at four aspects of EU macroeconomic policy, which illustrate the different ways in which an engagement with gender is (or is not) taking place.

Gender mainstreaming

Gender mainstreaming is used to describe the current stage of the EU's policy on gender equality. Its application at a high level was endorsed by the provisions of the Treaty of Amsterdam, 1997. It also figures largely in the recommendations of the Beijing Platform for Action, to which EU member states subscribe. As such it has been extensively studied and debated. I shall only make some brief points here.

Gender mainstreaming represents a new stage of policy, which in the EU at least, is characterized by a move away from narrow, targeted inter-ventions mainly in the employment field, towards a broader perspective which in theory at least brings gender awareness and action into all areas of policy. What does this entail? In this chapter, I shall use a definition developed by Teresa Rees in her role as consultant on gender mainstreaming to the European Commission over the last nine years.

Gender mainstreaming is the promotion of gender equality through its systematic integration into all systems and structures, into all policies, processes and procedures, into the organisation and its culture, into ways of seeing and doing.

(Rees 2004: 3)

This is similar to the definition developed by the Council of Europe's group of experts on gender mainstreaming (Council of Europe 1998: 13).

These definitions, which come from women with long experience in gender equality policy, represent an interpretation which emphasizes transformation. The focus is on location (everywhere) and thoroughness (systemic). As Rees points out, the adoption of gender mainstreaming in the EU is superimposed upon earlier forms of intervention: equal treatment in employment largely through legislation, and positive action to compensate specific groups of women for past or current disadvantage. The extent to which the application of gender mainstreaming accommodates and supports these earlier forms, or acts to downgrade them, depends on the precise coalitions of forces at particular moments and in particular fields.

Maria Stratigaki's detailed analysis of the history of gender-mainstreaming initiatives in the European Commission over the period 1996–2000 suggests that there was considerable confusion over what the term meant and its implications (Stratigaki 2005). As with any large bureaucracy, different interpretations existed, just as did different cultures and political ideologies. The interpretation and application of gender mainstreaming thus played its part in various political strategies and power plays.

Overall one can say that there was a mixture of commitment, lip service and indifference, not surprising perhaps in a policy that was expected to be applied everywhere. The commitment in the texts in formal terms was strong but this had little binding force and to be applied effectively would have required a strong budget line, political will at the top, together with staff to carry out the necessary studies and monitor developments. Very little of this was forthcoming. The highest level of commitment was shown by the five women Commissioners in the Santer Commission (1995–1999), all of whom initiated projects in their own areas of responsibility. General implementation was left to the Commission's Equal Opportunities Unit (EOU), already weakened by the removal or resignation of key staff and with little additional funding. The only new structures created were an informal group of Commissioners 'to oversee equality' and an interservice group of civil servants which operated in a fluctuating fashion. The most effective form of monitoring was that performed by the European Parliament's Committee on Women's Rights (from here on the EP Women's Committee) which also had some say on the budget.

Operating within this framework were committed individuals and groups in some Directorate-Generals (DGs), in some of the EU-funded projects and in relevant NGOs. These were particularly important in that together they had the capacity to work out what gender mainstreaming should mean in particular policy areas and put together a plan of action. It is significant that for the most part this only worked effectively in areas where there was a sympathetic Commissioner. None of this was sufficient to present a strong case for gender mainstreaming in the so-called 'technical areas' or areas where it was less obvious what the relevance of gender was or how gender imbalance might be tackled. It was certainly not sufficient to convince sceptical and indifferent civil servants, many of whom (and not only men) rated this broad view of gender mainstreaming as political correctness and a distraction from what they saw as their more urgent work. A survey of gender mainstreaming conducted in 1998–1999 suggested that progress was being made in certain areas, particularly research and development, structural funds and regional policy. Very little progress was being made in more technical and economic areas (the example chosen was competition policy) although the authors could see that there were gender issues that could have been taken up (Pollack and Hafner-Burton 2000). It was also clear by this stage that though some initiatives were being taken, no one had the authority to compel Commissioners to take gender issues seriously, if they were not so inclined. In a context where the whole Commission was forced to resign in March 1999 over accusations of fraud, gender mainstreaming was not an issue likely to be given a high priority.

For the period 2001–2006, gender mainstreaming has been administered under the Fifth Community Framework Strategy for Gender Equality.[3] This strategy involves an annual programme including money for projects, and a general overarching policy overseen by the Commission's EOU, located in the DG for Employment and Social Affairs. The remit for the EOU includes checking up on the level of gender projects in the different DGs of the Commission. Direction from the top appears to have been patchy. On the other hand, within three DGs concerned with the EU's external affairs (Trade, Development and External Relations – known as the Relex group) a small committee to co-ordinate gender-mainstreaming activity and compare practice and initiatives has been set up. A monitoring process, co-ordinated by the EOU, does now take place (for example, in April 2004), with DGs being asked to record what initiatives have been taken in the gender field. However, little pressure seems to be exerted if DGs, and some of them do, make a virtually nil return. Nevertheless, this process does mean that somebody in each DG has gender mainstreaming in his/her portfolio and has to get a reply drafted. In all of this there appears to be little capacity to initiate studies or draw together existing material, which would help to explain the relevance of gender in areas, like macroeconomic policy, where this is neither accepted nor immediately obvious.

Despite all this activity and formal rhetoric it is noticeable that high profile acts of the EU still tend to be taken without much regard for gender or the appropriate representation of women. This is true of the Commission's 2001 Governance White Paper, which makes no mention of gender, and the composition of the Convention on the Future of Europe, appointed to draw up the EU's draft constitution, which had only a tiny proportion of women members (Shaw 2001). At the time of writing, it is not clear yet how seriously the new Barroso Commission elected in 2005 will take gender mainstreaming or what kind of policy instruments will be devised.

It is in this context that I want to look at gender mainstreaming in four core areas of EU macroeconomic policy. Each of these areas has a different relation to gender politics both conceptually and in terms of previous EU policy development.

These four areas are:

European Employment Strategy (EES) – there is a long history here of EU activity in the field of equal treatment for women in employment and numerous EU-funded studies about different aspects of women's employment situation.

Broad Economic Policy Guidelines (BEPG) – little work has been done here from a gender perspective and attempts to initiate this have been met with some hostility.

Policy on Direct Taxation – this is seen as a technical issue where gender relations have little relevance.

Multilateral Trade Policy – for a long time this was regarded as a technical issue with little social relevance; however, more recently the linking of trade with development, and the degree of external campaigning around WTO negotiations, including much by women, is beginning to make DG trade more receptive to social lobbying.

European Employment Strategy (EES)

Up until the 1990s, the EC/EU played little direct role in employment policy across the member states. The main concern in this field was to encourage free movement of labour and make it easier for workers to take jobs wherever they were available. The EC's funding supported programmes for retraining workers and encouraging access to employment for disadvantaged groups including women. Certain core labour standards were embodied in European law, including equal pay and equal treatment for women in employment (Teague 1989). In addition, detailed statistics were compiled and numerous studies commissioned (including many on the situation of women in employment) which made aggregate measurements possible and encouraged debate on different labour market strategies. The EU-funded Expert Group on Gender and Employment (EGGE) has been in existence (under different names) since 1983.

As recession and unemployment hit in the early 1980s, the strategy adopted at European level was to go for an intensification of economic integration – the single market programme. Employment policy was not a central part of this, though it was hoped that the better operation of the market would in itself create jobs (Cecchini 1988) When unemployment remained high, the issue of employment moved higher up the agenda as demonstrated in the Commission white paper *Growth, Competitiveness and Employment* (CEC 1993). This text was remarkable for its failure to make any but the briefest reference to women's employment or equal opportunities, despite the amount of work that had been done on this topic. This indicated the extent to which at this stage women's issues were still ghettoized.

The continuing high levels of unemployment finally convinced states of the need for some co-ordination of employment policy at the EU level. This was in the context of the measures towards convergence under Economic and Monetary Union (EMU), which would make traditional ways of managing employment either more difficult or impossible. The result was the adoption of an employment title in the Treaty of Amsterdam in 1997 (Johansson 1999; Goetschy 2003). The process adopted under this title involved the setting of guidelines by the Council and Commission, the drawing up by member states of National Action Plans (NAPs) and the evaluation of these plans, together with country specific recommendations. There were no sanctions attached to this process, although quite rigorous tools and methods of evaluation have been devised since. The process for the first time commits member states to work towards 'a coordinated strategy for employment' and to view promoting employment as 'a matter of common concern'.

The central objective of the EES is to increase the employment rate – that is the rate of employed people relative to the whole population – to 70 per cent by 2010. By this means it is hoped both to reduce welfare costs and create the kind of flexible workforce the new economy is seen as requiring. To achieve this objective the guidelines were initially organized around four pillars. These are *employability* – developing 'active' unemployment policies including skills training; *entrepreneurship* – reducing red tape around setting up businesses and creating more employment-friendly tax regimes; *adaptability* – aiming at a flexible labour force and modernizing work organization and *equal opportunities* – removing barriers to women's participation in employment. All of these objectives can be interpreted differently; the aim was to steer a middle course which would involve flexibility and restructuring in the labour market while reforming rather than dismantling European welfare states (Trubek and Mosher 2003: 41–42). Overall, however, and in its application, the EES gives priority to market logic, downplaying or ignoring social relations and social reproduction. The EES is now widely regarded as the first example of the open method of co-ordination (OMC), the new and 'softer' way of developing policy at the European level, embodying greater respect for subsidiarity and the diversity of member state situations (Porte and Pochet 2002).

Given the general thrust of the EES, the attention paid to equal opportunities in its guidelines may seem surprising. This was partly the result of mainstreaming and partly of the level of work already done. But the main reason was economic. Since the objective was to increase the employment rate, the quickest way this could be done was by drawing women out of 'inactivity' and into some form of labour market participation. There is a realization that this will involve more than rhetoric and the guidelines mention 'reconciling work and family life', review of the tax/benefit system and (later) an increase in affordable childcare. The Commission has also asked EGGE to assist it in monitoring the NAPs from a gender perspective.[4] Crucially, however, there is little concern with the quality of jobs, and the measurement of the employment rate is by head count not full-time equivalent (FTEs), thus obscuring the extent to which the increase in employment rate rests on low-paid, fragmented jobs (EGGE 2001).

There is an assumption in the strategy that increased labour market participation equals gender equality. Though this may partly be true, Monica Threlfall points out that what the EES actually does is set targets for women's employment 'in a free floating manner' unanchored to gender equality or social context. As such it is unlikely to close the equality deficit (Threlfall 2002). Jill Rubery agrees. Employment participation may help to shift embedded patterns, but the kind of employment on offer may still cut women off from quality jobs and produce new forms of segregation (Rubery 2004). The key omission in the EES is its failure to address centrally the issues of care and unpaid work. Despite some gestures, the true link between domestic work and production is hidden. The EES pays attention to the 'weightless new economy' but not to the less mobile, one to one, care economy which lies behind it (Perrons 2003).

The case of the EES shows that even when women do play a central part in the economy, as now in the labour market, and even when analysis, research and critique is readily available, the issue of gender equality remains on the margins of policy. The new more open and fluid procedures, while letting a range of issues and attitudes come in, make concerted analysis and action less likely (Rubery 2005). Gender equality is accepted when it serves what are currently defined as macroeconomic interests – not when it might change or challenge them. The key strategy by which this disconnection is maintained is the separation of the social from the economic and the failure fully to incorporate social reproduction and its needs into conceptual and institutional thinking about the macroeconomy.

Broad Economic Policy Guidelines (BEPG)

The Broad Economic Policy Guidelines (BEPG) are developed through a somewhat similar process to that described for the EES. This has been characterized as the co-ordination of policy through 'multilateral surveillance' (Deroose *et al.* 2004). However, because the aim of the BEPG is to create a suitable macroeconomic framework for the EMU and the single currency, and because it relates to the stability and growth pact, the compulsion on member states to comply is much greater. Labour market objectives, fleshed out by the EES, are also included in the guidelines.

In contrast to the EES, there has been much less work by gender specialists and feminists around the BEPG, either in studies funded by the Commission or from outside. This seems to be partly because the gender implications of the BEPG are less obvious (there is a lack of gender-disaggregated statistics in most of the areas it covers) and also because there are relatively few women experts in this field. However, one area where substantial work has been done is gender budgeting. This refers to the development of a methodology for examining supposedly neutral public finance accounts of all kinds to reveal the differential effects on men and women and the way in which assumptions about gender are embedded in the texts (Elson 2004). Though gender-budget initiatives are now being taken up quite widely, the EU has been slow to respond.[5]

The idea of having guidelines for economic policy at the European level has a long history (Deroose *et al.* 2004). This correlates with the moves towards a single currency and was endorsed in the Delors report which laid the base for EMU (Delors 1989). Articles 98 and 99 of the Maastricht Treaty set the objectives and gave the Council primary powers and the Commission a strong co-ordinating role: the first guidelines were set out in 1993. Since then they have gradually evolved depending on the global economic climate, the particular problems created by the adoption of the single currency and the state of the European economies. The initial statement of intent was, however, to create a 'stable macroeconomic framework' characterized by:

- a stability-oriented monetary policy
- sustained efforts to consolidate public finances
- nominal wage trends – that is real wage trends below the increase in productivity[6]

All of these signal caution and a deflationary, budget-cutting ethos seen as essential to create stability around the adoption of the single currency. Gradually, over the years these objectives have been fleshed out to cover a wider range of topics and to encourage growth as well as stability. The 2001 guidelines, for example, cover public finances, labour, product and financial markets, entrepreneurship, the knowledge-based economy and sustainable development.[7] The preparatory text calls for budget positions 'close to balance or in surplus' and advocates the reform of pension systems in the light of an ageing population. Only in the labour market section is there any gender awareness. The objectives here include: to promote increased participation in the labour market, especially among women and older workers and 'to reduce gender pay differences due to de facto discrimination'.

It is customary for the member state holding the presidency of the EU to undertake one (or sometimes two) gender-mainstreaming initiatives during their time in office. These can involve high-level workshops, technical seminars or the commissioning of studies. In the second half of 2001, Belgium (the holder of the presidency and governed at that time by a red/green coalition) proposed that one of their initiatives should be on the BEPG. Though senior officials in the Commission's DG Employ-ment apparently attempted to discourage this, in the end it was agreed to hold a technical seminar in the Commission on gender mainstreaming in the BEPG. This was timed to take place the day after an international conference on gender budgeting was being held in Brussels.

The seminar took place on 18 October 2001 and was attended by experts, senior Commission officials and members of the Belgian pres-idency.[8] Papers were circulated beforehand on topics such as gender budgeting, public finance and gender mainstreaming in employment. Senior officials from the DG for Economic and Financial Affairs (ECOFIN) and from DG Employment attended.

The most controversial papers were the ones by Professors Bettio and Maier. Using the methodology of gender budgeting they subjected the BEPG to a rigorous critique, indicating the way in which the various stability provisions had a differential effect on women and men. So cuts in the public sector and public spending affected women more than men since they were more likely to be employed in the public sector and to be users of public services. Similarly the trend from direct to indirect taxation meant that women in general carried a higher tax burden than men and the long-standing linking of pensions to employment again disadvantaged women. Bettio in particular urged that caring should be seen as an economic category and that women should be more involved in the decision-making in these areas and in setting budgetary priorities if restrictions were necessary. Overall, the papers were critical of the fact that the only mention of gender was in the labour market sections of the BEPG, and urged policy makers to adopt a more gender-aware stance and to attach gender-impact statements to all proposals. These written texts are quite dramatic: by twisting the lens a bit they throw into question the carefully constructed arguments which lie behind the BEPG and the apparent inevitability of its provisions.

By all accounts, the officials present were dismissive of these argu-ments and in some cases downright rude. They maintained that the views expressed were 'irrelevant to these technical questions' and represented 'political issues which should be dealt with by parliaments'. Jill Rubery's paper, which was on gender mainstreaming in employment, was given a better reception although it was also hard hitting. This can be attrib-uted to the fact that gender is both a more visible factor in employment relations and that the arguments had been well rehearsed.

Despite this somewhat frosty reception, the organizers drafted a suc-cinct and telling report on the seminar for submission to the ECOFIN and Employment Councils in December. This contained the main conclusions and issues raised. There was some lobbying it seems within the Commission to have it suppressed, and direct political action (including an appeal back to Belgium) was needed to get it submitted. In the end, in the ECOFIN Council it was taken under 'any other business' at the end of the meeting. In the Employment Council it was incorporated in the final report on gender mainstreaming. There was no follow-up in subsequent presidencies. A similar battle took place in the following year over adopting an indicator within the BEPG on the gender-pay gap.

This history illustrates both the conceptual and institutional problems involved in gender mainstreaming in this area. Some of those present felt that the hostile reaction was caused by the sense among the officials that an invisible line was being crossed – a line which it was important to protect. It is interesting that this whole incident was sparked off by a political intervention by a member state and that those in the Commission responsible for gender mainstreaming showed no desire to challenge the male hierarchy in an unreceptive DG. There is a circular process here – because the DGs are unreceptive, there is little pressure for disaggregated statistics or impact assessment studies. As a result, little material is available unless it comes from outside to counter entrenched attitudes.

Policy on direct taxation

The issue of direct taxation, and particularly corporation tax, has long been controversial within the EC/EU. Given the existence of the single market and now the single currency, there should be at least harmonization of corporation tax, to prevent different tax regimes within the EU influencing decisions by businesses over where to invest and declare profits. Some would argue that part of corporation tax should go directly to the EU for administration and development, since it is business overall which has been the greatest beneficiary of the European single market. But the power to tax is seen as a key component of state sovereignty and this is an area where states have shown themselves only willing to take action by unanimity, that is, to retain the veto. As a result, effective harmonization has so far been limited to value-added tax (VAT), an indirect and regressive sales tax. The provisions on tax in the draft for the Constitution, which has now been rejected, maintained this position.

The existence of competition between states over levels of corporation tax and over business regulation more broadly has had the effect of reducing the contribution of business to tax revenues. This has been intensified by globalization which gives large companies the whole world to choose from – including a wide range of tax havens and offshore financial centres. The effect on the tax revenues of states over the last fifteen years has been dramatic. It has been calculated that in the UK in 1989–1990 income tax contributed £48.8 billion and in 2002–2003 £108.5 billion (more than double) to government revenues. For the same dates, and with a corporation tax rate of 30 per cent, corporation tax contributed £21.5 billion and £29.3 billion. This small increase was despite the vast increase in company profits over the same period. In addition, special concessions to companies meant that overall they were paying nearer a 15 per cent than a 30 per cent rate (Sikka 2003). The effect of this is to put the weight of maintaining the infrastructure and activities of the state more and more upon the taxation of individuals, despite the fact that companies benefit greatly from roads, rail, education, healthcare, embassies abroad and so on. The same trend can be seen even more starkly in the case of Brazil, where under the Cardoso presidency in the 1990s, employee's income tax rate rose by 14 per cent and social security contributions by 75 per cent. Tax on corporate profits, however, were reduced by 8 per cent over the same period (Tax Justice Network 2005: 15).

Over the past twenty years, an extensive industry has developed to help companies and wealthy individuals take advantage of the opportunities for tax avoidance. The line between tax avoidance (legal) and tax evasion (illegal) is blurred, as the scandals in the US involving Enron and WorldCom make clear. This does not only affect the richer countries. Oxfam calculates that around $50 billion a year is being taken from the revenues of poor states (through concealment of assets, clever financial engineering, transfer pricing and tax havens) roughly equivalent to the total annual aid budget (Oxfam 2000). Tackling this situation through international co-ordination is difficult: important interests are involved, and it is hard for any one country, or even a group of countries like the EU, to take action which might jeopardize investment.

As far as the EU is concerned, the Commission has for many years being trying to get measures adopted that would limit tax fraud and create a level playing field within the single market. This has been a slow progress given the importance of tax policy to individual states and the degree of autonomy already discussed. However, in recent years there has been some progress resulting from the setting up in March 1997 of an intergovernmental Tax Policy Group to take up 'harmful tax competition' affecting the single market. In addition, there has been the adoption in 2003 of a Directive on the taxation of (cross-border) savings income.[9]

The aim of this directive is to ensure the appropriate taxation of the income from the savings of residents of an EU member state, which may be held in other member states or dependencies offering lower tax rates. The negotiation of this has been long drawn out, particularly because to be effective it has to apply, not only to dependencies – Monaco and the Isle of Man, for example – but also to Switzerland, a non-member state. The Directive allows participating countries two options: either to exchange information with residents' home countries on the savings held, or to apply a withholding tax, 75 per cent of which would go to the home country. It is an important beginning to the tackling of tax avoidance/fraud and the taxation of income from capital held abroad. Significantly, however, it applies only to individuals and not to companies (Picciotto 2003).

Some of the impetus for greater action comes from heightened levels of public concern arising in particular from the major scandals of recent years. It is as a result of this that the US Senate finance committee began in 2004 to investigate the tax avoidance/tax evasion activities of some major companies and accountancy firms. Expert NGOs, in particular ATTAC (France) and the Tax Justice Network, are also carrying out monitoring and creating greater awareness.[10] The latter is an umbrella organization for groups in different countries which report on and identify government action, case law and the tactics of companies in respect of tax. As far as I know, there are no specific women's groups involved in these investigations.

Is there a gender aspect to these EU activities? Should gender mainstreaming apply? According to senior officials in the tax policy section of the Commission's DG Taxation and Customs Union (TAXUD), there is not much that is relevant. Any discriminatory treatment in the tax systems of member states should be dealt with under the EU's equal treatment legislation. Other forms of inequality are 'not the result of tax policy': the problem lies elsewhere. The effects of rates of corporation tax or loss of revenue are 'too distant' really to evaluate at this point. However, these officials are keen to increase public awareness on issues to do with tax avoidance/evasion and would welcome gender campaigning on these issues.[11] TAXUD has a member of staff who has responsibility for gender mainstreaming and liaises with DG Employment.

One could, however, go further than this.

- Regressive taxation, for example, VAT, the major EU revenue-raising instrument, affects the lower paid more than the wealthy (that is, takes up a larger share of their income). It therefore affects women more than men since they are more numerous in this category.

- The shift of the tax burden away from companies and onto individuals also affects women badly. They have less involvement in the former, and are less likely to hold shares; they pay a higher proportion of their income in tax.
- Cuts in social programmes as a result of tax cuts or loss of tax revenue to governments are likely to be more costly for women. The privatization of services which often results is also costly for women.
- 'Aggressive tax planning' and the hiding of assets offshore is at the moment an 'almost wholly male agenda'.[12]

Tax policy is an area which needs more investigation and study in order to challenge the view that it is a technical matter with only a distant social impact. Certainly within the EU it would seem to be in the interests of women's organizations to add a gender dimension to the campaigns against tax avoidance/evasion and for a more effective enforcement of corporation tax.

Multilateral trade policy

In contrast to tax policy, multilateral trade policy is an area where the European Commission has clear competence to act on behalf of the member states. Previously in the GATT, and now in the WTO, the EU can only comply with the rules if it negotiates as a single unit. As a result there is a complex procedure, centring on the little known Article 133 committee, whereby a mandate drawn up by the Commission is debated by the member state representatives and eventually approved by the Council of Ministers (Johnson 1998). This gives a strong trade Commissioner (Pascal Lamy, for example) a powerful position since in a complex negotiation, as in Cancun in 2003, there is little time for consultation.[13] There is virtually no democratic control of this procedure which during the 1990s contributed, with the United States and through the WTO, to the global reach of trade liberalization, and brought for the first time services as well as goods within the WTO remit (Dunkley 1997).

All this changed, however, with the collapse in 1998 of the Multilateral Agreement on Investment (MAI) and the demonstrations which disrupted the WTO ministerial in Seattle in 1999. From that point on, trade became closely linked with development and the well-organized lobbies on development issues, in the EU as elsewhere, turned their attention to trade and the operations of the WTO. In this new atmosphere, pressure from developing countries led in 2001 to the initiation of the Doha Development Round (DDR). The failure to make any real progress on this agenda, together with the demand for further concessions in trade liber-alization (the so-called 'Singapore issues'), led to the collapse at Cancun (CUTS 2004).

In response to the growing politicization, and also to a general feel-ing that the Commission needed to consult more broadly with civil society, DG Trade decided in 2000 to formalize what had been a series of ad hoc meetings and consultations into what is now called the Civil Society Dialogue (CSD). This involves a contact group, con-taining NGOs representing a broad range of interests, and a series of hearings in Brussels. Business organizations are seen as part of the CSD and regularly attend (Hocking 2004). Organizations can register to be part of the dialogue, and travel expenses are provided for cer-tain meetings (although apparently these have been little taken up). There are useful pages for the CSD on the trade section of the main Europa website.[14] The CSD is now a well-established part of DG Trade and the overall view seems to be that it is a 'normal and desirable' development.

The representatives of Women in Development Europe (WIDE), a net-work in Brussels which links a range of women's organizations active in the trade/development field, plays a full role in the CSD: accounts of the hearings are regularly included in the WIDE newsletter.[15] According to these representatives, the sessions are mainly of use for information; they do not lead to access or influence on policy making. They see their job as explaining why these complex trade issues are important to women, participating in advocacy work and doing detailed studies of the gendered impact of trade liberalization policies. The real ques-tion, they say, is how to move the debate on from seeing that there may be differential effects from trade liberalization to seeing that these do not happen in the first place.[16] It is perhaps significant that a WIDE representative was for the first time included in the Commission's offi-cial delegation to the WTO ministerial in Hong Kong in December 2005.

'Gender and trade' is recognized by EU trade officials as an issue which is coming up the political agenda. DG Trade made quite a full reply for the 2004 report on gender mainstreaming. NGOs including WIDE have also been consulted as to how to carry the agenda further.

It remains clear, however, that all of this is peripheral to the main work of the DG. The Trade Policy Analysis group has 'no time to do work on gender and trade – we don't have the tools'. There is also a feeling among some officials that trade is being 'demonised' for faults elsewhere. Despite all the commitments, gender expertise in the Relex group is normally provided from outside by officials on short-term secondments. Training on gender mainstreaming has also until very recently been of a low quality.[17]

As Debra Liebowitz shows in this book, it has proved extremely hard for women's organizations and activists to find an appropriate language and level through which to engage mainstream trade negotiators. This is also true of the EU. In contrast to the tax arena, however, the research and advocacy from outside, with which DG Trade has to deal, is already strongly gendered (Cagatay 2001; CIDA 2003; Young and Hoppe 2003; Williams 2005).

Outcomes

The accounts of gender mainstreaming in macroeconomic policy given here suggest very different degrees of incorporation, and levels and types of resistance. Nevertheless, in all these areas the possibility exists of a challenge to the assumed neutrality and technocracy of macroeconomic policy making. One of the advantages of gender mainstreaming, and this goes back to the definition by Teresa Rees given at the beginning, is that it is broad brush and all embracing. It also serves a democratic purpose in that it involves 'getting out', to at least part of the public, some idea of how these domains function. Gender mainstreaming and the gender equality it implies, however, has to be made very precise in each area and directed at specific targets, if it is to create a policy drive which sceptical officials cannot distort or bypass. Jackie True in this book shows that even in the most favourable circumstances that existed in the Asia-Pacific Economic Cooperation Forum (APEC) in the 1990s, there is still some doubt about the real impact of the measures adopted and their sustainability in the long term. As the trade example suggests, external events are crucial in creating this policy dynamism. But one should never underestimate the degree of resistance which complex bureaucracies can put up to deal with challenging and upsetting ideas of this kind. Even DG Trade, the most receptive of those studied, has only in real terms made minimal adjustments to its established procedures and policies.

The analysis given above suggests that gender mainstreaming and gender equality are unlikely to be delivered by macroeconomic policy, as it is currently formulated. The exclusion of social reproduction, caring and human needs from serious consideration, their relegation at best to another level of policy making, means that the power imbalances between women and men remain virtually unchallenged. What is needed is a new conceptualization which accords social reproduction its proper place as a crucial part of economic functioning. Defence of and support for social reproduction might then be seen as an integral aspect of macroeconomic planning: thus opening the way to a new social/sexual contract which embeds and tames neo-liberalism in the way that liberalism was at least partially tamed in the past.

The EU, as argued at the beginning of this chapter, represents at the moment the most advanced, and certainly the most structured, form of regional/global governance that we can examine. However, as must be evident from the above accounts, structures and procedures are not all. And while the influence of globalization, and one can see this in the case of the EU, has some effect in breaking up rigidities in state functions, it does very little to alter cultural and personal patterns of action which generate the kind of resistance discussed in this chapter. In some ways, these become more strongly held just because the global and state levels of policy making are becoming less secure and less controllable. Policies around gender are caught in these contradictions. The global market requires the freeing up of women as a labour force but the old assumptions about gender roles collude with the interests of capital to prevent this leading to equality and empowerment. The priorities and assumptions of the EES, and the way it has developed, show this very clearly. It is this nexus that prevents gender being taken seriously as a category in macroeconomic planning, in the EU as elsewhere. Using an institutionalist feminist approach, this chapter has argued that any strategies that attempt to engender global economic governance need to ensure that policies and analyses break down this separation of the economic from the social.

Notes

1. See for example the journal, *Feminist Economics*.
2. Ruggie, looking mainly at Europe and North America, theorizes the post-SWW period as one where trade liberalization was balanced by the capacity of states to mediate the social effects. This balance was facilitated by, on the one hand, the financial crises of the 1930s and on the other the degree of popular mobilization after the war. It is this sense of the need for balance on a worldwide scale between economic and social interests, which has now been lost (Ruggie 1982).
3. COM (2000) 335 final, Brussels, 7/6/2000.
4. For copies of these reports and other information, see EGGE pages in the gender mainstreaming section on the Europa website: *http://europa.eu.int*
5. But see the report by the EP Women's Committee: Gender Budgeting – building public budgets from a gender perspective. A5-0214/2003.

6. Council Recommendation of 8 July 1996 on the broad guidelines of the economic policies of the Member States and of the Community.
7. Council Recommendation of 15 June 2001.
8. This account is based on available documents and interviews with one of the organizers of the seminar and two of the experts who attended. The documents of the seminar and its conclusions have never to my knowledge been made public. Among the experts invited were Francesca Bettio, Professor of Economics, University of Sienna; Friederike Maier, Professor of Macroeconomics and Economic Policy, Berlin School of Economics; and Jill Rubery, the EGGE co-ordinator and Professor of Comparative Employment Systems, UMIST UK.
9. Directive 2003/48/EC, 3 June 2003, on the Taxation of Savings Income in the Form of Interest Payments.
10. See relevant websites: www.taxjustice.net; www.france.attac.org.
11. Interviews TAXUD, Brussels, 27 April 2004.
12. This is the view of an experienced accountant who campaigns against tax havens.
13. Pascal Lamy was EU trade commissioner from 2001–2005. He is now Secretary-General of the WTO.
14. http://europa.eu.int.
15. Available together with much other information on the WIDE website: www.wide-network.org.
16. Interviews WIDE, Brussels, 27 April 2004.
17. Interviews in DG Trade and DG Development, Brussels, 26 and 28 April, 2004.

6
Gender Mainstreaming and Regional Trade Governance in Asia-Pacific Economic Cooperation (APEC)

Jacqui True[1]

Introduction

Through various forms of direct and indirect action, civil society actors have challenged the elitist, technocratic decision-making power of regional and global governance organizations. They hold these organizations responsible for the global inequities – including the gender inequities – that are attributed to the increasing liberalization of global trade. Meanwhile, mainstream analysts assume that trade liberalization is a gender-neutral process. They consider the absolute gains from trade to be a rising tide that will lift all boats and are relatively silent about the inequalities that may result from greater dependence on global markets. Feminist scholars, activists and policy makers have questioned this neo-liberal view highlighting the mutual linkages between trade policy and gender, and the often adverse impacts of economic liberalization and crises on women (Molyneux and Razavi, this book; Van Staveren 2007; Willams 2003).[2] Responding to their critics, regional trade organizations have seen gender mainstreaming as a governance strategy for increasing domestic and regional trade capacity. Gender mainstreaming in this context aims to enhance women's economic participation, thus expanding trade, and to broaden the support for trade liberalization by ensuring that the opportunities and benefits from trade are distributed without gender bias. Towards those ends, organizations have begun devising means for integrating gender perspectives into their institutional policies and programmes. This chapter examines the efforts by one such regional organization, Asia-Pacific Economic Cooperation (APEC), to mainstream gender equality issues within its trade policy-making work. It addresses three key questions: (1) What are the gender-mainstreaming initiatives advanced by APEC? (2) How can we explain

APEC's commitment to integrating gender issues across its administrative and policymaking processes especially when compared with the relatively limited gender-mainstreaming efforts in trade governance in other regions? (3) To what extent has APEC's gender-integration framework been effective and in what sense?

The first part of the chapter discusses gender mainstreaming in regional organizations as an effort to improve the economic governance of markets and international trade. It explores the linkages between gender equality, markets and trade in different institutional contexts. The second part reviews the specific gender-mainstreaming initiatives advanced by APEC compared to the initiatives and achievements of other regional organizations. The third part analyses the factors that have shaped the APEC's capacity to promote and implement a gender perspective in trade policy. In a final section, the chapter considers the effectiveness of APEC's gender framework for trade governance taking into account both the novelty of its efforts among trade organizations and the difficulty of bringing gender issues to bear on trade policy as compared with other global policy areas such as human rights and development (see Chappell, this book; Hoskyns, this book).[3]

Gender mainstreaming and global governance

Gender mainstreaming is a governance strategy that attempts to put into practice many of the ideas and norms of feminist movements for gender equality. In order to bring about greater gender equality, mainstreaming requires institutional and policymaking processes at all levels to address the gender differences and disparities between women and men. Gender mainstreaming seeks to influence institutional rules and norms but it does so by promoting change in organizations (see Prügl 2004c and this book).[4] As Annica Kronsell (2006) has argued, feminist struggle is increasingly taking place within political and bureaucratic administrative organizations and is no longer solely restricted to grass-roots activism and the traditional women's movement. The goal of gender equality can only be attained when institutional rules and norms change to reflect and represent women's interests (Goetz 1995). As such, organizations and institutional processes – including regional and global governance organizations – are a worthy object of feminist study and activism (True 2003; Meyer and Prügl 1999).

The adoption of new gender-mainstreaming policies and institutional mechanisms is a successful outcome by any definition (True and Mintrom 2002). However, a critical feminist perspective pushes us further to analyse the outcomes and efficacy of such policy processes and mechanisms. Such a perspective asks: How far and in what ways does gender mainstreaming redress gender and other inequities and improve women's economic, political and social position and opportunities? One would expect differences across regimes and organizations in their capacity to achieve meaningful gender-equity outcomes. International organizations can make a difference to these outcomes even though most of them promote gender mainstreaming as means to an end, be it more transparent and democratic governance or more efficient markets, rather than seeking to achieve gender equity as an end in itself. As Elisabeth Prügl and Audrey Lustgarten (2005) observe, gender mainstreaming cannot be defined *a priori* but takes on meaning through specific organizational processes and policies. It is important therefore to study how gender is used as an analytical category in different organizations and institutional settings and with what consequences for global governance. This is what I propose to do here with respect to the governance of trade. However, before turning to the APEC case, I discuss the linkages between gender equality, markets and trade and show how trade-liberalization processes are constructed and regulated in gendered ways by governance institutions (cf. Polanyi 1944).

The gendered institutional contexts of trade governance

Increasingly it is recognized that trade liberalization may have a differential gender impact depending on women and men's location in gender-segregated divisions of labour, their position in power structures and access to credit, markets and knowledge within national and global economies. But gender analysis does more than highlight the impact of globalization processes on gender equality. It also seeks to reveal the gendered construction of the market in different institutional governance contexts. For instance, in the European Union (EU) gender equality realized through equal pay and anti-discrimination law and policy was a legal precondition for the establishment of a common market in Europe. During the creation of the European Steel Community in the 1950s, France successfully argued that unless all European member states adopted similar equal pay laws, investment capital might be attracted to those countries where unequal gender-pay structures allowed labour to be bought more cheaply (Hoskyns 1996). Thus gender-equity measures, albeit limited at the time, established a more level playing field to make trade integration among western European states politically feasible.

Contrary to the European governance model, the World Trade Organization (WTO), specifically its General Agreement on Trade in Services (GATS) and Government Procurement Agreement (GPA) makes it possible for corporations and governments to claim that national employment equity law and policy are constituting non-tariff trade barriers rather than enablers of trade integration.[5] "Free trade" among nations requires the dismantling of domestic regulatory structures and norms to allow all parties to access and benefit from market opportunities with transparency and predictability and without discrimination. The North American Free Trade Agreement (NAFTA) reflects this WTO governance logic to the extent that environmental and anti-discrimination employment provisions are contained in the second tier of the agreement where there are no sanctions for abrogation. Consequently, when a US-based multinational in Mexico decides to fire pregnant women workers despite Mexican national anti-discrimination law, there is only a very weak formal complaint process and no effective remedy for those workers under NAFTA. According to the WTO, opportunities for trade are maximized when trade occurs among neutral parties and is stripped of social and institutional baggage. By contrast, in the EU, trade is made possible and beneficial when it occurs among relative equals who share some foundational institutional, ostensibly "non-market", rules and norms.

The contrast between EU and WTO trade governance illustrates the gendered construction of the market, embedded as it is within specific institutional rules and norms that shape gender relations. Between the two extremes of the EU and the WTO, and the range of gender competency across the various (Directorate-General) policy areas within the EU Commission (see Hoskyns, this book), gender mainstreaming in the APEC is a unique governance strategy. Beginning in the late 1990s, APEC adopted an organization-wide strategy for integrating awareness of gender inequities into its trade and economic cooperation agenda and within and across the work programmes of its numerous committees and Working Groups. Compared with other regional organizations such as the Organization for American States (OAS) and the EU, APEC has done more so far to address gender-equity issues in trade governance. The OAS has also adopted a resolution promoting the integrating of gender perspectives across all its agencies and policy areas but is at an earlier stage of implementation than APEC although it has a more substantial secretariat. Together with the Inter-American Commission on Women, the OAS is collaborating with its trade unit and member states, to implement resolutions passed in 2004 by both the Second Meeting of Ministers Responsible for the Advancement of Women and the annual Meeting of

Trade Ministers. These resolutions involve conducting gender training across the organization and gender analysis within project profiles of the Hemispheric Cooperation Program of the FTA of the Americas for instance.[6]

As a single market, the EU has made substantial efforts to implement gender mainstreaming in its internal employment and social policy. However, as a trade organization it has largely neglected gender-equality issues, particularly in relations with developing countries. No EU trade body, most importantly the European Commission's Directorate-General on Trade, has given much attention to gender inequalities (see Hoskyns 2004). Empirical assessment of EU gender mainstreaming suggests an institutional norm which includes gender issues in inter-regional development cooperation but excludes them from trade relationships.[7] Thus, the relative novelty and extent of APEC's experience with integrating gender in trade governance makes it particularly important and relevant to study.

From its inception, APEC has developed a governance regime for trade and economic cooperation in Asia-Pacific that is gendered in several ways. Following a neo-liberal prescription it has sought to limit the influence of geopolitics, claiming to be concerned only with economic policy and integration as if economics could be so easily separated from politics (cf. Rai 2004: 582).[8] This economistic focus deliberately reduces the space for alternatives to neo-liberal globalization, and specifically gendered perspectives on political economy and development. Moreover, APEC gives business elites, mostly men, a privileged position in its structure and decision-making marginalizing non-elite perspectives in NGOs and civil society organizations. The APEC Business Advisory Council (ABAC) made up of three representatives from the business community in each member economy is one of the only bodies to have official observer status within APEC (the other two organizations being the highly male dominated PECC – Pacific Economic Cooperation Council – and ASEAN – Association of South-East Asian Nations). As well, government delegations typically involve economic actors from the transnational business community although bureaucrats play the major role. Unofficially, the APEC CEO Summit and Financiers Group takes place parallel to the government meetings. Civil society activists, including women's groups, have publicized APEC's links to business and failure to engage with other civil society actors. During parallel "People's Forums" in 1996 and 1997, activists assailed the organizations' lack of democracy, transparency and accountability (see Doucet 2000; Acharya 2004a). APEC's deficiencies were particularly noticeable following the Asian Financial Crisis in 1997 when the organization supported the IMF's financial intervention in the region and failed to respond to the deleterious social impacts of the crisis that negatively affected women and children particularly in the unpaid sector and in terms of the sex industry (Truong 2000; Young 2003a).

Not surprisingly given its organizational history, in advancing the integration of gender in trade governance, APEC has been motivated by instrumental and technocratic goals and to a lesser extent by normative concerns about equitable outcomes and broader participation in trade.[9] The "Beijing effect" may in part explain the high-level political support in 1996 by Leaders of APEC economies for an organizational strategy to increase the economic integration and participation of women. Further, following the Asian Financial Crisis in 1999 APEC Ministers formally recognized that institutional gender biases may result in the negative impacts of trade liberalization being disproportionately born by women.[10] APEC gender and trade advocates (inside and outside the multilateral organization) also argue that gender equality and trade capacity building are intrinsically linked and that gender awareness could increase the positive impacts of trade on populations. Greater gender equality expands human capabilities within member states, and thus the possibilities for accessing international markets. Countries will be better able to take advantage of the opportunities presented by trade liberalization when they address gender-related barriers to the economic activities of their workforce. Integration of gender perspectives in trade governance is presented in APEC official policies as a win/win strategy that will likely have economic payoffs for all member states. For APEC, addressing gender issues and increasing the participation of women in APEC economies may lead to an expansion of trade and prosperity as well as a fairer distribution of their benefits.

The following sections of this chapter explore the APEC case in greater depth, explaining how and why APEC, an exemplary neo-liberal organization that from its inception which has sought to exclude politics from trade policy, has embraced gender integration and opened itself to the influence of women's advocacy networks (cf. Bergeron 2003; Teightsoonian 2004). As Georgina Waylen (2004) has pointed out, there is not enough feminist analysis focused on the regional level despite the revival of regionalism in the 1990s and the development of women's networks around regional cooperation institutions such as NAFTA and the EU (see Liebowitz 2002, this book; Macdonald 2002; Hoskyns, this book).[11] Some feminists have argued that regional trade organizations are merely "conveyor belts" for the larger process of neo-liberal globalization (Runyan 1996). There has been even less feminist analysis of Asia-Pacific regionalism, perhaps due to Europe and North America's relative dominance in the international system and the more formal institutionalization in those regions. This chapter aims to address some of these gaps in the scholarship on gender, globalization and governance.

Mainstreaming gender in APEC

What is APEC?

APEC was founded in 1989 by Australian and Japanese foreign ministers (Ravenhill 2001). They saw the need for a new regional organization to capitalize on the economic dynamism of East Asia and the opening created by the end of the Cold War, bipolar international system. Building on previous initiatives in the post-war period, including the Greater East Asia Co-Prosperity Sphere, the academic, Pacific Trade and Development Forum (PAFTAD), the Pacific Basin Economic Council (PBEC) and the tripartite, Pacific Economic Cooperation Council (PECC), APEC sought to institutionalize regional economic cooperation among eleven countries bordering the Pacific. Since 1989 APEC has grown considerably; certainly one indicator of its successful region-building. It now comprises twenty-one economies that account for 56 per cent of world GDP and nearly half of all world trade (48 per cent) (See Appendix 3 for a profile of APEC member economies).

APEC is a unique trade forum and political project, based on a model of "open regionalism" where progress achieved in liberalizing trade is extended to non-member states. The forum thus aims to further rather than compete with multilateral trade in the WTO. Unlike the WTO, APEC does not have any trade dispute enforcement powers. Nor is it based on a formal trade agreement like the NAFTA. It differs from the EU style "common market" in that it is an open region and it does not have a large enough secretariat to form a intergovernmental policy think tank like the Organisation for Economic Cooperation and Development (OECD). Rather, through national government agencies, semi-autonomous regional inter-governmental committees and "virtual" associations APEC promotes voluntary policy coordination and functional cooperation among member states in three main areas; trade and investment liberalization, trade and investment facilitation, and economic and technical cooperation. In many respects the antithesis of a formal institution, APEC has adopted the "ASEAN way" of consensus. This is characterized by minimal bureaucracy, informal, non-legalistic process and non-binding resolutions in advancing regional integration (see Acharya 2004a: 181; 2004b). A guiding philosophy is that high levels of cooperation are possible with deliberately low levels of institution-alization (Zhang 2003), although this claim needs to be tested from a gendered perspective. As such, APEC has taken a "concerted unilateral" approach to trade liberalization, leaving decision-making about liberal-ization largely to individual member states, who devise their own action plans [Individual Action Plans (IAPs)] and timetables for reducing trade barriers. Thus, peer pressure among nation-states, or "economies" as they are called in APEC, is expected to be the mechanism of liberaliz-ation rather than reciprocal rules enforced by law.[12] However, within this essentially national framework the 1996 Bangor Declaration estab-lished a broad regional goal of free trade for APEC developed country members by 2010 and for less developed countries by 2020. In addition, APEC aims to diffuse information and best practices to allow individual nation-states to learn from one another and to harmonize their policies in order to facilitate economic cooperation and trade liberalization (see Kahler 1995).

Compared with the formal institutionalism of the EU and the move towards an ASEAN free trade area, APEC may seem no more than a "talk shop". Ravenhill (2001) has argued that APEC can claim few con-crete achievements outside of some positive low-key results on trade facilitation and economic and technical cooperation. At best, in his view, modest peer pressure may have "accelerated liberalization pro-cesses government had already committed themselves to" (p. 191). But to make these assessments is to miss the politics and possibilities for region-building nested within overtly technical, and often mundane eco-nomic governance processes (cf. Beeson 2004). As Hadi Soesastro asserts, "APEC is not fundamentally about liberalizing trade and investment. APEC is much more; it is first and foremost about community-building" (1998b: 95; 2003). It is regional "integration through regulation not lib-eralization" (Jayasuriya 2004: 10). Precisely because it is comparatively institutionally weak and based on voluntarism, APEC is able to exper-iment with policy and governance innovations. There is considerable space for bureaucratic activism within APEC and for the diffusion of policy innovations through peer demonstration. Although famous for its annual Leader's Meeting (and photo opportunity), the main work programme of APEC is organized by Senior Officials from member eco-nomies in four Committees, eleven Working Groups and Ad Hoc Special Task Groups that meet throughout the year (see Appendix 1 on the structure of APEC).

Mainstream IPE and global governance scholars increasingly dismiss APEC since it has not achieved big gains in outcomes for trade liberalization or economic union. Yet there has been little empirical evaluation of APEC's achievements in building voluntary commitment and consensus on key issues or in preparing the political and cultural ground for greater economic interaction including bilateral and regional trade agreements among western developed and Asian developing states. Neo-functionalist scholars of regional integration have long acknowledged that the intensification of seemingly innocuous transactions has spillover effects and unintended consequences for future political and economic community (see Deutsch 1957; Haas 1958). For example, scholars of the EU have documented how the single market initiative has had unintended consequences for social policy development (including gender-equality interventions) usually the preserve of nation-states (see Leibfried and Pierson 2005). Thus, we should not rule out the importance of APEC in trade governance, and more specifically we should pay attention to the minutiae of its gender and trade integration initiatives and their demonstration effects to which I now turn.

APEC framework for the integration of women

Is APEC's agenda for trade and investment liberalization gender-sensitive or does it have an adverse impact on women? For example, are the sectors most severely affected by liberalization (especially in the aftermath of the Asian Financial Crisis) also those which employ predominantly women workers? Until recently APEC did not have the capacity to undertake the analysis that could address these and other gender equity related questions. At the recommendation of the 1998 First Ministerial Meeting on Women held in the Philippines, the Framework for the Integration of Women in APEC ("the Framework") designed to address such questions was developed by the Ad Hoc Task Force for the Integration of Women in APEC and consensually endorsed by Ministers in 1999.[13] The adoption by APEC of the Framework is a significant example of how the "technical is political". It illustrates the potentially far-reaching nature of gender-aware institutional change in regional trade governance although it leaves off the question (and evaluation) of implementation.

The institution-wide framework is comprised of three guides on gender analysis, the collection and use of sex-disaggregated data and the participation of women. In the first guide, gender analysis is conceived as a methodology for examining trade and economic policy, a gender-differentiated perspective to ensure that trade benefits everyone. At the

Second Ministerial Meeting on Women held in Mexico in 2002, Ministers stated:

> We recognize that in some sectors women may bear a disproportionate share of the costs of trade liberalization, in addition to exacerbating existing gender inequalities. These differences must be taken into account when policies and programmes are being designed to ensure that trade liberalization contributes to shared prosperity.

The second guide on the collection and use of sex-disaggregated data makes it possible to describe the economic activity of women and men, which is important for agenda-setting, identifying and addressing the barriers to economic participation and for evaluation of APEC programmes and policies. The third guide on women's participation is vague in terms of its objectives and lacks indicators for judging progress and holding APEC accountable. It was intended to be broad, both to increase women's presence and enhance the quality of their participation in APEC bodies, including ABAC, or fora, activities (including meetings) and projects, and at the economy level as APEC focal points and delegates. However, APEC has interpreted this component of the Framework as involving the simply counting of the numbers of men and women at meetings.[14]

To strengthen the institutional capacity for the implementation of the Framework in 1999 the Senior Officials Meeting (SOM) appointed the Ad Hoc Advisory Group on Gender Integration (AGGI). The AGGI had a two-year mandate (extended to three years) to "develop APEC's awareness of the Framework; build capacity in gender analysis and the collection and use of sex disaggregated data; acquire knowledge of good examples of gender-integration policies and projects; and for APEC to gain experience with gender integration".[15] In its report to Ministers, the AGGI noted the "willingness of APEC to establish APEC as a world leader in the promotion of women in trade and economic development". At their meeting in Shanghai in October 2001, APEC leaders declared:

> We take satisfaction at the significant progress made, through the leadership of the AGGI, in the capacity of APEC to address gender equity in its work. Our commitment to a wide distribution of the economic opportunities of our era requires the application of gender perspectives in APEC's work, we welcome the opportunity . . . to make further progress.

Having laid the groundwork for gender mainstreaming in APEC, the AGGI's work was considered over. It was disbanded in 2002 but only after APEC agreed to establish a new, lower level institutional mechanism for gender mainstreaming, the *APEC Gender Focal Point Network* (GFPN).

The GFPN links Sectoral Working Groups directly with substantive gender expertise. It consists of APEC Fora Focal Points – an official focal point for gender issues in each Sectoral Working Group, Economy Focal Points – a focal point and typically a gender specialist representing each member state, and the Gender Integration Program Director, located in the small APEC secretariat in Singapore.[16] The GFPN is innovative in two ways. First, as the name suggests it takes a network form to ensure that gender is mainstreamed throughout APEC as a "cross-cutting issue" rather than a special interest. Second, the mainstreaming design rests heavily on gender expertise developed not in member states but transnationally across the economic sectors represented by the APEC Working Groups.[17] The GFPN's broad goal is to provide "linkages between APEC Fora (Committees and Working Groups), APEC economies, and the APEC Secretariat to advance the economic interests of women in the APEC region for the benefit of all economies".[18] It meets once a year and reports annually to the SOM on all APEC gender activities and outcomes.

Gender-based analysis is a formal requirement of all projects approved by APEC. Projects must address specific gender questions and criteria in both their proposal and evaluation stages. But APEC Fora are also encouraged to develop specific projects that utilize sex-disaggregated data, address gender-related issues and increase the involvement of women in projects and decision-making. Consider some examples of gender-related projects within different APEC Working Groups. Some of these projects were solely funded by APEC; other projects have been partially or fully funded by particular member economies.[19] Among the first APEC gender projects to be implemented in the 1990s were projects, among several, in the Human Resources Working Group that explored best practices in empowering women's earning capacity through lifelong learning, and in the Industrial Science and Technology Working Group that examined gender issues in science and technology policy in knowledge-based economies. The Small and Medium Enterprises (SME) Working Group has also carried out a number of gender projects, including projects on women entrepreneurs in APEC SMEs, on fostering SMEs and microbusiness through IT capacity-building for women, and on the gender dimension of the fast-growing SME sector in the APEC region (Chun 1999; Riddle 2004). Indeed experiences of member states in integrating gender in their SME promotion policies has become a regular SME meeting agenda item with Korea and Malaysia leading key pilot studies (Gibb 2002: 12). Importantly, gender mainstreaming in APEC has placed issues of concern to women entrepreneurs in micro and small enterprises on the APEC agenda, even though multinational businesses have been the primary partners and beneficiaries of APEC regional cooperation.

More recent APEC gender projects include the Transportation Working Group's development of a gender toolkit specific to transport issues to implement the Framework, the Fisheries Working Group's project on women in aquaculture and the Agricultural Technical Cooperation Group's study of gender and globalization in the agriculture. The APEC Group on Services commissioned a study partially funded by Chinese Taipei on the gender dimension of firm expatriation and practice in services trade (2001). This study analysed the transnational movement of women and men in the service trade, identified some discriminatory firm practices and suggested ways APEC business could address these gender disparities. One member said the committee's discussion on the gender dimensions of expatriation policy "enabled for the first time the forum to understand the gender implications ... in the services industry" (Gibb 2002). In 2003, the Committee on Trade and Investment (CTI) funded a project on "supporting potential women exporters" in six APEC member economies with lessons for all APEC countries. APEC delegates gave positive feedback on this project.[20] Their comments included: "the recommendations show that non-traditional fields have a gender dimension; the project shows how gender issues are inherent in CTI; CTI should make sure trade policy negotiators are aware of it; it is important to disseminate to our agencies domestically; the projects shows how the 'gender approach is very relevant for micro and small businesses and helps us find out what are the issues are for them;' the study shows that each country is quite different".[21]

As well as making an impact on regional trade discussions, a 2003 APEC project, "gender analysis in trade promotion" illustrates how addressing substantive gender issues at the regional level can have important impacts on policy debate and gender-equity outcomes at the national level. The Trade Promotion Working Group and the Chilean government held a "Gender Analysis in Trade Promotion" seminar to identify and address the gender-specific financial, market/regulatory and information technology and communications barriers to trade activities.[22] Concrete strategies and policies to address these barriers were discussed in workshops comprised of experts and officials from many APEC economies. The seminar also brought together a broad constituency of expert women, financiers, business executives, government and APEC officials, local Chilean Micro, Small and Medium Enterprise women entrepreneurs. It served as an education forum for all these groups; it was an opportunity for them to learn about each other's objectives and difficulties. For instance, local financial institutions were able to link up with women entrepreneurs, and some local women entrepreneurs even met with officials from the countries they were seeking to export their products/services to. In many respects, these deals struck were an unexpected outcome of the APEC seminar. However, Chilean "femocrats" from SERNAM, the State Ministry for Women's Affairs, were quite conscious in their efforts to leverage the prestigious regional trade capacity-building initiative and the presence in their country of international experts on gender equality in order to gain greater publicity and government support for Chilean women's equal rights.[23] Raising the status of women in member economies, that is, at the national and local level, is one of the most important benefits of APEC regional gender advocacy.

Women Leader's Network

As well as the official and formal institutional mechanisms, the informal, Women Leader's Network (WLN) of more than 2000 women in business, government, academe and civil society from the 21 APEC member economies, has played a major role in the integration of a gender perspective within APEC. The WLN started with a group of women leaders from several Asia–Pacific countries concerned about the gender issues facing women in the fields of science and technology at a meeting in Jakarta at the Indonesian Institute of Science and Technology and then again at a workshop hosted by NCRFW in the Philippines in 1996 (Lever 2006). Official accounts trace the origins of the gender-integration initiatives in APEC to the inaugural WLN conference held in Manila in 1996 (Kartini 2004).

   At this inaugural conference hosted by the Philippines, the 60 invited prominent and successful women leaders developed a strongly economic focus and lobbying strategy. Its mandate was to ensure that APEC incorporated gender as a cross-cutting issue in all of its programmes and policies. WLN members drafted a *Call to Action* and presented it to APEC Economy Leaders. This strategy was strongly supported by the APEC host economy leader, President Ramos.[24] APEC Leaders accepted and supported this document by including a gender-equity recommendation in their official Declaration at Subic. APEC Leaders emphasized the need "to jointly undertake economic and technical cooperation activities that will fully promote the full participation of men and women in the benefits of economic growth". This statement got in train a series of high-level political mandates for gender integration in APEC.

Each year subsequently an annual WLN meeting has been held supported by APEC host economies although not an official part of the APEC year. For the first four years these meetings were funded substantially by a grant from the Canadian International Development Assistance. In preparation for the 1997 WLN meeting in Canada, a primer on APEC "Gender: Front and Center" by Heather Gibb of the North-South Institute was commissioned by Canadian International Development Agency (CIDA) and United Nations Development Fund for Women (UNIFEM) to support WLN capacity-building for women on how to engage with and influence the multilateral trading system.[25]

Clearly, the leadership of both Canada and the Philippines was critical to the early success of the WLN. Canada in particular built on the WLN's initial engagement with APEC, during its year as APEC host. A federal government inter-departmental subcommittee on APEC and Gender was established to "advance in APEC, government commitment to promote and support global gender equality, target key entry points in the APEC structure and implement the 1996 APEC and Ministerial and Leaders' directives on women". Canada adopted a two track approach using high level APEC senior officials as champions for gender issues at senior officials meetings and also promoting gender-related initiatives in various APEC Working Groups (Hassanali 2000).

Following the 1997 WLN meeting held in Canada, APEC Leaders recommended that, "APEC should take specific steps to reinforce the important role of women in economic development". Within only three years of its formation, the WLN was able to get APEC economies to agree to organize a Ministerial Meeting on Women in Philippines in 1998. It was this meeting that led APEC Leaders to issue a directive that APEC develop a framework for the integration of women. The Ministerial Meeting on Women also enabled WLN advocates to collaborate with women colleagues in government to keep the momentum of gender integration in APEC going.

What allowed the WLN to achieve such high level influence so rapidly? There are several important reasons. As a relatively flexible transnational network, the WLN has been able to mirror the structures, themes and consensus model of the APEC. For instance, the WLN annual meeting closely follows the APEC host economy theme, while its network parallels APEC's structures through member economy focal points and workshops related to Working Group issue areas. The WLN's broad membership across different sectors also allowed it to comprehensively engage with APEC's policy agenda. In particular, the WLN has focused its energies on the Industrial Science and Technology and the Small and Medium Enterprise Working Groups. Those groups were targeted as institutional locations for initiating gender integration because of the strong and more apparent connections between their mandates and women's equality and entrepreneurship. WLN members were a strong presence at the 1998 SME business forum and policy-drafting process and made presentation to SME Ministerial that year as well and to the Meeting of Trade Ministers in New Zealand in 1999.[26]

Another factor critical to the WLN's success has been quality and commitment of its members and their embeddedness in APEC public and private sector networks. For instance, some WLN members have been members of the ABAC, established in 1995 as a permanent private sector group to advise economy leaders, which has given them direct access to power in the organization. This is significant since women's representation on ABAC has been slim, at approximately five per cent.[27] Other WLN members who have had access to the decision-making processes in their own economies have leveraged this national-level influence (for instance, Canadian members of the federal Parliament and Australian and New Zealand femocrats in the Ad Hoc Group on Gender Integration some of whom were members and some who had close ties to the WLN). As successful leaders in their own right then, these women have been able to frame gender equity as a positive sum issue that could benefit all APEC economies and the Asia Pacific region as a whole. WLN leaders, the AGGI and GFPN together have pushed "APEC to think of women as economic actors rather than victims and social safety net cases".[28] They aimed to improve the inclusiveness of the APEC trade liberalization and facilitation agenda rather than challenge its exclusions.

Critics have pointed to the elite-based membership of the WLN network and their reinforcement of neo-liberal economic approaches that privilege efficiency over equity concerns and growth over human development (Doucet 2000; Hassanali 2000).[29] The recent evaluation of the WLN noted tendencies in the network to focus more on women entrepreneurs and women-owned SMEs than on their formerly more diverse agenda that included issues affecting women workers and women in science and technology fields (that is, the Economic and Technical Cooperation Pillar of APEC) (Kartini 2004). At their 2003 meeting, many WLN members rejected the connotation that they were part "civil society", wishing to be seen primarily as businesswomen and leaders. Moreover, some participants in the 2004 evaluation of the network regretted that as the WLN membership has been democratized, its ability to influence APEC leaders and officials has diminished (Kartini 2004). As a strategic actor working inside and outside APEC, the WLN has helped to achieve the mainstreaming of a gender perspective in APEC by fitting them closely with the organization's existing institutional practices. Ultimately, agenda-setting and policy change in APEC member economies based on gender-equity perspectives will tell whether the WLN strategies have been justified.

Explaining gender mainstreaming in APEC

Having summarized the APEC gender integration framework, how can we explain APEC's commitment to integrating gender issues across its administrative and policymaking processes? A number of factors leading to the adoption of gender mainstreaming in APEC's can be identified: the transnational lobbying and networking of gender advocates, the oppositional discourse of regional civil society, the bureaucratic activism of "femocrat" government officials, APEC's informal institutional design, the emergence of a global gender-equality regime at the United Nations Beijing conference in 1995, and the leadership and financial support of several key activist states. Some of these factors are specific to the APEC context but most are potentially generalizable. Arguably the oppositional discourse of regional civil society, the emergence of a gender-equality regime at the global level and APEC's informal institutional design are necessary but not sufficient conditions in the adoption and implementation of APEC's gender-mainstreaming framework.

Critical theorists emphasize how the challenges by anti-capitalist globalization social movements to the legitimacy of global governance organizations may have a dialectical effect in causing organizations to enact reforms that address their critics (Payne and Samhat 2004). As Keck and Sikkink (1998: 35) argue, "without the disruptive activity of these actors neither normative change nor change in practices is likely to occur". In this way the promotion of the Framework for the Integration of Women and implementation of gender analysis in trade policymaking could be seen as positive albeit indirect outcomes of the highly public protests held by APEC's critics in parallel "People's Forums" during the APEC Leaders meetings in the Philippines in 1996, in Canada in 1997 and in Auckland in 1999 (Doucet 2000). It could also been seen as resulting from the growth and vibrancy of East Asian women's activism and resistance to neo-liberal globalization in various informal social networks, agricultural cooperatives, labour unions and NGOs around labour rights, migrant rights and human rights (see Hilsdon *et al.* 2000; Gill and Piper 2002; Yeoh *et al.* 2002; Piper and Uhlin 2003).

Conformity with the emerging global gender-equality regime, in particular, an opportunity to implement the Beijing Platform for Action that governments had ratified the year before at the Fourth UN Women's Conference, may have also persuaded APEC Leaders and government officials to support gender mainstreaming in a multilateral organization (cf. Elgstrom 1998). But the desire to conform to international norms and fulfil international obligations alone cannot fully explain the level of agency required to mainstream a potentially radical set of gender-equity concerns and procedures in a trade organization. It is likely that individual bureaucrats from typically marginalized national women's offices and ministries may have seen the potential to advance their own careers through international leadership on gender mainstreaming, and thus devoted significant resources to the AGGI.

APEC's informal institutional design and technocratic style has also affected the implementation of gender mainstreaming, although it cannot be responsible for the adoption of the gender-mainstreaming framework. Because APEC is trade discussion rather than a negotiating forum, there is less pressure and it has more room for broader economic agendas. However, the low level of political institutionalization in APEC is also a weakness when it comes to gender mainstreaming since there is a lack of administrative capacity and not the bureaucratic continuity that could drive the ongoing implementation of gender integration.

International relations scholars argue that the resonance between a new norm such as gender equity and the existing mission of the organization conditions the likelihood that gender issues are integrated (Keck and Sikkink 1998: 26; Staudt 2002). Gender equity and liberal trade are not directly resonant norms but the impact of the 1997 Asian financial crisis did make APEC leaders and officials more receptive to gender issues. The readily observable social impacts of the crisis in the region made the linkages between social and economic policy more apparent in APEC. At their 1999 11th annual meeting in Auckland, APEC Trade Ministers noted that, "the economic crisis has taken a heavy toll on the poorer and more vulnerable sectors of our societies and set back poverty alleviation programmes throughout the region" (paragraph 50), and agreed on the high priority of further work in this area involving greater coordination of activities among APEC fora such as the Human Resource Development Working Group and the Economic Committee (paragraph 51). Similarly, the Joint Statement of APEC Ministers at the 1998 First Ministerial Meeting on Women in the Philippines expressed concern that the adverse social impact of the economic and financial crisis in the region had fallen disproportionately on female youth and women. The Ministers suggested that APEC's response and regional recovery could be enriched by gender analysis.[30]

The combination of the "Beijing effect", global social movement pressure, APEC's institutional design and the social impact of the Asian financial crisis created a propitious climate for a new transnational advocacy network, the WLN, to put gender equity on the agenda of APEC. As a feminist constructivist perspective might suggest, the transnational advocacy of the WLN and the high-level political support of key activist states were the critical variables in leading to the adoption of the Framework (cf. True and Mintrom 2001).[31]

Evaluating gender mainstreaming in APEC

After nearly a decade of gender-mainstreaming initiatives, how effective has the APEC implementation process been? A formal mechanism for monitoring the implementation of gender-integrated policy within APEC has yet to be developed, so my findings here are tentative based on a 2002 preliminary evaluation of the APEC Framework for the Integration of Women (Gibb 2002), a comprehensive review of documents, observation at several key gender-relevant APEC meetings between 2003 and 2005, and ongoing networking with APEC gender advocates and specialists at regional and national levels.[32]

APEC's experiment with gender mainstreaming has evolved from its own "grass roots", beginning with a series of projects examining the gender dimensions of aspects of the APEC agenda (notably, in human resources development; small and medium size enterprises and industrial science and technology). A decade on, mainstreaming has been implemented throughout the institutional policies and procedures, if not the norms of APEC (which will clearly take much longer). On its own terms and with respect to making institutional procedures more gender aware, gender integration in APEC has been comparatively successful. Using Hafner-Burton and Pollack's (2002) five criteria for measuring effectiveness in terms of the procedural outputs rather than the outcomes of gender mainstreaming, APEC scores remarkably well: (1) It has completed a project designed to generate and build national capacity in the collection of gender disaggregated economic and trade statistics. (2) It has provided numerous gender-information sessions to APEC Working Groups. (3) It has funded many projects that analyse the gender dimensions of specific aspects of trade and economic policy. (4) It has developed gender criteria used to evaluate all APEC-funded project proposals, as well as a gender-information website and resource kit for APEC Working Groups. It has published a best practices handbook for member states and APEC Working Groups that demonstrates how to apply gender analysis to trade issues. (5) Finally it has required monitoring and evaluation of the Framework for the Integration of Women at several points and revised formats for reporting on progress so that all APEC Fora must report on their efforts to implement the Framework.

Privileging process over outcomes

To date, more effort has been devoted to putting in place institutional procedures for gender integration in APEC than in generating substantive gender-policy analysis. Certainly little effort within the regional organization has been made to evaluate whether or not the Framework for the Integration of Women's procedural reforms have changed behaviour by reporting instances of where a gender perspective resulted in a policy change or affected a policy outcome. In general, the APEC SOM is better set up to deal with process issues than substantive outcomes. The 2002 Review of Gender Integration in APEC found process or management APEC Fora to be far more aware and accepting of gender integration since they regularly approve gender criteria and checklists for APEC meetings and funding.[33] Other APEC groups felt that the various forms of compliance with gender integration (meeting gender criteria for project proposals and reports, reporting on gender breakdown at meetings, generating sex-disaggregated data) gave too much weight to gender issues in their policy work. Representatives from these groups also felt that the gender-information sessions provided by the AGGI were weighted more to theory than to demonstrating how policy or specific gender-equality outcomes could be improved through gender analysis (Gibb 2002).

At the first GFPN three-day meeting in 2003 most of the time was devoted to interpreting the terms of reference for the network. *Fora* gender focal points were not present unless they were also serving as *economy* focal points (USA, Mexico). There was considerable confusion about who could participate in the GFPN meeting, whether WLN members could attend as observers and the relationship of the WLN to the GFPN – despite the diagram drawn up by the AGGI to depict the institutional structure (see Appendix 2). Delegates from Canada, the USA, the Philippines and Mexico were well informed as to the history of the network's establishment and its brief but this knowledge was not widespread. In general, there was a lack of institutional memory about the intentions of the AGGI (documents, including the AGGI diagram, from previous years were not available, although some were hurriedly copied and distributed to delegates). Taking a formal bureaucratic approach, the chair from the host economy, Thailand, decided to exclude all those but economy focal points from speaking. Some participants have suggested expanding the network to include researchers and civil society organizations. Who participates in the GFPN is significant, since it will determine whether the network remains a purely technocratic governance mechanism or whether it is able to muster a sense of purpose and momentum in its work programme to be able to implement and monitor gender as a cross-cutting issue throughout APEC.

At the Khon Kaen meeting there was discussion about the use of gender criteria in evaluating projects for funding in the Budget and Management Committee (BMC). There was general misunderstanding among economy focal point delegates of how this evaluation was conducted and whether or not there were minimum standards that a project had to meet in order to be funded. The network was clearly having teething problems with the institutional procedures they had been deemed to carry out. Very little of substance was discussed at the meeting in terms of existing and future gender-policy analysis. For example, the USA economy focal point reported that the APEC sex-disaggregated data project was well under way but there was no input into what data would be generated or requested from economies or Working Groups (Apec 2003a,b).

Power relations between developed and developing countries were evident at the APEC gender meetings I attended (see Appendix 3 for the economic profiles of APEC members). For example, there was a perception among developing countries that Canada was far ahead in gender and trade policy analysis and therefore not a suitable model for other APEC economies. However, among the developed APEC members there is an assumption that the implementation of APEC gender mainstreaming is over and they can go back to their regular, unchanged policy agendas. For instance, Australian and New Zealand APEC officials devoted resources and energy to establishing the Framework in the AGGI (including two Chief Executive public servants) but consider that their gender work is now over. However, the potential gains from this work will be lost unless countries like New Zealand and Australia sustain APEC gender-mainstreaming efforts by actively participating in and supporting the implementation work of the GFPN.

Among developed-country officials the benefits of APEC's gender-mainstreaming initiatives to their economies are clearer and they have been strong defenders of the GFPN. For example, the Philippines has consistently taken a leading role in agenda-setting and project proposals

on gender-equality issues in APEC and includes women's NGO representatives in its APEC delegation. By contrast, a New Zealand APEC
official stated that gender equality had been achieved in New Zealand
("we have a woman leader after all!") and therefore gender-neutral trade
policy was adequate. It was the Asian countries, she argued, which had
cultural issues with respect to gender, that really needed to do the gender-
mainstreaming implementation work. Moreover, this official could not
understand why gender issues had to take up so much time in APEC
Working Groups and why they could not be dealt with solely in the
GFPN. This aside was also reflected in a comment from a WLN member
in the evaluation survey: "Gender issues are advanced in New Zealand
and APEC policy does not add much additional value to existing policies
and priorities."

These contrasting views among developed and developing countries
confirm Marceline White's (n.d.: 48) observation that trade is a lived
experience for women (and men) in the Global South compared with
women (and men) in the Global North. Nonetheless, most developing
country-led APEC projects do not show any greater understanding of
gender issues in trade policy than those led by developed countries. They
typically give one-sentence answers affirming or denying that women
workers would be negatively affected by the project or that women analysts would be involved in the project in order to fulfilling the mandatory
gender checklist that is required for APEC approval of all projects.[34]

Transforming trade policy and gender inequalities

While process evaluations of the implementation of gender mainstreaming are crucial, we also need to ask about the impact of APEC gender
mainstreaming on policy outcomes in member economies. Such an
analysis of regional policy transfer has yet to be conducted by APEC.
However, some preliminary findings from a survey of APEC economies[35] and a review of women's NGO shadow reports of country reports to
the United Nations Convention on the Elimination of All Forms of Discrimination against Women (CEDAW) committee[36] suggest that APEC's
policy impact at the national level is significant. Several APEC developing
economies have adopted an institutional structure and policy framework based on the APEC Framework for the Integration of Women to
address gender issues in economic governance (Thailand, Malaysia and
Indonesia).[37] For example, as a result of the various programmes and projects on supporting potential women exporters carried out by the APEC
Gender Focal Point Network together with the CTI and the Trade Promotion Working Group, in 2005, three member economies (Australia, Chile

and Malaysia) developed new gender-specific policies and programmes to facilitate the entry of women into exporting and to assist existing women exporters (in addition to wider policies to develop women-owned businesses and entrepreneurship among women). The Philippines, the United States and Canada already had export programmes targeted at women prior to 2003 but their policies and "best practice" experience were able to be learnt from and diffused through the APEC regional forums. In this way, certain member economies have an important impact on APEC gender-mainstreaming policies that in turn, have an impact on national policies in other member economies.

Ultimately the effectiveness of APEC's gender-mainstreaming framework and the GFPN rests on the quality of the gender projects and the economy level support for them in APEC policy working groups. The informal institutional design of APEC has to a large extent shaped the approach to gender mainstreaming that APEC has adopted through a series of ad hoc committees such as the AGGI with limited mandates. Gibb (2004b) observes that this approach has presented internal challenges to policy implementation across APEC's diffuse working groups and committees. The low-key and non-binding nature of APEC policies has facilitated gender mainstreaming by providing an institutional opening for gender advocates, especially the WLN to advance a new, potentially transformative initiative. But it has also made it difficult to deepen APEC's analytical capacity in order to adequately address the full complexity of gender-equity issues in specific areas of trade policy such as agriculture, transportation or trade promotion, for example.

Among multilateral organizations there is an ongoing process of diffusing "best practice" knowledge facilitated by epistemic networks of experts in gender and trade and activist governments like Canada who have been consistently funding multilateral gender-mainstreaming initiatives. The upshot of this global policy diffusion is that the design of gender integration in APEC may actually have as much influence on other institutional venues such as the Organization of American States that have devoted considerably more institutional resources to gender mainstreaming than APEC (with the employment of full-time gender specialists in their headquarters office). Future and ongoing research will assess whether gender mainstreaming as a regional governance strategy, such as APEC's Framework, makes a difference to gender-equity outcomes in different macro regions. Such research could trace the policy changes within member states, changes in women's participation in trade policymaking, entrepreneurship and export trade, as well as in women's organizing at the regional level.[38]

Conclusion

Feminist and constructivist scholars analyse how bureaucratic organizations passively resist change by formally institutionalizing new procedures and rules that divert the attention of critics, while informally ignoring them (Ferguson 1984; Keck and Sikkink 1998). Gender mainstreaming, like many bureaucratic strategies, may give the appearance of change in an organization without changing underlying gendered social relations or the degree of gender equality (Ferguson 1984). As this chapter has shown, APEC has been comparatively successful in integrating gender in governance processes. But it has been far easier for APEC to implement gender mainstreaming in organizational processes (governance, accountability) than operational outputs (programmes and policies) (Staudt 2003).

There is some preliminary evidence of the impact of these regional gender-mainstreaming processes on substantive policy outcomes in APEC member economies as well as the impact of particular member economies on regional gender-mainstreaming policy. This evidence suggests that the institutional strength and formal legalism of an organization are not necessarily the key factors affecting organizational and policy capacity to address gender inequities in trade (cf. Chappell, this book). Further, it shows that mainstreamed organizations, even when they have a relatively weak institutional mandate, can "provide a platform for change by encouraging new alliances and networking among feminist activists, scholars and policymakers inside and outside" the organization (True 2003: 373). Now that the APEC gender-integration framework has been formally implemented, domestic and regional civil society groups concerned with wider gender inequalities and not merely the plight of women entrepreneurs, can use its institutional procedures as opportunities for holding APEC states and accountable for gender-equity outcomes (see Keck and Sikkink 1998: 25).

Ironically, though the focus on the procedures for mainstreaming gender, that is, the gender checklists, criteria, information sessions and headcounts of women participants may have quietened the criticism about the male dominance of APEC regional governance and the gendered economic structures in the export-led economies of East Asia. Moreover, the new focus on women's entrepreneurship has served to shift the attention away from the situation of an increasingly precarious and feminized labour force in the region. While there is no consensus among feminists about gender mainstreaming (Waylen 2004; Rai and Waylen, this book), one interpretation of APEC's gender mainstreaming is that it is a new technical form of rule that is (re)constituting women as active subjects in liberalizing economic processes (cf. Prügl, this book). Given this possible interpretation, feminist analysis of regional and global governance needs to go beyond critical theory's emphasis on discursive procedure, albeit democratizing procedures (Payne and Samhat 2004). For APEC gender advocates and analysts the goal has been to transform gender inequality through supranational institutional mechanisms, not merely to make it more legitimate or illegitimate.

Appendix 1 Asia-Pacific economic cooperation structure

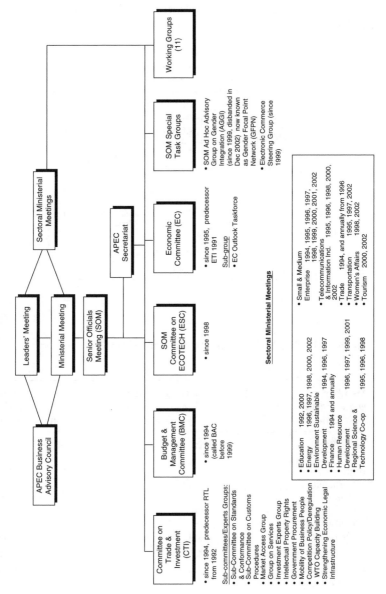

Committee on Trade & Investment (CTI)
- since 1994, predecessor RTL from 1992

Sub-committees/Experts Groups:
- Sub-Committee on Standards & Conformance
- Sub-Committee on Customs Procedures
- Market Access Group
- Group on Services
- Investment Experts Group
- Intellectual Property Rights
- Government Procurement
- Mobility of Business People
- Competition Policy/Deregulation
- WTO Capacity Building
- Strengthening Economic Legal Infrastructure

Budget & Management Committee (BMC)
- since 1994 (called BAC before 1999)

SOM Committee on ECOTECH (ESC)
- since 1998

Economic Committee (EC)
- since 1995, predecessor ETI 1991

Sub-group
- EC Outlook Taskforce

SOM Special Task Groups
- SOM Ad Hoc Advisory Group on Gender Integration (AGGI) (since 1999, disbanded in Dec 2002) now known as Gender Focal Point Network (GFPN)
- Electronic Commerce Steering Group (since 1999)

Working Groups (11)

Sectoral Ministerial Meetings
- Education   1992, 2000
- Energy   1996, 1997, 1998, 2000, 2002
- Environment Sustainable Development   1994, 1996, 1997
- Finance   1994 and annually
- Human Resource Development   1996, 1997, 1999, 2001
- Regional Science & Technology Co-op   1995, 1996, 1998
- Small & Medium Enterprise   1994, 1995, 1996, 1997, 1998, 1999, 2000, 2001, 2002
- Telecommunications & Information Ind.   1995, 1996, 1998, 2000, 2002
- Trade   1994, and annually from 1996
- Transportation   1995, 1997, 2002
- Women's Affairs   1998, 2002
- Tourism   2000, 2002

APEC Business Advisory Council

Leaders' Meeting

Ministerial Meeting

Senior Officials Meeting (SOM)

APEC Secretariat

Appendix 2 Asia-Pacific economic cooperation gender focal points network

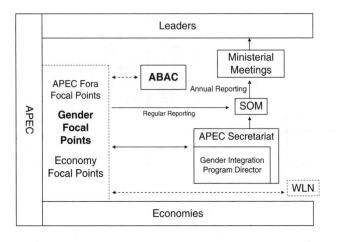

Appendix 3 APEC Economy Profiles (2005)

Member economy and year joined	Population (million)	GDP (US$ billion)	GDP per capita (US$)	Exports (US$ million)	Imports (US$ million)
Australia (1989)	20.2	692.4	33,629	86,551	103,863
Brunei Darussalam (1989)	0.4	5.7	15,764	4713	1638
Canada (1989)	32.0	1084.1	33,648	315,858	271,869
Chile (1994)	15.4	105.8	6807	32,548	24,769
China (1991)	1299.8	1851.2	1416	593,647	560,811
Hong Kong, China (1991)	6.9	174.0	25,006	265,763	273,361
Indonesia (1989)	223.8	280.9	1237	71,585	46,525

Japan (1989)	127.3	4694.3	36,841	566,191	455,661
Korea (1989)	48.2	819.2	16,897	253,845	224,463
Malaysia (1989)	25.5	129.4	4989	125,857	105,297
Mexico (1993)	105.0	734.9	6920	177,095	171,714
New Zealand (1989)	4.1	108.7	26,373	20,334	21,716
Papua New Guinea (1993)	5.9	3.5	585	4321	1463
Peru (1998)	27.5	78.2	2798	12,111	8872
Philippines (1989)	86.2	95.6	1088	39,588	40,297
Russia (1998)	144.0	719.2	5015	171,431	86,593
Singapore (1989)	4.2	116.3	27,180	179,755	163,982
Chinese Taipei (1991)	22.5	335.2	14,857	174,350	168,715
Thailand (1989)	64.6	178.1	2736	97,098	95,197
United States (1989)	293.0	12,365.9	41,815	818,775	1,469,704
Vietnam (1998)	82.6	51.0	610	26,061	32,734

Source: The APEC Region Trade and Investment 2005, http://www.apec.org.

Notes

1. I would like to thank Heather Gibb of the North-South Institute, Ottawa for her generous comments and insights that were extremely helpful in writing this chapter.
2. For guides to how to conduct gender analysis in trade policymaking, see Mariama Williams, *Gender Mainstreaming in the Multilateral Trading System*. London: Commonwealth Secretariat, 2003. Maree Keating ed. *Gender, Development and Trade*, Oxford: Oxfam, 2004. UN Inter-Agency Network on Women and Gender Equality Task Force on Gender and Trade, *Trade and Gender: Opportunities, Challenges and the Policy Dimension*. New York and

Geneva: UNCTAD Secretariat and United Nations, 2004. United Nations, *China's Accession to the WTO: Challenges for Women*, New York: United Nations Development Programme, 2003.

3. Several scholarly studies compare institutional frameworks for gender mainstreaming in different global governance organizations. Prügl and Lustgarten (2005) examine the ILO, the World Bank and the United Nations Development Program (UNDP) applying Jahan's distinction among the institutional strategies, operational strategies and policy objectives of gender mainstreaming. Razavi and Miller (1995) consider mainstreaming in the World Bank, UNDP and ILO. analyse the UNDP and the World Bank, and the OSCE and EU as well (2002) using a comparative opportunity structures framework adapted from social movement theory. No study that I know of has compared gender mainstreaming in either regional or trade organizations.

4. Prügl and Lustgarten (2005) distinguish an organization from an institution; the former are localized bureaucracies but also households, firms, but the latter are rules and norms, often embedded in organizations over time.

5. There is no test case of this possibility. But some scholars argue that government reluctance to improve employment equity laws reflects their awareness of WTO liberalization and of "free trade ideology". Similarly, corporate resistance to employment equity norms and practices also reflects their belief supported by global economic discourse that these interfere with their right to free trade. For a discussion of these points, see WEDO (1999) and Lamarche *et al.* (2005).

6. See Resolutions CIM/REMIN-II/RES. 5/04 and the OAS Resolutions on the Promotion of Women's Human Rights and Gender Equity and Equality. See also Trade Unit, OAS "Trade Liberalization, Gender, and development: What are the Issues and How can we think about them?", paper presented at the Second Ministerial Meeting for the Advancement of Women, 21–23 April, 2004. Gender training of OAS policy officials has been funded by the Canadian International Agency for Development (CIDA).

7. These points are substantiated in the study of gender mainstreaming in EU trade and development cooperation within Latin America, Caribbean and Asia. Claudia Mosimann, "Gender Equality – Absent from the EU's Trade Agenda?" MA Thesis, Department of Political Studies, University of Auckland, 2005.

8. However, since September the 11, 2001, APEC Leaders' Meetings have added regional security concerns with the US seeing APEC as a forum for promoting anti-terrorism cooperation in the Asia-Pacific.

9. Theme 3 of the 1999 11th APEC Ministerial Meeting held in Auckland, New Zealand, 9–10 September, was broadening support for APEC "both in terms of building greater understanding of APEC's goals, and ensuring that participation by our communities in economic activities as wide as possible". This is both a normative and instrumental goal to the extent that it aims to increase participation for its own sake and to generate greater social consensus around trade liberalization necessary for the regional organization to achieve its goals.

10. The 1998 APEC First Ministerial Meeting on women in its statement argued that "as a result of gender biases in institutions, women workers and women

in business are often less able to take advantage of the economic opportunities that may be created by trade and investment liberalization" (paragraph 8).

11. On the new regionalism in global politics see Grugel (2004); Marchand *et al.* (1999); Boas (2000).

12. Some analysts have argued that the model of open regionalism is explicitly political by design since it benefits the export sectors of economies while protecting politically linked business groups in the non-tradeable sectors of economies (see Jayasuriya ed. 2004).

13. The complex domestic and international political process that led to this agreement by Ministers from all APEC economies including those representing countries that consistently resist international human rights and women's rights norms in other fora such as the United Nations cannot be discussed in the chapter for reasons of length, but is the subject of another study by the author.

14. APEC has been especially open to claims that it is a club of globalizing elite men. In 2006, after the implementation of the Framework for the Integration of Women in APEC which recommended increasing women's participation in the organization, only six women were among the 63 members of ABAC.

15. Ad Hoc Advisory Group on Gender Integration (AGGI) Report to SOM III, December 2002.

16. See Appendix 2 for a diagram that depicts the structure of the GFPN.

17. The 11 Working Groups are: fisheries, transportation, human resources development, agriculture, industrial science and technology, marine resources conservation, telecommunications and information, small and medium enterprises, tourism, energy and trade promotion.

18. AGIGI, "A Sustainable Gender Integration Mechanism for APEC: The Gender Focal Point Network" (GFPN), APEC (2002). See www.apec.org.

19. Outside of the brief of this chapter but the subject of another study is the analysis of the origins of funding for gender projects in APEC. Identifying which APEC member states funded gender projects over time might help to explain the progress and or lack of progress in gender mainstreaming as changes in domestic politics and government affect both the funding streams and the political will for gender-mainstreaming initiatives.

20. Email communication with Heather Gibb (21 and 27 October, 2004) following a formal CTI "dialogue" about the project findings held during the SOM III in Chile.

21. At their 2004 meeting, Trade "Ministers commended the valuable contribution of the CTI project in identifying how APEC's trade liberalization and facilitation agenda can be inclusive of gender considerations" (Quoted from the Ministerial document found on the APEC website http://www.apecsec.org.sg/apec/ministerial_statements/annual_ ministerial/2004_16th_apec_ministerial.html.

22. Gender Analysis in Trade Promotion Seminar, Santiago, 3–6 September, 2003, at which I was a participant observer.

23. I participated in this APEC seminar as an international speaker. The local, Chilean politics at stake in the seminar became apparent to me when

expecting only to talk to a regional meeting, I found myself talking to a range of local media at the request of some very active Sernam "femocrats".

24. Filipino women leaders were strong and influential in catching the attention of the President and presenting a compelling case for his support for GI. Close, often kin, relationships with key political leaders in the country facilitated their case.

25. This primer has been used as a model for gender mainstreaming in other regional trade organizations.

26. In the EU, this approach to institutional change is termed "twinning", where a new agenda or partner is added to an existing initiative or partner in a type of mentoring relationship (Jacoby 2002).

27. One of the goals of the WLN has been to improve the gender balance of ABAC. The WLN recommends that at least one of three ABAC representatives from each economy is female in keeping with the approximately 35 per cent of SMEs run or owned by women (Wong 2001).

28. This was a comment made by a participant in the evaluation survey of WLN members (Kartini 2004).

29. The WLN was originally called the "Women Senior Leaders' Network" but the "Senior" was deleted from the network's name as it sought a broader and more cross-sectoral membership.

30. The relevant text of the Joint Statement reads: "In view of the economic and financial crisis in our region, we are concerned with its differential impacts on women and men. While the full social and economic consequences of the crisis have yet to be fully understood, we believe that a disproportionate share of the burden falls on female youth and women, particularly where there have been decreases of expenditures on education, training, health care and social services as well as supply shortages of basic needs such as food and medicines, and a general reduction in employment. We stress that women have a crucial role in the successful planning, design and implementation of economic recovery programs, not only as beneficiaries but also as decision-makers. Additional investments in training, retraining and upskilling women workers can aid in the recovery process."

31. Nuket Kardam (2004) argues convincingly that while neo-liberal institutionalism can explain the establishment of a global gender equality regime, constructivism is far better equipped as a theoretical approach to explain the processes through which new gender norms get interpreted, implemented and localized, and the factors shaping this norm diffusion.

32. I attended the first meeting of APEC Gender Focal Point Network, SOM I, Khon Kaen, Thailand, May 2003; the APEC Trade Promotion Working Group Meeting, Auckland, New Zealand, April, 2004, as an accredited New Zealand government delegate; the APEC Women Leaders' Network Meeting, Chiang Mai, Thailand, July–August, 2003 as a member; and the APEC Trade Promotion Working Group Seminar on Gender Analysis in Trade Promotion Activities, Santiago, Chile, September 2003 as an expert.

33. There are differences in perspectives on gender issues in APEC's "process" fora and the sectoral Working Groups, perhaps reflecting the closer relationship AGGI developed with the SOM and BMC. Officials from the "process" fora

felt that gender issues are very important, and that SOM provides strong support to AGGI and implementation of the *Framework*. One senior official noted that gender issues are "too important a mainstream value to ignore". Another cautioned that most senior officials are from trade, economic or foreign ministries and see gender as of secondary importance to their core business (Gibb 2002:15).

34. One test case of gender policy analysis will be how APEC Working Groups deal with the end of quotas under the Multi-Fibre Agreement in 2005, which is expected to lead to a reallocation of jobs worldwide and considerable uncertainly for women workers in particular across APEC economies depending on whether they are mainly consumers, raw material (agricultural) or manufacturing producers. A Chinese led project in 2005 sponsored by the Trade Promotion Working Group will investigate this issue.

35. These survey findings are taken from the survey of APEC economies policies for supporting women exporters coordinated by New Zealand in the second half of 2005. This survey was conducted in response to the completion of the CTI 2003 study on supporting potential women exporters (see Gibb 2004a). I had several opportunities to assist and consult with New Zealand officials during the design and reporting phases of the survey.

36. For example, Australia's shadow report on the implementation of CEDAW (Women's Rights Action Network Australia 2005) discusses Australia's role in the AGGI and establishing a gender perspective within APEC. In 2007 Australia will host APEC and the shadow report calls for the government to promote the routine – rather than selective – national adoption of gender impact assessments of trade agreements.

37. For evidence of this institutional and policy diffusion of gender mainstreaming see the 2006 economy reports to the Gender Focal Point Network available at www.apec.org.

38. On comparative institutional analysis see Alston *et al.* eds (1996); Aoki (2001); March and Olsen (1989); Chappell (2002).

7
The International Criminal Court: A New Arena for Transforming Gender Justice?

Louise Chappell

As with other institutions of global governance, international law – including that regulating human security and rights – has traditionally operated according to a strict gender code. Not only has it treated men and women differently when they experience the same crimes, but it has also failed to address the different acts of violence men and women experience in times of conflict. Until very recently, it has overwhelmingly been the case that men, and male experiences, have been used as the standard for international humanitarian law. Throughout the 1990s and into the new millennium this pattern gradually started to change through the decisions of the UN ad hoc International Criminal Tribunal for Rwanda (ICTR) and for the former Yugoslavia (ICTY) and, more particularly, through the advent of the International Criminal Court (ICC). This chapter explores these developments. It considers the objectives, successes and limitations of transnational gender-justice activists working through the ICC, and seeks to contribute to a growing comparative literature on gender and global governance by identifying the features of the political opportunity structure that have enhanced (and curtailed) the influence of these actors in this new arena of international law. It also assesses the extent to which changes to the international gender-justice regime have been transformative in terms of opening up new ways of defining women's experiences of war and conflict in ways which enhance their access to justice.

Working from a feminist institutionalist perspective, the chapter takes the view that the ICC is an important new body in a broader system of global governance. Despite it being weakened by the refusal of the United States and other key states to become signatories to the Court, it arguably has the potential to better regulate and protect human security across the globe. The Court also has the ability to create and enforce new norms of international criminal law. As such, it has been crucial that gender-justice advocates have engaged with the ICC to ensure that it does not replicate the existing gender blindness of the law. The chapter argues that these advocates have had a relatively high degree of success, compared with their counterparts engaging with other institutions of global governance such as the United Nations (UN) Human Rights treaty bodies, in terms making the structures and decisions of the ICC more focussed on substantive gender-equality issues. Yet it should not be presumed that theirs is a straightforward story of success: gender-justice advocates have had to struggle and make compromises with a range of forceful opponents, predominantly religious-based state representatives and lobby groups who have argued for the maintenance of the gender *status quo* under international law.

Measuring the 'success' of social movement actors, including those with a feminist perspective, is a difficult and contested terrain. For some commentators, the process of engaging with formal institutions – be they local, national or international level – is a sign of a sell-out and co-option (see Roth 2006). This criticism has been leveled at those gender-justice activists who have intervened in the creation of the ICC. It is argued that through their engagement with the Court, feminist-inspired activists are contributing to the expansion of a global legal system that is influenced by western-liberal ideals and is therefore gender-biased. Moreover, this engagement has done nothing to reconceptualize power relations between men and women or to address the social injustices arising from war and conflict (see Gardam and Jarvis 2001). While these broad critiques must be taken seriously, it is also important not to judge something against unrealistic or unfair criteria. In relation to this case, it is important to measure what has been achieved within the restricted ambit of what international humanitarian and criminal legal institutions are established to do – that is, ensure the survival of as many people as possible during the most extreme circumstances and to bring to account those who break the rules relating to established norms of behaviour under these circumstances. If this is an acceptable benchmark, then the ICC has led to some significant advances in terms of expanding women's access to international justice and in reformulating the normative bases upon which international law is based. Some of these advances can be seen in what Rai (2002) might refer to as being 'integrative' in nature – that is, mainstreaming a gender perspective into an institution without radically transforming it. However, to pick up an important theme of this book – there have also been some 'agenda setting' or transformative aspects of this engagement as well.

The most obvious transformative aspects of the gender-justice agenda at the ICC have been the expansion of the normative gender dimensions of international law. In examining this expansion it is useful to consider and Finnemore and Sikkink's norm lifecycle theory (1998). In their view, norms can move through three stages. The first stage is the *emergence* stage where social actors 'frame' new and contest existing normative frameworks. After the norm emerges and gains some resonance, there is a 'tipping point' where the norm is accepted by a critical mass of actors and moves on to the second phase of *institutionalisation*. During the third phase, a norm is *internalised* and comes to be taken for granted (1998: 906). As the following discussion illustrates, gender-justice advocates have been able to reframe existing norms around gender and were able, despite some strong opposition, to have these incorporated in the Rome Statute and associated ICC documents. Their success in achieving the first two steps of the norm lifecycle now leaves them with the difficult and final task of implementing these new gender frames so that they become a 'taken-for-granted' aspect of international law. The chapter advances three hypotheses to explain the relative success of gender advocates which may be useful in future comparisons of feminists' engagement with other institutions of global governance. These include the 'newness' of the Court; the willingness of gender advocates to utilize both 'inside' and 'outside' strategies in attempting to influence the Court, and most speculatively, that the nature of legal institutions – especially at national and international levels – make them more amenable than other institutions to the acceptance of gender-equality norms. In developing these arguments, the chapter relies on primary documents including transcripts from the ad hoc tribunals, as well as documents from the preparatory committees for the Rome Statute of the ICC. It also refers to speeches and papers from activists involved in the campaign to bring about gender justice through these institutions as well as secondary analysis of these developments.

The creation of the International Criminal Court: expanding the global governance of humanitarian law

According to Waylen (2004) global governance refers 'to the regulatory norms and practices that arise from the interaction not only of states, but also interstate systems and organizations of global civil society' (559–560). As Rai and Waylen note in the introduction to this book, governance structures are not neutral but are a gendered system of rules and regulatory norms that can be translated through the discourse of law and policy. This chapter looks at the gendered nature of a legal institution of global governance to demonstrate how international law translates new and existing gender concepts underlying international law.

The ICC, which came into being in 2002, can be seen as an important new feature of the system of global governance. The Rome Statute, upon which the ICC is based, is a multilateral treaty aimed at creating an inter-state system to regulate and create norms, rules and practices around the issues of human security, human rights and humanitarian law. As this chapter attests, global civil society had a significant influence on the shape and powers of the Court. And, since the inception of the Court, it is global civil actors – including the Women's Caucus/Initiatives for Gender Justice (WCGJ/WIGJ) and the Coalition for the ICC (CICC) who have played a prominent role in lobbying for worldwide ratification of the Rome Statute, pressuring States to develop implementing legislation and educating the global community about the role of the Court. The facilitating role played by CICC, which now includes over 2000 NGO members, has been officially recognized by the Assembly of State Parties to the Rome Statute (ICC 2003).

Although an international criminal court has been mooted since 1937, the proposal was not given serious international attention until the early 1990s. The timing was no coincidence; the process of devising and rati-fying the Statute for the ICC was facilitated by a number of factors. One important factor was the end of the Cold War. As Joachim (1999: 151) has noted, the thaw between East and West freed up agenda space at the UN. It also enabled greater consensus within the UN including the Security Council. In the early 1990s this consensus resulted in the Security Coun-cil creating two ad hoc tribunals to prosecute war criminals from the conflicts in the former Yugoslavia and Rwanda. These tribunals demon-strated that perpetrators of grave breaches of international law could, despite the difficulties, be brought to justice and strengthened demands from a rapidly expanding transnational human rights movement to establish a permanent body bring an end to immunity for perpetrators of international criminal law (Dieng 2002: 690–693). An additional factor leading to the development of the Court was the expansion of globaliza-tion during this period which subsequently led to an international push to entrench new legal codes (see Rai 2004: 582). The expectation held by many was that that strengthening the rule of law not only in the area of trade but also in the realm of human rights would result in greater stability of the 'new world order' (Kirsch and Oosterveld 2001: 1144).

The convergence of these political, ideological and historical factors meant that once the idea for the ICC re-emerged in the post-Cold War era, the institution developed relatively quickly. In 1993, a proposal to establish the ICC was put on the agenda of the General Assembly of the UN. In 1995, Preparatory Committee meetings (known as prepcoms) commenced and in June–July 1998, the Rome Conference was held to determine the details of the new Court. The conference was attended by a total of 148 states, 120 of which voted in support of the final outcome document *The Rome Statute of the International Criminal Court*. The Statute and two subsidiary documents, the *Elements of Crime Annex* (ECA) and *Rules of Procedure and Evidence* (RPE), devised at later prepcoms, combined to form important additions to 'hard' international humanitarian law.

The ICC came into being in July 2002 after it was ratified by 60 states. The Court agreed to at Rome is a unique institution; different to previous and existing ad hoc international criminal law tribunals. Unlike the ad hoc tribunals, the Court is a permanent, treaty-based organization. Although the global reach of the ICC is limited in some significant respects (see below), it extends further than any previous international court. It has jurisdiction over crimes committed within the territory of a ratifying state or by a national of a state to the treaty operating in other countries. The Statute also gives the UN Security Council the ability, under certain circumstances, to refer a crime to the Court that involves a non-state national or occurs on the territory of a non-signatory state.

The offences over which the ICC has jurisdiction fall into four main categories: genocide, crimes against humanity, war crimes and aggression.[1] Some of these crimes have previously been codified under international law such as in the Geneva Conventions and Protocols, the Convention on Genocide and the Convention against Torture.[2] However, these instruments have been difficult to enforce, allowing violators to escape justice. The ICC therefore provides the first permanent court with the capacity to enforce penalties against these execrable crimes. Also, under the Rome Statue and the ICC's two subsidiary documents, these crimes have been restated to give them greater currency (Lee 2002: 751). At least in relation to the first three categories of crime, the ICC Statute also reflects important recent developments in international criminal jurisprudence, especially at the ICTY and ICTR. As will be discussed below, the elaboration of these categories of crimes in the ad hoc tribunals, and their codification in the Rome Statute has provided an important opportunity structure for gender-justice activists wanting to reconfigure gender norms under international law.

At the heart of the ICC is an attempt to balance the central dilemma of international politics in a globalized world alluded to in Chapter 2 of this book: the desire for states to maintain sovereignty at the same time as facing an increased pressure/desire to co-operate to address supranational problems – in this case addressing grave breaches of human rights and human security. The ICC Statute recognizes that state sovereignty remains a fundamental principle of international law and politics. The most obvious way it does this is through the notion of *complementarity* which dictates that national courts should be the first choice for handling a breach of the Rome Statute. As is outlined in Articles 17–19 of the Statute, the ICC can only intervene to prosecute an alleged criminal when a state has demonstrated its *inability* or *unwillingness* to carry out an investigation (see Robertson 2000: 350). Moreover, the ICC Statute upholds the principle of double jeopardy, which means that once a national court has heard a case, so long as the proceedings are legitimate, it cannot be re-heard by the ICC.

At the same time as upholding the sovereignty principle, the Court also recognizes that to address the trans-border issues related to human security, the sanctity of sovereignty must be balanced against the Court's jurisdictional capacity to reach across state boundaries. The first way it attempts to do this is to recognize that it is *individuals*, not disembodied states (the traditional subjects of international law), who must be tried for actions that breach international humanitarian and human rights norms. In doing so, the Rome Statute raises the prospect of the ICC intervening, at least when states are unable or unwilling to take action, to bring to justice individuals who contravene international law. The second way the Court attempts to balance sovereignty with justice is through a more subtle and long-term process: the diffusion of new norms arising from ICC jurisprudence into the laws of nation states. Indeed, for some commentators (see, for example, Warbrick and McGoldrick 2001: 428), it is not the ability of the ICC to bring perpetrators to justice that makes the ICC so important but the obligation of signatory states to implement legislation to bring national law into line with the Rome Statute as well as the 'importation' of the jurisprudence of the ICC into domestic judicial and legislative arenas.

While there is no doubt that the ICC represents an important development in the governance of human security, the institution has a number of weaknesses in terms of providing a global system of justice. As noted above, the Rome Statute reflects a compromise between signatory states about its jurisdiction. It is also weakened by the refusal of key states including China, Israel and, most importantly given its 'superpower' status, the United States, to sign on to the treaty. The United States is in a particularly interesting position vis-à-vis the ICC given that it played such a key role at the prepcoms and Rome Conference in shaping the nature of the Court. Before leaving office, President Clinton made the United States a signatory to the Court but on coming to office in 2002 the Bush administration declared this act invalid and 'unsigned' the Statute. The new administration then took action through the American Servicemembers' Protection Act to protect US soldiers from the reach of the ICC at home and began initiating bilateral immunity agreements[3] with ICC state parties to ensure that US service personnel abroad were also immune from ICC prosecution (for a full discussion see Worth 2004). Whereas supporters of the Court argue because of its hegemonic position the United States is obligated to become a state party in order to bring greater legitimacy to the idea of an international system of the rule of law, the Bush Administration takes the opposite view. It argues that precisely because it is a superpower, the ICC would be used against the United States: it fears that hostile countries would instigate frivolous or politically motivated prosecutions of US nationals so as to embarrass the government. It also refuses to become a state party to the ICC because it argues that it would threaten the exercise of US sovereignty over its citizens and would weaken the government's exclusive jurisdictional authority over its territory. These arguments are entirely consistent with the current US Government's position in relation to other multilateral institutions including the United Nations (for an outline of these arguments see Casey 2002).

Because of the refusal of the United States and other significant global state actors to support the Court there are some grounds to fear that the ICC will be left to concentrate its efforts on human rights abuses in the developing world, especially in Africa, rather than to take a more international approach. That the first cases to be heard by the ICC relate to Uganda, the Democratic Republic of Congo and Sudan serves to reinforce these concerns.[4] Should this be the case, the ICC will be seen to offer only a form of 'victor's justice' with the winners of globalization – economically rich and politically powerful nations such as the United States and China – being able to remove themselves from the purview of international criminal law. It seems ironic that some of those states who have argued most strongly for an economically borderless world are those who also most vehemently seek to keep judicial borders in place.

Despite its imperfections, through the creation of the ICC, new opportunities have arisen for reconceptualizing international norms, rules and regulations related to human security. Taking advantage of these opportunities have been gender-justice advocates who have sought to challenge previous interpretations of international criminal law. The extent to which gender advocates were able to influence the final Rome Statute, in the face of strong opposition, is outlined below. But first it is necessary to briefly consider the gendered nature of existing international law to better understand what it was that these advocates were seeking to change.

The construction of 'Woman' under International Law

Women have never been entirely excluded in international law. Rather, where they have been included, women have been narrowly defined in limited roles and always situated in terms of their relationship with others – especially men or children. Charlesworth and Chinkin (2000: 308) succinctly summarize women's position thus:

> ... women's presence on the international stage is generally focussed in their reproductive and mothering roles that are accorded 'special' protection. The woman of international law is painted in heterosexual terms within a traditional family structure ... She is constructed as 'the other', the shadow complement to the man of decision and action.

International law has incorporated women primarily as victims of armed conflict and as mothers but never as independent actors. Women have neither been entitled to the protection afforded to men in similar circumstances, nor has the law taken into account their unique and varied experiences of and participation in armed conflict.

The construction of women as 'other' is obvious within the various key documents that have, until the Rome Statute, formed the basis of international humanitarian and criminal law. A few examples will help illustrate this point. In all four 1949 Geneva Conventions as well as the 1977 First Protocol to the Conventions, women are accorded 'special consideration' on account of their sex. Each of these measures is based on an underlying assumption about the ways biological differences between women and men define their appropriate behaviour and roles. Special measures include: separate quarters for women internees and prisoners of war, protection of women from sexual assault and protection for pregnant women and mothers of young children. The latter category, which emphasized women's reproductive capacity, provides the rationale for many of the provisions relating to women (Gardam and Jarvis 2001: 96).

Women have also been defined in international law through their relationship with men. Women are seen as the weaker sex and dependant on men in situations of conflict (Gardam and Jarvis 2001: 63). Moreover, they are assumed to possess gender-specific virtues derived from an archaic (that is, chivalrous) and male-centred moral code. This construction of women is especially obvious in provisions to protect women from sexual violence in armed conflict. Although sexual assault has been defined as a crime under international law,[5] until recently it has not been considered equivalent to other war crimes. Indeed, under the Geneva Conventions, rape along with other forms of sexual assault is categorized as a 'lesser crime' and not as a 'grave breach' of international law, which is subject to universal jurisdiction exercisable in national courts. Rape and sexual assault more broadly have been treated as a form of 'humiliating or degrading treatment' (in Geneva Convention I) or as an offence against a woman's honour (Boon 2001: 627).

The key conventions and jurisprudence of existing international law have obviously helped to actively construct women as mothers and dependents. But they have also contributed to the process of defining women and their rights in a more subtle way; that is, through silences and omissions. There are many examples of how this has occurred. The fact that the Refugee Convention does not include flight from continued sexual abuse as constituting a 'well founded fear of persecution' elides women's experience of armed conflict and leaves them without the ability to claim legitimate refugee status. Nowhere does international law address the fact that women are often as vulnerable to personal attack from 'friendly' as well as 'hostile' forces. When women experience violence from within their community in times of armed conflict, it is too often treated as a 'private' matter, or seen as an acceptable feature of the spoils of war (see MacKinnon 1994). Moreover, international law does not address the economic and social hardships that are created for non-combatants by armed conflict (see Charlesworth and Chinkin 2000: 255). The notion of women as objects rather than subjects of war and armed conflict has also been emphasized through their historical exclusion from combat roles (and the expectation that men will fulfil these positions) as well the lack of attention paid to women as the perpetrators of crimes. Whereas women's mothering roles have been embedded within international legal documents, there is a distinct absence of any reference to men's responsibility as fathers. Silence about many of the realities of women's lives in situations of armed conflict has served to reinforce a narrow view of women as victims, rather than active subjects in war, and has served to render them almost invisible in international legal discourse.

Advocating for gender justice

As the brief survey above illustrates, gender inequities have permeated the laws meant to enhance human security. However, it is wrong to assume that the law as an institution is fixed or static. Like other institutions, under the right conditions legal norms and structures are dynamic, permeable and open to challenge (see Chappell 2002). These conditions include having committed activists who are able to take advantages of shifts in the political opportunity structure, such as the building of new institutions which can open new avenues for the constructions and expression of interests (see Banaszak 1996: 30–31; Tarrow 1996: 76–80). For gender-justice advocates, new opportunities to challenge existing legal gender norms first arose through the creation of the International Criminal Tribunals for Yugoslavia and for Rwanda and then with the establishment of the ICC itself.

Advocacy at the UN tribunals

Throughout the 1990s, as part of a broader gender-mainstreaming agenda, women's NGOs began to argue for a revisioning of international law to take account of women's experiences of war and conflict. The issue of gender and the law was a feature of the 1995 Fourth World Conference on Women in Beijing, where feminist activists called for the international community to recognize women's rights' as 'human rights' including the recognition of sexually based crimes as egregious violations of humanitarian law (Freeman 1999; Copelon 2000: 219). At the same time, feminist lawyers were attentive to the creation by the UN Security Council of the ICTY) (1993) and the ICTR (1994) to prosecute war crimes arising from the conflicts in these countries and set to work, lobbying to have gender taken into account in the structures and processes of these institutions. It was hoped that through these initial steps, a gender-based legal culture could emerge which would be reflected in the jurisprudence of these new international bodies.

The first goal of gender-justice advocates at the ad hoc tribunals was to ensure that they better reflected the reality of women's unique and often ignored experiences of war and conflict. Relying on extensive evidence of the use of mass rape as an instrument of war and genocide in both the conflict in Yugoslavia and Rwanda,[6] women's groups successfully lobbied to have rape recognized as a war crime and a crime against humanity in the statutes of the ICTY and ICTR (Freeman 1999). Given the way in which the law has historically ignored this gender-specific crime, the recognition of rape as a war crime was a significant act. Further, by including rape as a crime against humanity[7] meant that women experiencing this form of violence outside times of war also had some recourse under international law.

However, this first step of including the gender-based crime of rape in the ad hoc statutes did not mean that gender-based violence was automatically prosecuted in applicable cases at either tribunal. While gender-based crimes, especially those experienced solely by women, were brought to the attention of prosecutors, they were initially reluctant to proceed with such charges due to 'a lack of evidence' (Copelon 2000). This reluctance meant NGOs, such as Human Rights Watch and the Canadian-based Coalition for Women's Human Rights in Conflict Situations (CWHRCS), had to intervene to draw attention to these issues and to seek support for pursuing these cases from the bench.

The efforts of NGOs and lawyers pursuing gender equality through these tribunals were initially rewarded with some significant developments in the international jurisprudence of sexual violence. At the ICTR, the case of *Prosecutor v. Jean Paul Akayesu* was one particularly noteworthy case which advanced the claims of gender advocates.[8] After the intervention of Judge Navanethem Pillay to have charges of sexual assault included in the case against the accused, the tribunal handed down a ground-breaking decision. It accepted that sexual violence was an integral part of the genocide in Rwanda; that rape and other forms of sexual violence were independent crimes constituting crimes against humanity and that rape should be defined in a broad and progressive manner – all arguments advanced by gender-justice advocates in their *amicus curiae* briefs before the ICTR (CWHRCS 1998; Askin 1999). Similarly, at the ICTY female judges, such as Florence Mumba, have followed through demands of gender-justice organizations to take sexually based crimes into account in prosecutions with the result that the tribunal has convicted several people on charges of rape as a form of torture and others on charges of rape as a war crime and rape as a crime against humanity (ICTY 2001). Another important development at the ICTY, given the publicity surrounding the case, was the inclusion of sexual assault charges in the indictment against former Yugoslav President, Slobodan Milosevic, was the result of extensive efforts of feminist lobby groups, including the CWHRCS (CWHRCS 2001).

These initial successful interventions at the tribunals in the area of sexually based crimes have been difficult to sustain overtime. One factor which has had a direct effect on gender-based outcomes at the tribunal has been the role played by key personnel, especially that of the Chief Prosecutor. At the ICTR, in the period immediately following the Akayesu judgement, the Chief Prosecutor, Louise Arbor, prioritised the issues of sexual assault investigations and gender awareness more broadly. As a result, existing cases were amended where relevant to include charges of sexual violence assault while new indictments were carefully scrutinized for elements of sexual assault. However, in 1999 Arbor was replaced as Prosecutor with Carla del Ponte, who was keen to accelerate the proceedings of the ICTR – in the view of some commentators, 'at any price' – which meant difficult (i.e., hard to prove) cases were laid aside (CWHRCS 2002). Many of these cases were those related to sexual assault; a crime notoriously difficult to prosecute because of problems in gathering evidence and in securing witness testimonies. During the period 1999–2003 when del Ponte held the position of prosecutor at the ICTR there was a steep decline in the number of indictments which included sexual violence.[9] Such an outcome serves to demonstrate the point made by feminists that it is not sufficient to simply add women to senior political and legal positions in order to successfully challenge gender norms.

The primary gender-justice advocacy group working to influence the ICC was the Women's Caucus for Gender Justice (WCGJ). Despite some significant and ongoing difficulties in keeping the tribunals focussed on gender-based crimes, they nevertheless offered both the framers of the ICC and activists wanting to challenge existing norms of international law a good basis from which to proceed: they not only learned from the limitations of the tribunals but were keen to ensure that advancements in terms of gender-sensitive legal structures and jurisprudence served as the foundation for the new Court. Lobbying hard for a gender-inclusive approach to international law, equality activists helped to shape the ICC statute in three significant ways – in terms of its criminal articles, structures and processes – and ensured that the Court became the most gender sensitive of any international legal institution to date.

Advocacy at the ICC

The primary gender-justice advocates working to influence the ICC were the WCGJ). Drawing on their experience at the tribunals and at other UN meetings, including the Vienna, Cairo and Beijing conferences, a number of New York-based feminist activists set about forming a permanent organisation to lobby for the inclusion of a gender perspective in the ICC Statute (Facio 2004). Created in 1997, the WCGJ came to include over 300 women's organizations and 500 individuals from across the world and was an independent member of the broader NGO Coalition for the

International Criminal Court (CICC). The WCGJ operated with three primary goals in mind: to ensure a worldwide participation of women's human rights advocates in the negotiations of the ICC treaty and to lobby for an effective and independent court; to educate government delegations and mainstream Human Rights NGOs on their commitments to women and the need to integrate a gender perspective into the UN; to raise the public awareness of the horrific nature of crimes committed against women (Facio 2004: 315). Since the creation of the ICC in July 2002, the Women's Initiatives for Gender Justice (WIGJ) has replaced the WCGJ. The WIGJ's role is different to the Caucus reflecting the fact that the ICC is now focussed on the implementation of the Statute. The primary work of the WIGJ is to provide training on gender and the law for state parties and ICC officials, scrutinize state-based implementing legislation and to lobby for greater sensitivity to gender concerns within both the judicial and prosecutorial aspects of the Court (see http://www.iccwomen.org/).

The WCGJ arguably had a strong influence on the outcome documents of the ICC forums. In relation to the Statute, it helped shape articles relating to the categories of crimes, Court procedures and structure. Frustrating the efforts of the feminist-inspired coalition were conservative religious forces that clashed with the WCGJ over a range of gender-related issues. The following discussion will outline the major advances made by feminist activists at the ICC and briefly consider the key areas of contestation.

Crimes

The WCGJ and other like-minded activists had some success influencing the nature of crimes included ICC Statute as well as the ECA and the RPE documents. Due in part to their efforts, Article 7, relating to crimes against humanity and Article 8, concerning war crimes, included reference to sexual violence as acts constituting such crimes. These articles removed the moral element of these offences – which linked such acts to 'honour' and the lesser crimes of 'humiliating and degrading treatment' – found in the Geneva Conventions and placed them in the category of 'grave breaches' of international law. Further, to emphasize the gravity of sexually based crimes against humanity, feminist activists successfully lobbied to have these crimes enumerated in a separate sub-paragraph (Moshan 1998: 177).

Gender-justice advocates also had success in securing a broad-based definition of types of sexual violence constituting war crimes and crimes against humanity. Included under the category of war crimes were:

Rape, sexual slavery, enforced prostitution, forced pregnancy, enforced sterilization, or any other form of sexual violence of comparable gravity.

(Article 7 (h))

Similar crimes were enumerated under the category of crimes against humanity (see Article 8 (b) (xxii)). The codification for the first time of the offences of sexual slavery and forced pregnancy (discussed in detail below) as an element of war crimes and crimes against humanity represented a transformation in the way international law represented and understood women's experience in situations of armed conflict.

In addition to the advances noted above in relation to women's rights, gender activists were also successful in having the term gender 'mainstreamed' in sections of the Statute. For instance, Article 7 (h) provided that gender to be included as a ground for persecution (alongside political, racial, religious and other such categories), under international law. Similarly, Article 21, prohibiting discrimination based on gender in the application and interpretation of the Statute reflected an attempt to integrate gender concerns within the ICC. Gender activists hoped that this article would be applied in cases where state parties prove 'unwilling or unable' to investigate and prosecute gender-based crimes.

Structures

The influence of gender advocates was also apparent in the structural aspects of the Court. After much lobbying from the WCGJ, effort was made at the prepcoms to ensure that the staff of the ICC represented women and gender interests more broadly. As a result, the Statute included the statement that there should be '[a] fair representation of female and male judges' (Article 36 8(a) (iii)) and noted that in nominating judges, state parties 'shall also take into account the need to include judges with legal expertise on specific issues including . . . violence against women or children' (Article 36 (8) (b)). Elections for the first bench of the ICC were held between 3 and 7 February 2003. At the conclusion to a drawn-out election procedure, seven women and eleven men were elected as judges. Of the female judges, most had extensive experience in dealing with issues related to violence against women (ICC 2002). When the second round of judicial elections was held in January 2006, six women and six men were elected, bringing the overall number of women on the bench of the ICC to 8 out of a total of 18 judges on the Court (WIGJ 2006). As a result of their experience with the ad hoc tribunals, activists were also alert to the importance of gender representation in the

Office of the Prosecutor, and actively lobbied for gender representation in the prosecutorial arm of the Court. In 2004, after the appointment of men to two of the three senior Prosecutor positions, gender advocates argued strenuously for the third post to be given to a woman. The willingness of the Prosecutor to put forward three female nominations for the position ensured that Assembly of State Parties elected a woman (Schense 2004: 3). The second Deputy Prosecutor position was filled by Ms Fatou Bensouda from Gambia, a woman with a strong background in gender issues and the law, an appointment that met with a favourable response from the WIGJ (Inder 2004).

Procedures

An additional area where gender concerns have been reflected in the ICC Statute is in relation to procedural matters. Drawing on (mostly negative) experiences from the UN ad hoc tribunals, the WCGJ pushed to ensure that the Prosecutor was obligated to address gender issues. As a result, the Prosecutor was charged with investigating and prosecuting crimes in a way that 'respect[s] the interests and personal circumstances of victims and witnesses, including . . . gender'. He or she was also required to 'take into account the nature of the crime, in particular where it involves sexual violence, gender violence or violence against children' (Article 54 (1) (b)). Article 68 of the Statute, which gives the Court the authority to protect victims and witnesses, specified the need to give due attention to victims of sexual violence, which may include the use of *in camera* evidence to shield victims from confronting their aggressors in the court room. It is still too early in the life of the Court to assess how well it will address gender concerns related to procedural matters. However, the initial signs are encouraging with the Prosecutor making clear in relation to the Court's first referrals concerning Uganda and Democratic Republic of Congo that issues related to rape and other forms of sexual violence are being investigated (Moreno-Ocampo 2004). The Prosecutor has also made mention of the importance of ensuring that victims and potential witnesses are provided with adequate protection (CICC 2004:1).

Challenging gender advocacy at the ICC

Given the significant normative shift that gender advocates were proposing throughout the process of framing the Rome Statue their position was highly contentious and not surprisingly met with some stiff opposition. This opposition came primarily from religious-based state and non-state actors and was concentrated in three main areas: the development of an international definition of gender, the inclusion of new crimes related to women's experience of war and conflict and the recognition of gender-based violence in the private realm.

Defining gender

When gender was first debated at the preparatory meeting for the ICC, the Holy See and a group of Arab League countries including Syria, the United Arab Emirates and Qatar contested the inclusion of the notion of gender-based – as opposed to sex-based – crimes (Bedont 1999: fn 15; Copelon 2000: 236). A particular fear held by these groups was that gender crimes could provide the grounds for homosexuals to claim rights under the Statute. Later in Rome, gender again became a focus of dispute. The issue came to a head when the Guatemalan delegation, representing a strongly Catholic state, formally proposed the deletion of the term 'gender' wherever it appeared in the Statute (Facio 2004: 327). After much debate, gender remained in the text of the Statute under Article 7 (3) which stated:

> the term 'gender' refers to the two sexes, male and female, within the context of society. The term 'gender' does not indicate any meaning different from the above.
>
> (Copelon 2000: 236)

The confused statement seeks to appease both the gender advocates pushing for a social understanding of gender and more conservative forces who wish to see it treated as a biological fact. This latter, essentialist approach rules out the possibility of any degree of fluidity in a person's gender/sexual identity, thereby foreclosing the possibility of recognition of homosexual or transgender identities.

Enforced pregnancy

A second area of contention concerned the elaboration of the newly recognized crime of (en)forced pregnancy[10]. With testimonies about this crime still fresh in their minds from hearings at the ICTY and ICTR, WCGJ members were determined to see this crime codified in international law through the ICC Statute. In doing so, they met with strong opposition from the Holy See and other pro-life lobbyists and state representatives from Ireland who argued that the term was ambiguous, and that it could be interpreted to mean denial to terminate a pregnancy (Holy See 1998: 2; Lifesite 1998; REAL Women of Canada 1998). Some state representatives from Muslim-populated countries including

Nigeria and a number of Gulf Arab countries also opposed to the pro-vision, though their concern was less about its effect on abortion laws and more about a fear that it could open the door to international inter-vention in domestic laws more generally (Terraviva 1998). The Vatican expressed some sympathy with the position of these delegates, arguing that states should have the right to make their own laws without external interference (Holy See 1998).

Eventually, the crime of forced pregnancy was included in the Rome Statute. Under Article 7, the crime is defined as 'the unlawful confine-ment, of a women forcibly made pregnant, with the intent of affecting the ethnic composition of any population or carrying out other grave violations of international law'. However, as with the definition of gender, an important rider was added to the Statute: 'this definition shall not in any way be interpreted as affecting national laws related to preg-nancy'. In relation to this crime, feminists could claim a qualified success: they achieved their main goal of codifying forced pregnancy under the Statute but were forced once again to accept compromises over the text.

Contesting gender-based violence in the private realm

A third area of contention between feminists and religious forces related to criminalizing the practice of domestic violence under the crime against humanity (CAH) provisions of the ICC Statute. The issue did not receive a great deal of attention at the Rome Conference but came to a head in November 1999 at a ECA prepcom meeting when eleven Arab League countries[11] introduced a petition to 'exclude crimes of sexual or gender violence when committed in the family or as a matter of reli-gious or cultural concern' from the category of CAH (WCGJ 2000: 2). These states were concerned that, among other things, under Article 7 women working at home may be interpreted as enslavement.

The WCGJ rejected this interpretation and strenuously objected to the exclusion of 'private' acts of violence from the CAH provisions. The Caucus also criticized the US delegation for entering into negotiations on the issue with certain Arab League states in order to win concessions on other matters, specifically raising the threshold for all crimes against humanity (WCGJ 1999: 10). Eventually, lobbying by the WCGJ helped to ensure that sexually based crimes remained under the category of CAH in the ICC Statute without allowing any derogations based on cultural spe-cificity. However, it lost an important battle in terms of the threshold test for CAH. As a result of pressure from conservative countries, the ECA states crimes against humanity must be demonstrated to be part of a 'widespread and systematic' attack, and state and non-state actors must be seen to 'actively promote or encourage' the commission of the crime. As the WCGJ and other sympathetic commentators subsequently pointed out, this threshold test creates potential problems for addressing women's experiences of armed conflict. Often attacks on women are isolated events and, at least in the case of the crime of forced pregnancy, a perpetrator can use a defence of not having knowledge of actually impregnating the victim (Moshan 1998: 183).

The disquiet about the efforts of gender-justice advocates have not only come from 'without'. Some feminist commentators have expressed reservations about the strategies and arguments of gender-justice advocates but for distinctly different reasons to those defending the gender status quo. Charlesworth and Chinkin (2000: 334) have noted three concerns with developments at the ad hoc tribunals and the ICC. First, they argue that violence against women in situations of armed conflict and peacetime is 'part of the same spectrum of behaviour'. Therefore, by focussing on violence in times of conflict, recent developments do little to challenge the 'acceptability of violence and . . . the private order of the domination of women' at other times. Second, in their view, international criminal law continues to emphasize women's sexual and reproductive identities. The emphasis on sexual violence, including acts of forced pregnancy, keeps women in the role of 'other' – identified only through their relationship with men and children. Finally, the social burden that falls on women in armed conflict remains unacknowledged, and women continue to be cast as passive victims rather agents of change or survivors. Gardam and Jarvis agree that recent advances do little to alter the social, economic and health aspects women experience as a result of armed conflict (2001: 229). Another feminist legal scholar, Julie Mertus (2004), raises additional concerns about over-reliance on an international adversarial litigation system for advancing the interests of survivors of rape in times of conflict. The report of the CWHRCS into the prosecution of Sexual Assault at the ICTR gives some weight to her concerns (CWHRCS 2002).

Assessment and hypotheses: a transformation in gender norms under international law?

Confronting the critiques of the conservative lobby and other feminist positions, gender-justice advocates working through the ICC can argue that they have been successful in expanding gender norms and gender-equality practices in significant ways. In terms of crimes, it is the case

that feminists have been limited to working within the bounds of existing international law that continues to emphasize women' sexual and
reproductive identities. Nevertheless, within these confines, they have
been able to make sure the law's construction of these identities is more
complex than ever before. Women are no longer understood solely as
mothers or as the dependents of men, but as individuals who have
the right to sexual autonomy and who can be harmed both mentally
and physically through acts of violence such as rape. Crimes previously
ignored in international law, such as forced pregnancy, have been given
due recognition. Moreover, to some degree, gender is 'mainstreamed'
in the ICC statute which should make it more difficult to ignore these
concerns in future prosecutions and judgements. Securing a place for
women on the ICC bench and signs of an increasing sensitivity to gender
issues in the procedures of the court has been a significant advance
on previous practice not only in other international legal bodies but
in institutions of global governance more broadly (see Rai 2002: 11).
Another important potential outcome of the engagement of these activists at the international level is the diffusion of these new legal norms
to the domestic level. Because of the new norms institutionalized in
the Rome Statute and through the jurisprudence of the UN ad hoc
tribunals, there is an increased possibility that domestic level courts
will, for example, recognize women fleeing domestic violence as refugees
and will use a victim-centred view of the crimes of rape and sexual
assault.

   The ability of gender advocates at the ICC to (re)frame and institutionalize new gender norms is even better understood when compared
with the experience of similar activists in other international arenas.
An apposite example here is the attempt of other feminist activists
to pursue gender equality within the United Nations, an organization
which pledges a commitment to equality of the sexes. In two detailed
studies of UN treaty bodies, Rahmani (2005) and Charlesworth (2005)
both demonstrate that while activists were able to frame new gender-
equality norms, they have been much less successful in having these
principles 'mainstreamed' or institutionalized (let alone internalized)
in the work of the committees. Rahmani argues that while there were
some small differences between the treaty bodies in terms of the acceptance and implementation of gender-equality norms, overall these norms
have been tokenized and 'there has not been any transformation of the
kind envisaged by the promoters of the gender mainstreaming strategy'
(2005: 227). In Rahmani's view, the main reason for the resistance to
gender-equality norms within each of these bodies relates to the ongoing

adherence by treaty members to the original, restrictive treaty mandates which either excluded any reference to gender equality or mentioned it in an extremely limited way (229).

It is clear that the ICC Statute does not fully meet the expectations of gender-equality advocates nor does it have the capacity to expand women's rights in every aspect. However, as has been outlined in detail in this chapter, it has transformed international criminal law in some important respects. Gender-equality norms have been framed and institutionalized or embedded within the criminal, structural and procedural aspects of the Court. While the challenge still exists to ensure that these norms become taken-for-granted both at the international and domestic level, achieving the first two stages of the norm lifecycle is a major advance both in terms of what existed previously in terms of international humanitarian law and what has been possible within analogous UN institutions. These positive outcomes raise questions about the factors that have contributed to these developments, and the broader issue of the engagement of feminist actors with institutions of globalization and global governance.

This chapter proposes three hypotheses which are aimed at contributing to the ongoing research agenda on gender activists and institutions of global governance. The first hypothesis suggested by this study is that the success of gender-activist strategies has a temporal element; that it relates directly to the age of the institution as well as the context in which it is being argued. The fact that the ICC is a *new* institution provided a positive opportunity structure for gender advocates wanting to influence the nature of the Court. The creation of the Court gave gender advocates a new arena to state their claims, which was free from the biases and vested interests, or the 'congealment' of norms that can be found in existing institutions. Moreover there was a broad view within the international legal community that although the ICC could not completely 'start from scratch' in terms of its legal codes, that it should reflect contemporary legal standards. By 1998, especially after the developments at the ad hoc tribunal, these standards included a growing acceptance of the need for a more gender-sensitive view of the law. While those framing new gender-equality norms faced opposition and hostility to their position from those defending the status quo, evidence emerging from the tribunals meant it was increasingly difficult to support a gender blind view of the law. The fact that this was happening in the broader context of general debates about the need for/acceptance of a better understanding of gender in other fora, such as the UN Conferences on Women (see Molyneaux and Razavi, this book), the UN Security Council (see

Cohn, this book) and within other international institutions, served to further reinforce the legitimacy of those advocating for gender justice. It appears then that in the context in which the ICC was being built, the tide was flowing with, rather than against the demands of these advocates. As we know, tides can turn, and quickly. Given the changes in international politics since 1998 when the Court was being formulated, it is questionable whether these gender claims would have the same resonance today.

A second hypothesis that requires further comparative analysis is that to be successful, any gender-equality strategy requires the co-operation of insider and outsider advocates to work towards its incorporation. My research on the relationship between feminist activists and 'femocrats' demonstrates that has been important in challenging bureaucratic and legal norms in national level political institutions (Chappell 2002: especially Chapter 4). Jaqui True (2003) has also discussed the importance of this relationship in other arenas of global governance, including the WTO and UN forums. In this study, it was very obvious that both at the ad hoc tribunals and the ICC gender advocates played a pivotal role in bringing to the attention of official delegates the importance of considering gender issues in their discussions. The WCGJ was tireless in its efforts throughout the drafting process, and now the WIGJ has taken up the challenge of monitoring the implementation of the Rome Statute. However, as the ad hoc tribunals demonstrated, having gender-based crimes formally recognized is not the same as having them prosecuted; in other words, there is a limit to the effectiveness of lobbying as a strategy on its own. In order to translate the demands of gender advocates into reality, it is necessary to have 'insiders' – especially senior prosecutors and judges – take up these demands in their decision-making processes. As was seen in relation to the decisions of Justices Mumbo at the ICTY and Pillay at the ICTR and the role of Louise Arbour at the Rwandan tribunal, key personnel can have a positive influence on the outcome of cases by being alert to the gender-based aspects of crimes. A potentially crucial development at the ICC is that a number of women and some men, who have expressed a concern about gender justice, have been appointed to judicial and prosecutorial positions. The ability to alter the gender-normative framework within institutions requires a willingness on behalf of gender advocates to enter institutions and to maintain contact with, and respond to, the demands of external advocates, who continue to push from the outside for internal change.

The third and most speculative hypothesis to emerge from this study is that it is easier to bring about more gender-sensitive outcomes through legally, rather than bureaucratically based institutions. This proposition is based on the view that compared with domestic and international bureaucratic institutions, which exist to provide a permanent, regularized and consistent framework for implementing government decisions; legal institutions are more amenable to change[12]. It is true that legal norms related to women's equality remained static for centuries. However, the willingness at times of courts to respond to new arguments and reflect these arguments in precedent-setting judgements means that judicial decision-making can *potentially* reframe and redefine norms, and do so relatively quickly. My work concerning the ability of gender activists in Canada to use the Charter of Rights to successfully argue a number of important cases related to gender equality before the Supreme Court – at the same time as a being blocked in their efforts to challenge gender norms in the bureaucracy – shows that this pattern can operate at the level of the nation state (see Chappell 2002 especially Chapter 5). The above discussion suggests that a similar pattern might exist in the international arena. Judicial rulings made at the ad hoc tribunals, which reflected the arguments of gender advocates effectively, broke through the silence on women's experiences of war and conflict. Once this reality was exposed, it could no longer be ignored and has become the basis for reformulating international legal norms. By contrast, gender advocates have had much less success in bringing about a normative shift in the more bureaucratically structured UN Human Rights Treaty bodies due to the unwillingness of actors within these bodies to challenge their restrictive mandates.

While the legal *nature* of the institution is important, it may not be this factor alone which has influenced the prevailing opportunity structure open to gender advocates. An additional intervening variable – that of the level of the institution – might also have some bearing on the extent to which legal institutions are more amenable than others to gender claims[13]. The question is whether it is through legal institutions per se or whether it is through higher level courts, such as the ICC or Supreme Courts that gender norms are more salient? The importance of a 'level-based' analysis is highlighted in Shirin Rai's work which found that in India the Supreme Court 'has provided an important resource which they can mobilize against the more repressive institutions of the state' (2002: 188). However, at the same time, lower level courts have not been as useful to women, especially in pursuing responses to violence issues. Rather, she found that, 'local courts were just as amenable to socially constructed patriarchal explanations and interpretations of norms as were the administrative bodies, whereas at the national level, the court was much more "dis-embedded" and able to open new spaces of contesting dominant social norms' (2002 and personal correspondence). Concerning gender advocates and the ICC, it may be that their success relates both to the fact that it is a legal institution *and* that it is a global institution which is expected, along with the highest-level domestic courts, to establish new norms. By contrast, local level courts are closer to the social and cultural roots of societies, and thus, as far as women tend to maintain and reinforce existing gender biases within these societies. Obviously, much more comparative research examining the opportunities across local/national/regional and global legal and non-legal institutions is required before these propositions about the *nature* and *level* of the institution can be substantiated.

Conclusion

It has been vitally important that gender advocates have been involved in the creation of the ICC. The process in which they were engaged was a highly contentious one and although they were unable to secure all of their objectives, through their efforts a foundation now exists for a much more nuanced understanding of gender under international law. At both the international and national level the ICC has the potential to act as a transformative global governance institution. By embedding new gender norms in the Rome Statute, activists now have a tool to argue for the recognition of women's experiences of war and conflict at the international level. But these developments are also relevant at the level of the nation-state, because these new norms can recast decision-making within domestic legal institutions. Through the implementation of the statute at the domestic level, states will be encouraged to bring their criminal law up-to-date to reflect the ICC provisions including the groundbreaking gender provisions. Further, it is expected that over time the jurisprudence stemming from the ad hoc tribunal and ICC cases will shape national law. Some possible advances include redefinition of key crimes such as rape and sexual assault to reflect a victim rather than a perpetrator point-of-view, wider recognition of gender-based violence as a basis for claiming refugee status and the introduction of newly defined crimes such as enforced pregnancy. Of course, the ongoing salience of state sovereignty means that these changes will not be automatic. As with the debates at the international level, shifts in these legal norms will be hotly contested and interpreted and reinterpreted to suit national contexts. The task now confronting gender advocates will be to work simultaneously at the global and national level, both inside and outside legal institutions, to ensure that these recent steps towards transforming international law to better reflect principles of gender justice is made a reality. Advocates will know that they have achieved their goals if and when there is no longer a need to think about the uniqueness and importance of these developments but when they have become a taken-for-granted feature of international and national law.

Notes

1. This latter category is yet to be defined under international law, and will not come under the jurisdiction of the court until state parties to the ICC can agree on its meaning.
2. The full title of these treaties are: *The Convention of the Prevention and Punishment of the Crime of Genocide*, 9 December 1948, 78 UNTS 277; *Geneva Conventions I–IV* 12 August 1949 and *the Protocol I and II to the Geneva Conventions of 12 August 1949*, June 1977; *Convention against Torture and Other Cruel, Inhuman or Degrading Treatment or Punishment* 10 December 1984, 1465 UNTS 85.
3. These agreements prohibit the surrender to the ICC of a broad scope of persons including current or former government officials, military personnel and US employees (including contractors) and nationals (CICC 2005). In an attempt to secure compliance, the United States has introduced legislation (known as the Nethercutt Amendment to the US Foreign Relations Appropriations Bill) to authorize withdrawal of aid from those states refusing to enter into a BIA. As of June 2005, the US State Department reports that it has signed 100 BIAs. The chief monitoring agency of the ICC, the CICC is aware of only 91 of these. The CICC reports that of the 57 States who have refused to enter into a BIA, 27 have lost US aid (CICC 2005).
4. However, news in July 2005 that three British servicemen have been charged with war crimes related to the inhumane treatment of detainees in Iraq under the UK's domestic International Criminal Court Act 2001 may go some way to ally these fears and reinforce the view that the 'diffusion effect' of the ICC is working.
5. Although rape has not been given serious attention under international law it has been prohibited by the law of war since the time of Richard II in 1385. It was treated as an infringement of the Lieber Code of 1863 during the American Civil War. More recently, it was prosecuted as a war crime under the Tokyo Tribunal after Second World War, and included in the Geneva Conventions (Merom 1993: 425).
6. The UN estimates that upwards of 20,000 women were raped between 1992 and 1994 in the former Yugoslavia (quoted in Nahapetian 1999: 127). Figures for Rwanda are difficult to find, but estimates indicate that hundreds of thousands of women experienced some form of sexual violence during this conflict (Nahapetian 1999).
7. Crimes against humanity are defined as 'inhumane acts of a very serious nature committed as part of a widespread or systematic attack against a

civilian population on political, ethnic or religious grounds. They may be committed in times of peace or war' (in Robertson 2000: 295).

8. Akayesu, who served as the equivalent of a mayor at the Taba commune, was tried and convicted of ordering, instigating and aiding and abetting crimes against humanity and acts of genocide against Tutsi's during the 1994 Rwandan Civil War.

9. It is interesting to note that between February 2001 and November 2002 (during del Ponte's period as prosecutor) only 6 of the 15 indictments included acts of sexual violence while in 2000, in cases flowing on from the Arbor period, 6 of the 6 indictments included such crimes (CWHRCS 2002: 10).

10. The crime of enforced pregnancy is usually understood to involve raping a woman until she is made pregnant then confining her with the intent that she will bear a child of a different 'ethnicity'. As witnesses had testified to both the ICTY and ICTR, enforced pregnancy, where women were raped until made pregnant and then held in captivity until they bore the child, has become a commonly used weapon of war (see Boon 2001: 656–667).

11. They included *inter alia*: United Arab Emirates, Libya, Oman, Sudan, Lebanon and Bahrain.

12. This is not to argue that gender advocates have no success in bureaucratic institutions (for a discussion of this see Chappell 2002, Chapter 4). However, the permanent pattern of decision-making leads to the 'congealment' of existing norms. Trying to unsettle these practices requires the co-ordinated effort of supportive governments, insider and outsider gender advocates, as well as sympathetic senior bureaucrats. Aligning these forces may be more difficult than the strategic selection of legal cases by advocates and judges to challenge existing laws.

13. I would like to thank Shirin Rai for raising the significance of a level-based analysis in relation to the ICC.

8

Mainstreaming Gender in UN Security Policy: A Path to Political Transformation?[1]

Carol Cohn

In October of 2000, the UN Security Council (SC) unanimously adopted Resolution 1325 on women, peace and security (WPS).[2] Resolution 1325 is often called a landmark resolution because it represents the first time the SC directly addressed the subject of women and armed conflict, beyond a few passing references to women as victims, or women as a "vulnerable group." It not only recognizes that women have been active in peace-building and conflict prevention but it also recognizes women's *right* to participate – as decision-makers at all levels – in conflict prevention, conflict resolution, and peace-building processes. Further, it calls for *all* participants in peace negotiations "to adopt a gender perspective," and "expresses its willingness to incorporate a gender perspective into peacekeeping operations." Gender perspectives, in this context, are taken to include attention to the special needs of women and girls during disarmament, demobilization, repatriation, resettlement, rehabilitation, reintegration, and post-conflict reconstruction, as well as measures supporting local women's peace initiatives. Resolution 1325 recognizes that women are disproportionately victimized in wars and calls upon all parties to armed conflict to take special measures to respect women's rights, to protect women from gender-based violence, and to end impunity for crimes of violence against women and girls. It calls for gender training for peacekeepers and others involved in peace operations. And it calls for better representation of women throughout the UN system itself.

In other words, although "gender mainstreaming" has been official UN policy since 1997,[3] Resolution 1325 represents the first time that gender has been mainstreamed in the *armed conflict and security* side of the UN.[4] It was the product of a sophisticated feminist initiative – launched by NGOs and later picked up by women's advocates within the UN. The struggle to move it from rhetorical commitment to practical implementation is currently the focus of a massive mobilization of women's political energies in many different countries.

The idea of mobilizing to influence the SC, to get a SC resolution passed, and to then try to change the functioning of the security apparatus of the UN represents a new, daring, and ambitious strategy for anti-war feminists. While feminists internationally have long been active in trying to shape the UN agenda in areas such as development, human rights, and violence against women, the main focus of their work has been the General Assembly (GA) or the substantive Commissions of the Economic and Social Council (ECOSOC) such as the Human Rights Commission and the Commissions on the Status of Women (CSW), Sustainable Development and Social Development. Although the NGOs discussed the possibility of continuing to work in the GA, the SC represented a more potent venue for action. As the primary UN decision-making body in the area of international peace and security, the SC is at the center of UN power. Not coincidently, it is also an overwhelmingly male and masculinist domain, devoted to the "hardcore" issue of military threats to international peace and security.[5]

Thus, the initiative to pass and implement 1325 can be seen as a bold move to influence what is arguably the most powerful global governance institution in the area of international peace and security. It can also be seen as a strategy that has channeled tremendous amounts of women's energies and resources into engagement with the micropolitics, processes, and paradigms of a conservative institution, as well as with interstate diplomatic political machinations. What is certain is that the strategy has provoked an extremely complex process of reciprocal re-shaping, at both individual and organizational levels.

An assessment of the impact of the initiative to pass and implement Resolution 1325 reveals some of the challenges and complexities that feminist political analyses and practice face in the process of engaging with global governance institutions. In this chapter, after providing a brief account of the genesis and diffusion of 1325, I first explore what it means to "assess the impact" of such an initiative, suggesting that it is a far more complex and multifaceted project than it might first appear. Drawing on my study of 1325 and informed by my experiences as both a feminist researcher and a participant observer, I articulate a series of questions meant to tease out some of those many dimensions of impact, both inside the global governance institution and outside its bounds, in an attempt to ensure attention to the full range of actors engaged in and by this initiative when "assessing impact." I then go on to address just a fraction of those questions, focusing on the question of the degree to which this "policy victory" reflects the original motivations, beliefs and purposes of the NGOs, both the explicitly feminist and the non-feminist, that fostered it, and on the political implications of the discursive strategy used to achieve this victory. I end with a number of personal reflections on the implications of the construction of women as "peacemakers."

The genesis of 1325

The conceptual roots of 1325 lie in the 1995 Beijing Platform for Action's chapter devoted to women and armed conflict.[6] It was at the 1998 UN CSW debate about the obstacles to implementing that chapter that a group of NGOs, the Women and Armed Conflict Caucus, started to think about taking the issue of "women, peace and security" (WPS) to the SC. Two years later, the 2000 CSW (known as "Beijing +5") served as the review of the Beijing Platform for Action as a whole, and here again, issues of women and armed conflict became a focus of discussion. In participants' accounts, the March 2000 International Women's Day Presidential Statement by (then) Security Council President Anwarul Chowdhury of Bangladesh (2000),[7] in which he called for the SC to examine the intersections between gender, peace, and security, emerges as a crucial rhetorical act, which NGOs could then use as legitimization for their assertions that a discussion of women and security could and should be on the SC's agenda. At the end of the March 2000 CSW, the NGO Working Group on WPS, http://www.womenpeacesecurity.org/ (hereafter "the Working Group") was formed to advocate for a SC resolution. The six founding members were: Women's International League for Peace and Freedom (WILPF); Amnesty International; International Alert; Hague Appeal for Peace; Women's Commission for Refugee Women and Children; and Women's Caucus for Gender Justice.

The drafting and passage of the resolution is ultimately an enormously multifaceted and complex story with many different actors. For the purposes of this chapter, I want to focus on the Working Group and two points that are crucial. First, the entire groundwork for this resolution, including the initial drafting and the political work of preparing SC members to accept that the resolution was relevant to and had precedents in the SC's work, was done by NGOs. This is perhaps the only SC resolution of which that can be said. The NGOs accomplished this through an extremely sophisticated strategy. They worked to educate the Council, finding as much high-quality relevant literature as they could, and presenting it, along with summaries, to the Council delegations.

They combed through every UN document from the institution's inception, finding every reference in any way relevant to the WPS agenda, and provided the Ambassadors with a compendium of "agreed language" which showed the basis for committing themselves to the language of the resolution. They met with Council members (learning the protocol for how and when to approach them) and also worked to develop relationships with relevant departments of government in the member states' capitals. They supplied information about poorly understood conflicts from women's groups "on the ground," thus providing Council members with a valuable resource. Toward the end, they brought women from conflict zones to address the Council in an Arria formula meeting,[8] bringing to men who rarely left New York a concrete, personal awareness of both women's victimization in war and their agency.[9] Generally, the Working Group self-consciously decided to position themselves as "helpers" to the Council, rather than confrontational adversaries.

The second crucial point is that although other actors eventually became very important – including the United Nations Development Fund for Women (UNIFEM) and individual Council members such as Namibia, Jamaica, and Canada – the Working Group initiated and carried this project for months *despite* what they felt was a clear message from women's advocates within the UN that "the time isn't right, it couldn't happen, it isn't worth the effort." It was not until the NGOs had made considerable political inroads that the advocates inside the UN really signed on to the project. It is one of the ironies of the Working Group's 1325 success that group members are now accorded much more status and access within the UN, and have closer personal relationships with UN and member state insiders, resulting, I think, in a diminished willingness to take positions or actions that are advised against by UN insiders.[10]

When the resolution was adopted in October 2000, still containing some of the language from their draft resolution, the Working Group was exultant. It was immediately apparent to all of the resolution's advocates, however, that the work had just begun, and that getting the resolution implemented would be an even more difficult task than getting it passed. So ever since 1325's passage, feminists inside and outside the UN have put tremendously creative thought and energy into making it a living document – an ongoing commitment for the SC, rather than a one-time rhetorical gesture. Around the UN, 1325 is known as the only resolution that has such an active constituency – and the only one that has an annual anniversary, when there are multiple panel discussions, SC meetings, and other events organized to try to advance the women, peace, and security agenda.[11] Additionally, new groups have been formed within the

UN, including the UN Inter-Agency Task-force on Women, Peace, and Security (with members from the Secretariat, as well as NGOs), as well as group of governments called Friends of 1325, to try to bring gender perspectives into the daily procedures and mechanisms of the SC and relevant UN departments.

Throughout this period, the NGO Working Group has not only directed its efforts to changing the practices of the UN itself; it has also focused on making 1325 a known and useful tool for grassroots women's organizations in conflict zones, via publicizing the resolution in many international venues, and organizing regional consultations and trainings. The UN office of WILPF has created the PeaceWomen website, www.peacewomen.org, to share information among women peace activists from around the world – information about the resolution itself, about UN system, and topics related to women and war, and women's organizing in specific conflicts. On a bi-weekly basis, news and updates to the website are distributed in the 1325 E-news which reaches thousands of NGOs, governments, and UN staff. One of the PeaceWomen projects is to increase the accessibility and potential impact of the resolution by translating it into as many different languages as possible – 71 as of January 2006[12] – although some might argue that for 1325 to be maximally useful, it also needs to be translated out of local versions of UN-ese. Two years after PeaceWomen went online, UNIFEM launched a complementary web portal, www.womenwarpeace.org, to provide national and international actors with timely information on the impact of conflict on women and their role in peace-building and to show how and when gender issues should be addressed in preventive actions and in post-conflict peace-building. One of their primary goals is to foster the inclusion of gender perspectives in resolutions, mandated missions, and debates of the SC and regional organizations focused on peace and security, and in the reports of the Secretary-General, which too often lack attention to specific gender issues in individual countries. The method is to provide high quality information, so that the excuse that "we had no way of knowing" is no longer unavailable.

One of the most interesting aspects of the diffusion of the resolution to grassroots organizations is the variety of ways women "on the ground" have found to make use of it. Resolution 1325 was never designed as an organizing tool for women's movements; instead, it was shaped as an intervention in the functioning of a global governance institution, and its paragraphs mostly speak to actions to be taken by different actors within the UN system itself (e.g., the Secretary-General, the Department of Peacekeeping operations, and so on), as well as by member states.

Yet women's NGOs in conflict zones have used it in multiple strategic ways, including for consciousness raising amongst their own constituencies about women's right to participate in peace-making and political decision-making more generally; as a tool to try to hold the UN accountable in its peacekeeping operations in their own country; and as a lever for attaining political access and influence with their own local and national governments, by holding their governments accountable to commitments they made at the UN. For example:

- After women from the Democratic Republic of the Congo (DRC) heard about 1325 from UNIFEM, they wrote a memorandum to their government, telling them that as signatories to the resolution, they now needed to implement it! For two years, they lobbied extensively for 1325's implementation in the DRC, both nationally and internationally, including writing to the SC. When the UN peacekeeping mission arrived in the DRC in 2000 without a gender component, they lobbied the director of the mission for a gender office and perspective in the mission. Since a Gender Advisor became a part of the mission in March 2002, the women have been working closely with her (and later, the rest of the gender unit) on projects such as translating 1325 into the four official languages and strategies for inserting a gender perspective into all levels of the government.
- Women from Melanesia have formulated a plan of action to implement 1325 at local, regional, and national levels. They have established women's community media as a way to spread information, and to make 1325 a reality at the community level, and have established a quarterly regional magazine, *FemTalk 1325*, to highlight women and peace initiatives in the Pacific region as well as increase awareness of the implementation of 1325.
- Women in Kosovo/a have not only translated 1325 into local languages, but have also translated it out of "UN language" into more accessible terms. Among their many initiatives, they negotiated with a women's group in Italy and got some financial support from the UN to sponsor about 20 shows on TV explaining the resolution. They also organized several roundtables, not only in Kosovo/a, but also in Macedonia and Albania, and built a network around the resolution.
- At their July 9th 2003 conference on democracy in Baghdad, Iraqi women held a workshop in which they explained 1325 to the many participants (including lawyers, university lecturers, and so on) who had never heard of it. At the end of the day, they came up with recommendations, saying that, "We need equality between men and women

with regard to rights and responsibilities." They used 1325 to support their call.

- The Russian Committees of Soldiers' Mothers has used the resolution to support their own claim of legitimacy as actors working for military reform, and as a means to increase their access to institutions of state power. "Now," according to one activist I interviewed, "when we go to talk to political or military leaders, we take it with us. And because the Russian leadership is now very concerned about their international legitimacy, they feel that they have to listen to us, because that's what the resolution says."

Viewing the campaign to pass and implement 1325 from the perspective of the gender in global governance framework developed by Meyer and Prügl (1999), it is clear that all three kinds of phenomena they identify have been important dimensions of the development of the "women, peace and security agenda" at the UN. The resolution was born in the interchange between an intergovernmental organization and international NGOs. In the NGOs' organizing and lobbying to influence the SC, they also reached out to women who were diplomatic and political agents in different bodies of the UN, as well as to grassroots women's groups. (Some of the women leaders of the NGOs also eventually took jobs in the UNIFEM.) Ultimately, each of these sets of actors organized activities and structures of their own; they also have come together (along with a few researchers) into what can best be described, in Keck and Sikkink's term, as a transnational advocacy network (TAN) (Keck and Sikkink, 1998). The objectives of this TAN range from the extremely concrete and particular (e.g., make sure the SC mandate for the Haiti peacekeeping operation includes a P5 level gender advisor,[13] *with* a budget; or make sure that peace-keeping forces get "gender training"), to the fundamental contestation of the rules and discursive practices in international peace and security institutions (e.g., what counts as "security"? Who should be at peace negotiation tables? What are the elements necessary to building sustainable peace?)

Assessing the impact

An assessment of the impact of the initiative to pass and implement Resolution 1325 reveals some of the challenges that feminist political analyses and practice face in the process of engaging with global governance institutions. But before looking at those challenges, it is important to pause, and recognize that "assessing the impact" itself presents quite a challenge. Which impacts, exactly, is it important for us to assess when analysing feminist engagement with global governance institutions? (see also Prügl and True, this book)

In the case of my research on 1325, the impacts that seemed most salient, most important, shifted and multiplied. During my fieldwork with the NGOs and UN entities campaigning for 1325, the impacts that seemed most apparent were the phenomenal success of the "women, peace and security" advocates in transforming some of the SC's rhetoric around women and war, coupled with the incredibly slow and comparatively minuscule progress in transforming the SC's, UN Secretariat's, and member states' organizational and programmatic practices. The other issue I could not avoid thinking about was the impact on activists of re-shaping their activities and political agenda into a form that would make them acceptable, even attractive and valuable participants in UN policy-shaping processes.

Both of these impact questions – how has the UN changed? how have the activists changed? – are, in a sense, the "close-in" questions, the questions that almost demand one's attention when intimately engaged in the process. Stepping back a bit, but still deriving the questions out of an empirical study of the 1325 process, it is apparent that there is a more intricate series of questions embedded in each of those two. At the same time, viewing the process from the context of the gender, governance and globalization literature (Waylen and Rai 2004; introduction, this book) suggests a broader range of questions that need to be asked. Put together, these questions comprise a list that might have at least some applicability in assessing the impact of other feminist engagements with institutions of global governance as well. It is not meant to be comprehensive, but rather an illustrative set of questions that I have found useful in seeking a more textured description and analysis of impact, and of what might in the past have been framed in terms of "cooptation versus empowerment."[14]

In assessing the impact *within* the UN . . . .

1. *To what degree have there been changes at the rhetorical and discursive levels?* Even if the changes appear "merely rhetorical," what are the social and political processes through which rhetorical change becomes something more than that? How are rhetorical changes connected to experiences that lead to changes in understandings and actions? In *what* ways are *which* actors using rhetorical statements (not even commitments – just statements) as a tool to initiate *what* kinds of political processes?

2. *To what degree have there been changes in organizational policies and practices?* At headquarters? In the field? If there have been changes made, do they depend on the accident of committed actors in the right positions at the right time, or have they been institutionalized?

3. *Are there mechanisms in place to facilitate change?* To inform, educate, motivate, empower, reward, and hold accountable? Is there an organizational infrastructure/location to implement and facilitate the process? Does it have economic resources, and organizational status and power? Is it staffed with people who are there because they are knowledgeable and committed, or for some other reason? Are there effective means of communication between different parts of the system, to avoid reinventing the wheel, and to facilitate intra-organizational learning?

In assessing the impact on women *outside* the UN . . . .

4. *Has the resolution (or other kind of policy commitment of an institution of global governance that has been fought for by women) made a difference to women on the ground?* To what extent does a hard-fought, much celebrated "victory" by feminists working in the international arena translate into concrete effects in the lives of the women whose situation was the original motivation for the initiative? That is, has it been operationalized by state and interstate actors? And specifically, in ways that are beneficial to women?

5. *Can the resolution/policy commitment be used by women on the ground as an effective vehicle for their own organizing, mobilization, and political action?* How closely does it serve their purposes and open useful pathways? Does it re-shape their actions in ways that derail them from their own integrally developed purposes and strategies?

6. *What impact has work on the initiative had on the political practices and efficacy of the (often internationally identified) NGOs that initiated it?* How has it affected their use of their human and economic resources, and their political reputation? To what degree has it enhanced or diminished their status and ability to communicate with *which* actors? How has it affected their own political analyses and priorities, and their ability to act on them? Have some of the NGO activists been recruited into the global governance institution, and if so, what has the impact been on the NGO? What is the background, political experience, and political analysis of the people who replaced them in the NGO?

7. *What were the root values, beliefs, and objectives that motivated this particular initiative/engagement in attempting to influence the global governance*

institution in the first place, and to what degree does a policy "victory" actually reflect them?

In assessing the impact both *within and outside* the UN....

8. *What kinds of political arguments were used to "sell" this policy innovation to the global governance institution, and how were "women" constructed in the process?* What are the implications for women themselves, and for the likelihood of future political successes and failures within the institution?

9. *Has the resolution/policy commitment fostered discursive change at the level of foundational concepts?* If so, do the operational outcomes of that commitment actually reflect/construct that conceptual re-casting?

Each of these questions arises out of my participant observation in the community of "women, peace and security" advocates in and around the UN; to begin to do justice to discussing them, each would require its own paper. What I will do for the purposes of this book is to focus on the last three, starting with #7; in the process of addressing #7, I will also briefly discuss #9. Then, the last section of the chapter explores some answers to #8, which, of course, is not to say that answering questions 1–6 is not vitally important, but that it is not possible to do it within the confines of this chapter. It would require a more institutionalist focus that would fit more directly into a gender-mainstreaming framework (similar to that used by Chappell and True in this book), whereas I adopt a more discursive approach that provides us with some different but complementary insights.

The strangest dream: gender equality, ending wars, and an end to war[15]

Question #7 asks, "What were the root values, beliefs, analyses and objectives that motivated this particular initiative/engagement in attempting to influence the global governance institution in the first place, and to what degree does a policy 'victory' (1325 in this case) actually reflect them?" This is a crucial, and in practice too rarely asked, question.[16] In the space between a group of NGOs' motivations for action and the actual plan of action they come up with, and, in the space between their plan and the form in which a policy initiative ultimately materializes, multiple factors are at work re-shaping, and usually narrowing, the parameters of the final outcome. Yet, once the policy victory has been won, advocates' energies tend to be poured into assuring that it is actually implemented. At that point, after months or years of concerted action invested in the initiative, activists are likely to be well aware of some of the initiative's shortcomings. But at the same time, the activity of stepping back, consciously reconnecting to the original motivations and assessing the kinds of actions they might now suggest, is too often swallowed up in the time-urgent business of trying to hold the governance institution accountable to its commitments.

Asking about the relation between 1325 (and the whole "women, peace and security agenda" it has made possible at the UN) and the objectives of the NGOs that initiated it immediately suggests a further set of questions. One question of particular interest to me is, what were all of the different factors that contributed to constructing the final shape of the resolution? Tracing the path of 1325, from the initial perception that there was a problem, to the words on the paper adopted unanimously in October 2000, reveals a myriad of factors at work. Among the most salient: the particular make-up of the NGO Working Group (e.g., which NGOs were members of it, and what were the characteristics of the main activists in each); the boundaries of the SC mandate; the institutional precedent and template set by a prior "thematic resolution" (on children and armed conflict); the Council's structural division into permanent and non-permanent members; the accident of which countries were on the Council at that time, and their histories; the role of political horse-trading (and the many non-substantive reasons that diplomats might vote for something); and the gender-related policy tools and framings already extant in the UN at the time of the resolution initiative – most critically, the UN's official adoption of "gender mainstreaming" as an institution-wide policy. Or, in a more abstracted version, understanding this policy outcome requires analysis of political motivations, institutional structures, and discursive framings – all the while being attentive to the serendipity of personal relationships, upon which much of this rests.

But there is a question that is logically prior to this historical tracing of 1325's path: what were the motivations of the NGO activists in the first place? The answer is not simple. Public documents suggest that when the idea of a SC resolution was first discussed among the NGOs of the Women and Armed Conflict Caucus, and later the NGO Working Group on WPS, there were two fundamental problems they hoped to find a way to ameliorate – the terrible suffering women experience as victims of war, and the barriers women face in their quests to participate in peace negotiations. These two problems, in turn, were compounded by a third – the absence of any kind of real institutional awareness of women (much less gender analysis) in the parts of the UN specifically mandated to deal with armed conflict and security. So in public accounts, "protection" (of women in war) and "participation" (of women in peace-making and peace-building) appear as the key goals. And the method to achieve these was envisioned as "mainstreaming gender" in the work of the SC.

Interviews and archives suggest a more complex picture in many ways. In the NGO Working Group, as in any coalition, there were a variety of political analyses, self-definitions, and motivations. About the closest one can get to a starting point (as mealy mouthed as this is) is that all Working Group members were concerned with women and war: the terrible things that happen to women in war; the failure of the UN and the international humanitarian aid community to meet women's needs; the exclusion of women from peace processes; and the failure to see and acknowledge the incredibly hard organizing and peace-building work that women in war zones undertake. And, as NGOs that had war as their concern, and that saw the UN and UN processes as important arenas for action, changing the behaviour of the UN and its member states was seen to be best accomplished through an initiative to transform policy in an institution of global governance. (I stop to note this perhaps self-evident fact because one of the notable absences from the Working Group was that of US feminist NGOs, most of which do not see influencing the UN as a high priority.)

Although all of the Working Group members were concerned about what was happening to women in wars, the majority of Working Group NGOs defined themselves neither as "anti-war," per se, nor as feminist. Amnesty International defines itself as a *"human rights"* organization; the Women's Commission for Refugee Women and Children describes its mission as "working to improve the lives and defend the rights of *refugee and internally displaced women,* children and adolescents. For both, issues of women's protection were paramount. International Alert more directly addresses war, but its emphasis is *on peace-building* (and it now has a program to promote the role of women in peace-building). The Women's Caucus for Gender Justice was founded to bring feminist perspectives into the founding documents and practices of *the International Criminal Court.* It is only the Hague Appeal for Peace and the WILPF that are explicitly anti-war, anti-militarist, and pro-disarmament. And of the two, only WILPF also explicitly identifies itself as feminist.

What these differences meant concretely was that although all group members agreed that something had to be done to increase women's protection and participation, their own conceptual framings for how to do that were quite divergent. Humanitarian and human rights groups talked about themselves as "not political," (a descriptor that puzzled me for a very long time), and for some of them, anything that smacked of an analysis of the *causes* of women's victimization and exclusion was "too political." (In fact, it was over the "too political" issue that Amnesty actually left the Working Group, although it returned three years later). Certainly, talking about the international arms trade, "militarism," or even worse, militarism's relation to masculinities (as WILPF wanted to do) was deemed by these groups to be in the "too political" category. While these same terms might have been "too political" for the Council as well, I think it is significant to note that the self-censorship that was the product of working in this coalition foreclosed even the possibility of conversation with member state delegations about these issues.

It is also important that when addressing *causes* of war and militarism is "too political" and off the agenda, it radically narrows the range of the kinds of policy initiatives one might take to solve a problem. If rape's use as a weapon of war is your concern, for example, you can safely contest the meanings of "war crime" or "crimes against humanity," and hope that through redefining rape as a war crime, rather than a "natural," "inevitable," "boys-will-be-boys" inherent aspect of war, there will be some deterrent effect. But if it is off-limits to address the intersections of gender and ethnicity, and the gender regime that makes a physical, sexual attack on a woman a blow against the "honour" of a man and his community, how likely is it that rape will stop being used as a weapon? Or, another example, if sexual exploitation and abuse by peacekeepers is your concern, you can write a Code of Conduct for peacekeeping troops that has a strict prohibition against "fraternization" with local women, and hope that it will be possible to widely train troops about the code, and that commanders will take it seriously. But if it remains off-limits to address the nexus of militarized power, constructions of masculinities, gendered inequalities in access to paid work, and global economic inequality, how likely is it that that Code of Conduct will make a significant difference?

These examples not only demonstrate the narrowed realm policy initiatives that are possible when political analyses of the causes of war, militarism, and armed violence are off the table; they also begin to suggest something about the degree to which the "women, peace and security" agenda both does and does not represent a fundamental contestation of the rules and discursive practices in international peace and security institutions (*question #9*). The assertions that women have a right to be at the peace table, or that women are central to national and international security, for example, do, in fact, represent fundamental contestations of those rules and practices. Yet they do not, in and of themselves, address the gender constructs that underwrite war-making as a practice, nor the gendered inequalities that underlie women's vulnerability in war and post-conflict settings; thus, they leave many significant rules and discursive practices of international peace and security institutions in place. There are many other examples that merit discussion; for the moment, I will confine myself to two.

First, the NGO framers of 1325, while insisting on building awareness that "women suffer the impact of war disproportionately," had as one of their main goals the recasting of the image of "women" in the SC. Many of their interactions with SC members, as well as the language they drafted for the resolution, were focused on prying women out of the "womenandchildren"-as-helpless-victims construct,[17] and constructing women as active agents, already engaged in peacebuilding in civil society. Although "agency" was a word that some of the NGOs used, in the process of the 1325 campaign, "agency" too quickly became narrowed into a new construct, "women as peacemakers." While this construct has gained quite a bit of rhetorical currency in the UN, it has significant difficulties of its own, not the least of which is that it leaves the construct of "men-as-naturally-aggressive, women-as-naturally peaceful" firmly in place. I will return to a discussion of some of the troubling consequences of this using this construct in *Fragment Two* and *Fragment Three* below. For the moment, however, I think it is fair to say that one success of the 1325 campaign is that it has, in fact, brought women as actors (not just vulnerable victims) into SC discourse.[18]

Second, we should note that while claims for women's rights to "protection" in war and to "participation" in peace-making and peace-building are actually quite radical (for all that there should be nothing radical about it), in another light these claims do not represent a contestation of some of the fundamental assumptions of international peace and security institutions. Protecting women *in* war, and insisting that they have an equal right to participate in the processes and negotiations that *end* particular wars, both leave *war* itself in place. That is, it is a kind of late intervention – once the war occurs, we will try to protect women, and we will have them try to help end it – rather than an intervention that tries either to prevent war, or to contest the legitimacy of the systems that produce war – that is, "to put an end to war." In this sense, it fits comfortably into the already extant concepts and discursive practices of the SC, where the dominant paradigm holds a world made up of states that "defend" *state* security through *military* means.

This limitation of the resolution is seen as a problem by some of the actors involved, and not recognized by others – as might have been predicted from the earlier discussion of the different political position-ing, self-definitions, and goals of the NGOs involved. Among those who see it as a problem is Cora Weiss, director of Hague Appeal for Peace. She acutely expressed the central dilemma early on, exclaiming in a meeting, "Look, we are not just trying to make war safe for women!" More recently, some 1325 advocates (both in NGOs and the Secret-ariat) have responded to this limitation by adding a third "P" – that is, they have reframed the WPS agenda as being about "the 3 P's" – prevention, protection, and participation. This is certainly an improve-ment – but not as much of one as it might first appear. Before the agenda-expanding report of the Secretary-General on conflict preven-tion in 2001,[19] "prevention" tended to be rather narrowly construed in the SC and the international security community generally – as relat-ing to so-called "early warning mechanisms," interventionary forces in an impending genocide, and so on. Although the issue is addressed by the Secretary-General in his reports,[20] "prevention" of war is all too often *not*, for example, taken by governments to mean disarmament. Nor is it typically taken to mean the abolition of the military–industrial complex, nor a revolution in gender regimes such that societies are no longer producing one category people seen as having the nurturing, collaborative, empathetic qualities of peacemakers, and another "cap-able of being schooled into thinking that killing, and being killed, in the name of nation is the ultimate badge of honour and manhood." (Cockburn 2004: 224) Even so, when advocates tried to get the narrow "prevention" on the agenda of the 2004 CSW meetings (which again had women and armed conflict as one of its two annual themes, under the agenda item "Women's equal participation in conflict prevention, man-agement and conflict resolution and in post-conflict peace-building"), they were stymied by other women inside the UN system and in mem-ber state delegations, who insisted that one had to be "realistic about accomplishing things," and that therefore the agenda should be limited to women's participation in peace processes and in post-war electoral processes.[21]

In thinking about the question of whether 1325 actually serves the purposes intended by its NGO originators, I have, thus far, attempted to be quite specific about the ways the different NGOs have named their objectives and framed them in the context of the institution of the SC. At this point, I want to step back and say that essentially, they all wanted to do something that would be good for women, and good for peace.

(I think this is a fair generalization, although not all of the NGOs would use this kind of language). So will it be good for women? Will it be good for peace?

In conclusion I want to sketch out some fragments of personal rumination in response to the questions I have raised above.

Fragment one

Listening to the speeches of (male) SC ambassadors during the October 2003 day-long SC Open Debate on "Women, Peace and Security in the Context of Peacekeeping Operations," one might have imagined that feminist dreams and tireless organizing had succeeded in radically remaking the world. The men said:

> In our view, only the full participation of women in global affairs can open up greater opportunities for achieving global peace.
> (Ambassador Cristian Maquieira, Deputy Representative of
> Chile to the UN, 29 October 2003; http://www.peacewomen.org/
> un/SCOpenDebate2003/Chile2003es.pdf.)

> Peace is inextricably linked to equality between women and men.
> (Ambassador Marcello Spatafora, Permanent Representative
> of Italy to the UN, speaking on behalf of the European
> Union, 29 October 2003, http://www.peacewomen.org/
> un/SCOpenDebate2003/EU2003.pdf)

> No approach to peace can succeed if it does not view men and women
> as equally important components of the solution.
> (Ambassador John D. Negroponte, United States
> Representative to the United Nations, 29 October 2003;http://
> www.peacewomen.org/un/SCOpenDebate2003/USA2003.html)

When I think about these statements, I am struck by two things. First, the obvious – they do not mean it. This is immediately apparent when you consider, for example, Ambassador John Negroponte's statement. Any analysis of US foreign and security policies makes it impossible to believe that they are based on the view that "peace depends on men and women as equally important components of the solution." (I think I need not belabour this point.)

Second, I am not at all sure that I believe it either. I do not actually know if peace – in the way they mean it, as the absence of war – is impossible without gender *equality*. I am, however, certain that *equality* between women and men – in the way they mean it, a liberal version of political equality – does not begin to get at the pernicious, pervasive complexities of the gender regimes that undergird not only individual wars themselves, but the entire war system.

Fragment two

The rhetorical strategy that has been used to sell the idea that women should have decision-making roles in peace-making and peace-building has largely rested on the "women-as-untapped-resource" or "use-value" argument.

> We [at UNIFEM] argue that women should be included because they provide a perspective and offer resources that would otherwise not be considered. We say that this is important because it supports the kind of monitoring (by women's groups) that is essential to ensure that peace agreements are implemented as intended.[22]

As I have always understood it, when (natural) resources are tapped, it is to use them, exploit them, transform them into a product of someone else's design, for someone else's profit.

And then again, I am told by women in New York and Washington that the use-value argument is used because it works, because it is a much more effective way to get women in the door than talking about "rights."

And I am told by some women "on the ground" that they could not care less what argument gets them in – just get the damn door cracked open before we all perish.

Fragment three

The use-value argument, in turn, rests on a particular construct of women – the construct of women-as-peacemakers. We hear it in the words of women's advocates:

> Women can more readily embrace the collaborative perspective needed to cut through ethnic, religious, tribal and political barriers. They also embrace a more sustainable concept of security.
>
> (Noeleen Heyzer, Executive Director, UNIFEM; http://www.accord.org.za/ct/2003-3/foreword.pdf)

And the SC echoes this construct:

> Women are not just victims of violence. They are often the driving force for peace.
> (Ambassador Stefan Tafrov, Permanent Representative of the Republic of Bulgaria to the United Nations, 29 October 2003; http://www.peacewomen.org/un/SCOpenDebate2003/Bulgaria2003.pdf)

I know that I – who have spent years teaching women's studies and feminist theory – am extremely uncomfortable with the women-as-peacemaker construct for many, many reasons.

I also know that in many (although by no means all) of the interviews I have done with women grassroots activists from war zones around the world, many of the women – who have spent many years struggling with incredible courage against devastating armed violence – have themselves expressed the same belief in women's greater ability and motivation to end wars and create sustainable peace.

Feminist theorists and researchers have exhaustively catalogued the dangers of these kinds of constructs for women. They erase differences among and between women. Gender appears as though it were a separable identity from race, class, religion, ethnicity, religion, sexuality, a set of meanings not entwined with other structures of power. Gender appears as a fixed identity, instead of a process, a doing, a making. Resting our claim to legitimacy as a political actor on a construct of who we are and what we can do (for you), rather than on a claim of rights, means that we can easily be excluded (again) when we fail to embody and enact the construct. The construct of difference that we argue makes us fit to participate can be turned into an argument for why it would be dangerous to allow us to participate. And on and on.

We can and should also catalogue the dangers of these constructs for how we understand the making of war and the building of peace.

While I do not think one can begin to understand war without gender; while I understand gender, war, nationalism, ethnicity, religion, capitalist forms of production, and consumption (how long should I make this list?) as mutually constitutive, I fear that "Women-as-peacemakers" place too much of war on gender. And in so doing, actually leaves the dominant political and epistemological frameworks untouched.

I fear that it is the easy way out. That it obscures all the parts of the war system, including, perhaps paradoxically, the working of gender regimes themselves.

To say it another way – If women are peaceful and men are warriors, will putting women in charge of peace work? This is not one of those silly and annoying "what about Margaret Thatcher?" questions. Nor is it one of those equally silly and annoying Francis Fukuyama questions – of how those poor peaceful women will protect themselves from being overthrown by testosterone-driven, power-hungry, war-loving men.[23] It is a question about what will happen if peaceable women hold peace talks while:

- the global arms trade continues apace, with 80 percent of the mammoth profits going to the five permanent members of the SC;
- international financial institutions and trade organizations continue to impose policies that foreclose the possibilities of creating a citizenry that can get what it needs without fighting for it, or a citizenry that is free enough from want that its government need not be oppressive to maintain power, or a citizenry democratically empowered enough to not need to turn to religious or political demagogues who promise to give them the kind of life they really want;
- "security" is understood as state security, and huge standing armies and armories are understood as legitimate;
- investments in armaments, arms industries, and private militaries are understood as an inviolate part of free enterprise;
- and when the centrality of gender regimes to all of the above remains largely invisible.

At this point, letting (some) women into decision-making positions seems a small price to pay for leaving the war system essentially undisturbed. And, at the same time, yes, 1325 has the potential to have tremendously important effects on the lives of women who are already being ripped apart in the clutches of war.

Notes

1. I want to thank Felicity Hill for opening so many doors into the world of 1325 for me, as well as for her helpful comments on an earlier draft of this chapter. I also want to thank Ayala Wineman for her extremely able research assistance, and Shirin Rai for her supportive style as editor. Finally, I am grateful to the Ford Foundation, whose generous support made this research possible.
2. S/2000/1325 on Women, Peace and Security was adopted unanimously on 31 October 2000 under the Namibian Presidency of the Security Council, E/1997/L.30, 14 July 1997.
3. The 1997 ECOSOC Agreed Conclusions emphasize the need to incorporate gender perspectives into the mainstream of all areas of the United

Nations' work, including macroeconomic questions, operational activities for development, poverty eradication, human rights, humanitarian assistance, budgeting, disarmament, peace and security, and legal affairs. The concept of gender mainstreaming was defined as "... the process of assessing the implications for women and men of any planned action, including legislation, policies or programmes, in any area and at all levels. It is a strategy for making the concerns and experiences of women as well as of men an integral part of the design, implementation, monitoring and evaluation of policies and programmes in all political, economic and societal spheres, so that women and men benefit equally, and inequality is not perpetuated. The ultimate goal of mainstreaming is to achieve gender equality." E/1997/L.30, 14 July 1997.

4. Gender mainstreaming grew out of women activists' efforts to ensure that women would be included in and benefit from the programs and projects of international development agencies. When they saw that Women in Development programmes too often resulted in the addition of small, marginal projects for women, while the major development projects proceeded unchanged, they sought a new strategy that would bring women into the mainstream of development activities. By 1995, the Beijing Platform for Action (BPA) established gender mainstreaming as a global strategy for achieving gender quality. While the BPA addresses peace and security issues, in the early years of gender mainstreaming attention was much more focused on development, and then human rights issues. Until 1325's passage, there was no concentrated effort to apply gender mainstreaming in the security realm. For accounts of the origins of gender mainstreaming, see Hafner-Burton and Pollack (2002); Riddell-Dixon (1999); and True (2003).

5. At the UN, I have heard the Third Committee of the GA – the committee that works on social, humanitarian, and cultural issues – referred to in-house as the "ladies committee." In this trivializing framing, there is no question that power, and the "real," "hard" issues, are seen to reside elsewhere.

6. The Fourth UN World Conference on Women generated the Beijing Platform for Action, which is organized around 12 Critical Areas of Concern, the fifth of which is Women and Armed Conflict. http://www. un.org/womenwatch/daw/beijing/platform/plat1.htm. It aims at accelerating the implementation of the Nairobi Forward-looking Strategies for the Advancement of Women agreed at Nairobi in 1985.

7. "Peace Inextricably Linked with Equality between Women and Men says Security Council, in International Women's Day Statement," Security Council press release SC/6816, 8 March 2000 http://www.un.org/News/Press/docs/2000/20000308.sc6816.doc.html

8. By inviting members of the Security Council to gather over coffee to hear the views of a Bosnian priest in 1993, Ambassador Arria of Venezuela created what has become known as the Arria Formula, an informal exchange between Security Council members and NGOs. The Arria Formula has been used more regularly since 1999 to provide expertise and testimony on thematic issues taken up by the Security Council, in particular on humanitarian issues, the protection of civilians in armed conflict, children and armed conflict, and, more recently on women, peace and security.

9. The speakers were: Isha Dyfan from Sierra Leone; Inonge Mbikusita-Lewanika from Zambia; Luz Mendez from Guatemala; and Faiza Jama Mohamed from Somalia. Additionally, the Working Group presented a statement.

10. For an extended examination of the ways that activists in WILPF, in particular, changed in response to this closer relation with UN insiders, see Sheri Gibbings (2004).

11. While the anniversary of 1325 is emphasized by advocates as the only one celebrated, other resolutions and issues receive annual attention through being a formal item on the Security Council agenda. If resolution 1325 had contained a date by which the Secretary-General needed to report back to the Council, Women, Peace and Security would have automatically become a regular item on the SC. In the absence of this commitment, advocates make the most of the anniversary.

12. http://www.peacewomen.org/1325inTranslation/index.html

13. P5 refers to the grading system in the UN, with P standing for Professional, which includes 5 levels. A P5 is the highest Professional level ranking before Director or "D" level posts.

14. In a 2003 article, Jacqui True reframes the question, saying it is "not how feminist scholars and activists can avoid cooptation by powerful institutions, but whether we can afford not to engage with such institutions, when the application of gender analysis in their policymaking is clearly having political effects beyond academic and feminist communities." True (2003: 368) If we do engage, we need to analyse the complexity of the impacts of that engagement along many different dimensions.

15. For readers who may be unfamiliar with it, "The Strangest Dream" reference is from a song, "Last Night I had the Strangest Dream," written in 1950 by Ed McCurdy. It begins, "Last night I had the strangest dream, I ever dreamed before. I dreamed the world had all agreed to put an end to war. I dreamed I saw a mighty room, and the room was filled with men. And the paper they were signing said they'd never fight again." The song was frequently sung by US peace activists in the 50s, 60s, and 70s. Obviously, for some of us, the room is no longer filled only by men.

16. The gender-mainstreaming literature frequently addresses the question of whether policy-implementers themselves are keeping in mind gender mainstreaming's original goal (i.e., gender equality) or the original problem (the pervasive system of gender inequality) (e.g., Meier *et al.* 2004; Verloo 2002). It also criticizes femocrats' and policy-makers' lack of continuous reflection upon gender-mainstreaming policies as they are being implemented (e.g., Carney 2004). But the mainstreaming literature tends to ignore the challenge faced by feminist activists in remaining true to their political goals when they are caught up in a mainstreaming policy "victory" that may be very real, but also very compromised.

17. The useful phrase/framing "womenandchildren" comes originally from Cynthia Enloe's "Womenandchildren: making feminist sense of the Persian Gulf Crisis", Enloe (2000), and also appears in her book, *The Morning After*, Enloe (1993).

18. The cynical caveats here: into SC rhetoric far more than daily deliberation or practice; and only at certain times of the year, notably around 1325 anniversary events.

19. Secretary General's Report on Prevention of armed conflict 7 June 2001, S/2001/574 http://www.un.org/Docs/sc/reports/2001/574e.pdf

20. Secretary-General Kofi Annan remarks that rather than using the UN to prevent and resolve conflicts, member states have spent funds on "military action that could be available for poverty reduction and equitable sustainable development." (Prevention of Armed Conflict: Report of the Secretary-General (A/55/985-S/2001/574) 7 June 2001) The Secretary-General repeats the message to governments that they should discourage competitive arms accumulation and create an enabling environment for arms limitation and reduction agreements as well as the reduction of military expenditures. The Secretary-General also observes that war costs a great deal of money – quoting the Carnegie Commission on Preventing Deadly Conflict that estimated at least US $200 billion was spent on the seven major interventions in the 1990s – in Bosnia Herzegovina, Somalia, Rwanda, Haiti, the Persian Gulf, Cambodia, and El Salvador (not including East Timor and Kosovo). A preventative approach would have cost the international community $130 billion, saving $70 billion.

21. Despite the lack of appetite for the issue of women's participation in conflict prevention, the Swedish delegation, known for its leadership on conflict prevention, pushed through language that was adopted (ironically) that called for support of women's organizations' capacity to intervene and contribute to conflict prevention. "In regard to conflict prevention The Commission on the Status of Women calls on Governments, as well as all other relevant participants in these processes, to a. improve the collection, analysis and inclusion of information on women and gender issues as part of conflict prevention and early warning efforts; b. ensure better collaboration and coordination between efforts to promote gender equality and efforts aimed at conflict prevention; c. support capacity building, especially for civil society, in particular women's organizations, to increase community commitment to conflict prevention; d. continue to make resources available nationally and internationally for prevention of conflict and ensure women's participation in the elaboration and implementation of strategies for preventing conflict." An important and emblematic sidebar on the CSW: the second of the two themes was "the role of men and boys in achieving gender equality," but never were the two themes discussed in conjunction, nor any connection between them made.

22. Maha Muna, former Programme Manager and Officer in Charge at the Governance, Peace and Security unit of UNIFEM, in Cohn *et al.* (2004: 136).

23. This question is based on the logic of Francis Fukuyama's argument (Fukuyama 1998).

9
Governing Globalization: Feminist Engagements with International Trade Policy

Debra J. Liebowitz

As I stood in the international terminal of the Cancun, Mexico airport on the afternoon of September 14, 2003, I was struck by how the scene epitomized the condition, complexity, and contradictions of the current debate on globalization. A buzz of energy filled every inch of the space as thousands of people – women and men of every colour, clothed in an incredible array of hues and styles – streamed into the airport following the collapse of the 146 nation World Trade Organization (WTO) negotiations. Some of the people who had been inside the conference center just a few hours earlier knew that the negotiations had broken down and that delegates from a number of governments walked out as it became clear that core conflicts among them could not be resolved and consensus could not be reached. However, many inside the conference center, and the thousands of protestors kept out by the fortress-like fencing and the slews of police and military officers blanketing this tourist "Mecca", had little information about what was actually occurring. In this environment of militarized mistrust, rumors spread like wildfires: "Delegates from the G-21[1] stormed out", "G-21 Delegates coordinated an action and all marched out of the negotiations", "Brazil walked out", "There was a big demonstration in the conference center", "The US negotiators called it quits and said the meeting was over", "backup military forces were called in to quell the riot like atmosphere", "NGO delegates were arrested", "Government delegates were arrested". Strangers talked easily to one another sharing information as we waited in unbelievably long lines. Easily distinguishable by the colour-coded identification badges we still wore around our necks, people pointed out that various government delegates were trying to leave Mexico. In that moment, this observation served as evidence that the rumors were indeed fact.

The airport scene was interesting not just because it buzzed with energy, but because of the vastly different sentiments that circulated amidst the buzz. Some who were attempting to leave appeared to be in somber moods. For them it seemed that the breakdown of the talks represented failure. Some government delegates appeared to be uncomfortable interacting with "protestors". A large group of NGO folks were visibly jubilant – a complete breakdown of the negotiations warranted celebration. These wildly divergent reactions are important because they call attention to the debates surrounding and the challenges of governing globalization.

My experiences in Cancun match the conclusions reached by the World Commission on the Social Dimension of Globalization, a twenty-six member independent body established by the International Labour Organization (ILO) in February 2002. As they put it, "[g]lobal governance is in crisis" yet, a more robust and fair *governing of globalization* is necessary if worldwide problems such as poverty, hunger, lack of housing, and inadequate employment are to be addressed (2004). Indeed, the collapse of the Cancun WTO negotiations is important on a myriad of levels and could be used in the service of many stories about global governance. This paper, explores one of these: The important and often invisible role gender analysis and women's rights advocates play in the governance of globalization. Although the international community has at least rhetorically recognized that gender-based inequities have detrimental consequences for women's and men's lives, they have been slower to acknowledge that the significant economic and political changes often referred to as globalization may reinforce and reinscribe these inequities. When such recognition has occurred, like in the document negotiated by United Nations' member states on the occasion of the tenth anniversary of the organization's World Conference on Women held in Beijing, China in 1995, the recognition is largely the product of feminist activist work (see United Nations General Assembly 2000, Paragraph 35 for language about how globalization presents "new challenges" and obstacles for realizing gender equality). Increasingly, feminists target their efforts to affect the discourses, policies, and practices of international economic governance. Such activism is premised on the belief that influencing the rules and structures that govern international economic order(s) is critical to more just economic, political, and social relations.

Examining the role of feminist activists to shape the governance of globalization is important since most mainstream accounts of globalization paint all protestors with one sweeping stroke where their ideas and concerns are under-examined and overly homogenized. Such over-generalized and simplistic depictions of activists contesting the discourses and rules of global governance mean that only certain critiques and critics are noticed (even if they are, in reality only occasionally heard). For example, the concerns of labour union activists, those working on agricultural issues, and consumer advocates are more likely to be noticed than those issues raised by advocates of indigenous, immigrant, and women's rights or racial, ethnic, and religious minorities.

This chapter examines the efforts of feminist activists struggling to influence the governance of globalization – particularly those efforts targeting the governance international trade policy. I argue that while these efforts have become more numerous, they confront significant obstacles. While feminist activists efforts to influence the governance of globalization share many concerns with the broader oppositional (or "anti-globalization") movement, feminist activism is clearly distinct from it. Indeed, the rationale propelling feminist activists to engage the governance of globalization as well as the challenges they face in so doing are different from those of the broader global economic justice movement. Both feminist activism and the larger movement emanate from a critique of neo-liberal economic policy, yet gender-based concerns are often overlooked or marginalized when women's organizations are not at the table. Since the broader movement is not generally attentive to feminist concerns and, indeed, in some cases, the inclusion of women is tokenist, feminist activists bring a critical analysis to this sphere (Eschle 2005).

Critique of anti-globalization activism

As activists attempt to shape the governance of globalization, a series of critiques have been levied against them. The first set of critiques claim that "anti-globalization" activists[2] do not understand the nature of international trade and finance and thus their critiques are simplistic. In other words, they are naive, uninformed, or use inadequate information to support their arguments (e.g., Friedman 2004). Less generous critics tend to paint such activism as "untrue, exaggerated, or just plain silly" (Gilpin 2000: 294) or as simply blinded by ideological concerns rendering them unworthy of serious debate or dialogue.[3] Such critics do not exclusively target feminist analyses and activism but tend to lump all non-governmental critics of globalization in the same undifferentiated heap. Indeed, it is this line of thinking that allows media and policymakers to mostly dismiss the concerns articulated by women's rights advocates. If even labour and environmental issues are seen as marginal, then women's rights can easily be framed as simply irrelevant.

The second type of critique does indeed stem from feminist literature and focuses on questions of representation and elitism among activists working in the international arena. Feminist scholar Sonia Alvarez, for instance, expresses this concern by arguing that there is an increasing gulf between women's grassroots activism and the more specialized and professionalized non-governmental organizations (NGOs) working in this arena (1998: 295). This "NGOization" is of critical concern because such activism can reinscribe and magnify preexisting unequal power relations.

This chapter addresses both sets of critiques by arguing that feminist activists engage the governance of globalization for clear, important, and well-thought out reasons and have developed strategies that are attentive to the obstacles to such participation. I show that the first set of critiques are neither useful nor accurate descriptions of feminist activism in this arena and that the second set of critiques, while articulating a valid concern, cannot take account of the difficulties feminists encounter in trying to shape the governance of globalization. Here I show that feminist activism makes theoretical and empirical contributions to the study of gender and globalization. Discussing the reasons why feminist activists engage the governance of globalization can lead us to rethink the critiques of globalization as not analytically or politically useful. What follows is a discussion of three key reasons why feminist activists are increasingly trying to shape the governance of international trade policy and an analysis of the key obstacles they confront in so doing.

This analysis is synthetic of my previous work looking at gender, global governance and trade policy and, as such, is not focused on a single empirical site (e.g., Liebowitz 2002). Rather, it is based on data gathered and observations I have made while monitoring activist efforts focused on the North American Free Trade Agreement (NAFTA), the Free Trade Agreement of the Americas, the World Trade Organization, as well as the United Nations Conferences on Women, Financing for Development, and Sustainable Development. My research focused on feminist activism and the governance of globalization has included more than 50 interviews with key activists, participation in a host of meetings organized by women's groups held in conjunction with meetings of global trade bodies, extensive review of organizational materials and research, as well as media coverage of gender and global trade issues. It is from this previous empirical work that I offer these thoughts about women, gender, and the governance of globalization.

Why "engender" the governance of globalization?

International women's activism is by no means a new phenomenon. In the first half of the twentieth century, women used international organizations and networks to advocate for women's rights and to demand the elimination of inequalities between women and men (Stienstra 1994; Meyer 1999). Indeed, in the 1930s and 1940s, women's organizations as well as individual women have played significant, if circumscribed, roles in the United Nations (U.N.) and in its predecessor, the League of Nations (D'Amico 1999). Their work even crossed borders, as Leila Rupp's work details, to address issues such as war and peace, suffrage and labour protection (1997). While the United Nations has not been the only site of this work, it has provided a host of structural opportunities and openings for women's activism and has been key to the "internationalization of feminism" (West 1999). Many local, national and regional groups and networks have been created or strengthened as women used the various structures provided by the U.N. to come together to share stories, cross-fertilize their analysis, and engage in joint strategy development.

In various forms, economic issues have always been part of this internationalist agenda. While the past 50 years have clearly brought economic wealth to many parts of the world, inequalities have also increased. Of the 1.3 billion people estimated to live in poverty in the mid-1990s, seventy percent were women. And, in a twenty-year span from the mid-1970s to the mid-1990s, absolute poverty among rural women rose by close to 50 percent (United Nations Development Programme 1995: 36). The surge of women's anti-globalization activism in the past ten years stems from an attempt to address these growing inequalities. It is also a product of the increasing importance of multilateral financial institutions and agreements in structuring the economic realities of national economies. While there remains much debate over the extent to which the nation-state is the key actor in international and national politics, anti-globalization activists argue that international institutions like the World Trade Organization or the International Monetary Fund approach policy as though the interests of all states are the same. In addition, the interests of states and capital are assumed to be co-terminus with the interests of citizens. This 'cookie-cutter' approach to international economics, advocates argue, is fundamentally flawed as it does not actually take account of differences within and between nations. Instead, it inaccurately assumes that macro-economic growth and integration will positively affect all groups of people. Dominant neo-liberal economic discourse may acknowledge some limited deleterious consequences of this approach, but such consequences are minimal or insignificant when compared to the overall benefits of increased international trade. As a result, political remedies to address the negative consequences of global economic restructuring are relegated to the margins of policymaking.

The promotion of market-based strategies for economic development, feminists argue, has, indeed, benefited some women. However, approaches that rely primarily on the market to provide for basic needs also tend to exacerbate poor women's structural economic disadvantage. Frequently the theoretical (and, I would argue, ideological) foundation of market-based models of economic development depends upon and perpetuates gendered assumptions about women's and men's roles and labour. It is from this point that feminist anti-globalization activism takes off.

In this section of the chapter, I address, in turn, three key reasons why feminist activists are increasingly attempting to influence the global governance of trade policy. First, I explore how feminists are challenging the architecture of the international economy, increasingly in the realm of global governance. Second, I look at how many feminists are eager to challenge the ideological hegemony of neo-liberal globalization by struggling to win a war of ideas. Third, I argue that an increasing number of feminist activists see this work as providing an opportunity to hold governments accountable for gender-based inequalities. After analysing each of these in turn, I move to a discussion of the constraints that feminist activists face as they attempt to engage in these efforts.

Do we really have a choice? The necessity of focusing on the institutions governing globalization

In a context where feminists engage the governance of globalization with the hope of breaking down the ideological hegemony of current debate and policy, it is clear that the increasing importance of global governance in the post-cold war era has elicited responses on the part of women's organizations (Meyer and Prügl 1999). Indeed, as I noted above, women's and feminist groups have long been in the forefront of efforts to make alliances across borders (Sternbach, *et al.* 1992; Stienstra 1994; Rupp 1997). Women have demanded inclusion (with varying degrees of success) in arenas of global governance, and at times have inserted feminist analyses in the discussion. Indeed, part of what we see when we look at women's and feminists' engagement in global governance is how the reshaping of economic and political relations on a global scale has reconstructed the space within which governments, citizens, civil society actors, and non-governmental organizations operate (Smith *et al.*

1997; Tarrow 1998). As global political and economic changes occur, the role of the state and the relations between states, citizens, and NGOs are restructured as well (Smith *et al.* 1997; Gills 2001; Rosenau 2003).

Importantly, for my purposes here, the "changing logic of collective action" (Cerny 1995) has affected the calculations made by women's organizations about engaging in global economic governance (see also Staudt this book). Joanna Kerr, Executive Director of the Association for Women's Rights in Development, a Canada-based international organiz-ation, explains "[g]lobalization is radically transforming both the issues women's organizations are addressing and the strategies used to address those issues". She continues, "[w]hile the sites of struggle for the women's movement have traditionally been related to the household, the work-place, and the state, women now must engage with supra-national actors including international financial institutions and private sector corpor-ations" (2001: 4). In other words, many feminist activists believe that they must monitor and engage the institutions of global economic governance in order to protect and affirm women's rights.

More specifically, feminist transnational activist attention is increas-ingly addressing the governance of global trade policy. In the mid-1990s when I first began doing work on gender and the NAFTA, there were only a few organizations that spoke about a link between women's rights and trade policy. Canadian feminists, under the umbrella National Action Committee on the Status of Women in Canada, took early leadership to articulate connections between gender and trade policy. Their efforts were significant enough to help spark feminist activism on the issue in both Mexico and the United States (Cohen 1987; Pierson *et al.* 1993; Arteaga 1996; Yanz 1996; Liebowitz 2001). In the past ten years, atten-tion to the nexus of gender, women and trade has increased dramatically. Now, women's groups in most regions of the world have incorpor-ated these issues onto their agendas. Moreover, many older organiza-tions like the Women's Environment and Development Organization (a US-based international organization) and Development Alternative with Women for a New Era (DAWN), the twenty-year-old network of women scholars and activists from the South have also jumped into the fray.

DAWN's approach is instructive. The organization was founded in 1984 in anticipation of the 1985 World Conference on women as an effort to give voice to feminist alternative development perspectives. DAWN's General Coordinator, Claire Slatter suggested that the organ-ization "strategically locat[es] itself as a feminist network within the paradoxical spaces opened up by globalization, and engaging with other networks in its advocacy for economic and gender justice" (Slatter 2003: 1). In other words, DAWN's work self-consciously tries to transform global governance through its engagement with the structures, policies, and discourse of the international economy.

New feminist organizations have been created to specifically address the nexus of gender, trade, and governance. Most importantly, the International Gender and Trade Network (IGTN) was formed following a strategic planning seminar on gender and trade held in Grenada in December 1999. The purpose of the Network is to "increase the engagement of the Global Women's Movement in the discourse and negotiations on regional and global trade and investment agreements" (IGTN n/d). Since its founding, the IGTN has become the key actor on gender and trade-related issues and is organized in seven regions of the world.[4] Indeed, collaboration across traditional North/South lines is one of the hallmarks of the IGTN's success. It has undertaken significant research and analyses and has contributed substantially to knowledge about the gendered construction of trade policy. Even more importantly, it has used its research to facilitate feminist activism in the institutions which govern the globalization of trade policy (e.g., IGTN at Cancun; IGTN at Miami; IGTN May 2001–August 2005). The daily briefings provided by the IGTN and its members during the September 2003 WTO meeting in Cancun were critical locations for gathering information and for consulting about advocacy strategies. Briefings like these, held during meetings of key international organizations, are indicative of increasingly sophisticated feminist communication and advocacy strategies.

As this brief discussion shows, one consequence of the shifting "logic of collective action" is that there is now more transnational feminist coordination, collaboration, and activism to shape the governance of globalization than ever before. While it is clear that feminists have been working across borders for hundreds of years, more and more organizations believe that weighing in on the substantive issues of the day requires transnational collaboration and attention to the politics of global governance. As Chandra Mohanty argues, "cross-national feminist solidarity" to organize against the effect of global capitalism is more necessary than ever (2003: 509). It is also important to mention that international organizations governing globalization are increasingly addressing gender-related issues from the inside. However, as chapters by Catherine Hoskyns, Jacqui True, and Elisabeth Prügl in this book demonstrate these efforts are context-specific and confront serious obstacles.

Challenging ideological hegemony

Feminist activists' engagement with the institutional architecture of trade policy is first and foremost an effort to challenge the hegemonic ideological tenor of the globalization debate (for a review of feminist interventions in conversations about global governance see Rai in this book). By attempting to transform the practice and discourse of global governance, women's organizations give voice to their policy priorities and concerns (López 2001). While the meaning of the term "globalization" has been highly contested, ideological support for neo-liberal economic policies remains hegemonic. Policymakers, business executives, and policy analysts from all parts of the world extol the virtues of globalization and stress its inexorability even while they begin to acknowledge (some might argue "co-opt") critiques articulated by the global movement for economic justice. Indeed, mainstream proponents of neo-liberal economic globalization now rhetorically employ some key activist critiques. For instance, the theme of one of the primary sessions at the 2004 Davos Summit[5] was "Globalization or Deglobalization for the Benefit of the Poorest". Discussions such as this one are a recent addition to the Davos agenda which used to be limited entirely to representing the interests of global capital.

What is important here is that mainstream policymakers use language which rhetorically mimics their detractors while simultaneously promoting the precise policies being criticized. A comment made at the 2003 Davos Summit by former Mexican President Ernesto Zedillo, a long-time enthusiast of neo-liberal economic policies is indicative of the way that proponents of neo-liberal economic restructuring are reshaping their rhetoric. Zedillo said, "the question is not whether globalization is good or bad; the question is how to make it inclusive" (Davos 2003). The articulation of similar concerns have become commonplace at the World Bank following James Wolfensohn's reign as President. In the flack over Paul Wolfowitz's 2005 nomination to succeed Wolfensohn, for instance, the nominee went to great lengths to validate the Bank's role in reducing poverty, protecting women's rights, and generally tackling problems affecting poor countries.

While such acknowledgment of activist concerns can be framed as an important step toward creating more just global economic order, it remains to be seen whether the rhetoric will be translated into concrete policy action. This remains an important question since eradicating all forms of inequality is framed, by policymakers, as commensurate with neo-liberal economic globalization while critics often see this pairing as wholly incompatible. For instance, the final declaration of the 2002

United Nations World Summit on Sustainable Development (WSSD) states that economic development is synonymous with globalization which is synonymous with international trade which is synonymous with "progress" (A/CONF.199/20*, 2002). Addressing this logic, the Fiji-based DAWN network criticized the WSSD for reinforcing the neo-liberal model of economic globalization. DAWN advocates stressed their alarm at how the WSSD focused on debating international trade rather than thinking holistically about sustainable development (Charkiewicz 2003). Similar tensions can be read into the U.N.'s Millennium Development Goals which, for example, promote the development of a more "open trading and financial system that is rule-based, predicable and non-discriminatory" and is also committed to "poverty reduction" and "access to affordable essential drugs in the developing world" (http://www.un.org/millenniumgoals/, MDG #8).

In many ways, feminist activists' desire to challenge the ideological hegemony of a pro-corporate, neo-liberal agenda is consonant with the goals of the broader movement for global economic justice. However, feminist activities therein are substantively distinct from the work of labour, consumer, human rights, and environmental organizations. Without feminist interventions, other global justice activists might easily concede critical rhetorical, material, and conceptual territory, often without even being aware of doing so, because of their lack of awareness (some might even say lack of interest) in the gender implications of economic policies. Given the structure of the current political terrain of economic integration and economic justice advocacy, feminist activists increasingly recognize that it is critical to try to reframe the globalization debate to address the ways that certain policies can mitigate while other exacerbate gender-based inequalities.

For feminist activists, attempts to shape the governance of globalization are especially critical since globalization is generally considered to be "gender-neutral" by proponents, detractors and co-opters alike. Since there is "a growing consensus among women's...groups that many aspects of globalization and trade liberalization have exacerbated existing gender inequalities and deepened asymmetrical power relations between men and women internationally" the decision to stay out of the fray would risk further marginalizing these concerns and would concede the terrain to ideological opponents (Canadian Gender & Trade Consultation 2002: 1). As the Association for Women's Rights in Development's 2002 meeting theme "Re-inventing Globalization" suggests, feminist organizations are becoming increasingly concerned with the nexus of global governance and globalization. Along these lines, the report of AWID's 2002 meeting states,

> ...women of the world are poorer and more marginalized, they continue to be victims of gender-based violence, and they are excluded from public decision-making positions. Maybe gender has been mainstreamed and women are now included in discussions with the power players, but can we really say that we are making progress? We must be savvy to change the course of globalization – this is a different time.
> (Symington 2002: 11)

Engaging the institutions of international trade is necessary if feminists are to challenge dismissive characterizations of their concerns and to stem the tide toward locating decision-making in inter-governmental or transnational arenas that are less and less open to gender-based concerns. Feminist disengagement from this arena is thus not viable. Failure to enter debates about the governance of trade policy would leave definition of the substantive and ideological tenor to those who have no interest in acknowledging or addressing gender-based concerns. Globalization discourse – as articulated by mainstream policymakers and business interests – does and will continue to play a large role in national and international political arenas. Opting out would mean conceding important material, political, and ideological ground and this is true even if the activists who are able to participate in this arena represent a relatively elite cross-section of women's rights advocates. Furthermore, feminist activists engage arenas of global economic governance knowing full well that the "gendering" of current policy and structure is unlikely.

Holding governments accountable

Feminist engagements in debates over the governance of globalization are designed to highlight how gendered economic inequalities are constructed and regularly re-enacted through the process of economic integration and restructuring policies. In particular, feminist activists aim to explode the myth that neo-liberal economic policies are by definition economically progressive and that they uniformly benefit all groups of people. These alternative policy positions challenge the predominant understandings of globalization as actor-less and inexorable, where poverty, scarcity, and inequality are assumed to be "normal" or "permanent" features of the world system. Such advocacy calls attention to the ways that *current* national and international economic policies and practices actually create, recreate, and reinforce particular forms of social, political, and economic inequality.

Indeed, this spotlight on accountability is central to feminist efforts to shape the governance of globalization. A statement issued by the members of the Women's International Coalition for Economic Justice (WICEJ) during the United Nations Beijing +5 Conference, for instance, highlighted the issue of accountability and in so doing, they called attention to the ways that stereotypes about "progressive" Northern countries and "conservative" Southern ones were actually hampering the negotiations.[6] They wrote,

> The position taken by some Northern government delegates and non-governmental organizations (NGOs) – that all would be fine if a right-wing "cabal" of countries were less rigid – is not only false, it smacks of racism and exacerbates the North/South divide in the UN. A common tendency is for the US, European Union and other Northern states to smugly point the finger at corrupt Southern governments, calling for better governance and accountability and scolding them for not upholding UN agreements on social development indicators, human rights and women's human rights. At the same time, these Northern nations set the macro-economic policies, through the International Monetary Fund (IMF), World Bank and World Trade Organization (WTO), that are devastating developing economies, cutting social service and regulatory budgets, and violating women's economic human rights to jobs, housing, healthcare and an adequate standard of living. The history of colonialism and Northern-supported corrupt Southern dictators makes such remonstrations ring hollow. This is a cynical game being played in the name of advancing women's rights, while pushing forward a neo-liberal economic agenda that hurts women of both South and North.
>
> (Women's International Coalition for Economic Justice 2000)

Coordinated efforts by the Economic Justice Caucus at Beijing +5 were indeed successful in getting government delegates to acknowledge that *current policies* are exacerbating *and* creating gender-based economic inequalities. The Beijing +5 Outcomes document itself (formally known as *Further Actions and Initiatives to Implement the Beijing Declaration and Platform for Action*) concludes that contemporary policies of economic globalization are having "negative social and economic impacts" in women's lives (Paragraph 135 c). It further acknowledges that:

[g]lobalization has presented new challenges for the fulfillment of the commitments [governments] made [in 1995 in Beijing].... and that the changes brought by processes of globalization have transformed patterns of production and accelerated technological advances in information and communication and affected the lives of women, both as workers and consumers. In a large number of countries, particularly in developing and least developed countries, these changes have also adversely impacted on the lives of women and have increased inequality.

(Paragraph 29, B+5 OD)

It is important to remember that the Outcomes Document (as in the case of all U.N. documents) was drafted through an intergovernmental process. Thus it represents the positions, policy prescriptions, and ideological premises to which governments have agreed. In this light, Paragraph 29 of the Outcomes Document is particularly important because it concedes that contemporary policies of globalization have had deleterious consequences in some women's lives. Indeed, it echoes the above quoted NGO statement by highlighting the fact that policies of globalization have, in some cases, exacerbated North/South inequalities. It suggests that gender-based inequities are not simply the product of some ancient patriarchal system but are, in part, the product of contemporary policies. Members of the Economic Justice Caucus argued that this admission was a key step in achieving economic justice for all.

For governments, the process of coming to consensus on the globalization language in the B+5 Outcomes Document was extremely contentious. Indeed, the language on globalization was agreed on at the end of the negotiations and was still unsatisfactory to many. The U.S. government, for instance, disassociated[7] itself from the Document's agreed language on globalization [paragraphs 29, 30, 135(I)]. The U.N. press release at the close of Beijing +5 reported on the U.S. government's position. The U.S. contends that those paragraphs dealing with globalization and economic issues:

characterized globalization and debt as significant obstacles to achieving gender equality. National governments had *primary* responsibility for social and economic development and for ensuring the equality of women. Most aspects of equality for women had no direct link to international economic and financial issues.

(Press Release, GA/9725, June 10, 2000, emphasis is mine)

In other words, the U.S. government disavowed any responsibility for gendered economic inequalities, instead, asserting that globalization has primarily positive consequences for individual women's lives. Moreover, the poverty, discrimination, or economic inequality that women in a particular country face is the responsibility of *their* government alone. Evident in the U.S. government's position is a desire for distance from a key feminist activist contention: those contemporary neo-liberal economic policies pushed by the U.S. (as well as many other countries) are themselves partly responsible for gendered inequalities.

As the above discussion illustrates, feminists engage the institutional spaces of neo-liberal economic globalization in order to demonstrate that globalization is neither an inexorable nor a gender-neutral process. When possible, they also use these opportunities to push governments to concede that neo-liberal policies have not had a uniformly positive impact and that countries of the Global South have often borne the brunt of them.

Obstacles to feminist engagement in the governance of global trade policy

Up to this point, I have focused on the three key reasons why feminist activists are working to shape the governance of globalization. My goal here has been to demonstrate the myriad ways that such efforts are substantively sophisticated and politically strategic. In other words, feminist engagement with the institutions that govern neo-liberal economic globalization are not the work of unsophisticated "globofobicos" who lack an adequate understanding of the complexities of governing the global economy. Rather, they are activists, from the Global South and North, who believe that gender justice requires shaping the policies, practices, and discourse of global governance. In many cases, they are extremely experienced global political actors, in some cases with nearly thirty years of advocacy experience in global governance arenas.

Now, I turn my attention to the other side of the coin by examining the three key obstacles feminist activists face as they attempt to influence the governance of globalization. First, I examine the problems posed by focusing on global governance structures that operate in a largely anti-democratic political field. Second, I look at the challenges activists face when attempting to translate feminist critique into concrete policy interventions that target international governance organizations. Finally, I explore the difficulties feminist groups face when they try to work with mainstream NGOs that repeatedly ignore gender-based concerns.

The challenge of working in an anti-democratic field

It is, perhaps, an understatement to note that the challenges associated with trying to shape the governance of globalization in accord with feminist analyses and values are considerable. On the one hand, feminist activists are increasingly arguing that "[w]omen's economic advocacy in the future will need to address the major power brokers, if its agenda of human rights, equity and sustainable social development is to be realized" (Riley 2001: 4). On the other hand, working with international institutions that lack meaningful avenues of democratic accountability, like the World Trade Organization, presents enormous obstacles. While much could be said about the anti-democratic norms and institutions that govern the global economy, here I will highlight how the anti-democratic structures of these institutions have particular consequences for feminist activists.

Moving away from the United Nations

Historically, the United Nations has provided an important space for transnational feminist activism and has, at least in recent years, been increasingly hospitable to feminist analyses, concerns, and activists, especially as the U.N. itself has made a commitment to "gender mainstreaming" throughout all of its operations (Pietilä 1999; West 1999; Friedman 2003; Cohen, this book). The series of world conferences in the 1990s, for instance, helped foster cross-national feminist collaboration, served as locations for movement-building, and challenged individuals to conceptualize their work in more interconnected ways (e.g., Clark *et al.* 1998; Bunch & Hinojosa 2000; Dutt 2000). Yet, neo-liberal globalization has hampered the potency of the most "democratic" of international spaces – the United Nations. At the 2002 United Nations Financing for Development Conference held in Monterrey, Mexico, the Women's Caucus stressed the crucial role of the U.N. as an organ of global governance. Because the U.N. has a history of being relatively open to feminist ideas and initiatives, the Women's Caucus urged "that a process be established that places the UN at the center of global economic governance" as opposed to simply strengthening organizations like the WTO or IMF at the U.N.'s expense (FfD Women's Caucus 2002). Because the international center of gravity governing globalization is located in organizations that are highly secretive and actively skirt civil society input (like the WTO, IMF, APEC, or negotiations over the FTAA), feminists face significant obstacles to participation.

A parallel development in the world of global governance is the fact that the U.N. itself is ever less likely to provide a space open to feminist activists (Pheko 2002). Indeed, in recognition of the diminishing usefulness of the U.N. as a space open to feminist concerns, women's organizations from all parts of the world worked to ensure that the tenth anniversary commemoration of the 1995 IV World Conference on Women held in Beijing would involve no inter-governmental negotiations. Many argued explicitly against a Beijing +10 inter-governmental conference, because they feared it would result in backpedaling on previous commitments and agreed language. These concerns are the product of the incremental increase in the mobilization and power of conservative and fundamentalist governments (in conjunction with the Vatican) and right-wing NGOs in U.N. Anti-feminist women's organizations actively support this "unholy alliance" thus challenging the legitimacy of feminist voices and advocacy within the United Nations (Buss and Herman 2003). For feminists concerned about the governance of globalization, the weakening of the United Nations is particularly disconcerting as it has historically been one of the only global inter-governmental institutions where gender issues have been addressed in a meaningful way. While the U.N. is by no means wholly supportive or attentive to gender, it is clearly more so than the international organizations that govern global economic activity.

Insiders and outsiders

The anti-democratic functioning of the institutions that govern global trade policy circumscribes the composition of feminist activism in this arena. Most importantly, it has reified a divide between feminist 'insiders' and 'outsiders' where 'insiders' have some access to the locus of decision-making and 'outsiders' are literally and figuratively cut out of the conversation altogether. In her work on the feminist non-governmental organizations (NGOs) in Latin America, Sonia Alvarez, problematizes this divide. She suggests that there is a widening gap between women's grassroots activism and the more specialized and professionalized feminist NGOs (Alvarez 1998; on this point see also Ammar and Lababidy 1999). The gap Alvarez identifies, and the exclusions that accompany it, are also evident in women's activism to shape the governance of globalization. This "NGOization" is of critical concern because such activism can reinscribe and magnify unequal power relations. Yet, the structural requirements of participating in the governance of trade policy require a high level of expertise and specialization. When this need for highly specialized knowledge is combined with restricted access to the poli-cymaking arena, the result is the reification of a hierarchy where the voices of many women's rights advocates remain literally and figurat-ively 'outside' the arena of global governance debates. Interestingly, this "insider"/"outsider" dynamics does not clearly follow North/South lines. Rather, a relatively few feminist NGO "elites" from the Global North and from the Global South gain access to these spaces while the vast major-ity of women's NGOs from all regions of the world are unable to or uninterested to participate.

It is my contention that the anti-democratic practices of the major institutions governing globalization severely constrain the abilities of women's rights activists to organize more comprehensively. The anti-democratic structure of the WTO creates both feminist and non-feminist 'insiders' and 'outsiders', indeed any study of the global movement for economic justice will show that such hierarchies are present. However, this hierarchical organizational structure is a particularly potent obstacle to women's activism since such divisions expressly contravene key tenets of feminist thought and practice. Take organizing at the WTO meeting in Cancun as a case in point. The IGTN coordinated feminist advocacy on the "inside". The group had many members with official NGO con-sultative status and they came from the Global South and North. This status allowed participants access to venues and meetings within the cordoned off perimeter of the official space. In Cancun, the security restrictions were so intense that without this official NGO consultative status individuals were virtually unable to get within five miles of the negotiations. On the "inside", the IGTN's daily strategy meetings were key to information sharing and strategy building.

However, there were representatives of many other women's and fem-inist NGOs who were literally kept on the "outside". Among them were many who had participated in the two-day long Women's Forum (*Foro Internacional Mujeres: Mujeres Hacia Cancún*) organized by a coalition of Mexican NGOs held in downtown Cancun immediately before the offi-cial WTO Ministerial commenced. There were also scores of women who were actively working in the Mexican *campesino* movement whose physical access to the official negotiations were limited by large metal fences and thousands of police officers. As the official WTO Ministerial began, it was immediately obvious that there was essentially no con-nection between women's rights advocates organizing on the outside of the security perimeter and the IGTN discussions on the inside. At a number of the IGTN daily briefings, concern was raised about this dis-connect. As a result, junior staff members of the Association for Women's

Rights in Development (AWID) and the Women's Environment and Development Organization (WEDO) tried to establish a space for linking "insiders" and "outsiders". However, their efforts were largely unsuccessful in bridging the gap. The clear division between those who had access to the official space and those who did not proved too great an obstacle to overcome.[8]

The division between "insiders" and "outsiders" in Cancun were mapped on to both class and colour hierarchies. This anti-democratic structure had the effect of reinscribing the marginality of certain women's struggles for gender justice (in this case indigenous, *campesina*, and many Mexican women). While these divisions are not new to women's or feminist activism, the anti-democratic structures and practices of global economic institutions, like the WTO, reinforce and exacerbate them. In this case, it was women from international NGOs based in the North trying to bring grassroots women activists (who in this case were largely Mexican) into the process. However, the division was not one that readily obeyed North/South lines since many feminists from Mexican women's NGOs (largely based in Mexico City) had official NGO credentials and thus, functioned as NGO "insiders" and many of the key participants in IGTN's daily briefings were themselves from the Global South.

These hierarchies are likely to become even more entrenched as the WTO (and other similar institutions) structures their activities so as to avoid civil society monitoring and protest. Such anti-democratic strategies (like holding meetings in Qatar or doing work through lower profile meetings at WTO headquarters in Geneva) create additional layers of exclusion that further limit participation to an elite few – some of whom will undoubtedly come from the United States and Europe, but others will come, as they did in this case from El Salvador, Brazil, and Figi.

The challenges of translating feminist critique into concrete policy interventions

Women's rights advocates' ability to influence the governance of globalization is constrained by the fact that feminist discourse and critique have no legitimacy in the international policy arena. The intensity of this feeling of "disenfranchisement" is palpable in the words of *Articulación Feminista Marcosur*, a South American feminist collective. They argue that the "Market" is seen as "a kind of contemporary...[deity], which occupies the place of the one and only God...." (Articulación Feminista Marcosur). In essence, *Marcosur* is suggesting that the "Truth" of neo-liberal economic policies render feminist contestation illegitimate or even sacrilege.

Myriad examples of this illegitimacy exist. In 1993, for instance, during the U.S. debate over the NAFTA, Senator Ted Stevens a Republican from Alaska, introduced an amendment to the NAFTA implementing legislation designed to separate any discussion of social or environmental issues from the substance of international trade policy. In arguing for the amendment, Stevens suggested that "social" issues like labour and the environment were completely irrelevant to the substance of trade policy[9] (United States Senate 1993). In the ensuing years, some concessions have been won by activists challenging neo-liberal economic globalization. In the main, however, Stevens' argument remains illustrative of the challenges feminist and other activists in the movement for global economic justice face when trying to articulate alternatives to the dominant policy paradigm. Even while there have been some substantive and rhetorical concessions in the past decade about the relevance of social and environmental issues to trade policy, feminist activists trying to influence the governance of globalization still struggle to locate themselves in these conversations.

Women's EDGE, a US-based coalition organization that focuses on trade, development and aid policies has extensive experience attempting to engender these conversations. Yet, as Marceline White, Director of the Global Trade Program at Women's EDGE has suggested, satisfactorily representing feminist critiques while articulating viable political strategies very difficult. On this point, White noted, "[w]hile we would love to craft a perfect argument that speaks to the paradigm of free trade and to the systemic flaws in the current model, we are cognizant that those arguments are not heard" (quoted in Runyan 2002: 264). Furthermore, White suggests that trade negotiators are loathe to concede that there is a connection between development and trade (echoing Senator Stevens earlier argument). "If someone objects to something in a trade agreement, negotiators may ask for a suggested alternative but it must fit into the confines of the agreements. You can suggest a **'must'** as opposed to a **'make every endeavour to'** but that is the scope of alternatives that they really would like to hear" (quoted in Runyan 2002). In other words, feminist activists confront clear structural impediments to their participation in the trade policy arena because the dominant discourse governing globalization is narrowly circumscribed.

Policymakers' assumption that the rules governing globalization are gender-neutral requires that feminists wage an uphill battle – first to gain acknowledgement that there are gender-specific impacts, and then to articulate the complexity and seriousness of their concerns. They function in a political context, and in a language, where feminist critiques of globalization are nearly incomprehensible. As a result, activists tend to simplify their critiques, advocating sweeping changes as opposed to articulating specific policy alternatives. For example, feminist activists often narrow their critique to highlighting the ways that women are negatively affected by trade policy, as opposed to underscoring the gendered structuring of the norms, policies, and practices governing globalization. In other words, the constraints of the policy environment may provide enough space for activists to talk about issues where women are seen (e.g., as workers or as victims of sexual violence), but not how the system itself reifies gendered notions of "knowledge" like in the rules governing trade in intellectual property.[10] Or, in cases where activists provide a broader gender analysis of trade policy they end up recommending that the entire system be altered which automatically positions them as irrelevant to the internal debates.

In December 2001, Canadian women's groups, for instance, convened a consultative meeting designed to assess the movement's response to international trade. This meeting was particularly important since Canadian feminists had been in the forefront of international efforts to shape the governance of trade policy during the 1980s and 1990s, but their participation had been declining. Attending the meeting were most of the key Canadian feminist activists and academics working in the area, as well as a few representatives of the women's rights division of the Canadian federal government. During the meeting, the two representatives of the government office of the Status of Women Canada talked about how policymakers want "very specific suggestions for developing positions and find it difficult to respond to general recommendations" (Canadian Gender & Trade Consultation: 7). They emphasized the fact that sympathetic policymakers need help linking the concerns articulated by feminist organizations with specific ideas for changing trade policy in light of them.

However, the group was unable to respond to the challenge posed by the government officials. Instead, the report of this meeting ended with a discussion of the "Key Points" that emerged. These include the assertion that "The WTO and FTAA cannot be 'fixed'. They are based on the wrong assumptions and aim to extend a corporate and neo-liberal agenda" (Canadian Gender & Trade Consultation: 8). The conclusions also suggest that "[t]here are alternatives.... We have consensus on a broad strategic vision, although that does not necessarily translate into a single strategic plan of action. We are working on various tracks" (8).

Indeed, the group ended up recreating the very same problem that officials from the Status of Women Canada warned about. They set out a meta-level critique of trade policy, hinted that there are in fact alternatives, but highlighted their "vision", without developing specific ideas which could be useful to activists and policymakers in the governance of trade policy.

Of course, this problem is not limited to Canadians working on the issue. The statement of the Women's Caucus at the United Nations Financing for Development Conference for instance, demands "democratic global governance; binding mechanisms for the full implementation of all human rights; equitable redistribution of resources, and; changes in power relations within and between countries inclusive of women, the poor, and racially and other marginalized groups" (FfD Women's Caucus 2002). In the end, the most concrete proposal in the Declaration calls for women's organizations to be included in the decision-making and follow-up to the Conference.

Even those feminist organizations with the most developed analysis and resources face this conundrum. The IGTN's policy statement about the 2003 WTO Ministerial meeting in Cancun, for example, that the proposed Agreement on Agriculture (AOA) will disproportionately burden women. They posit that "women everywhere become default providers of food and other demands of social reproduction in the face of market and state failures" (IGTN 2003a). Their conclusion, however, does not include specific suggestions about how to address this, but instead argues that the proposed AOA be removed from the WTO negotiating table. This pattern is repeated over and over again, in this, and in other activist critiques of trade policy. Activists articulate a critique of the gendered construction of trade policy and then suggest the scraping of the proposed agreement rather than articulating substantive changes to the draft text. Here I am not judging whether scrapping the AOA is, or is not, the best solution, my point is rather that fundamentally different values make engaged conversation between policymakers and feminist activists extremely difficult and, as the current system is configured, unlikely.

The above examples represent only a small sample of the significant work done by women's organizations in the past five years to address the governance of globalization. However, this work must now, according to Joanna Kerr, executive director of Association for Women's Rights in Development, "concentrate on the much tougher agenda of developing viable alternative economic models" (Kerr 2001: 5). In part, the inability to do so stems from working within an environment inhospitable to feminist critique. In other words, it is not simply that feminist

organizations are "doing it wrong." Rather, It is extraordinarily difficult, maybe impossible, to move from a feminist meta-level critique
of neo-liberal international economic policy's discourse and practice
into policy proposals that are concrete, viable, and yet accurately reflect
the nuanced and multifaceted nature of feminist political-economic
analysis. As a result, many feminist activist interventions in the governance of global trade policy make only general critiques, suggesting
further study of the ways women are affected (because it is also true
that we do not fully understand the complexity of the impact of such
policies on women), and then either arguing for a totally different system
(but obviously without a map to get from here to there), or suggesting
policy interventions that will barely shift the gender structuring of the
economy.

As the above examples show, there are only very limited ways to
actually engage the governance of globalization and none of them facilitate levying a feminist critique of trade, let alone a contestation of
the gendered epistemology of the current policies, structures, and discourses that govern globalization. Moreover, it is difficult to articulate
critiques that can capture the fine distinctions and complexities of feminist analyses. As a result, policy analysis and proposals focus on the way
that women are materially situated, downplaying critiques that address
how gendered ideologies shape the structure of international economic
policy. In part, as a result of this dilemma, the policy proposals that get
"air time" tend to be those that are either extremely general or very specific. In other words, feminist interventions end up being articulated at a
meta-level or at a very micro-level – both of which have significant limitations. The result, I argue, is a mismatch between what policymakers
can use given the current structure of global governance of international
economic policy and the knowledge and recommendations feminist
activists and scholars are producing.

The challenge of working with mainstream NGOs

Up to this point, I have emphasized the structural considerations shaping feminist activism in the realm of trade policy. In this final section, I
examine how feminist analyses and activism fit within the broader spectrum of organizing to shape the governance of globalization. In fact, this
field of oppositional organizing often constitutes yet another challenge
for feminists to overcome in their quest to influence the governance
of globalization. In attempting to influence the discourses, policy, and
practice of globalization, feminist activists have to bring on board not
only those (re)designing the architecture of the international political

economy, but they also have to enlist the support of mainstream activists who tend not to embrace a feminist politic (Riley 2001: 8). This
lack of support or is not surprising given that much anti-globalization
rhetoric and activism renders women, girls, and gender analyses invisible
much like the neo-liberal paradigm they contest (Mohanty 2003: 515).

While inadequate attention to the nexus of gender and globalization
has been an unfortunate constant in nearly all mainstream trade organizing, a few key examples demonstrate the intransigency that feminist
activists frequently confront. Contemporary activism around international trade policies came to the fore while the U.S. and Canada were
negotiating their Free Trade Agreement (signed in 1987) and then again
when they moved to include Mexico in a North American FTA (signed
in 1993). When discussions began about extending NAFTA to include
all of the countries of the Americas (minus Cuba), civil society organizations began collaborating on a process to develop "concrete and
viable alternatives" to the Free Trade Area of the Americas (FTAA). The
Hemispheric Social Alliance (HSA), the network that emerged, compiled
a document called "Alternatives for the Americas: Building a People's
Hemispheric Agreement" (1998). This document was organized into
chapters according to thematic issues and constituencies. Interestingly,
the "Alternatives" document failed to include a chapter on women or
gender until its third edition (Hemispheric Social Alliance 2001). The
latent inclusion of gender was catalyzed by the creation of a Women's
Committee of the HSA (White 2000; Guillen 2003). Patty Barrera of
Common Frontiers in Canada noted that gender was not even considered at the first meeting of the Hemispheric Social Alliance and
that the ratio of men to women was high (Canadian Gender & Trade
Consultation: 7).

In my interviews with feminists trying to shape the governance of
globalization, I was told again and again that non-women's organizations in the movement for global economic justice were often insensitive,
uninterested, or simply inattentive to the gender-related aspects of the
issues they were addressing. Recent reports of sexual harassment of young
women in the "youth camp" at the 2005 World Social Forum in Porto
Alegre present yet another, even more disturbing element of "gender-
blindness" by progressive organizers. This inattention is manifest both
in terms of a lack of substantive interest in gender issues as well as
a lack of attention to whether or not feminist activists are invited to
be part of key discussions and presentations. For instance, in preparation for the September 2003 WTO meeting in Cancun, civil society
groups held a planning meeting in Mexico City in November 2002.
More than 230 people from 16 countries attended that meeting, yet

only two women's organizations had representatives present[11] (Symington 2003). The extremely small representation of women's organizations in the Cancun-WTO planning process is emblematic of a marginalization that surfaces over and over again. In 2002, for instance, Naomi Klein a well-known activist and author of the book *No Logo*, expressed her hope that this inattention to gender was abating within the global movement for economic justice. In 1999, she said:

> I think that the moment we're in now is drawing on social movements of the past and present – it's finding new intersections to develop a coherent analysis. But so far when attempts have been made to develop that coherent analysis, feminist theory and the globalized feminist movement have been marginalized again. We saw this in Porto Alegre – the World Social Forum. But I do think that ever since then there's been growing awareness that recognizing the power of capital does not mean saying that gender and race no longer matter, quite the opposite, they matter more than ever.
>
> (quoted in Thomas 2002: 49)

Here Klein acknowledges feminist marginalization in the broader movement and "hopes" that gender issues will be taken more seriously in the future. However, as the November 2002 planning meeting for the WTO meetings in Cancun makes clear that change is slow in coming.

The marginalization of women's rights activists and gender-issues (and, indeed, too often, women themselves) continues to be a problem in the movement for global economic justice and this means that feminist activists face an even greater obstacle to establishing the legitimacy of feminist critiques of global economic governance (e.g., Rebick 2002). As a result of the continued inattention to gender and trade by mainstream NGOs, feminist groups are grappling with how to work with male-led NGOs and networks. Some important organizations like DAWN, have decided to make a concerted effort to work with non-women's organizations, but are often frustrated by the difficulties. As Gigi Francisco notes,

> ...DAWN is continuing to work to make "friendly bandits" within Southern networks and organisations more gender-aware or conscious, and more committed to taking on board the struggle for gender justice. The work has not been easy either. It is one thing to have separate panels addressing "gender issues"; quite another to be included in the main panels and plenaries, and there is much territoriality around

certain globalisation issues.... [A]ttempts by feminist to raise gender issues in the lead up to the Seattle ministerial in 1999 were denigrated by a "progressive" NGO which, in an article on its web-site, referred to 'gender activists and animal welfarists baying for space within the multilateral trading system.

(Francisco quoted in Slatter: 5)

However, DAWN remains hopeful that working with male-led NGOs will lead to more gender-aware analysis and advocacy in the future (Slatter 2003: 5).

As the above makes clear, feminist organizations that attempt to shape the governance of globalization must deal with not just the structural obstacles to working in this anti-democratic, highly specialized policy environment. They must also be ever vigilant to ensure that the voices of the opposition incorporate a gender-analysis and that women's rights advocates are represented at all appropriate tables.

Conclusion

Feminist political engagements with processes of globalization are increasingly focused at the places where the global political and economic rules are made – the World Trade Organization, World Bank, International Monetary Fund, Summit of the Americas, and the Asia Pacific Economic Cooperation, among others. This focus is the result of the "acceptance that equality will depend more on changing the structures of organizations, and most importantly, the institutions (or rules of the game) that embody them" (Kerr 2001: 8). Indeed, there has been a massive increase in feminist activism to shape the governance of globalization. Here I have argued that feminist activists engage the governance of international trade policy because they see doing so as a political imperative and because they believe that so doing gives them a space and framework for articulating their concerns. In other words, their actions, musings, etc., are not the product of uninformed "globofobicos" but rather the reasoned and increasingly sophisticated work of a well-organized, transnationally coordinated, and strategically thoughtful group of feminist activists. These activists believe that the gender dimensions of globalization will not be addressed without intentional and concerted targeting – by feminists – of the policies, practices, institutions, and discourses of global governance.

Interestingly, however, the barriers to success have not declined commensurate with the increase in the level of activism. Feminist activists are fighting a number of very tough battles for recognition of their concerns. First and foremost, the political/policy terrain is an epistemologically and materially inhospitable location for feminist analyses and activism. While all critics of neo-liberal economic policy find activism at the WTO, for instance, arduous, the masculinist discourse, practices, and institutional structures that constitute the politics of global trade policy are particularly anathema to feminist engagement.

In addition to trying to figure out how to articulate their concerns in a policy environment that refuses to understand gender analysis, feminist activists confront internal contestation and hierarchies. These challenges arise on two key fronts: from within the feminist movement itself as well as in relation to the mainstream movement for global economic justice. Despite the increasing media and policy attention paid to those contesting the current governance of globalization, it remains an uncomfortable location for feminist activism, particularly given its exclusionary character. However, the political significance of these venues means that they are read as politically and materially critical to constructing a more just economic order.

Notes

1. The main undercurrent of the WTO talks was a clash between developing and rich countries. The clearest manifestation of this tension could be seen in the formation of the Group of 21 (G-21), a collection of developing countries publicly led by Brazilian Foreign Minister Celso Amorim, but including at various points Argentina, Bolivia, China, Chile, Colombia, Costa Rica, Cuba, Ecuador, Egypt, Guatemala, India, Mexico, Pakistan, Paraguay, Peru, Philippines, South Africa, Thailand, Venezuela, El Salvador, and Nigeria. The G-21's focus was on trying to push the US and EU to agree to deep cuts in the subsidies they dole out to their own farmers. The G-21 posture had the effect of intensifying the North–South rhetoric and it emerged as the leading voice in opposition to an agreement without an adequate solution to the issues in agriculture.
2. Indeed, the use of the label "anti-globalization" is part of that contested territory. Increasingly, the label is used in the media and by political opponents to characterize activist efforts with the intention of delegitimizing them (Alldred 2002; Klein 2002). Given the politics of the term, I use it only to invoke the label ascribed to these organizing efforts and when so doing, I enclose it in quotations. The label that I use instead is "movement for global justice" (MGJ).
3. The Mexican government, for instance, created a "black list" of "anti-globalization" activists or in Spanish "globofobicos." The Mexican government denied visas to some on the list and the Mexican press reported that authorities planned on watching closely the activities of more than 100 people during the WTO meetings in Cancun (Xinhua News Agency 2003).

4. The seven regions are: Africa, Asia, Caribbean, Europe, Latin America, North America, and the Pacific.

5. Formally called "The World Economic Forum" the Davos Summit is an annual meeting (usually held in Davos, Switzerland) of the world's foremost business elites (with membership from the "world's 1000 leading companies" as well as "200 smaller businesses"). Also invited to the Summits are key world leaders from government, academia, religion, NGOs, and the arts (World Economic Forum).

6. The purpose of this meeting, held in 2000 in New York City, was to review the progress toward the goals and commitments made by governments at the United Nations IV World Conference on Women in Beijing, China in 1995.

7. In U.N. parlance this is referred to as "reserving" or issuing a "reservation" on a particular part of the agreed document. Reservations facilitate negotiations since they give states a way to disagree with particular language while preserving the possibility of achieving consensus adoption of the whole document.

8. I attended the meetings designed to connect women's organizing on the outside to the negotiations on the "inside" and quickly realized that the obstacles to communication were too structurally significant to address in this matter.

9. The amendment was defeated by a vote of 73-26 (Senate vote #389).

10. Trade rules governing intellectual property tend to value "man-made" products like synthetic pharmaceuticals and treat the fruits of the earth as commodities that can be patented, controlled, and sold (Shiva 1999).

11. The two organizations are Women's Environment and Development Organization and Association for Women's Rights in Development. In addition, there were a few other women at the meeting who have actively worked on gender and trade issues but they were not there as official representatives of women's organizations.

10
Gender, Governance, and Globalization at Borders: Femicide at the US–Mexico Border

Kathleen Staudt

Globalization, free trade ideologies, and migration raise questions about the extent to which the nation-state is or should be the primary governance institution for citizens and residents. If not national, what then is the appropriate level: local, global, or regional? Considerable attention has been paid to global governance, whether active players are with International Organizations (IOs) such as United Nations affiliates, national governments, multinational corporations, and/or International Non-Government Organizations (NGOs) such as women's and human rights organizations. But many decisions are made locally, framed by global and national constraints and opportunities. Few studies of women/gender have been grounded in and at border "places," or *borderlands*, omnipresent in all nations save those surrounded by water. This chapter focuses on the "local," from the standpoint of the US–Mexico borderlands region, as it engages in national and international governance around the murders of girls and women.[1]

In *Activists Beyond Borders*, Keck and Sikkink develop path-breaking analyses of international human rights, environmental, and women's organizations. They differentiate among four different "politics" pursued in such networks: informational, symbolic, leverage, and accountability (1998: 18–26). Their focus is on established organizations— the kinds that are registered in the *Yearbook of International Organizations*, affiliated with the United Nations and/or with national governments as tax-exempt organizations in order to raise funds for their staff and mission. These organizations have achieved admirable progress in making issues visible and getting them on the policy agenda. However, Keck and Sikkink do not analyse networking *at or with border activists*, despite the book's title, except for the global networking through communication across national territorial lines, that is transnational activism. Moreover, the four types of politics that networks pursue are hardly differentiated in practice, as this study of US–Mexico cross-border networking demonstrates: local border networks connected with national and international networks to their advantage through seizing any and all opportunities for visibility, yet the connections occurred with some ambivalence and tension, including local questions about "who profits from the pain" (of the victims' families). These border networks, most of which are not formally registered or affiliated with their governments, the United Nations, or the *Yearbook of International Organizations*, seek to move beyond agenda-setting, called "Stage I" in this chapter, to concrete policy implementation, requiring Stage II actions that move beyond visibility and awareness-raising activity into actual, systemic changes.

This chapter begins with the consideration of the "politics of place." It then moves to discuss border theory, in both concrete and metaphoric forms, and borderland categories. It outlines the peculiar form of local governance at borderlands where multiple sovereign governments sit side by side. Next, the chapter grounds analysis at the US–Mexico borderlands, along with factors that facilitate and impede cross-border organizing. The heart of the chapter is devoted to cross-border organizing around the murders in Ciudad Juárez affecting approximately 370 girls and women, a third of them raped and mutilated (Benítez 1999; Portillo 2001; Washington Valdez 2002; Monárrez Fragoso 2002; Amnesty International 2003). Governmental responses have been limited, for reasons outlined in the body of the paper. Binational activists, grounded at the border, have raised awareness with high-visibility, but media-dependent events; cultural imagery, colours, and icons; reports and resolutions. The process of raising awareness occurs at some costs, including division, co-optation, and the unintended consequence that seems to demonize Mexico for those unfamiliar with the country. Ultimately, the chapter argues that cross-border activists have challenged (patriarchal) policy paradigms that render women's lives and work of little value, but that agenda-setting public awareness and symbolic concessions have not changed local, regional, and binational governance coalitions with the resources to address the toleration of violence against women, the non-enforcement of law, and the obscene levels of economic inequality between working women and people generally in both the United States and Mexico.

The politics of place: globalized borderlands

People's common interests span national borders, whether borderlands are densely or sparsely populated. In community development parlance, this is known as the "politics of place" or among activists, "place-based organizing." Geography shapes the political terrain. Contexts matter enormously in these politics, including governmental systems, practices, institutions, decision makers, and stakeholders in civil society. Two or more sovereign nations cohabit the land near territorial lines, with their own particular governance systems, creating peculiar local politics. While different versions of federalism, centralization, or decentralization bump against one another at borderlands, economic players seem to navigate crossing borders better than government officials. The North American Free Trade Agreement (NAFTA) consolidated these collaborations in 1994. One commonality shared near virtually all borders is transcendent male privilege: gender imbalance in governance and gender injustices, including a tolerance for violence against women and for lower valuations of their labour.

The metropolitan region of El Paso-Juárez, a densely settled population of two million people, is a case in point. The US–Mexico border runs through the metropolitan area, with different versions of sovereign federal "democracies" on either side. The economies are interdependent, and the inequalities, rampant: legal minimum wages in El Paso are 10 times the minimum wages of Juárez. Investors and corporate managers, with assistance from local and state government economic development agencies in both countries, interact in trade associations, chambers, and social networks that exhibit regional governance. Well before free trade agreements and the consolidation of post-1970s neo-liberal economic dogma as dominant hegemony, the dogma needed pilot testing, and the US–Mexico border was a major site. Mexico developed a border industrialization program in the 1960s, and US tariff codes provided incentives for "off-shore" export-processing assembly in factories known as *maquiladoras*. At their high point, in the year 2000, Juárez employed 250,000 *maquiladora* workers, a female majority workforce (down to 60 percent from 80 percent at the program's inception). Most jobs pay the official minimum wage of US$4–5 daily, plus fringe benefits. On each side of the border, men earn approximately twice what women earn (Staudt 1998; Kopinak 2004; Romero and Yellen 2004).[2] On both sides of the border, high levels of domestic violence exist, but on the Mexico side, the decade of female murders and atmospheric intimidation and threat take a huge toll; a third of the victims experience rape and mutilation.

At the "politics of place" around borderlands, people share common interests, but they encounter obstacles in efforts to organize across borders around such issues as air quality, living wages, health, water, violence, and human rights. Border controls and delays inhibit crossing; political constituencies are contained within sovereign countries; economic, language, and cultural differences are difficult to bridge; and nationalist education does its work from childhood ages on (Rippberger and Staudt 2003; Staudt and Coronado 2002). Yet some cross-border organizing has emerged around trade, labour, the environment, and human rights (Staudt and Coronado 2002; Brooks and Fox 2003). Ironically, NAFTA facilitated transnational networking among anti-free trade activists from Mexico, Canada, and the United States (Liebowitz 2001; Domínguez 2002), though not enough to halt the economic elite cohesion around the perpetuation of NAFTA through its 10-year anniversary celebrations in 2004.

Borders in comparative perspective

The late poet Gloria Anzaldúa (1987) put borders on the map for many feminist scholars. Her eloquent, philosophical accounts mixing English and Spanish about crossing visible and invisible borders at the US–Mexico border gave rise to a decade's worth of post-modern discourse on border "hybridity" and crossing metaphors, suggesting that "de-bordering" processes were taking hold. Anzaldúa's words are vivid: At the border's "open wound," the "third world grates against the first and bleeds...[and] the lifebloods [merge] to form a third country—a border culture" (1987: 3). More recent scholars, also in post-modern and critical perspectives, identify differentiation and segregation among the many "others" (Mexicans, Mexican Americans of first-, second-, and third generation, Anglos, more and less privileged, bilingual, Spanish and English speakers, identities across all of which gender and class cut) at the US–Mexico borderlands (Vila 2003). Ortiz-González argues that the border image is like "a fetish of the border region," mystifying and trivializing "the conceptual challenge of dealing with the new heterogeneity" (2004: 20, 24).

Staudt and Spener summarize the explosion of border scholarship as falling into material and metaphoric traditions (1998). They discuss simultaneous "bordering," "de-bordering," and "re-bordering" in the US–Mexico border context with the mix of migration, militarization (Dunn 1996), and reduced obstacles to commerce.

Historian Oscar Martínez is perhaps the quintessential border scholar, developing a typology of borderlands interaction (1994: 6–10). Martínez identifies four models. The *alienated borderlands* model exhibits tension, with minimal cross-border interaction. In *coexistent borderlands,* limited cross-border interaction exists, but relations are not stable. *Interdependent borderlands,* like the US–Mexico border, are usually stable, with extensive cross-border interaction among complementary economic and social forces. At *integrated borderlands,* economies merge and people and goods move across boundaries without restrictions. Parts of Europe fall into this category, including the Regio Basiliensis transfronter zone wherein cooperation exists between Switzerland, France, and Germany. Mathias Albert and Lothar Brock analyse such "debordering" processes (1998), but without regard to women or gender.

Analysis of the US–Mexico borderlands offers patterns and insights for other border regions. The literature on governance at borders is limited, only rarely addressing gender. Analysts have looked at border controls, including the movement of labour and of drugs. Extensive literature exists on the European Union, including policies on women and gender (Hoskyns 1999; Ellina 2003), but governance at EU borders has not been examined with gender lens. Until the recent expansion of the European Union, US–Mexico per capita incomes and wage gaps have been wider than those at borders within the European Union, but perhaps match the kinds of gaps that coincide with "Fortress Europe," differentiating member and non-member countries. While the US–Mexico border is complex enough, it is merely a binational context unlike the many trinational contexts or the nations that share borders with multiple double-digit national "others," as with the national neighbors of Brazil, China, Congo, Russia, and elsewhere. The research terrain is open and needy.

The European Union, with its transnational social policies and movements, is a model, but remains the regional exception rather than the global rule. The North American countries associated with NAFTA – Mexico, Canada, and the United States – have limited comparable "institutional shrouds" (explained in Staudt and Coronado 2002) that could provide policy norms for leverage to human rights and feminist activists as they struggle for professional anti-violence law enforcement, human rights, and living wages for the female-majority workforce in the export-processing factories known as *maquiladoras.*

It is important to keep in mind that contemporary nations were once "imagined," (Anderson 1991). National boundaries undergo constant change, most recently in the Balkans region. And if nations were once imagined and can change, then borders were also once imagined and borders can and do change. Colonial powers carved up the continent of Africa, drawing borders and boundaries through and in between cultural and linguistic groups, containing men and women. Wars and purchase also altered boundaries, common in the US–Mexico border region in the nineteenth century, when much of the now-southwestern United States was once Mexico. And boundaries change through negotiation as well. The latest changes in the US–Mexico border occurred in the 1960s, when the meandering Rio Grande River in Juárez-El Paso was channeled in a concrete bed.

US–Mexico border governance: a focus on Ciudad Juárez-El Paso

Mexico and the United States call themselves democracies. They are both federal systems that divide authority at the national, state, and local levels, with local municipal governments in Mexico, and city, county, and school district governments in the United States. Both Mexico and the United States are presidential, rather than parliamentary forms of government that claim division among the executive, legislative, and judicial branches. Two or more political parties compete in regular elections for limited terms of office.

On the surface, both government structures appear to be similar, but in practice, they operate quite differently. Mexico is far more central-ized than the United States, where local taxing and spending authority is comparatively greater but fragmentation makes accountability diffi-cult for citizens to decipher. In Mexico, the executive branch reigned supreme for much of post-1910 revolutionary history, although the legis-lative branch has gained more power since the 1990s with its multi-party system, one that elects almost twice as many women to the national Congress than does the United States (Rodríguez 2003).[3] Mexican schol-ars and reformers argue that the "rule of law" is limited (Domingo 1999; Human Rights Watch 1999), problematic for the impunity with which officials have dealt with the murders of women and girls.

El Paso's city budget is approximately 10 times the municipal budget of Juárez, a city approximately twice as large as El Paso (Staudt 1998). El Paso is home to multiple law enforcement agencies, ranging from the Sheriff's Department for the County, the Police Department for the City, and fed-eral agencies with a border presence: Drug Enforcement Administration, Federal Bureau of Investigation (FBI) regional office, Border Patrol dis-trict office, and others. El Paso ranks as the second-"safest" large city in the United States, according to recent national crime statistics, although its domestic violence reports average 2400 monthly or approximately 28,000 annually in a city of 600,000 (Romero and Yellen 2004).

Both Mexico and the United States not only embrace global neo-liberal economics, but they also share a rightward, quasi-religious ideological shift and polarized partisan politics, all of which have bearing on gender tensions, of which violence is one reflection (Staudt and Vera 2006). As the conservative National Action Party (PAN) competed with the long-dominant Institutional Revolutionary Party (PRI) in elections, it triumphed at Mexico's northern frontier since 1983, when PAN won the Municipal Presidency and most of all subsequent elections. PRI, however, controlled not only the governorship in the State of Chihuahua (where Juárez is located) for all terms (except 1992–1998) but also the national presidency until 2000 with PANista Vicente Fox's emergent victory. In Mexico's federal system, budgetary allocations are heavily centralized, and partisan conflicts influence the distribution of money to states and municipalities. With PAN and PRI controlling different levels of government, it was in the interest of the federal, state, and/or municipal governments to tarnish one another's image, depending on which party was in control. The major casualty was prioritizing and professionalizing the search for the serial killers of women.

The State of Texas (where El Paso is located) is under Republican Party control in both the executive and legislative branches, as is the federal government, while the borderlands vote heavily for the Democratic Party. Moderate Republicans are in the minority of Texas government, while extremely conservative Republicans are in the majority. While US-style federalism is more decentralized, with revenue-generating capability at the local and state levels, El Paso's poverty undermines its ability to generate sufficient property-tax revenue to fund effective local public services. The police and sheriff departments, however, respond professionally to murder and domestic violence cases.

In Juárez, the State Judicial Police of Chihuahua are responsible for serious crimes, though municipal police are usually first at crime scenes. Domestic violence reports are not counted and reported as distinctive crimes. The number of female victims over the last decade is contentious, and numbers float up and down, depending on whether the PRI or the PAN controls the governorship. During the 1990s, officials of both parties discounted the murders, often blaming the victims. The police mistreat victims' families, most of them of modest economic means. Since 2000, partisanship undermined coordination between PAN President Fox and PRI State of Chihuahua Governor Patricio Martínez. Many theories circulate about the killers, some of them bizarre (organ harvests) and others of them plausible (police collusion; sons of wealthy families [an overlapping category with drug cartel families]; hunting women as "sport;" trafficking in women; snuff videos). Studies in Mexico document that large percentages of people distrust the police (Giugale *et al.* 2001), a rational response to the often-unprofessional police behaviour.

What precedents exist for binational cooperation? Mexico and the United States have seventy-some treaties, ranging all the way from insect to air traffic controls and drug trafficking. No specific human rights treaty is in place. While international and inter-American human rights treaties are in place, the abuse and accusation agendas are full, with a variety of formal complaints. Only recently have the murders of women been elevated to high visibility, although even in the international NGO community, Amnesty International developed its position rather belatedly (2003), part of its 'turf,' rather than Human Rights Watch, another international NGO. Local, extensive informal cooperation exists among governments in El Paso and Juárez over major government functions, such as police, fire, and child protection. Business communities interact extensively, sometimes with co-owned/managed "twin-plant" operations on both sides of the border.

Thus far, various levels of border 'governance' have been identified, from official, governmental bodies to cross-border networking and organizing to joint business ventures. Governments on both sides of the border facilitate business and commerce, with their government-subsidized chambers and economic development staff. NAFTA created institutions that legitimize cross-border interests in environment and labour practices, however weak the accountability tools. The North American Development Bank, a symbol of cooperation, makes resources available for infrastructure at borders, far less than its public relations imply. However, the facilitation of democracy gets neither subsidies nor an institutional shroud that legitimizes cross-border organizing.

Underneath these binational institutions and networks, people share common interests that transcend the border in the peculiar local politics of the US–Mexico border. They breathe the same air, drink water from similar sources, and grapple with mosquitoes and health problems that do not respect borders. In El Paso, approximately 80 percent of its residents share Mexican heritage; 70 percent speak Spanish. People have relatives, friends, and colleagues on both sides of the border. Factors like these facilitate cross-border organizing around common interests.

Yet many obstacles exist to cross-border organizing. As noted above, different governments, constituencies, and accountability relationships complicate activists' goals and strategies. Technically, the Mexican Constitution prohibits foreigners from active involvement in politics in Article 33.[4] To cross the border itself requires documents, bureaucratic gaze, and lengthy waits at the international bridges. Income differences plague activists' ability to organize on similar terms with such seemingly mundane technology tools like telephones, faxes, and Internet. Given language and cultural differences, misunderstandings emerge, even down to the way Mexican Americans speak Spanish, or the use of English in the US or European press and the way it privileges English over Spanish (Staudt and Coronado 2002: Ch 3).

On top of, or underneath, all the connections is a seeping 'cartelization' of Juárez that, like Tijuana, is home to drug transit operations that grew once the US War on Drugs shifted the Colombia connection from Miami to the 2000-mile long US–Mexico Border. The enormous amounts of drug-money profits generate corruption and collusion with officials (Andreas 2000). US drug consumption is as strong as ever, and the prospect for legalization (and greater control) is dim. When the US War on Drugs is effective, the border plug helps spread drug use in Juárez.

Cross-border organizing around violence: local, national, global

Violence against women transcends the border, but Juárez has achieved infamy in the world for the murders of over 300 girls and women during the last decade, 100 victims of whom have been raped and mutilated before death (Benítez 1999; Monárrez Fragoso 2002; Washington Valdez 2002; Amnesty International 2003; Staudt and Coronado 2005a). Mexican police, at both the municipal and the state levels, respond with indifference, impunity, and incompetence. Many residents mistrust or fear the police generally, and more specifically view them as complicit and/or paid to protect the perpetrators, allegedly sons of the wealthy and/or narco-traffickers. The majority of Juarenses live below the poverty line, earning little more than the rock-bottom wage totaling US$25 weekly, in a city with hundreds of foreign export-processing factories, most of them US-owned.

Extensive organizing and networking has occurred around the murders, and the El Paso-Juárez Coalition Against Violence toward Women and Families is one of many groups involved in mobilizing awareness and pressuring governments to respond. It has a special place in organizing efforts because it is based in the border region, with deeper knowledge of the issues, people, and setting than the distant, weakly linked cyber activists. The networking links and Coalition activists' use of local cross-border space produced extraordinary attention that exploded in exponential ways over a three-year period, as outlined below.[5]

The Coalition Against Violence toward Women and Families at the US–Mexico Border, hereinafter called the Coalition, is an example of human rights networking at global to local levels. It is co-chaired by an academic (female) and a former labour union organizer (male), with an organizational and individual base made up of anti-violence center staff, feminists, union activists, and university students. Coalition volunteers network in non-hierarchical fashion. The Coalition draws on activists from young to old with an ideological and/or personal interest in the problem. Although clergy are sometimes present to open and close rallies with prayer, the institutionalized church has dedicated little effort to the cause, despite the victims' families and Juárez NGOs' inventions of religious icons and imagery as discussed below.

The Coalition was born at a labour solidarity meeting in Juárez with anti-violence activists in November 2001. It rarely misses the opportunity to critique the tenfold minimum-wage salary difference between El Paso and Juárez, and complicit US-owned factories. The Coalition consciously avoided US tax-exempt status and the concomitant fund-raising, reporting, and bylaws structure. It contrasts with, but allies with the first cross-border organization to address the murders, the Las Cruces-based Amigos de las Mujeres de Juárez, which raises awareness and funds, then allocates the latter to several NGOs in Juárez. Participants, all of them volunteers rather than paid staff or organizers, expand and contract, depending on opportunities for actions. Actions emerge around crises—bodies found in the desert or city ditches—and culturally significant seasons. Documentaries, like Lourdes Portillo's *Señorita Extraviada*, provide compelling visuals that rouse people to action.

Coalition stakeholders conceptualize violence against women as a binational problem, with binational solutions. Of the hundreds of victims, most of them Mexicans, victim lists count four El Pasoans, one Dutch, one Honduran, and one Guatemalan. Some of the dead once worked at US-owned *maquiladoras*. The borderline is busy: 250,000 million people cross legally on an annual basis (Ganster and Lorey 2005: xviii). Inside the border zone, Mexican authorities exert little oversight for crossers, while US authorities ask for identification, resident alien cards, or local passports for shopping and visiting. Some of the crossers could be registered sex offenders, 700 of whom live in El Paso, with their names and addresses posted on the Texas government website. The State of Chihuahua counts neither sex offenders nor domestic violence victims.

Activists in and outside the Coalition create events to heighten visibility to the problem and pressure authorities into action. They use dramatic symbols, some of them quasi-religious, and occasions: Public Día de los Muertos/Day of the Dead altars in October and November, to mourn and remember the victims; International Women's Month/Day (March), and V-Day (February) events to march against violence; violence against women (Latin America) day in late November. The colours and icons are pink and black, contrasting a crucifix-shaped cross and its background. At the downtown international border crossing bridge, a large wooden crucifix sits on which nails are hammered with names of the victims.

Drawing on existent informal binational cooperation, in 2002, Coalition members called attention to police cooperation over stolen vehicles. When a stolen car is reported in El Paso, police authorities immediately coordinate with their counterparts in Juárez. Coalition members wondered publicly, over and over: If police can cooperate over stolen cars, why cannot they cooperate over murdered girls and women? El Paso political representatives at the city and county levels unanimously voted for an anti-violence resolution and its relative low-cost binational police cooperation. The *cabildo* in Juárez, a partisan council, is relatively closed to agenda setting and public participation.

In 2003, after a series of marches, El Paso Mayor Caballero, Police Chief Leon, and their counterparts in Juárez held a press conference to announce binational cooperation over training and an international 800-tip line into the El Paso Police Department, with assistance from the FBI. Of course, systemic changes like these are delicate matters, treading on national sovereignty issues. Moreover, with alleged police complicity with the murders, activists are understandably ambivalent about police involvement.

Coalition activities are planned through face-to-face meetings and speedy listserv dissemination. Participants identify targets of opportunity, such as resolutions in City and County bodies, to educate the community. Under two El Paso mayoral administrations, council members voted unanimously for largely symbolic resolutions against the violence and in favour of call for binational cooperation, resolutions difficult to oppose. The Coalition also worked with State Senator Eliot Shapleigh and Representative Norma Chávez who introduced and negotiated passage for a resolution in the Texas legislature, complete with April 2003 hearings in Austin, at which Coalition testimony was given. The state legislature in Chihuahua City consists of 30 deputies, three of whom are women who each belong to one of the three major parties (the PRI, the PAN, and the left-of-center PRD). While the women across partisan lines agree on the need for action, the issue is not a high legislative priority and three legislators among 30 have never amounted to a majority. State legislative deputies exercise little oversight of the state government, including the judicial police. Coalition efforts to encourage the business community and Maquiladora Association to pressure government have not been successful, although the business community concedes that Juárez's tarnished image probably discourages investment.

During the summer of 2003, the Mexico Solidarity Committee networked with the Coalition and the Washington Office on Latin America to facilitate a US Congressional delegation to visit Juárez, to meet with victims' families, including the mother of a disappeared US national (from El Paso), officials, and NGO activists. Congresswoman Hilda Solis (Democrat, Los Angeles) led a delegation to Juárez with representatives from Chicago, San Antonio, Tucson, and El Paso. They visited sites inside the city and at the desert periphery where multiple bodies had been found, and pink-coloured wooden crosses were erected to mourn their memory. Amnesty International released a 70-page monograph detailing human rights abuses and police corruption (2003). In November, 2003, another Congressional delegation followed, focused on NAFTA; Amigos de las Mujeres briefed them on the murders. The media on both sides of the border and from afar engaged in frenzied-like attention. Elites and officials in Juárez periodically express outrage at their city's image internationally, although they no longer publicly blame the murder victims as was common during the 1990s. However, Governor Martínez dismissed the activists as exaggeration, citing average murder rates (not genderdisaggregated) in other cities in Mexico and the United States. Others wonder about the inattention to men's murders, killed at higher rates than women, but often execution style, leading people to conclude that drug cartels are to blame for deals gone bad.

Coalition activists prize networking at the local, binational metropolitan, national, and international levels, while maintaining personal contact with activists who work with anti-violence counseling centers and victims' mothers in Ciudad Juárez (for the binational "digital divide" is even greater across border and class lines between Mexico and the United States than within the United States). Networking through cyber activism has an anarchic quality that allows speedy response among those who may have only tenuous, virtual relationships.

In both 2002 and 2003, Coalition activists organized marches that brought activists together at the international border, with hundreds crossing into Juárez. Journalists covered the murders and events, including papers from Mexico City, New York, Los Angeles, Washington, D.C., and European cities. Border activists had invested considerable labour in speaking to visiting journalists and researchers. Playwright Eve Ensler, famous for authoring the *Vagina Monologues* and authorizing its performance for fund-raising around violence, named Esther Chávez Cano, who heads Casa Amiga, an anti-violence counseling center in Juárez, one of "21 International Leaders for the 21st Century." Her involvement shifted the networking process to a whole new level.

Ensler visited Juárez on V-Day, 2003, for a protest at the Juárez office of the State Attorney General. Several universities later held conferences on the issue, including UCLA's "Maquiladora Murders" conference from October 31 through Day of the Dead. The conference attracted 1000 participants, including a New York-based cyber activist who broadcast the conference on the Internet and organized a Floodnet of Mexican government agencies, inducing the Mexican Consulate in Los Angeles to respond with a lengthy fax authorizing a series of coordinating committees. Congresswoman Solis, leader of the October delegation, spoke at the conference. At this writing, resolutions associated with resources to assist in DNA testing and technology testing have been introduced in both the US House and Senate with more than a hundred co-signers and bipartisan support. Similar activities occurred in Mexico City, putting pressure on the federal government. After lengthy delays, PAN President Fox finally appointed special prosecutors at the federal level to investigate what had heretofore been defined as a state and local problem. Special Prosecutor Guadalupe Morfín issue a report in June 2004 linking the murders to the social climate of poverty and inadequate municipal infrastructure.

V-Day 2004 produced a crescendo of international visibility, with Eve Ensler and entertainers from Mexico City and Hollywood performing Ensler's *Vagina Monologues*, with a new monologue on the Juárez murders, to huge audiences in Juárez, El Paso, and over a thousand cities around the world. A cross-border solidarity march was organized, the largest ever in El Paso–Juárez history, drawing from 5000–8000 crossers from local to distant locales. Ensler was present at the University of Texas at El Paso *Vagina Monologues* performance, with a 1200-person audience that honored four Coalition women, one of them a university student, as "vagina warriors." Language like this, and VMonologues' celebration of female sexuality, does not always resonate well with some of the NGOs in Juárez, especially those that represent the murder victims' mothers. Yet the size of the events set frenzied precedents. Layers of networked activists, grounded at the border with national and international visitors, created a crescendo that was difficult to match, especially with limited response from governments. To sustain commitment over time, organizations, whether cross-border or not, need "wins," or the achievement of concrete goals.

As a loose network, the Coalition draws creative political energy from a variety of sources, all maintaining the constant pressure on governments, primarily Mexico, to respond. Cristina, talk-show host on Latin America's Spanish UNIVISION television network, (equivalent to Oprah Winfrey in the United States), interviewed victims' mothers and activists. TV Azteca, a privately owned station telecasting from Mexico City across Mexico to Juárez (and El Paso), broadcast a soap opera from July 5–9, 2004, translated to "As Infinite as the Desert," focused on a fictitious family, murder victims, police disdain and complicity, yet running script from Federal Prosecutor Morfín's report at the bottom of the screen. After it ended, some argued that the story was over, while others said TV Azteca bowed to pressure from Juárez elites to cancel the show.

Loose networking among activists in scattered locations, at the border and far from it, has not surprisingly produced misunderstandings, defensiveness, and competition over accountability: who is and should be authorized to speak about the murders and domestic violence generally? Who is and should be authorized to strategize over solutions? And who profits from the pain of victims' mothers? Funds are generated both locally and afar in amounts people only speculate about, but the allocation process is not transparent. One NGO in Juárez diminished to a handful of activists, seized whatever opportunity possible to criticize Ensler, Mexico City and Hollywood celebrities for disrespect and broadening the agenda to violence against women generally rather than the murders alone. New York-based activists criticize localism or align themselves with some NGOs against others, without deep knowledge of the local terrain. Capital-city-based organizers behaved, some thought, like *chilangos/as* (arrogant know-it-alls), whether they worked in the capital cities of Mexico City or Washington, D.C.. Electronic communication, if cryptic and culturally insensitive, sparked a bitterness all its own, leading to rude emails and ugly exchanges. Some activists deleted, rather than read messages. In these difficult circumstances, the Coalition operates carefully, trying to maintain bridges with all groups, in a contested terrain.

The successes of the anti-violence movement have been remarkable, but may stem in part from its dramatic character. Economic inequality at borders generates no comparable interest to murders. Public awareness has been heightened, issues have been framed, and gender agendas have been set. But little concrete change occurred in law enforcement. Several men have been convicted, the first Abdel Latif Sharif Sharif, an Egyptian national, but he died in jail. The murders continue.

Cross-border activism needs to move to another level, one that produces more than awareness-raising activity. Will the organizing move to another stage, beyond movement activism to strategic decision-making in a binational or single-side-of-the-border governing coalitions? Stage II organizing would go beyond awareness to strategic actions and decisions that could reduce, hopefully end the deaths and address the widespread climate of tolerance of both violence and poverty at the border. Despite the 1.5 million population of Juárez, the government supports and funds no battered women's shelter. Domestic violence is hardly taken seriously, as state law requires independent witnesses and physical scars to last more than 15 days for cases to be adjudicated. Although impressive national laws have been passed, through feminist coalitions in civil society and across partisan lines in Congress (Rodríguez 2003: 170), legal change and action are necessary in Mexico's states and municipalities in this federal system, deep in the bowels of bureaucracy. Existing polices and new policies require the political will and budgetary resources necessary to change implementation and administration, with the continuation of civil society pressure. The activities involve deepening democracy at and across borders. Meanwhile, the consolidation of a global neoliberal agenda, coupled with conservative ideological controls over strategic places in federal governance, does little to enhance corporate social responsibility, require living wage-levels for the minimum wage, or address the social needs of the majority-poverty population in Juárez. Such policies would appear to require challenge rather than withdrawal from the political process.

Juárez activists have been reluctant to engage with state and municipal government, campaigns, and elections. While frequent complaints have been made to Mexico's National Commission on Human Rights, the Commission issues strong reports, but has no enforcement authority. Activists' reluctance to engage in the electoral political process stems from past and present co-optation and government manipulations. Through co-optation, government hires or appoints critics whose voice is then muted. Through manipulation, government sows seeds of division among likely allies and undermines the credibility of individuals and groups. Mexico is hardly unique in engaging in such practices, highly destructive to civil society.

A case in point involves former anti-violence activist, Vicky Caraveo. PRI Governor Martínez (1998–2004) appointed Caraveo to the Instituto Chihuahuense de la Mujer (ICHIMU) for the State of Chihuahua, a form of "women's machinery in government" that extends from national to state levels. At the national level, the Instituto Nacional de la Mujer (ES: INMUJER) has been a powerful voice for agenda setting and reports on women, although its guidance under President Fox comes from PAN appointees (Rodríguez 2003). Caraveo recruited a group of victims' mothers and provided them with stipends, a reproduction of the ways once-critical voices are muted. ICHIMU's budget, reputed at US$400,000, has no transparency. NGOs participate in no councils to advise or prioritize the Institute's programs. Elsewhere in the world, women's machineries, including femocrat activism in Australia, have been "insider" tools to secure greater government accountability to women (Alvarez 1997, on Brazil). To be effective, however, insider activism must be coupled with "outsider" representation and civil society oversight. In Juárez, NGOs have been silent on this issue, disgusted and cynical about state-level women's machinery.

During the summer 2004 elections for governor (a six-year term) of Chihuahua, NGOs avoided engagement with campaigns and elections. In the Mexican constitution, there is a "no-succession" principle, a relief for anti-violence activists, given Governor Martínez's disinterest in the murders. However, the PRI won the election. The odd-bedfellow coalition of PAN and PRD gave attention to the violence in party platforms and campaign speeches, yet that party coalition had no comparable campaign money equivalent to the PRI. When governor-elect Reyes Baeza made the ICHIMU appointment, it was unclear to whom he went for advice or recruitment pools. Anti-violence activists were likely left out, and if there is no consultation or budgetary transparency, ICHIMU may become mere bureaucratic decoration, lacking dedication to issues important to various constituencies.

Another case in point involves divisions among NGOs, largely over fund-raising and allocations. Activists need resources to raise resources, but if their accounting practices are not transparent, suspicions may be raised. Past accounts suggest that activists generate informal earnings through their leadership (Staudt 1998; Gaspar de Alba 2003), a practice institutionalized among many national and international NGOs that need operational and staff budgetary support. A quarter to a third of Mexico's workforce generates money informally, and entrepreneurial hard work is a US–Mexico border trademark. Fund-raising for the victims' families occurs not only at the border, but all over the world. On various university campuses, feminist activists raise money and send it to groups with track records and accountability, including Casa Amiga, an anti-violence counseling organization, and Amigos de las Mujeres de Juárez. Some groups get funds, and others do not, leading to resentment and exclusion. The government and media have put extensive efforts into 'investigating' the sources of 'foreign' funds, alleging corruption. In May, 2004, local television stations in Juárez aired a series on this topic, and Juárez newspapers ran these stories, especially the Diario de Juárez, the largest newspaper, reputedly aligned with the PRI and self-acknowledged recipient of the equivalent of millions of US dollar equivalents from Mexico state and municipal government advertising revenue. Anti-violence activists and victims' family members would rather the government investigated the murders.

Thankfully, fund-raising continues, for activists need resources, victims' families must bury their dead and deal with grief, and shelter must be offered to battered women through private fund-raising since the government allocates no funds for shelters. Casa Amiga has recently opened a shelter, but it holds a mere 10 families. The government provides no funding for battered women's shelters. But the entrepreneurial, even hustling spirit continues: flyers at the Juárez airport around V-Day, 2004, offering "macabre tours" (where bodies have been found); Save Juárez, a patronizing name for a California-based organization claiming tax-exempt status, is a church front seeking a quarter million dollars for women's self-defense training in Juárez. Garage sales evoke the victims and their families to generate customers. Such actions cheapen the tragedy and undermine legitimate activity.

Meanwhile, the victims' families, from modest economic backgrounds, challenge, wait, and wonder about the kind of governments and economies that fail to respond to them. Journalists come from all over the world, wanting testimony for fresh stories, but after repeating stories over and over, many family members are reluctant to relive the pain. One television reporter from a small European country proposed that the Coalition help establish contact with a victim's family, preferably with the victim's sister working in a *maquiladora*, who would allow a cameraman in their house for a week to film them. Although the few minutes aired might make an interesting story across the Atlantic, what good would it do for those grounded at borders, seeking solutions from intransigent governments in their regional terrain? At the five-year anniversary of their daughter's death, the Dutch family came to Juárez in September 2004 with a television cameraman, hoping to follow up on the investigation. The police said the records were misplaced or lost.

Conclusions

This chapter has addressed the common interests that people share at borderlands along with the difficulties organizing solutions to common problems, given the multiple governments and obstacles to cross-border organizing. In the body of the chapter, analysis focused on cross-border organizing around the extensive violence against women, resulting in the murders of hundreds of girls and women over a decade. Border activists are grounded: they know the terrain, the details, and strategic players and decision points. They are personal, often friends, who have face-to-face relationships of trust with one another, despite the obstacles that a borderline presents. However, their visibility, resources, and tools are limited unless they are networked with other NGOs at the national and international levels.

At the US–Mexico border, ties with other networks generated great strength with multiple pressures and means to address the problems of violence. But these ties were weak and impersonal, expanding, neigh exploding in their potential. Weak-tied individuals took actions that sometimes only tenuously tied to the purpose and people around which cross-border organizing occurred. In some reports, Mexico is demonized along with Juárez, mystified as an evil locale of corrupt and violent people, rather than the complex, multi-faceted near-global city that it is. There is tension and ambivalence in the connection between border and non-border transnational activists, for their standpoints diverge and their stakes in the issue range from up close and personal to distant and abstract. Border activists live with continual murders; cyber transnational activists do not.

Analysis also emphasized the shortcomings of movement-oriented networking for awareness-raising alone. Much energy has been invested in process, but the outcomes have been meager: an international 800-tip phone line, symbolic resolutions, coordinating committees, new appointees who are occasionally mere bureaucratic decoration. A few "heads roll" (i.e. political appointees are replaced or corrupt police officers discharged), but the systemic inattention to violence continues. Stage II organizing requires comparable support for local, border resources and staff that existing global, national, and local governance, commerce, and even some international NGOs enjoy. Above all, borderlands require professional law enforcement that includes and prioritizes violence against women, respect for human rights, and living wages.

And who or what are the targets of the concrete and systematic changes necessary for Stage II actions? The analysis in this chapter suggests that while global governance allows rules and ideological frameworks that transform women into casualties of violence and cheap labour, it is national and subnational governments that can and should make change. At borderlands, with their peculiar local politics that join two or more sovereign countries at the hip, accountable regional governance is in order.

More research is necessary at borders in all their glorious varieties, from alienated to co-existent, interdependent, and integrated models. If transnational organizing at the UN, capital city, or cyber levels is to have more meaning and impact on policy and implementation decisions and outcomes, it needs to connect with and understand the standpoints of stakeholders and activists at borders and local terrains. Academics could devote great energy to connecting their analysis to action and practice. To do so, they must learn organizing and political skills, hardly the stuff of most graduate training. Staudt and Coronado (2005b) have called for a kind of feminism that engenders responsibility and commitment to the people and issues studied.

Transnational organizing and networking create the appearance that tools are readily available to address the ways women's human rights have been undermined. Global level acceptance of principles may have little bearing on national or regional enforcement and implementation, including staff and resources therefore. Surely extensive violence and serial murders would be enveloped in human rights discourse and annual reports. Mexico's Instituto Nacional de las Mujeres prepared a 303-page compilation of the principal instruments of women's human rights (INMUJER 2004). Its five-year, post-1995 Beijing synthesis is a beautifully packaged document that addressed the Fifth Principle, Violence Against Women (though no mention of the Juárez murders is found therein). Mexico ratified the international convention that would eliminate "all forms" of discrimination against women (CEDAW) in 1981. Internationally, and in many countries, formal laws and reports operate at far distance from implementation and practice. Political will is necessary to enforce the laws, and status-quo bureaucrats rarely act on their own to address embarrassing and outrageous human violations without the push from civil society. Transnational, cross-border activists and academics have key roles to play in making symbolic laws real, but that involves real, concrete organizing on the ground over sustained time periods.

Notes

1. Governance refers to the rules, institutions, games, and decisions in public and private market spheres. For the last two decades, international institutions have focused on "good governance," although meanings differ. The World Bank and International Monetary Fund seem to privilege stable, efficient, and honest contexts for business and contractual negotiations. The US Agency for International Development emphasizes political characteristics, such as elections (www.usaid.gov). Feminists would do well to incorporate professional, honest law enforcement, safety from domestic violence and murder, human rights law and *enforcement*, and "living wages" at borders into notions of good governance, as implied in this chapter. In the United States, living wages refer to wages with health benefits that more adequately cover the cost of living. Over a hundred local governments in the United States have passed living-wage ordinances that require businesses that contract with government to pay a living wage. El Paso is not one of them. Living wages generally amount to 2–3 times the legal minimum wage (www.livingwagecampaign.org). The living wage concept can and should be transnational.
2. While men and women earn the legal minimum wage in *maquiladoras*, there is increasing evidence that the diversification of Juárez *maquiladoras* and the flight of some to China with its extremely low-cost labour has been a *gendered* labour segmentation; women are relegated to bottom-level jobs and pay. See selections in Kopinak, 2004. Drawing on Census data, Romero and Yellen report that Hispanic women earn 37 percent of Anglo men's wages in El Paso (2004). In Staudt's study of informal economies at the US–Mexico border (1998), men earned approximately twice of women's earnings even through informal means, with the relatively lucrative cross-border buying and selling of goods and services. (Drug trade questions were not included in the research.)
3. According to the Inter-Parliamentary Union (www.ipu.org), consulted in September 2004, women make up 23 percent of Mexico's lower house and 16 percent of its upper (the Senate). In the United States, comparable figures are 14 and 13 percent.
4. According to Article 33 of the 1917 Constitution, foreigners should in no way get involved in the political affairs of the country. *Los extranjeros no podrán de ninguna manera immiscuirse en los asuntos políticos del país.*
5. This research is based on participant observation for three years in the Coalition, field notes, documents, electronic communication/listservs, television and newspaper clippings. Thanks to Irasema Coronado, co-chair of the Coalition, with whom I have co-authored several papers and a book and shared many conversations. Thanks also to Research Assistants including Alejandra Martínez Márquez and Gabriela Leticia Montoya.

11
Transforming Global Governance: Challenges and Opportunities

Georgina Waylen

Introduction

The purpose of the last chapter of this book is twofold. It will not only assess the evidence and arguments presented in the rest of the book but in so doing it will reflect upon the opportunities for and limitations to the transformation of global governance for feminists. As we have seen from many of the contributions, there is ample evidence that governance regimes also reflect and construct gendered processes of power (Prügl 1999, 2004). Both understanding and transforming these regimes is therefore central to any feminist project of lessening gender inequality. But there are serious questions to be answered about the extent to which changing global rules and international bureaucracies can be a potential source of improving levels of women's equality. And if these can be changed, what strategies should be used and what are the potential results of such a transformation?

There is no consensus among feminist scholars about the extent to which the transformation of global governance is possible, what form it should take, and indeed to what ends global governance could and should be transformed. Some have voiced the now familiar scepticism that it is not possible to 'use the master's tools to transform the master's house' (Staudt 1998), while others have developed strategies of engagement with the institutions of global governance. The sceptics would argue that engagement with global governance institutions will inevitably lead to the co-optation of feminist agendas and will cement gender hegemony, whereas others argue that there is evidence of the real gains that can be achieved through engagement (often using strategies that fall under the rubric gender mainstreaming) and that the potential for further gains exists. But most feminists would agree that even if engagement is necessary, it can only be one strategy of transformation among many, rather than the solution to problems of gender inequality, as the transformation of institutions does not equate in any direct or simple way to the wider transformation of social relations. The chapters in this book reflect many of these debates and disagreements and have drawn on a wide range of sources to inform their analyses.

Despite the lack of consideration of gender issues in the mainstream governance literature pointed out by Shirin Rai in this book, this body of work has provided a useful starting point for our endeavour. We have seen, both in the mainstream literature and in the contributions to this book, that definitions of global governance are broad. It can encompass a range of global rules, regulations, regimes and institutions. Many mainstream analyses of global governance have usefully interrogated how global governance has developed, its fluid and changing nature, how it might link to the diminishing power of the nation state, and its relationship to globalization and to the rise of new global actors. But only some of this literature is concerned with changing and improving global governance either by enhancing global governance through improving its capacity or alternatively by refashioning and transforming it (Wilkinson 2005).

The little of this mainstream literature that has engaged seriously with transformation often sees transformation in a rather narrow sense as the incorporation of global social movements and bottom-up social change (Wilkinson 2005). Its focus is therefore on how global civil society can help to make global governance more democratic through its greater involvement and participation, rather than looking at how to fundamentally transform the ways in which institutions are organized (Scholte 2002).[1] As we have already seen in this book, one of the two major strands of the gender literature on governance to date has also focused primarily on one part of global civil society – women's movements and their efforts to influence a number of governance regimes – rather than on the question of transformation from the perspective of the institutions themselves (Meyer and Prügl 1999). But this chapter argues, in keeping with the analysis that runs through all of this collection, that approaches that focus primarily on previously excluded groups are limited, as transformation requires more extensive change than simply increasing the influence of previously excluded groups within global institutions.

The heterogeneity and pluralism within this collection – recognized also as one of strengths of feminist scholarship overall – allows us to develop these broader analyses. The range of feminist analyses put forward by the contributors to this book utilize different methodological and theoretical approaches such as governmentality and institutionalism. As a result, their understandings of how different institutions of global governance are gendered is bound to vary. But perhaps unsurprisingly given that the stated aims of the book are to understand global governance institutions from a gendered perspective and to move away from a bias towards the actions of women actors organizing in movements outside of institutions, different kinds of feminist institutionalist analysis are predominant. But these are also sensitive to the importance of agency and the diverse roles played by a range of actors both inside and outside institutions of global governance.

The chapters demonstrate the extent of the gender-blindness of the existing mainstream analyses of many of these institutions, showing how they often act to reinforce patterns of gender inequality at the global level. But the heterogeneity of these different institutions of global governance is also striking. They do not all act in the same way. For example, the gender regimes, the way issues are framed and the functioning of the institutions of the United Nations family differs considerably from the international financial and trading institutions. The contrasting examples of the case studies of the International Criminal Court (ICC), World Bank and the European Union in this book have demonstrated yet again how different global institutions and regimes vary considerably and institutions are not homogeneous and monolithic. Individual institutions themselves are often made up of complex and sometimes contradictory structures. Broad generalizations are therefore difficult to make and detailed research is necessary for any comprehensive understanding.

But feminist perspectives are, of course, about more than developing gendered analyses; developing strategies for change that derive from those analyses is also a central task. The chapters in this collection have shown that any feminist analysis that sees gender as fundamentally constitutive of these global processes and institutions must itself interrogate more profoundly what is meant by the transformation of global governance. If institutions construct as well as reflect power relations, then in order to transform them more is necessary than just incorporating previously excluded actors. The chapters have shown that we need to focus on changing the governance regimes and institutions themselves as well as the ways in which they operate. These regimes and institutions are not fixed and immutable and some possibilities for change exist. We therefore need to have a good understanding of the ways in which institutions of global governance and their rules operate in gendered ways in order to see how they could be made to become more open to gender concerns and as a result more democratic, transparent and accountable to different groups of women regardless of their race, location or class position.

This concluding chapter therefore also takes an avowedly institutionalist perspective, and in line with the growing body of work being identified as 'feminist institutionalism', understands institutional analysis as fundamentally concerned with the interaction between institutions and actors and accepts that different institutions will present actors with different opportunities and challenges. But it recognizes that, although they are linked, the transformation of institutions and their practices is not the same as the transformation of wider social relations.

Therefore, as the previous chapters have demonstrated, analysing the transformation of global governance is not just question of looking at either strategies emanating from inside institutions such as gender mainstreaming implemented as a technocratic policy doctrine or at the activities of women's movements outside institutions as separate entities. In this vein any analysis of actors must also include the actions of 'sympathetic insiders' (or gender policy entrepreneurs as they are sometimes called) within those institutions as well as any alliances that exist between 'insiders' and 'outsiders' and the ways in which both can interact together. Here again it is important to recognize the complexity and diversity of institutions, the issue areas they are involved in, and the very different opportunities they can present. We therefore have to be more specific about the particular nature of the relationships between different institutions and actors, namely about the relationship between structure and agency. Furthermore because the political opportunity structure varies in different institutional contexts, actors (both insiders and outsiders) adopt different strategies in different contexts with different ways of framing issues and their actions have different outcomes.

The primary aim of this chapter therefore is not to answer the question: how can women's movements successfully influence international organizations but how can global governance be transformed along gender lines? As such, the starting point will be that strand of the gender literature that we have already encountered in the many chapters in this collection that have a directly institutional focus. We have seen in a large number of the preceding chapters (Cohn, Chappell, True, Hoskyns) that a range of different actors operating within different global governance regimes, including trade, economic governance, human rights and security, have heralded gender mainstreaming as the most influential potential strategy for transforming global governance. This concluding chapter therefore offers an opportunity to draw this material together and to reflect in some detail not only on the meaning of gender mainstreaming but also on its potential as a strategy for change in different global institutional contexts.

The chapter will begin with an overview of the gender mainstreaming literature to set the experiences described elsewhere in this book in the context of the general debates on gender mainstreaming. To extend the analysis of these key themes, I will contrast the developments in two different areas of global governance. I will explore the global human rights regime associated with the UN system that forms the background to the experiences discussed in Cohn's and Chappell's chapters and compare it with the World Bank – as a central part of the global economic regime originally established at Bretton Woods – that underlies Bedford's chapter. The changes achieved in the global human rights regime with regard to gender rights and domestic violence are often seen as a successful transformation of one aspect of global governance. This is in stark contrast to economic governance where fewer positive gender outcomes have been identified. Finally, building on Chappell's analysis of the ICC (considered a relative success), I will briefly consider how far the creation of new institutions and rules can offer opportunities for the creation of more gender-sensitive institutions. I will then be in a position to draw some more general conclusions about the challenges and opportunities that exist for the transformation of global governance and the extent to which gender mainstreaming can provide a successful strategy of transformation. This chapter will therefore reinforce the findings of the preceding chapters and show how complex an undertaking transformation is. It will also argue that although there is no one blue print for change, it is possible to discern some general themes relevant to a range of diverse contexts. The chapter will therefore pull together the conclusions of the other contributions to the book not only about the gendered analyses of global governance, but also about the contribution of those analyses to attempts to effect its transformation.

Institutional strategies: gender mainstreaming

Gender mainstreaming has been the most common label used to describe almost any institutional gender strategy employed to change aspects of global governance in both the contributions to this book and in the wider literature. Indeed Sylvia Walby (2005a: 464) argues 'that gender mainstreaming is a leading edge example of the potential implications of globalization for gender politics' as it often draws on transnational processes and involves transnational networks. The term has been adopted by academics as well as practitioners and as a result has been used both analytically and descriptively to refer to the majority of strategies implemented to get gender concerns taken more seriously in institutions, whether on a national, regional or global level. But as a result of its varying and widespread usage there is no consensus or clarity about gender mainstreaming's potential, and indeed whether efforts to implement gender mainstreaming have been a success or failure to date. Sylvia Walby (2005b) has even termed gender mainstreaming an essentially contested concept and practice. But in addition to the large number of empirically based studies that describe various efforts to introduce gender mainstreaming in different contexts, there is now a growing body of literature that considers the more theoretical issues surrounding gender mainstreaming (Squires 2005; Walby 2005a,b). Informed by this work, we will now consider the different meanings of the term 'gender mainstreaming', how and why it has been adopted and with what impact. We will then be in a position to consider our case studies.

Most commentators do agree on what is meant by gender mainstreaming, citing either the definition adopted by ECOSOC in 1997 or that of the Expert Group commissioned by the Council of Europe in 1998. For ECOSOC:

Mainstreaming a gender perspective is the process of assessing the implications for women and men of any planned action, including legislation, policies or programmes, in all areas and all levels. It is a strategy for making women's as well as men's concerns and experiences an integral dimension of the design, implementation, monitoring and evaluation of policies and programmes in all political, economic and societal spheres so that men and women benefit equally and inequality is not perpetuated. The ultimate goal is to achieve gender equality.

(Cited in Charlesworth 2005: 4 and Moser 2005: 577)

In a similar vein the Council of Europe defines gender mainstreaming as

the (re)organization, improvement, development and evaluation of policy processes, so that a gender equality perspective is incorporated in all policies at all levels and at all stages, by the actors normally involved in policy making.

(Cited in Hafner-Burton and Pollack 2002: 342)

Disagreements then emerge over the interpretations of these definitions and the significance that can be attached to gender mainstreaming. The greatest controversy centres on whether gender mainstreaming is 'integrationist', 'agenda-setting' or 'transformative' (Jahan 1995; Rees 1998; Rai 2003). Namely does gender mainstreaming simply introduce a gender perspective without challenging the existing policy paradigm and therefore can be promoted instrumentally on the basis that the adoption of gender mainstreaming will enable other policy goals to be achieved more easily and efficiently? Or does gender mainstreaming result in more profound change – transforming and re-orientating existing policy paradigms, prioritizing gender equality and changing decision-making processes (Walby 2005b: 323)? In an extension of these debates, gender mainstreaming has then been interpreted as either a technocratic policy tool or more far-reachingly as an important feminist strategy (and sometimes as both simultaneously). Moser (2005: 577), for example, sees it as a twin track strategy attempting to increase both gender equality within institutions and women's empowerment through increasing women's participation in decision-making processes.

Each of these differing interpretations has implications for the ways in which gender mainstreaming is implemented and by whom. If it is considered a technocratic doctrine or policy process, compatible with an integrationist interpretation, it can be implemented by the 'normal' policy actors (as was envisaged by the Council of Europe). However, if gender mainstreaming is associated with a transformative agenda, the process becomes more deliberative, requiring much greater participation and involvement by civil society thereby resulting in more fundamental change (Squires 2005). But others argue that it is possible to reconcile expertise and democracy. Walby (2005b) cites Woodward's 'velvet triangle' of academics, feminist bureaucrats and organized women, arguing that they can increase accountability by creating alliances that integrate networks outside institutions with actors inside those institutions. But as we will see when we consider how and why mainstreaming was adopted, gender mainstreaming has more frequently been understood as a technocratic doctrine to be implemented primarily by normal policy actors than a transformative strategy involving the resources of deliberative democracy.

The overall assessment of gender mainstreaming's potential and success as a strategy also varies tremendously, depending again in part on whether analysts have an integrationist or agenda-setting/transformative view of it. Sceptics, often adhering to a transformative view, claim that 'the strategy of gender mainstreaming has deployed the idea of gender in a very limited way and has allowed the mainstream to tame and derad-icalize claims to equality' (Charlesworth 2005: 2). Indeed Charlesworth believes that gender mainstreaming diverts attention from the ways in which gender inequality is a fundamental part of the international sys-tem and so a radical transformative strategy of mainstreaming would require more than allowing women into international institutions. But others – often coming from a more integrationist perspective – argue that the implementation of gender mainstreaming policies have achieved significant things and that engagement with these processes and insti-tutions is a necessity for feminists (True 2003: 368). Moser (2005), for example, cites seven principal achievements of gender mainstreaming that were identified by an Expert Group consultation on the Beijing Platform for Action and extend beyond simply institutional factors. These include greater awareness of gender inequality, the strengthen-ing of the capabilities and advocacy of women's organizations and women's machineries, legal reforms, as well as the collection of more sex disaggregated data.

Before we can form our own assessment of the transformative poten-tial of gender mainstreaming, we need to examine its emergence and implementation. Gender mainstreaming first permeated the work of the UN when it appeared at the third Women's Conference in Nairobi in 1985 and then appeared in EU parlance in 1991 (Charlesworth 2005: 3, Pollack and Hafner-Burton 2000: 435). It received widespread exposure when it featured in the Beijing Platform for Action adopted at the Fourth World Conference for Women in 1995 and governments and other actors were exhorted to 'promote an active and visible policy of mainstream-ing a gender perspective in all policies and programmes' (Charlesworth 2005: 3). But prior to its prominence in the Beijing platform for Action, gender mainstreaming had been growing in importance in the develop-ment sphere for some years. In the context of shift from the liberal WID (Women in Development) approach to GAD (Gender and Development), gender mainstreaming was identified as a mechanism that could help to ensure that all development policies were more relevant to women. WID had focused primarily on integrating women into existing devel-opment strategies, often in women-only projects; whereas the new GAD approach focused on the impact of relations between women and men on development and therefore on altering development practice as a whole.

After the 1995 Beijing Women's Conference, gender mainstreaming was soon adopted by a large number of organizations in the interna-tional arena, including organizations closely associated with the United

Nations such as UNDP and UNESCO, as well as the World Bank, ILO and the WHO. Multilateral and bilateral development agencies such as CIDA and IDB as well as other regional organizations such as the OSCE and the Commonwealth also endorsed mainstreaming. The European Union itself adopted gender mainstreaming in 1996 and much of the subsequent analysis of gender mainstreaming has been done in the context either of development policies overseen by international institutions or of EU policies. Therefore only a decade after the Beijing women's conference, mainstreaming as a doctrine had been widely endorsed at the international, regional and even national levels (Rai 2003).

Why had this happened apparently relatively easily and quickly? Commentators have pointed to a number of factors that enabled the adoption of gender mainstreaming in global institutions (Pollack and Hafner-Burton 2000; True and Mintrom 2000; Hafner-Burton and Pollack 2002; True 2003). All stress the important role played by women's advocacy. Without the actions of organized women, gender mainstreaming would not have become widespread. Jacqui True (2003) identifies three factors that were crucial in allowing a range of actors to successfully advocate for the adoption of gender mainstreaming: discursive change, for example allowing women's rights to be framed as part of human rights discourses; transnational networking by women's organizations; and gender policy entrepreneurs acting within global institutions. In a similar vein, Hafner-Burton and Pollack (2002), using social movement theory, argue that favourable political opportunity structures – namely in institutions with relatively open input structures, together with suitable mobilizing structures and the strategic framing of issues – enabled gender mainstreaming to become widespread.

However, as Caroline Moser (2005) argues, formally adopting gender mainstreaming or even having gender policies in place is not the same as actually implementing them. Far-reaching agreements on gender equality have been sanctioned at various regional and international conferences and the terminology of gender equality and mainstreaming is now widely used (Friedman 2003; Moser 2005). But in order to assess the impact of gender mainstreaming, we first have to see what has actually happened in practice before being able to make a final judgement about how far gender mainstreaming has either worked in its own terms or can be transformative. In their empirically based analysis of gender mainstreaming, Moser and Moser (2005) argue that the robust monitoring and evaluation of policies is necessary in order to assess its implementation. Moser (2005: 584) outlines three concepts that can be operationalized to do this. It is necessary to evaluate the extent to which: first evaporation (a situation where positive policy intentions are not followed through in practice); second invisibilization (where what happens on 'the ground' is not captured by monitoring and evaluation procedures); and finally resistance (where essentially political opposition creates mechanisms that block gender mainstreaming) occur. Using this framework, Moser claims that far more has been achieved in the initial stages of adopting the terminology and creating the policies than in the subsequent stages of implementing or evaluating gender mainstreaming.

Confirming the findings outlined in many of the chapters in this book, most analysts agree that the implementation and outcomes of gender mainstreaming strategies is very variable. It differs between institutions, policy domains and divergent circumstances. Mirroring Hoskyn's arguments in this book, Pollack and Hafner-Burton (2000), for example, detail significant differences in adoption and implementation between five issue areas of EU policy. Therefore before we can make any overall assessment of gender mainstreaming as the most important strategy adopted to gender global governance to date, we need to consider how its adoption and implementation has fared in different contexts, considering the different political opportunity structures, how issues are framed, the roles of actors inside and outside those institutions. Building on the evidence presented already, we will consider the fate of gender mainstreaming in two contrasting contexts to help to develop our argument. Then we will be in a better position to make a judgement about how transformative it has been as a strategy.

Engendering the global human rights regime

The gendering of the global human rights regime (including the security issues and the ICC discussed by Cohn and Chappell) has been seen as the prime example of successful gender mainstreaming at the international level. According to the conventional wisdom, gender issues were incorporated into human rights thinking because of the activities of international women's movements operating primarily but not exclusively at a range of international conferences, particularly those held in the 1990s (Kelly 2005). However, sceptics argue that although the language of gender mainstreaming is now widely deployed throughout the international human rights regime, the actual implementation of gender mainstreaming has been disappointing. And in spite of rhetorical changes and new policy commitments, gender has remained marginal (Riddell-Dixon 1999; Charlesworth 2005). Perhaps understandably most of the literature that has looked at changes to the human rights regime has focused on the initial stages of women's activism and the process of gendering the human rights agenda, often from the perspective of social movement theory (Friedman 1994; Weldon 2006). Much less work has considered what has happened to the implementation of this agenda and outcomes within the actual institutions. And therefore little has considered the extent to which the global governance of human rights has been transformed. In this section we will focus on both areas.

The adoption of the mainstreaming of women's rights within human rights discourses and the UN human rights regime is a major achievement of the international women's movement. The slogan 'women's rights are human rights' has become widely accepted and great strides have been made in ensuring that gender-based violence within the private sphere is considered as a human rights violation (Waylen 2004). Several analysts have detailed the processes by which the transnational women's rights movements developed as part of second wave feminism from the 1970s onwards. One key factor supporting this phase of the development of international women's networks was the international conferences associated with the United Nations system (Keck and Sikkink 1998). The transnational women's movement gathered momentum during the UN International Women's Decade (1975–1985). The three conferences that took place during that decade (Mexico City 1975, Copenhagen 1980 and Nairobi 1985) and the activities that took place around them served as the spur for the mobilizing and networking of large numbers of women (True 2003). The numbers of international women's NGOs grew exponentially as did women's international advocacy networks. Although there were divisions between women activists, particularly between Northern and Southern feminists, sufficient common ground existed, for example around issues of violence against women, to form alliances (Weldon 2006).

By the early 1990s, women's NGOs and networks had begun to move away from using the 'discrimination' frame embodied in CEDAW to a 'human rights' frame. Until then human rights bodies and treaties had paid little attention to women's rights and the public/private divide within rights discourses meant that many gender-specific violations could easily be ignored (Keck and Sikkink 1998). But facilitated by funding from a number of foundations, a women's human rights network that aimed to ensure that women's rights were integrated into the human rights agenda grew exponentially in the 1990s. A major organizing force, the Global Campaign for Women's Rights, consisting of 90 NGOs, was launched in 1990 (Clark *et al.* 1998) and it played a key role in the planning of the activities that centred on the preparations for the

World Conference on Human Rights to be held in Vienna in 1993. And in 1991, a global petition calling for the recognition of women's rights as human rights was initiated (Friedman 1995). After the Global Campaign organized satellite meetings and engaged with governments prior to the Vienna conference, a Women's Caucus co-ordinated lobbying efforts, made plenary presentations and organized a Tribunal during the NGO forum that highlighted human rights abuses endured by women globally (Keck and Sikkink 1998).

Largely as a consequence of these activities, the final document from Vienna had women's human rights mainstreamed throughout together with a section dealing with 'the equal status and human rights of women'. There were also recommendations for protecting women's human rights within old and new mechanisms (Friedman 2003). In addition, violence against women was firmly established as a human rights violation as the Vienna conference produced the 1993 Declaration on the Elimination of Violence against Women (Kelly 2005; Weldon 2006). These declarations were subsequently followed up by increasingly strong resolutions passed by various UN bodies including the Commission for Human Rights. In addition to the Commission on Human Rights' resolutions on integrating the rights of women throughout the UN system referring, for example, to gender sensitive guidelines, the Commission has also requested sex disaggregated data in reports, and that women-specific violations of human rights are addressed (Charlesworth 2005).

What are the explanations for this apparent success? The global women's movement was obviously very effective in its organizing around this issue. In comparison to global women's movements organized around a number of other issues, it managed to overcome potential internal divisions, it made effective alliances with other more mainstream human rights NGOs and received funding at important moments in its development. It also framed the issue of women's rights as human rights very strategically enabling the effective use of the human rights discourse. Finally the political opportunity structure was relatively favourable as the UN system, and the conferences, in particular, were relatively open enabling the global women's movement to lobby effectively over a range of different venues using a number of strategies.

There are far fewer accounts of the actual implementation of gender mainstreaming in the international human rights regime. But Riddell-Dixon (1999) and Charlesworth (2005) both detail what they see as the 'muted response' to gender mainstreaming that in practice has meant that little has been done to mainstream women's rights. The most comprehensive statement on gender mainstreaming policies was set out in the widely circulated Report of the Expert Group on the Development of Guidelines for the Integration of Gender Perspectives into Human Rights Activities and Programmes that Riddell-Dixon (1999) argues can be used as a yardstick with which to assess progress.[2] Using Moser's categories of evaporation, invisiblization and resistance, we can document how far these outcomes match up to these stated aims.

First both Charlesworth and Riddell-Dixon describe the ways in which policy intentions were not followed through in practice. No clear mandate was established within Office of the High Commissioner for Human Rights/Commission on Human Rights (HC and CHR) requiring the mainstreaming of women's rights (Riddell-Dixon 1999: 153). How far different committees implemented the policies therefore appeared to depend on the commitment of individual committee members and has often been done inconsistently even within the different committees themselves. For example, the Human Rights Committee which monitors the International Covenant on Civil and Political Rights only considered gender issues in some contexts and not others. Even when gender was raised as an issue, concerns were often limited to comments about the numbers of women in public life and the need for statistical information about women (Charlesworth 2005: 9). The composition of mainstream human rights bodies also remained very male-dominated as, despite commitments to increase female membership, few new women were included. So while women made up 40 per cent of the overall membership in 2004, most women (74 per cent) were on two committees: the Committee on the Elimination of Discrimination Against Women and the Committee on the Rights of the Child. The overall proportion of women on other mainstream committees was only 15 per cent (Charlesworth 2005: 7). Furthermore managerial and strategic level positions within the HC/CHR were occupied almost exclusively by men, and few women were appointed to 'mainstream' Special Rapporteur positions. As a result, there have been few notable and influential sympathetic insiders or gender 'policy entrepreneurs' active within the international human rights institutions.

Second, it has been hard to discern what has happened on the ground as there has been inadequate expertise to conduct gender-based analysis or monitoring and little training has been provided to improve skills. Widespread staff shortages have also detracted from the ability to undertake mainstreaming activities as well as their evaluation. The lack of co-ordination, information sharing and co-operation evident between different bodies has been further exacerbated by a failure to establish a focal point on women. Finally these technical problems and the lack of a policy mandate have been intensified by resistance to gender mainstreaming in some quarters. Charlesworth (2005: 10) argues that the reports of the 'mainstream' Special Rapporteurs on Human Rights demonstrate a resistance to gender mainstreaming or at best a misunderstanding of what it means, giving only brief and broad brush information. She also cites the example of the Committee on the Elimination of Racial Discrimination (which had only 2 women out of its 18 members) that was initially reluctant to refer to gender considerations in its reports. Indeed its Chairman stated in 1996 that directives to integrate gender into reports were 'fundamentally misconceived' (quoted in Charlesworth 2005: 8). Even when it did adopt a general recommendation on the gender-related dimensions of racial discrimination this was done in a desultory manner (Charlesworth 2005: 8). Overall there is evidence to suggest that a decision to implement mainstreaming in any aspect of human rights work is determined not by policy but personality (Riddell-Dixon 1999: 152). Not surprisingly, given the lack of 'sympathetic insiders' efforts have been limited and not very effective.

Therefore despite some apparent success – measured in terms of the widespread presence of the language of mainstreaming – institutional inertia and resistance has confined its impact to a rhetorical one (Charlesworth 2005: 16). We may debate the significance of this change in rhetoric and discursive framing but it is clear that, from both an integrationist and a transformative perspective, human rights institutions and governance regimes have not changed significantly. The achievement of a commitment to the mainstreaming of gender into human rights is therefore very different to its implementation as an effective strategy that has changed institutions and practices.

Engendering economic governance: the World Bank

There are some significant differences between the UN human rights regime and that part of the global economic regime embodied by the World Bank. Three in particular stand out: the different institutional context; the very different framing of the issues; and the absence of a coherent global women's movement organizing around the World Bank's activities. As a result few commentators have felt able to herald the success of global women's movements in getting gender integrated into the World Bank's concerns. At the same time the World Bank has, over the years, paid increasing attention to gender issues and formally adopted gender mainstreaming. Before we build on Bedford's analysis and examine the development of the World Bank's gender policies, exploring how they have been implemented in practice, it is useful to examine these three differences in some detail as they have broader implications for our understanding of the potential and limits of strategies of transformation.

The World Bank is a multi-lateral economic institution that was established at Bretton Woods in 1944. It has acted to provide finance, research and policy advice to developing countries. Its structures are relatively closed and hierarchical. Formal power lies with its owners – nation states who are represented by the board of governors and the executive board on which country representatives sit – and with the Bank's President and his top management team (Tzannatos 2006). In 2002, 94 per cent of the board of governors were men as were 91.7 per cent of its board of directors. As the United States is the largest donor and the World Bank is located in Washington, the United States also wields considerable influence over the institution. Despite this, the Bank is not monolithic and parts do retain some degree of autonomy (O'Brien *et al.* 2000). This structure, combined with the Bank's organizational culture, means that there are few entry points for outside actors such as NGOs to try to influence the Bank's activities (Hafner-Burton and Pollack 2002). As Bedford (this book) and others have argued, the dominant belief system at the World Bank is based on conventional economic analysis (Bergeron 2003). The policies that it advocates are framed in terms of micro-economics, and, for example, its structural adjustment policies of the 1980s are seen by many critics as a paradigmatic example of neo-liberal Washington Consensus. Even with emergence of a post-Washington Consensus that puts greater value on participation, good governance and stakeholding, the underlying commitment to market solutions remained dominant. Policies are justified primarily in terms of the business case and economic efficiency (or more recently 'Gender Equality as Smart Economics') rather than their contribution to human rights or equality for its own sake.

As a consequence of both the World Bank's structures and world-view, global women's movement activists have tended to have more interaction and contact with UN organizations based in part on greater shared beliefs and outlook as well as the differential relative openness of the structures and location of some friends in 'high places' according to Moghadam (2005). Indeed despite the relatively upbeat assessment of some scholars like Moghadam (2005) about levels of gender advocacy around global economic issues, it has not been possible to discern a coherent global women's movement actively trying to engage the World Bank on the same scale as the gender and human rights movement. O'Brien *et al.* (2000) argue that several additional factors mitigate against this. First, the divisiveness of the issues surrounding global economic justice in contrast to human rights mean that a common position among feminists from different backgrounds and regions is harder to achieve as class, racial and spatial divisions separate them. Second, in order to engage with the World Bank, activists need specialist knowledge and technical expertise in economic analysis that many women's NGOs lack. And finally because the World Bank is located in Washington, effective interaction requires greater interest and engagement from the US-based women's movement that has not been forthcoming to date. As a result the advocacy organizations that have emerged have often been relatively small, often dependent on a small number of individuals and not always very long-lived. Despite these differences, the World Bank has declared itself to be increasingly committed to gender equality and mainstreaming over the last thirty years. If it cannot be attributed primarily to the actions of organized women, how has this happened?

Writing in 2002, Hafner-Burton and Pollack identify three phases of Bank gender activity. The first phase began in 1977 when the Bank appointed its first WID Adviser who had few resources and no effective power (O'Brien *et al.* 2000). Located on the research and policy side her brief was to provide advice on WID issues throughout the Bank and defend its operations to the outside world rather than initiate policy or monitor bank activities effectively (Zuckerman and Qing 2005). But then, coinciding with the preparations for the Nairobi conference, the Bank's activities around gender increased in the mid-1980s. The first WID guidelines on gender were adopted in 1984, and in 1985 the office of the WID advisor was upgraded to a division with more staff and resources. The new advisor, appointed in 1986, oversaw the production of research that demonstrated the economic gains to be had from investing in women, for example, through healthcare or girls' education.

Tzannatos (2006) claims that the World Bank's emphasis on gender issues started to accelerate in the first half of the 1990s partly in preparation for the Beijing Conference. By the middle of the decade each region had funding for a WID co-ordinator or focal point in the regional offices and in 1994 the Bank produced its first official policy paper on gender *Enhancing Women's Participation in Development* (World Bank 1994). New operational policy also provided guidance on how to achieve women's enhanced participation and reduce gender disparities by integrating gender considerations (Hafner-Burton and Pollack 2002; Zuckerman and Qing 2005).

Therefore by the time of the Beijing Women's conference in 1995, the World Bank had already endorsed the adoption of some measures to mainstream gender in bank lending. Two further developments enhanced this process. First, the new World Bank president James

Wolfensohn appeared to take gender issues far more seriously to the extent that he has been called a gender policy entrepreneur (True 2003). He led the World Bank delegation at Beijing and partly as a result of consultation with civil society groups there set up an External Gender Consultative Group then comprised of 14 gender activists and academics from around the world (O'Brien *et al.* 2000).[3] Institutional change within the bank also followed. A GAD approach was formally adopted, gender and development activity was located in the Poverty Reduction and Economic Management (PREM) Technical Network and a Gender Sector Board was also set up.

Second, the Bank also came under increased pressure from external actors around the time of the Beijing conference. After Wolfensohn was presented with a letter with over 800 hundred signatures at Beijing, a number of women's groups formed a gender advocacy group, Women's Eyes on the Bank (WEOB), demanding increased participation by women in Bank policymaking, increased Bank investment in women, for example, in education, health, income generating and financial opportunities, and gender mainstreaming in all Bank policies and projects (Hafner-Burton and Pollack 2002; Long 2006). Although WEOB remained active in the United States and Latin America for the rest of the decade, the US campaign dissolved after four key individuals left their NGO jobs in 1999 (Long 2006). Since 2000, a couple of other small US-based advocacy NGOs, Women's Edge and Gender Action, have tried to focus some of their efforts on pressuring the World Bank (Long 2006).

The Bank's attention to gender has also continued since 2000. Indeed in 2001 the Bank produced *Engendering Development*, its first ever policy research report on gender. Synthesizing a large quantity of research, it argued that there are significant positive correlations between greater gender equality and higher levels of economic growth and reductions in poverty thereby endorsing the economic efficiency arguments for gender equality (World Bank 2001). It was followed in 2002 by a new gender strategy *Integrating Gender into the World Bank's Work: A Strategy for Action* endorsed by the Bank's directors. After laying out the business case for mainstreaming gender, it puts forward a range of strategies and tools such as the Country Gender Assessment (CGA) that could operationalize gender mainstreaming in practice (World Bank 2002b). These measures then should feed into the Country Assistance Strategies (CAS) and Poverty Reduction Strategy Papers (PRSPs) that now form the key to Bank lending. And a new four-year programme, Gender Equality as Smart Economics, began in 2007 (World Bank 2006b). The importance accorded to the integration of gender issues as well as the mechanisms to implement it into the World Bank's activities have therefore grown and changed over time. But it is a technocratic view of gender mainstreaming that has been adopted by the Bank, advocating the promotion of gender equality as a means of achieving other goals, primarily economic development.

Before we can reach a judgement about the transformative potential of the World Bank strategy, we need to assess its operation in practice. Have these ideas been widely implemented? Does the Bank achieve its own strategy targets? There are few analyses that deal with these questions but even in one that has been seen by some feminists like Bergeron (2004b) as sympathetic, Zuckerman and Qing (2005: 1) claim that 'while some progress has been made, success has been limited'. For example, the Bank now collects a range of gender disaggregated data and gender figures prominently on its website. However, if we use Moser's concept of evaporation, we can see that implementation has been inconsistent. Gender mainstreaming has at no time been made mandatory. Therefore while it is mandatory for Bank staff to assess the environmental impact of every operation, this is not the case for gender, and without incentives to include gender in day-to-day activities it does happen uniformly (Zuckerman and Qing 2005). 'Soft' social sector activities, such as health and education, have traditionally had more gender input than the 'harder' economic and financial sector activities, although over the years gender has gradually moved into 'harder' areas such as PREM. Zuckerman and Qing (2005) concluded that, although the situation has improved, Gender Country Assessments are often ignored in the preparation of the key Country Assistance Strategies and PRSPs that themselves vary significantly in the extent to which they incorporate gender. For example, Zuckerman and Qing (2005) claim that in 2002 only 3 of the 13 PRSPs addressed gender adequately.

The resources and staff allocated to gender activities, although they have increased over time, have been insufficient and limited. For example, some incentive funding ($600,000) was provided to facilitate the implementation the Gender Strategy but for one year only. Although the number of 'gender experts' in the Bank had grown from 1 in 1977 to around 115 in 2005 (still less than 1 per cent of Bank staff), environmental experts grew from 1 in the early 1980s to around 700–800 over the same period. Furthermore the core figure of 10–12 centralized gender unit staff has not expended since the mid-1980s. As a result the majority of the 'experts' are located in country-based gender focal points, and they often lack specific gender expertise and sometimes spend as little as 10–15 per cent of their time on gender issues (Zuckerman and Qing

2005). But some regions such as Latin America and the Caribbean and parts of some networks such as Environmentally and Socially Sustainable Development have greater gender expertise than others such as the Financial and Infrastructure networks that are virtually devoid of gender experts (Zuckerman and Qing 2005). Bank staff therefore divided into two groups: a small number with gender expertise and the vast majority who have little knowledge about gender and feel that they lacked the time and incentives to increase their knowledge about the Bank gender strategy (Zuckerman and Qing 2005). Therefore despite increased attention to gender, it remains a relatively low priority for the Bank and despite some measurable changes in policies, personnel and procedures, gender concerns have not been fully mainstreamed into current Bank operations.

As a result, even from an integrationist perspective, gender mainstreaming has not been an unqualified success in the Bank. More profoundly, there are serious questions about how transformative gender mainstreaming that is based on incorporating the 'business case' for gender equality into Bank's activities could be. As Hafner-Burton and Pollack (2002) argue, this kind of gender mainstreaming has not and cannot fundamentally shift the Bank's goals. Without changing the Bank's relatively closed and hierarchical institutional culture and an ideological approach that still prioritizes neo-classical economic analysis (despite more recent attention to equality and welfare), it is hard to envisage greater democracy and participation in both its structures and policy outcomes.

Possibilities for transformation?

The contrasting examples of the incorporation on gender issues into the World Bank and the global Human Rights regime show how limited change, even from an integrationist perspective, has been in both these arenas to date. The two cases offer useful lessons for the analysis of other attempts to incorporate gender into institutions of global governance both in this book and more broadly. In each case more has been achieved in terms of the adoption of the language of integrating gender than in terms of implementing any strategies and policies to achieve this. These very different cases demonstrate that the formal adoption of the language of equality, although significant in its own right, is not sufficient to transform institutions of global governance. The ways in which issues have to be framed in order to successfully place them on policy agendas can also set limits to their subsequent transformatory capacity but this is often a necessary condition for their acceptance within those institutions. And as demonstrated by the case of the human rights regime, under certain circumstances global women's movements can effectively articulate gender issues and even place them on the policy agendas of international institutions, but more must happen inside these institutions if these commitments are to be translated into outcomes in terms of changed institutional structures, governance and policies. Although the World Bank has greater implementation capacity than the human rights institutions, it too shows that several other factors contribute to successful implementation. Change will be more likely if powerful actors within institutions can ensure that changes are mandatory and resourced in terms of both staff and funding. This outcome will only be likely if effective alliances can be made between sympathetic 'insiders' and 'outsiders'. Entrenched structures, hostile ideas and resistant personnel only make this more difficult.

As Molyneux and Razavi (2005) have argued, the global context has also become less favourable since a global policy framework to advance gender equality was adopted at the Beijing Women's conference in 1995. This landmark in policy terms marks a high point of the global women's movement. Since then a conservative backlash, led by the rise of religious fundamentalisms and the political Right in the United States, has made the climate for measures to the enhance gender equality or even defend existing rights – for example in the area of reproductive rights – much more hostile. The task of transforming global institutions of governance has therefore become more challenging. But at the same time, the international climate towards the adoption of measures to promote the equal representation of women in decision-making has become more favourable. But while quotas – as one aspect of transforming global institutions – have become more acceptable in legislatures and some other institutions, increasing scepticism has been voiced about the concept of 'critical mass' with evidence growing that 'sheer numbers' of women are less significant than the presence of key actors who are feminists or sympathetic to gender issues in influential positions.

There is also some evidence to support the belief that the creation of new institutions can offer opportunities for gender concerns to be incorporated more easily and fundamentally at the outset of an institution's life than it is to 'add them in' at a later stage. Chappell (this book) gives some indications of these possibilities and drawbacks in her analysis of the International Criminal Court (ICC). However, it is clear from other cases of institution-building at the national, regional and international levels that a number of similar conditions apply. The contrasting examples of constitutional design – for example in South Africa, in the devolved institutions in Scotland and Wales and the (to date failed) efforts in the European Union – have demonstrated that new constitutions can protect and also enhance gender rights but this is by no means inevitable and indeed will only happen under certain conditions (Dobrowolsky and Hart 2003; Waylen 2006b). The political opportunity structure during the process of institutional design must be a favourable one. It must be relatively open, democratic and transparent if it is to be one in which interventions by feminists are possible. Crucially key institutional participants within these processes also have to be open to gender concerns and prepared to take them on board. This is often more likely if women activists have already made gender issues legitimate and framed them effectively in ways that resonate with the dominant discourses. As the example of the human rights regime has already made clear, organized women 'outsiders' can play a key role but, on their own, cannot effect significant change. In some cases women activists pressing gender concerns from both within and outside the processes of institution building can form alliances with other sympathetic insiders. Without the presence of all these factors, it is unlikely that the gender rights will be enhanced or even existing rights protected in new institutions.

Therefore as this book has demonstrated, feminist perspectives on global governance are diverse and varied, using different definitions of and approaches to global governance. But these perspectives do share certain characteristics. First, they believe that it is necessary to understand how the mechanisms and structures of global governance are gendered, both reinforcing and helping to create relationships of inequality. Second, they believe that it is important to use that understanding to achieve change. The strategies for change also vary. But as we have seen many of them focus on achieving institutional change often falling under the rubric of gender mainstreaming. All agree that strategies for change that involve multiple agents and sites do exist, and that these involve action both inside and outside institutions. More research, both empirical and conceptual, that goes beyond exploring the actions of women's movements and particular gender policy doctrines, is now needed to fill the remaining gaps in our knowledge. We still do not know enough about attempts to implement these policy doctrines or about a whole range of governance structures. Attention should focus on institutions, how they operate and how they can be altered in terms of their practices, policymaking procedures and outcomes. In addition, we need to understand the role of key actors. Improved understanding of these areas will improve our understandings of how global governance can be made more effective from a gender perspective, thereby helping to ensure that not only is gender embedded as a fundamental concern within all governance structures at all times, but that those structures are also democratic and accountable and open to participation by all women regardless of their location.

Notes

1. But unusually, in the only instance in which this literature does pay any attention to gender issues, some work falling within this category does consider women's organizations as part of global civil society (Clark *et al.* 2000; O'Brien *et al.* 2000; Waylen 2004, 2006a).
2. Recommendations centre on three broad categories: first, the collection and analysis of gender-disaggregated data; second, the development of effective responses to violations of women's rights; and third, the improved co-ordination and exchange of information among human rights bodies within the UN system (Riddell-Dixon 1999: 154).
3. Although reduced in size to eight members in 2000 and lacking significant resources, it has continued to function and according to Long (2006) acts as an important reference group for the gender anchor.

Bibliography

Acharya, A. (2004a) 'Democratisation and the Prospects for Participatory Regionalism in Southeast Asia'. In K. Jayasuriya (ed.) *Governing the Asia Pacific: Beyond the 'New Regionalism'*. Third World Quarterly Series, Basingstoke: Palgrave Macmillan, pp. 177–192.

Acharya, A. (2004b) 'How Ideas Spread: Whose Norms Matter? Norm Localization and Institutional Change in Asian Regionalism'. *International Organization* 58: 239–275.

Adams, B. (2002) 'The Gendered Time Politics of Globalization: Of Shadowlands and Elusive Justice'. *Feminist Review* 70: 3–29.

Adams, V. and Prigg, S. L. (eds) (2005) *Sex in Development: Science, Sexuality, and Morality in Global Perspective*. Durham, NC: Duke University Press.

Agarwal, B. (1997) 'Editorial: Re-sounding the Alert – Gender, Resources and Community Action', *World Development* 25(9): 1373–1380.

Agarwal, B. (2003) 'Gender and Land Rights Revisited: Exploring New Prospects via the State, Family and Market'. *Journal of Agrarian Change* 3(1–2) (January and April): 184–224.

Agathangelou, A. (2004) *The Global Political Economy of Sex: Desire, Violence, and Insecurity in Mediterranean Nation States*. New York: Palgrave Macmillan.

Agathangelou, A. and Ling, L. H. M. (2004) 'The House of IR: From Family Power Politics to the Poisies of Worldism'. *International Feminist Journal of Politics* 6(1): 21–49.

Aggarwal, V. K. and Morrison, C. E. (eds) (1998) *Asia-Pacific Crossroads: Regime Creation and the Future of APEC*. Basingstoke: Palgrave Macmillan.

Albert, M. and Brock, L. (1998) 'New Relationships Between Territory and State: The U.S.–Mexico Border in Perspective'. In D. Spener and K. Staudt (eds) *The US-Mexico Border: Transcending Divisions, Contesting Identities*. Boulder, CO: Lynne Rienner Press, pp. 215–231.

Alexander, M. J. (1994) 'Not Just (Any) Body Can Be a Citizen: The Politics of Law, Sexuality and Postcoloniality in Trinidad and Tobago and the Bahamas'. *Feminist Review* 48: 5–23.

Alldred, P. (2002) 'Thinking Globally, Acting Locally: Women Activists' Accounts'. *Feminist Review* 70: 149–163.

Allen, J. (1990) 'Does Feminism Need a Theory of "The State"?' In S. Watson (ed.) *Playing the State: Australian Feminist Interventions*. London: Verso, pp. 21–27.

Alston, L., Thráinn Eggertsson, J. and North, D. C. (eds) (1996) *Empirical Studies in Institutional Change*. New York: Cambridge University Press.

Alternatives for the Americas: Building a People's Hemispheric Agreement. Prepared for the Peoples' Summit of the Americas. Santiago, Chile, April 1998. In possession of Debra Liebowitz.

Alvarez, S. (1997) 'Contradictions of a "Women's Space" in a Male-Dominant State: The Political Role of the Commissions on the Status of Women in

Postauthoritarian Brazil'. In K. Staudt (ed.) *Women, International Development, and Politics: The Bureaucratic Mire.* Philadelphia: Temple University Press, 2nd edition.

Alvarez, S. (1998) 'Latin American Feminisms "Go Global": Trends of the 1990s and Challenges for the New Millennium'. In S. E. Alvarez (ed.) *Cultures of Politics, Politics of Culture: Re-visioning Latin American Social Movements.* Boulder, CO: Westview Press, pp. 293–324.

Amigos de las Mujeres de Juarez. http://www.amigosdemujeres.org.

Ammar, N. H. and Lababidy, L. S. (1999) 'Women's Grassroots Movements and Democratization in Egypt'. In J. M. Bystydzienski and J. Sekhon (eds) *Democratization and Women's Grassroots Movements.* Bloomington: Indian University Press, pp. 150–170.

Amnesty International (2003) *Intolerable Killings: Ten Years of Abductions and Murders of Women in Ciudad Juarez and Chihuahua.* http://www.amnesty.org.

Amoore, L. (2005) Globalizing Resistance. London: Routledge.

Amt für Landwirtschaft und Forsten – Regen (n.d.) Daten und Fakten aus unserem Dienstgebiet. http://www.alf-rg.bayern.de. Accessed 10 March 2006.

Anderson, B. (1991) *Imagined Communities: Reflections on the Origins and Spread of Nationalism.* London: Verso.

Andreas, P. (2000) *Border Games: Policing the U.S.–Mexico Divide.* Ithaca, NY: Cornell University Press.

Anzaldua, G. (1987) *Borderlands/La Frontera: The New Mestiza.* San Francisco: Spinsters/Aunt Lute Press.

Aoki, M. (2001) *Toward a Comparative Institutional Analysis.* New York: Cambridge University Press.

APEC Group on Services (2001) *Firm Expatriation Policy and Practice in Service Trade: The Gender Dimension.* APEC.

Arteaga, M. (1996) Frente Autentico del Trabajo y Red Mexicana de Acción Frente al Libre Comercio. Interview. Mexico City, November 27.

Articulación Feminista Marcosur. 'Against Fundamentalisms, People are Fundamental'. http://www.mujeresdelsur.org.uy/campania/foro1a.htm. Accessed 22 February 2003.

Asia Pacific Economic Cooperation (APEC) (2002) Second Ministerial Meeting on Women: Joint Ministerial Statement. Guadalajara, Mexico, 28–29 September.

Asia Pacific Economic Cooperation (APEC) (2003a) GFPN Summary Report to SOMII. Senior Officials Meeting II, Khon Kaen, 29–30 May 2003/SOMII/048.

Asia Pacific Economic Cooperation (APEC) (2003b) APEC Secretariat's Report at the First GFPN Meeting. Gender Focal Point Network, Khon Kaen, Thailand, 20–22 May, 2003/SOMII/GFPN/001.

Askin, K. (1999) 'Sexual Violence in Decisions and Indictments of the Yugoslav and Rwandan Tribunals: Current Status'. *The American Journal of International Law* 93(1): 97–123.

Aulestia, A. and Quintero-Andrade, R. (2001) Informe Del Taller Sobre Conceptos Básicos Y Herramietas (Sic) Metodogicas De Género, Regionales Amazonia Norte Y Sur. P.R.O.D.E.P.I.N.E: Quito.

Bachmann, K. (1999) 'Die Gemeinsame Agrarpolitik der Europäischen Union: Die Bevormundung der "BürgerInnen Europas"' In P. Teherani-Krönner, U. Hoffmann-Altmann and U. Schultz (eds) *Frauen und nachhaltige ländliche*

Entwicklung: Beiträge der III. International Tagung 'Frauen in der ländlichen Entwicklung'. Pfaffenweiler, Germany: Centaurus-Verlagsgesellschaft, pp. 162–166.

Bakker, I. (1999) 'Identity, Interests and Ideology: The Gendered Terrain of Global Restructuring'. In S. Gill (ed.) *Globalization, Democratization and Multilateralism*. New York, Tokyo and Paris: Macmillan, pp. 127–139.

Bakker, I. (2003) 'Neo-Liberal Governance and the Reprivatization of Social Reproduction: Social Provisioning and Shifting Gender Orders'. In I. Bakker and S. Gill (eds) *Power, Production and Social Reproduction: Human In/Security in the Global Political Economy*. Houndsmill: Palgrave Macmillan, pp. 66–82.

Bakker, I. and Gill, S. (eds) (2003) *Power, Production and Social Reproduction: Human In/security in the Global Political Economy*. Basingstoke: Palgrave Macmillan.

Banaszak, L. A. (1996) *Why Movements Succeed or Fail: Opportunity Culture, and the Struggle for Woman Suffrage*. Princeton: Princeton University Press.

Barber, B. (1996) *Jihad vs. McWorld*. New York: Ballantine Books.

Barker, G. (1998) 'Boys in the Hood, Boys in the Barrio: Exploratory Research on Masculinity, Fatherhood and Attitudes Toward Women Among Low Income Young Men in Chicago, USA, and Rio de Janeiro, Brazil'. Paper Prepared for the IUSSP/CENEP Seminar on Men, Family Formation and Reproduction, 13–15 May. Buenos Aires, Argentina.

Barrett, M. (1980) *Women's Oppression Today: The Marxist/Feminist Encounter*. London: Verso.

Barrig, M. (2005) 'What is Justice? Indigenous Women in Andean Development Projects'. In J. Jaquette and G. Summerfield (eds) *Women and Gender Equity in Development Theory and Practice*. Durham: Duke University Press.

Barrientos, S., Dolan, C. and Tallontire, A. (2003) 'A Gendered Value Chain Approach to Codes of Conduct in African Horticulture'. *World Development* 31(9): 1511–1526.

Barry, A, Osborne, T. and Rose, N. (eds) (1996) *Foucault and Political Reason: Liberalism, Neo-Liberalism, and Rationalities of Government*. Chicago: University of Chicago Press.

Bayerisches Staatsministerium für Landwirtschaft und Forsten (2004) *Bayerischer Agrarbericht*. Website of the Bavarian State Ministry for Agriculture and Forests: http://www.stmlf-neu-bayern.de/agrarpolitik/daten_fakten/ab2004. Accessed 3 September 2004.

Baxi, U. (1996) ' "Global Neighborhood" and the "Universal Otherhood": Notes on the Report of the Commission on Global Governance'. *Alternatives* 21: 525–549.

Baxi, U. (2002) 'Global Justice and the Failure of Deliberative Democracy'. In O.Enweror *et al.* (eds) *Democracy Unrealized*. Kassel: Hatje Cantz Publishers, pp. 113–132.

Baxi, P., Rai, S. M. and Sardar Ali, S. (2006) 'Legacies of Common Law: "Crimes of Honour" in India and Pakistan'. *Third World Quarterly* 27(7): 1239–1254.

Becker, G. (1991) *A Treatise on the Family*. Cambridge: Harvard University Press.

Beckmann, M., Bieling, H. and Deppe, F. (eds) (2003) *'Euro-Kapitalismus' und globale politische Ökonomie*. Hamburg: VSA Verlag.

Bedford, K. (2005a). 'Empowering Women, Domesticating Men, and Resolving the Social Reproduction Dilemma: The World Bank's Employment Policies in Ecuador and Beyond'. PhD Dissertation. New Brunswick, NJ: Rutgers University.

Bedford, K. (2005b) 'Loving to Straighten Out Development: Sexuality and "Ethnodevelopment" in the World Bank's Ecuadorian Lending'. *Feminist Legal Studies* 13: 295–322.

Bedford, K. (2007) 'The Imperative of male Inclusion: How Institutional Context Influences World Bank Gender Policy'. *International Feminist Journal of Politics* 9(3): 289–311.

Bedont, B. C. (1999) 'Gender-Specific Provisions in the Statute of the ICC'. In F. Lattanzi and W. Schabas (eds) *Essays on the Rome Statute of the ICC*. Naples: Editorial Scientifica. http://iccwomen.addr.com/recourses/genderprovs.html14. Accessed June 2004.

Beeson, M. (2004) 'The Origins of Regionalism: Western Europe and East Asia in Comparative Historical Perspective'. Paper presented at the Oceanic Conference on International Studies, Canberra, July 14–16.

Bell, E, (2001) 'Gender and Governance: A Bibliography,' *BRIDGE*, Brighton: Institute for Development Studies, University of Sussex.

Benería, L. (2003) *Gender, Development, and Globalization: Economics as If All People Mattered*. New York: Routledge.

Benería, L. and Feldman, S. (eds) (1992) *Unequal Burden: Economic Crises, Persistent Poverty, and Women's Work*. Boulder, CO: Westview Press.

Benería, L. and Lind, A. (eds) (1995). 'Engendering International Trade: Concepts, Policy, and Action'. *A Commitment to the World's Women*, pp. 69–86.

Benitez, R. *et al.* (1999) El Silencio que la Voz de Todad Quiebra: Mujeres y Victimas de Ciudad Juarez. Chihuahua: CHIH: Azar.

Bergeron, S. (2003) 'The Post-Washington Consensus and the Economic Representations of Women in Development at the World Bank', *International Feminist Journal of Politics* 5(3): 397–419.

Bergeron, S. (2004a) *Fragments of Development: Nation, Gender, and the Space of Modernity*. Ann Arbor, MI: University of Michigan Press.

Bergeron, S. (2004b) 'Bringing Gender In: Acts of Translation and Gender Mainstreaming at the Bank'. Paper delivered at the ISA meeting, Chicago, March.

Berlant, L. and Warner, M. (1998) 'Sex in Public'. *Critical Inquiry* 547–566.

Bernhards, U., Klockenbrink, C., Plankl, R. and Rudow, K. (2003) *Pilotfallstudie zur Bewertung der Ausgleichszulage in benachteiligten Gebieten im Landkreis Freyung-Grafenau*. Braunschweig: Bundesforschungsanstalt für Landwirtschaft, Institut für Betriebswirtschaft, Agrarstruktur und ländliche Räume.

Bieling, H-J. and Steinhilber, J. (eds) (2001) *Die Konfiguration Europas. Dimensionen einer kritischen Integrationstheorie*. Münster: Westfälisches Dampfboot.

Birdsall, N. and Kapur, D. (2005) *The Hardest Job in the World: Five Crucial Tasks for the New President of the World Bank. An Agenda for the Next World Bank President*. Washington, DC: Center for Global Development.

Blacklock, C. and Macdonald, L. (2000) 'Women and Citizenship in Mexico and Guatemala'. In S. Rai (ed.) *International Perspectives on Gender and Democratisation*. Basingstoke: Palgrave Macmillan.

Bloch, F. and Rao, V. (2000) 'Terror as a Bargaining Instrument: A Case Study of Dowry Violence in Rural India'. Policy Research Working Papers 2347 (May). Washington DC: World Bank.

Block, F. (1990) *Postindustrial Possibilities, A Critique of Economic Discourse*. Berkeley: University of California Press.

Boas, M. (2000) 'The Trade-Environment Nexus and the Potential of Regional Trade Institutions'. *New Political Economy* 5(3): 415–432.

Boon, K. (2001) 'Rape and Forced Pregnancy under the ICC Statute: Human Dignity, Autonomy, and Consent'. *Columbia Human Rights Law Review* 32: 624–675.

Boris, E. and Prügl, E. (eds) (1996) *Homeworkers in Global Perspective: Invisible No More*. New York: Routledge.

Boserup, E. (1970) *Women's Role in Economic Development*. New York: St. Martin's Press.

Bothfeld, S., Gronbach, S. and Riedmüller, B. (eds) (2002) *Gender Mainstreaming – eine Innovation in der Gleichstellungspolitik*, Frankfurt/M.; New York.

Brah, A. (2002) 'Global Mobilities, Local Predicaments: Globalization and the Critical Imagination'. *Feminist Review* 70: 30–45.

Braithwaite, M. (1994) *The Economic Role and Situation of Women in Rural Areas*. Luxembourg: Office for Official Publications of the European Communities.

Bretherton, C. (1998) 'Global Environmental Politics: Putting Gender on the Agenda?' *Review of International Studies* 24(1): 85–100.

Bröckling, U., Krasmann, S. and Lemke, T. (eds) (2000) *Gouvernementalität der Gegenwart*. Studien zur Ökonomisierung des Sozialen, Frankfurt/M: Suhrkamp Verlag.

Brodie, J. (2004) 'Die Re-Formierung des Geschlechterverhältnisses. Neoliberalismus und die Regierung des Sozialen'. *Widerspruch* 46.24.1: 19–32.

Brodie, J. (2005) 'Globalization, Governance and Gender: Rethinking the Agenda for the Twenty-First Century'. In L. Amoore (ed.) *Globalizing Resistance*. London: Routledge.

Brooks, D. and Fox, J. (eds) (2002) *Cross-Border Dialogues: U.S.–Mexico Social Movement Networking*. La Jolla, CA: Center for U.S.-Mexican Studies, University of California, San Diego.

Brown, W. (1995) *States of Injury: Power and Freedom in Late Modernity*. Princeton, NJ: Princeton University Press.

Bruce, J. and Dwyer, D. (1988) *A Home Divided: Women and Income in the Third World*. Stanford, CA: Stanford University Press.

Bunch, C. and Hinojosa, C. (2000) *Lesbians Travel the Roads of Feminism Globally*. New Brunswick, NJ: Center for Women's Global Leadership, Rutgers University.

Bundesministerium für Verbraucherschutz, Ernährung und Landwirtschaft (2003) *Ernährungs- und agrarpolitischer Bericht 2004 der Bundesregierung*. Berlin: BMVEL. Webpage of the BMVEL at http://www.verbraucherministerium.de/index-0005BCF0323B1050A9746521C0A8D816.html. Accessed 6 September 2004.

Burch, K. (1998) *'Property' and the Making of the International System*. Boulder, CO: Lynne Rienner.

Burnham, P. (1999) 'The Politics of Economic Management in the 1990s'. *New Political Economy* 4(1): 37–54.

Buss, D. and Herman, D. (2003) Globalizing Family Values: The Christian Right in International Politics. Minneapolis: Minnesota University Press.

Butler, J. (1990) *Gender Trouble: Feminism and the Subversion of Identity*. New York: Routledge.

Cable, V. (1995) 'The Diminished Nation-State: A Study in the Loss of Economic Power', *Daedalus, Journal of the American Academy of Arts and Sciences*, Spring.

Cagatay, N. (2001) *Trade, Gender and Poverty*. New York: UNDP.

Canadian Gender & Trade Consultation (2002) 7–9 December 2001. Report issued January 1–12.

Canadian International Development Agency (CIDA) (2003). *Gender Equality and Trade Related Capacity Building*. Toronto: CIDA.

Caporaso, J. A. (1996) 'The European Union and Forms of State: Westphalian, Regulatory or Post-Modern?' *Journal of Common Market Studies* 34(1) (March): 29–52.

Carabine, J. (2000) 'Constituting Welfare Subjects Through Poverty and Sexuality'. In G. Lewis, S. Gewirtz and J. Clarke (eds) *Rethinking Social Policy*. London: SAGE, pp. 78–93.

Carney, G. (2004), 'Researching Gender Mainstreaming: A Challenge for Feminist IR', Paper prepared for International Studies Association Annual Convention, Montreal, March 17–20. http://archive.allacademic.com/publication/index.php?PHPSESSID=f0a099a46ab703b02e932243431b4f40.

Casey, L. A. (2002) 'The Case Against the International Criminal Court'. *Fordham International Law Journal* 25: 840–844.

Castells, M. (1996) *The Rise of the Network Society*, Cambridge, MA: Blackwell.

CEC (1993) White Paper on Growth, Competitiveness and Employment.

Cecchini, P. (1988) *The European Challenge – 1992 and the Benefits of a Single Market*. Aldershot: Wildwood House.

Cerny, P. G. (1995) 'Globalization and the Changing Logic of Collective Action'. *International Organization* 49 (Autumn): 595–625.

Chang, K. A. and Ling, L. H. M. (2000) 'Globalization and Its Intimate Other: Filipina Domestic Workers in Hong Kong'. In M. H. Marchand and A. S. Runyan (eds) *Gender and Global Restructuring: Sightings, Sites and Resistances*. London: Routledge, pp. 27–43.

Chappell, L. (2002) *Gendering Government: Feminist Engagement with the State in Australia and Canada*.Vancouver: UBC Press.

Charkiewicz, E. (2003) 'Sustainable Development in a Neo-Liberal Frame'. *DAWN Informs* April, 16–17. http://dawnnet.org/publications/newsletters/ DAWNInforms/DIApril03.pdf. Accessed on 17 November 2007.

Charlesworth, H. (2005) 'Not Waving but Drowning: Gender Mainstreaming and Human Rights in the United Nations'. *Harvard Human Rights Journal* 18 (Spring): 1–18.

Charlesworth, H. and Chinkin, C. (2000) *The Boundaries of International Law: A Feminist Analysis*. Manchester: Manchester University Press.

Chin, C. B. N. (1998) *In Service and Servitude: Foreign Female Domestic Workers and the Malaysian "Modernity" Project*. New York: Columbia University Press.

Chun, B. J. (1999) 'Women Entrepreneurs in SMEs in the APEC Region'. APEC SME Working Group.

Clark, A., Friedman, E. and Hochstetler, K. (1998) 'The Sovereign Limits of Global Civil Society: A Comparison of NGO Participation in UN World Conferences on the Environment, Human Rights and Women'. *World Politics* 51(1): 1–35.

Cleaver, F. (ed.) (2002) *Men and Masculinities: New Directions in Gender and Development*. London/New York: Zed Books.

Coalition for the International Criminal Court (CICC) (2004) 'ICC Receives First State Referral', *ICC UPDATE* 37, 1.

Coalition for the International Criminal Court (2005) 'Status of US Bilateral Immunity Agreements'. http://www.iccnow.org/documents/USandICC/ BIAs-ByRegion_current.pdf. Accessed 22 July 2005.

Coalition for Women's Human Rights in Conflict Situations (1998) 'Amicus Brief Submitted to the International Criminal Tribunal for Rwanda Respecting the Amendment of the Indictment and Supplementation of the Evidence to Ensure the Prosecution of Rape and Other Sexual Violence Within the Competence of the Tribunal'. http://www.womensrightscoalition.org/index_en.htm. Accessed 22 July 2005.

Coalition for Women's Human Rights in Conflict Situations (2001) 'Women's Groups Congratulate ICTY on Charges of Sexual Violence Against Slobodan Milosevic' Press Release 29 October. http://www.womensrightscoalition.org/ newsReleases/2001-10-yugo_en.php. Accessed 22 July 2005.

Coalition for Women's Human Rights in Conflict Situations (2002) 'Analysis of Trends in Sexual Violence Prosecutions in Indictments by the International Criminal tribunal for Rwanda (ICTR) from November 1995 to November 2002'. http://www.womensrightscoalition.org/advocacyDossiers/rwanda/rapeVictims. Accessed 22 July 2005.

Cockburn, C. (2004) *The Line: Women, Partition and the Gender Order in Cyprus*. London: Zed Books.

Cohen, M. G. (1987) *Free Trade and the Future of Women's Work: Manufacturing and Service Industries*. Toronto: Garamond Press and the Canadian Centre for Policy Alternatives.

Cohen, M. G. (1995) 'Feminism's Effect on Economic Policy'. In R. R. Pierson and M. G. Cohen (eds) *Canadian Women's Issues: Volume II—Bold Visions*. Toronto: James Lorimer, pp. 263–298.

Cohen, C. (1997) 'Punks, Bulldaggers, and Welfare Queens'. *GLQ* 3: 437–465.

Cohn, C., Kinsella, H. and Gibbings, S. (2004) 'Women, Peace and Security: Resolution 1325', *International Feminist Journal of Politics* 6(1) (March): 130–140.

Colloreado-Mansfeld, R. (1999) *The Native Leisure Class: Consumption And Cultural Creativity in the Andes*. Chicago: University of Chicago Press.

Comision Nacional de la Mujer (former name of INMUJER) (2004) *Mexico: Sintesis del Informe de Ejecucion*. Mexico, DF: CNM.

Commission on Global Governance (1995) 'Our Global Neighbourhood'. Oxford: Oxford University Press.

Conejo, M. (2002–2003) Hablando de Sexualidad con Adolescentes Indígenas: Escuelas del Sistema Intercultural Bilingüe Imbabura. Otavalo: Jambi Huasi.

Conférence Agricole des États membres de la Communauté Économique Européenne. Recueil des Documents, Stresa, 3 au 12 Juillet 1958.

Connell, R.W. (1998) 'Masculinities and Globalization'. *Men and Masculinities* 1(1) (July): 3–23.

Cook, J. (1998) 'Flexible Employment: Implications for Gender and Citizenship in the European Union'. *New Political Economy* 3(2): 261–277.

Cook, J., Roberts, J. and Waylen, G. (eds) (2000) *Towards a Gendered Political Economy*. Basingstoke, Hampshire: Palgrave Macmillian.

Cooper, D. (1995) *Power in Struggle: Feminism, Sexuality and the State*. Buckingham, England: Open University Press.

Copelon, R. (2000) 'Gender Crimes as War Crimes: Integrating Crimes against Women into International Law'. *McGill Law Journal* 46: 217–240.

Correia, M. (2000) *Ecuador Gender Review: Issues and Recommendations. A World Bank Country Study.* Washington DC: World Bank.

Correia, M. (2002) 'Gender Dimensions of Vulnerability to Exogenous Shocks: The Case of Ecuador'. In P. Beckerman and A. Solimano (eds) *Crisis and Dollarization in Ecuador: Stability, Growth, and Social Equity.* Washington DC: World Bank, pp. 177–215.

Council of Europe (1998) Gender Mainstreaming. Conceptual Framework, Methodology, and Presentation of Good Practice. Strasbourg: Council of Europe.

Cox, R. (1983) 'Gramsci, Hegemony, and International Relations: An Essay in Method'. *Millennium* 12(2) (Summer): 162–175.

Cox, R. (1999) 'Civil Society at the Turn of the Millennium, Prospects for an Alternative World Order'. *Review of International Studies* 25(1): 3–28.

Crain, M. (1996) 'The Gendering of Ethnicity in the Ecuadorian Andres: Native Women's Self-Fashioning in the Urban Marketplace'. In M. Melhaus and K. A. Stolen (eds) *Machos, Mistresses, Madonnas: Contesting the Power of Latin American Gender Imagery.* London: Verso, pp. 134–158.

Cravey, A. (1998) *Women and Work in Mexico's Maquiladoras.* Lanham, MD: Rowman & Littlefield.

Cruikshank, B. (1994) 'The Will to Empower. Technologies of Citizenship and the War on Poverty'. *Socialist Review* 23(4): 29–55.

Cruikshank, B. (1999) *The Will to Empower. Democratic Citizens and Other Subjects.* Ithaca, NY: London.

CUTS (2004) *We've Been Here Before: Perspectives on the Cancun Ministerial.* Jaipur, India: CUTS.

D'Amico, F. (1999) 'Women Workers in the United Nations: From Margin to Mainstream?' In M. K. Meyer and E. Prügl (eds) *Gender Politics in Global Governance.* Lanham, MD: Rowman & Littlefield, pp. 19–40.

Davos (2002) 'The Silent Voices on Globalization' Annual Meeting, 1 February http://www.weforum.org/site/knowledgenavigator.nsf/Content/The%20 Silent%20Voices%20on%20Globalization_2002?open. Accessed 6 February 2003.

Davos (2003) 'Globalization, Poverty and Inequality' Annual Meeting, 23 January http://www.weforum.org/site/knowledgenavigator.nsf/Content/Globalization, %20Poverty%20and%20Inequality_2003?open. Accessed 6 February 2004.

Dean, M. (1999) *Governmentality. Power and Rule in Modern Society.* London, Thousand Oaks and New Delhi: Sage.

Debord, G. (1967) *The Society of the Spectacle.* Translated by Donald Nicholson-Smith. New York: Zone Books, 1995.

Debord, G. (1998) *Comments on the Society of the Spectacle.* London: Verso.

de la Cadena, M. (1995) 'Women are More Indian: Ethnicity and Gender in a Community near Cuzco'. In B. Larson and O. Harris, with E. Tandeter (eds) *Ethnicity, Markets, and Migration in the Andes: At the Crossroads of History and Anthropology.* Durham: Duke University Press, pp. 329–348.

de la Torre, C. (2000) 'Populist Seduction in Latin America: The Ecuadorian Experience'. Latin American Series 32. Athens, OH: Center for International Studies.

Delors, J. (1989). *Report on Economic and Monetary Union in the European Community.* Luxembourg: OOPEC.

Delphy, C. (1984) *Close to Home: A Materialist Analysis of Women's Oppression*. Amherst: University of Massachusetts Press.

Delphy, C. (2000) 'Rethinking Sex and Gender'. In K. Oliver (ed.) *French Feminism Reader*. Lanham, MD: Rowman & Littlefield, pp. 63–76.

Delphy, C. and Leonard, D. (1992) *Familiar Exploitation: A New Analysis of Marriage in Contemporary Western Societies*. Cambridge, UK: Polity Press.

Deroose, S., Hodson, D. and Kuhlmann, J. (2004) 'Economic Governance in the EU: Lessons from the First Five Years of EMU'. Paper presented at UACES research conference, Birmingham, September.

Desai, M. (2002) 'Transnational Solidarity: Women's Agency, Structural Adjustment, and Globalization'. In N. A. Naples and M. Desai (eds) *Women's Activism and Globalization: Linking Local Struggles and Transnational Politics*. New York: Routledge, pp. 15–33.

Deutsch, K. (1957) *Political Community in the North Atlantic Area: International Organization in the Light of Historical Experience*. Princeton: Princeton University Press.

Deutsch, F. (1999) *Halving It All: How Equally Shared Parenting Works*. Cambridge: Harvard UP.

Devetzi, S. and Schmitt, V. (2002) 'Die offene Methode der Koordinierung im Bereich Alterssicherung in der EU – eine kritische Bestandsaufnahme', *Deutsche Rentenversicherung* 4–5: 234–249.

Dieng, A. (2002) 'International Criminal Justice: from Paper to Practice – A Contribution from the International Criminal Tribunal for Rwanda to the Establishment of the International Criminal Court'. *Fordham International Law Journal* 25: 688–707.

Division for the Advancement of Women (UN/DAW) (1999) *World Survey on the Role of Women in Development*. New York: UN.

Dobrowolsky, A. and Hart, V. (eds) (2003) *Women Making Constitutions: New Politics and Comparative Perspectives*. Basingstoke: Palgrave Macmillan.

Domingo, P. (1999) 'Rule of Law, Citizenship and Access to Justice in Mexico'. *Mexican Studies/Estudios Mexicanos* 15(1): 151–191.

Dominguez, E. (2002) 'Continental Transnational Activism and Worker Networks under NAFTA'. *International Feminist Journal of Politics* 4(2): 216–329.

Doucet, M. (2000) 'Asia-Pacific Economic Cooperation (APEC) and the Parallel "People's Summits": Theorizing the Political and Democracy in International Theory'. PhD dissertation. Canada: University of Ottawa.

Dunkley, G. (1997) *The Free Trade Adventure: The WTO, the Uruguay Round and Globalism—A Critique*. London: Zed Books.

Dunn, T. (1996) *The Militarization of the U.S–Mexico Border, 1978–1992: Low-Intensity Conflict Doctrine Comes Home*. Austin: Center for Mexican American Studies, University of Texas.

Dutt, M. (2000) 'Some Reflections on United States Women of Color and the United Nations Fourth World Conference on Women and NGO Forum in Beijing, China'. In B. G. Smith (ed.) *Global Feminisms Since 1945: Rewriting Histories*. New York: Routledge.

EGGE (2001) 'Gender Equality and the European Employment Strategy: An Evaluation of the National Action Plans for Employment'. Posted on EGGE website April 2002 (see Note 6, Chapter 5).

Eguiguren, A., Maldonado A. and Marchán, M. (2002) Seis Estudios De Caso Sobre Identidades Y Roles De Género En Las Nacionalidades Y Pueblos Del

Ecuador: Estudio De Caso Sobre El Pueblo Chachi—Fecche, Norte De Esmeraldas. Quito: P.R.O.D.E.P.I.N.E.

Ehrenreich, B. and Hochschild, A. R. (eds) (2002) *Global Women: Nannies, Maids, and Sex Workers in the New Economy*. New York: Metropolitan Books, Henry Holt and Company.

Einhorn, B. (2000) 'Gender and Citizenship in the Context of Democratisation in East Central Europe'. In S. Rai (ed.) *International Perspectives on Gender and Democratisation*. Basingstoke: Palgrave Macmillan, pp. 103–124.

Elgstrom, O. (1998) 'Norm Negotiations: The Construction of New Norms Regarding Gender and Development in EU Foreign Aid Policy'. *Journal of European Public Policy* 7(3): 457–476.

Ellina, C. A. (2003) *Promoting Women's Rights: The Politics of Gender in the European Union*. London: Routledge.

Elson, D. (1996) 'Gender-Aware Analysis and Development Economics'. In K. P. Jameson and C. K. Wilber (eds) *The Political Economy of Development and Underdevelopment*. New York: McGraw Hill.

Elson, D. (2000) 'Gender at the Macroeconomic Level'. In J. Cook *et al.* (eds) *Towards a Gendered Political Economy*. Basingstoke: Palgrave Macmillan, pp. 77–97.

Elson, D. (2004). 'Engendering Government Budgets in the Context of Globalisation(s)'. *International Feminist Journal of Politics* 6(4): 623–642.

Enloe, C. (1993) *The Morning After*. Berkeley: University of California Press.

Enloe, C. (2000) 'Womenandchildren: Making Feminist Sense of the Persian Gulf Crisis'. *The Village Voice* 25 September.

Eschle, C. (2000) *Global Democracy, Social Movements and Feminism*. Boulder, CO: Westview Press.

Eschle, C. (2005) ' "Skeleton Women": Feminism and the Antiglobalization Movement'. *Signs: Journal of Women in Culture and Society* 30(3) (Spring): 1741–1770.

Eschle, C. and Maiguashca, B. (eds) (2005) *Critical Theories, International Relations and the Anti-Globalization Movement*. London: Routledge.

Escobar, A. (1995) *Encountering Development. The Making and Unmaking of the Third World*. Princeton/New Jersey: Princeton University Press.

European Commission (2004) *Employment in Europe. Recent Trends and Prospects*. Luxembourg.

European Commission (2007) *General Budget of the European Union for the Financial Year 2007*. Luxembourg: Office for Official Publications of the European Communities.

European Communities (2002) *Agriculture: The Spotlight on Women*. Luxembourg: Office for Official Publications of the European Communities.

Evans, A. (1993) 'Contracted-out: Some Reflection on Gender, Power and Agrarian Institutions'. *IDS Bulletin* 24(3) (July).

Evers, B. (2003) 'Broadening the Foundations of Macro-Economic Models through a Gender Approach: New Developments'. In M. Gutierrez (ed.) *Macro-Economics: Making Gender Matter*. London: Zed Books.

Facio, A. (1999) 'Integrating Gender into the World's First Permanent Criminal Court'. http://iccwomen.org/archive/resources/bplus5/part1.htm. Accessed 9 November 2004.

Facio, A. (2004) 'All Roads Lead to Rome But Some are Bumpier than Others'. In S. Pickering and C. Lambert (eds) *Global Issues: Women and Justice*. Sydney: Federation Press.

286   *Bibliography*

Falk, R. (2000) 'Global Civil Society and The Democratic Prospect'. In B. Holden (ed.) *Global Democracy*. London: Routledge.

Fausto-Sterling, A. (2000) *Sexing the Body: Gender Politics and the Construction of Sexuality*. New York: Basic Books.

Ferber, M. A. and Nelson, J. A. (1993) *Beyond Economic Man: Feminist Theory and Economics*. Chicago: The University of Chicago Press.

Ferguson, K. E. (1984) *The Feminist Case Against Bureaucracy*. Philadelphia: Temple University Press.

Fernandez-Kelly, M. P. (1983) *For We are Sold, I and My People: Women and Industry in Mexico's Frontier*. Albany, NY: SUNY Press.

Ferrándiz, F. (2003) 'Malandros, Maía Lionza, and Masculinity in a Venezuelan Shantytown'. In M. Gutmann (ed.) *Changing Men and Masculinities in Latin America*. Durham, NC: Duke University Press, pp. 115–133.

FfD Women's Caucus (2002) 'A Presentation to the Financing for Development Ministerial Roundtable on "Looking Ahead"'. Monterrey, Mexico, March 21. http://www.wedo.org/ffd/looking.htm. Accessed 2 April 2002.

Finnemore, M. and Sikkink, K. (1998) 'International Norm Dynamics and Political Change'. *International Organization* 52: 887–917.

Fligstein, N. (2001) *The Architecture of Markets: An Economic Sociology of Twenty-First-Century Capitalist Societies*. Princeton: Princeton University Press.

Folbre, N. (1994) *Who Pays for the Kids? Gender and the Structures of Constraint*. New York: Routledge.

Foucault, M. (1990) *The History of Sexuality: An Introduction*. Vol. 1. New York: Vintage Books.

Foucault, M. (1991a) 'Governmentality'. In G. Burchell, C. Gordon and P. Miller (eds) *The Foucault Effect: Studies in Governmentality*. Chicago: University of Chicago Press.

Foucault, M. (1991b) *Discipline and Punish: The Birth of the Prison*. Translated from French by Alan Sheridan. London: Penguin.

Foucault, M. (1994a) 'Omnes et singulatim. Zu einer Kritik der politischen Vernunft'. In J. Vogl (ed.) *Gemeinschaften. Positionen zu einer Philosophie des Politischen*. Frankfurt/M, pp. 65–93.

Foucault, M. (1994b) *Überwachen und Strafen. Die Geburt des Gefängnisses*. Frankfurt/M.

Foucault, M. (1999) *Botschaften der Macht: Der Foucault Reader, Diskurs und Medien*, Stuttgart.

Foucault, M. (2000a): 'Die Gouvernementalität'. In U. Bröckling, S. Krasmann and T. Lemke (eds) *Gouvernementalität der Gegenwart. Studien zur Ökonomisierung des Sozialen*. Frankfurt/M, pp. 41–67.

Foucault, M. (2000b) 'Staatsphobie'. In U. Bröckling, S. Krasmann and T. Lemke (eds) *Gouvernementalität der Gegenwart. Studien zur Ökonomisierung des Sozialen*, Frankfurt/M, pp. 68–71.

Fox, J. and Brown, D. (1998) *The Struggle for Accountability: The World Bank, NGOs, and Grassroots Movements*. Cambridge: MIT Press.

Fraser, N. (1997) 'From Redistribution to Recognition? Dilemmas of Justice in a "Poststructuralist" Age'. *New Left Review* 212, July-August.

Freeman, M. (1999) 'International Institutions and Gendered Justice'. *Journal of International Affairs* 52(2): 513.

Fremont, J. (2001) 'Agriculture in Europe: The Spotlight on Women'. *Statistics in Focus: Agriculture and Fisheries* Theme 5–7.

Freyung-Grafenau, L. (2004) 'Land- und Forstwirtschaft'. http://www.freyung-grafenau.de/index.phtml?NavID=376.34. Accessed 24 August 2004.

Freyung-Grafenau, L. (2005) 'Arbeitsmarkt'. http://www.freyung-grafenau.de/index.phtml?NavID=376.3. Accessed 3 March 2006.

Friedman, E. (1994) 'Women's Human Rights: The Emergence of A Movement'. In J. Peters and A. Wolper (eds) *Women and Human Rights: An Agenda for Change*. New York: Routledge, pp. 18–35.

Friedman, E. (1995) 'Women's Human Rights: The Emergence of a Movement'. In J. Peters and A. Wolper (eds) *Women's Rights, Human Rights: International Feminist Perspectives*. London: Routledge.

Friedman, E. (2003) 'Gendering the Agenda: The Impact of the Transnational Women's Movement at the UN Conferences of the 1990s'. *Women's Studies International Forum* 26(3): 313–331.

Friedman, T. L. (2004) 'No Dumbo in Davos'. *The New York Times*: 7.

Fuhr, D. (1995) 'Nachlese zur Bäuerinnen-Rente: Änderungen zur Agrarsozialen Gesetzgebung ab 1995'. In *Der kritische Agrarbericht*. Rheda-Wiedenbrück: Arbeitsgemeinschaft Bäuerliche Landwirtschaft.Bauernblatt e.V.

Fukayama, F. (1991) *End of History and the Last Man*. New York: Free Press.

Fukuyama, F. (1998) 'Women and the Evolution of World Politics'. *Foreign Affairs* 77(5): 24–40.

Ganster, P. and Lorey, D. E. (eds) (2005) *Borders and Border Politics in a Globalizing World*. Lanham: SR Books.

Gardam, J. G. and Jarvis, M. J. (2001) *Women, Armed Conflict and International Law*. The Hague: Kluwer Law International.

Gaspar de Alba, A. (2003) 'The Maquiladora Murders, 1993–2003'. *Aztlan: A Journal of Chicano Studies* 28(2): 1–17.

Gibb, H. (1997) *Gender Front and Center: An APEC Primer*. Ottawa: North-South Institute.

Gibb, H. (2002) 'Review of Gender Integration in APEC: Overview'. Ottawa: North-South Institute, September.

Gibb, H. (2004a) 'Supporting Marginalized Women Exporters: An Overview of Issues and Strategies'. APEC Committee on Trade and Investment, September.

Gibb, H. (2004b) 'Speaking Notes for the Gender and Trade Panel', East Block, Parliament Hill, Ottawa, November 5.

Gibbings, S. (2004) 'Governing Women, Governing Security: Governmentality, Gender Mainstreaming and Women's Activism at the UN'. MA Thesis, Anthropology. York University.

Gilbert, C. and Vines, D. (eds) (2000) *The World Bank: Structure and Policies*. New York: Cambridge University Press.

Gill, S. (1995) 'Globalization, Market Civilization, and Disciplinary Neoliberalism'. *Millennium: Journal of International Studies* 24(3): 399–423.

Gill, S. (2002) 'Privatization of the State and Social Reproduction? GATS and New Constitutionalism'. Paper presented at the GATS: Trading Development? International Workshop, Centre for the Study of Globalization and Regionalisation, University of Warwick, 20–21 September.

Gill, S. (2003) *Power and Resistance in the New World Order*. Houndsmill, Basingstoke: Palgrave Macmillan.

Gill, D. and Piper, N. (eds) (2002) *Women and Work in Globalizing Asia*. USA: Routledge.

Gills, B. K. (2001) 'Introduction: Globalization and the Politics of Resistance'. In B. K. Gills (ed.) *Globalization and the Politics of Resistance*. New York: Palgrave, pp. 3–1.

Gilpin, R. (2000) *The Challenge of Global Capitalism: The World Economy in the 21st Century*. Princeton, NJ: Princeton University Press.

Gilpin, R. (2002) 'A Realist Perspective on International Governance'. In D. Held and A. McGrew (eds) *Governing Globalisation: Power Authority and Global Governance*. Cambridge: Cambridge University Press.

Giugale, M., Lafourcade, O. and Nguyen, V. (2001) *Mexico: A Comprehensive Agenda for the New Era*. Washington, DC: World Bank.

Goetschy, J. (2003) 'The European Employment Strategy, Multi-level Governance and Policy Co-ordination: Past, Present and Future'. In J. Zeitlin and D. M. Trubek (eds) *Governing Work and Welfare in a New Economy*. Oxford: Oxford University Press.

Goetz, A. (ed.) (1995) *Getting Institutions Right for Women*. IDS Bulletin 26(3). Sussex: IDS.

Gordon, C. (1991) 'Governmental Rationality: An Introduction'. In G. Burchell, C. Gordon and P. Miller (eds) *The Foucault Effect. Studies in Governmentality*. Hemel: Hempstead, pp. 1–51.

Granovetter, M. (1974) 'The Strength of Weak Ties'. *American Journal of Sociology* 78(6): 1360–1380.

Grugel, J. B. (2004) 'New Regionalism and Modes of Governance – Comparing US and EU Strategies in Latin America'. *European Journal of International Relations* 10(4): 603–626.

Guillen, R. (2003) 'Mujeres Transformando la Economía'. Interview. Cancun, Mexico, September.

Gutierrez, M. (ed.) (2003) *Macro-Economics: Making Gender Matter*. London: Zed Books.

Gutmann, M. (ed.) (2003) *Changing Men and Masculinities in Latin America*. Durham: Duke University Press.

Haahr, J. (2004) 'Open Co-ordination as Advanced Liberal Government'. *Journal of European Public Policy* 11(2): 209–230.

Haahr, J. and Walters, W. (2005) *Governing Europe. Discourse, Governmentality and European Integration*. New York: Routledge.

Haas, E. (1958) *The Uniting of Europe*. Stanford: Stanford University Press.

Hafner-Burton, E. and Pollack, M. (2002) 'Mainstreaming Gender in Global Governance'. *European Journal of International Relations* 8(3): 339–373.

Hall, B. R. and Biersteker, T. J. (eds) (2002) *The Emergence of Private Authority in Global Governance*. Cambridge, UK: Cambridge University Press.

Hamilton, S. (1998) *The Two-Headed Household: Gender and Rural Development in the Ecuadorian Andes*. Pittsburgh: University of Pittsburgh Press.

Hancock, G. (1989) *Lords of Poverty: The Power, Prestige, and Corruption of the International Aid Business*. New York: Atlantic Monthly Press.

Hardt, M. and Negri, A. (2000) *Empire*. Cambridge, MA: Harvard University Press.

Harriss-White, B. (1998) 'Female and Male Grain Marketing Systems, Analytical and Policy Issues for West Africa and India'. In C. Jackson and R. Pearson (eds) *Feminist Visions of Development*. London: Routledge.

Hassanali, S. (2000) 'International Trade: Putting Gender into the Process, Initiatives and Lessons Learned'. Discussion paper prepared for Status of Women Canada.

Hayzer, N. (2003) 'Forward', http://www.accord.org.za/ct/2003-3/foreword.pdf and http://www.peacewomen.org/un/SCOpenDebate2003/Bulgaria2003.pdf.

Hedley, B. (1977) *The Anarchical Society: A Study of Order in World Politics*. New York: Columbia University Press.

Held, D. (2002) 'Cosmopolitanism: Taming Globalization'. In D. Held and A. McGrew (eds) *Governing Globalization: Power, Authority and Global Governance*. Cambridge: Polity.

Held, D. and McGrew, A. (eds) (2002) *Governing Globalization: Power, Authority and Global Governance*. Cambridge: Polity Press.

Hemispheric Social Alliance (2001) *Alternative for the Americas: Towards an Agreement between the Peoples of the Continent*. Second Peoples' Summit. Quebec City, Canada, April. In possession of Debra J. Liebowitz.

Herrera, M. G. (2001) 'Introducción'. In *Antología De Estudios De Género*. Quito: FLASCO-Ecuador/ILDIS, pp. 9–50.

Hewson, M. and Sinclair, T. J. (eds) (1999) *Approaches to Global Governance Theory*, New York, State University of New York Press.

Hilsdon, A., Macintyre, M., Stivens, M. and Mackie, V. (2000) *Human Rights and Gender Politics*. New York: Routledge.

Hocking, B. (2004). 'Changing the Terms of Trade Policy Making: From the "Club" to the "Multistakeholder" Model'. *World Trade Review* 3(1): 3–26.

Hollander, G. M. (1995) 'Agroenvironmental Conflict and World System Theory: Sugarcane in the Everglades Agricultural Area'. *Journal of Rural Studies* 11(3): 309–318.

Holy See (1998) 'Intervention of the Holy See Diplomatic Conference of Plenipotentiaries on the Establishment of An International Criminal Court, Working Group on War Crimes'. http://147.222.27.5/people.dewolf/hs.html. Accessed 14 June 2004.

Hooper, C. (2000) 'Masculinities in Transition: The Case of Globalization'. In M. H. Marchand and A. S. Runyan (eds) *Gender and Global Restructuring: Sightings, Sites and Resistances*. London: Routledge. pp. 59–73.

Hooper, C. (2001) *Manly States: Masculinities, International Relations, and Gender Politics*. New York: Columbia University Press.

Hoskyns, C. (1996) *Integrating Gender: Women, Law and Politics in the European Union*. London: Verso.

Hoskyns, C. (1999) 'Gender and Transnational Democracy: The Case of the European Union'. In M. K. Meyer and E. Prügl (eds) *Gender Politics in Global Governance*. Lanham: Rowman & Littlefield, pp. 72–87.

Hoskyns, C. (2004) 'Mainstreaming Gender in the EU's Macroeconomic Policy. Institutional and Conceptual Issues'. Paper presented to ECPR conference, Bologna, June.

Hoskyns, C. and Rai, S. M. (1998) 'Gender, Class and Representation: India and the European Union'. *European Journal of Women's Studies* 5(3–4): 347–365.

Hoskyns, C. and Rai, S. M (2005) 'Gendering International Political Economy', *CSGR Working Paper No. 170/05*.

Human Rights Watch (1999) *Systemic Injustice: Torture, 'Disappearance,' and Extrajudicial Execution in Mexico*. New York: HRW.

Hunt, A. and Wickham, G. (1994) *Foucault and Law: Towards a Sociology of Law as Governance*. London: Pluto Press.

Huntington, S. (1996) *The Clash or Civilisations and the Remaking of World Order*. New York: Simon and Schuster.

ICC (2003) 'Resolution ICC-ASP/2/Res.8 Recognition of the Coordinating and Facilitating Role of the NGO Coalition for the International Criminal Court'. http://www.iccnow.org/inroduction/ciccbackground.html. Accessed 21 July 2005.

Inder, B. (2004). 'Short-Changing Global Justice'. *The International Criminal Court Monitor*, November.

Inhetveen, H. and Blasche, M. (1983) *Frauen in der kleinbaeuerlichen Landwirtschaft*. Opladen: Westdeutscher Verlag.

Inhetveen, H. and Schmitt, M. (2004) 'Feminization Trends in Agriculture: Theoretical Remarks and Empirical Findings from Germany'. In H. Buller and K. Hoggart (eds) *Women in the European Countryside*. Aldershot, England: Ashgate, pp. 83–102.

Ingraham, C. (2005) 'Introduction'. In *Thinking Straight: The Power, the Promise, and the Paradox of Heterosexuality*. New York: Routledge: pp. 1–11.

Instituto Nacional de las Mujeres (2004) *Compilacion de los principales instrumentos internationals sobre derechos humanos de las mujeres*. Mexico, DF: INMUJER.

International Criminal Court (2002) 'ICC Judges, Facts and Background, Resumes'. http://www.iccnow.org/building the court/judges/statusofnominations/resumes. html. Accessed 6 January 2003.

International Criminal Tribunal for Yugoslavia (2001) *Press Release. Judgment of Trial Chamber II in the Kunarac, Kovac and Vukovic case*. http:www.un.org/icty/pressreal/p566-html. Accessed 6 January 2003.

International Gender and Trade Network (2001–2005) *Monthly Bulletin* Vols 1–5 (May 2001–August 2005). http://www.igtn.org/Bulletins. Accessed 5 June 2004.

International Gender and Trade Network (2003a) *International Gender and Trade Network at Cancun*. WTO Fifth Ministerial Meeting, Cancun, Mexico. IGTN.

International Gender and Trade Network (2003b) *IGTN at Miami: Advocacy Position for the Eighth FTAA Ministerial Meeting*. November 20.

International Gender and Trade Network (2003c) 'History'. IGTN, July 7. http://www.igtn.org/History/history.html.

Jackson, C. (ed.) (2001) *'Men at Work' Men and Work: Labour, Masculinities, Development*. Portland OR: Frank Cass.

Jacobsson, K. and Schmid, H. (2002) 'Real Integration or Just Formal Adaptation? – On the Implementation of the National Action Plans for Employment'. In C. de la Porte and P. Pochet (eds) *Building Social Europe through the Open Method of Co-ordination*. Brussels, Bern, Berlin, Frankfurt/M., New York: Wien, pp. 69–96.

Jacoby, W. (2002) 'Talking the Talk and Walking the Walk: The Cultural and Institutional Effects of Western Models'. In F. Bonker, K. Muller and A. Pickel (eds) *Postcommunist Transformation and the Social Sciences: Cross Disciplinary Approaches*. Lanham, MD: Rowman & Littlefield, pp. 129–152.

Jaggar, A. (1997) 'Love and Knowledge: Emotion in Feminist Epistemology'. In S. Kemp and J. Squires (eds) *Feminisms*. Oxford: Oxford University Press, pp. 188–193.

Jahan, R. (1995) *The Elusive Agenda: Mainstreaming Women in Development*. London: Zed Books.

Jaquette, J. and Wolchik S. L. (eds) (1998) *Women and Democracy: Latin America and Eastern Europe*. Baltimore: Johns Hopkins University Press.

Jayasuriya, K. (ed.) (2004) *Governing the Asia Pacific: Beyond the 'New Regionalism'*. Third World Quarterly Series, Basingstoke: Palgrave Macmillan.

Jessop, B. (2003) 'Changes in Welfare Regimes and the Search for Flexibility and Employability'. In H. Overbeek (ed.) *The Political Economy of European Employment. European Integration and the Transnationalization of the (Un)employment Question*. London/New York: Routledge, pp. 29–50.

Joachim, J. (1999) 'Shaping the Human Rights Agenda: The Case of Violence Against Women'. In M. K. Meyer and E. Prügl (eds) *Gender Politics in Global Governance*. Lanham, MD: Rowman & Littlefield.

Johansson, K. M. (1999) 'Tracing the Employment Title in the Amsterdam Treaty: Uncovering Transnational Coalitions'. *Journal of European Public Policy* 6(1): 85–101.

Johnson, M. (1998). *European Community Trade Policy and the Article 113 Committee*. London: Royal Institute of International Affairs.

Kabeer, N. (2004) 'Globalization, Labor Standards and Women's Rights: Dilemmas of Collective (In)Action in an Interdependent World'. *Feminist Economics* 10(1): 3–35.

Kahler, M. (1995) *International Institutions and the Political Economy of Integration*. Washington DC: Brookings Institution.

Kardam, N. (2004) 'The Emerging Global Gender Equality Regime from Neoliberal and Constructivist Perspectives in International Relations'. *International Feminist Journal of Politics* 6(1): 85–109.

Kartini International, Dana Peebles (2004) *Evaluation of the Women Leader's Network*. La Serena, Chile.

Katz, C. (2003) 'Vagabond Capitalism and the Necessity of Social Reproduction'. In S. Aronowitz and H. Gantrey (eds) *Implicating Empire—Globalisation and Resistance in the 21st Century World Order*. New York: Basic Books, pp. 255–270.

Keane, J. (2003) *Global Civil Society?* Cambridge: Cambridge University Press.

Keating, M. (ed.) (2004) *Gender, Development and Trade*. Oxford: Oxfam.

Keck, M. E. and Sikkink, K. (1998) *Activsts Beyond Borders: Advocacy Networks in International Politics*. Ithaca, NY: Cornell University Press.

Kelly, L. (2005) 'Inside Outsiders: Mainstreaming Violence against Women into Human Rights Discourse and Practice'. *International Feminist Journal of Politics* 7(4): 471–495.

Kelly, R. M., Bayes, J. H., Hawkesworth, M. E. and Young, B. (eds) (2001) *Gender, Globalization, and Democratization*. Lanham, MD: Rowman & Littlefield.

Keohane, R. O. (2005) 'Global Governance and Democratic Accountability'. In R. Wilkinson (ed.) *The Global Governance Reader*. New York: Routledge, pp. 120–138.

Kerr, J. (2001) 'International Trends in Gender Equality Work.' http://www.genderatwork.org/updir/Joanna-internationaltrends.htm. Accessed 13 January 2003.

Kirsch, P. and Oosterveld, V. (2001) 'Negotiating an Institution for the Twenty-First Century: Multilateral Diplomacy and the International Criminal Court'. *McGill Law Journal* 46(4): 1141–1161.

Klein, N. (1999) *No Logo: Money, Marketing, and the Growing Anti-Corporate Movement*. New York: Picador USA.

Klein, N. (2002) *Fences and Windows: Dispatches from the Front Lines of the Globalization Debate*. New York: Picador USA.

Knickel, K. and Seibert, O. (1990) 'Freyung Grafenau Study Area Germany'. In *Agrarian Change and Farm Household Pluriactivity in Europe: Second Research Report for the Commission of the European Communities on Structural Change, Pluriactivity, and the Use Made of Structures Policies by Farm Households in the European Community*. Vol. II: *Study Area Analysis*. The Arkleton Trust (Research) Ltd., pp. 152–172.

Kofman, E., (2000) 'Beyond a Reductionist Analysis of Female Migrants in Global European Cities'. In M. Marchand and A. S. Runyan (eds) *Gender and Global Restructuring*. London: Routledge.

Kolbeck, T. (1990) 'Direktvermarktung—Bedeutung fuer die Baeuerinnen frueher und heute'. In S. Hebenstreit-Mueller and I. Helbrecht-Jordan (eds) *Frauenleben in laendlichen Regionen: Individuelle und strukturelle Wandlungsprozess in der weiblichen Lebenswelt*. Bielefeld: Kleine Verlag GmbH, pp. 143–169.

Kooiman, J. (2003) *Governing as Governance*. London: Sage.

Kopinak, K. (ed.) (2004) *The Social Costs of Industrial Growth in Northern Mexico*. San Diego: US-Mexico Studies, University of California at San Diego.

Kronsell, A. (2006) 'Studying Silences on Gender in Institutions of Hegemonic Masculinity'. In B. Ackerley, M. Stern and J. True (eds) *Feminist Methodologies for International Relations*. Cambridge: Cambridge University Press, pp. 108–128.

Kuiper, E. and Barker, D. (eds) (2006) *Feminist Economics and the World Bank: History, Theory and Policy*. New York: Routledge.

Kyle, D. (2000) *Transnational Peasants: Migrations, Networks, and Ethnicity in Andean Ecuador*. Baltimore: John Hopkins University Press.

Lamarche, L. in collaboration with Bachand, R., Arnaud, A. and Chagnon, R. (2005) *Retaining Employment Equity Measures in Trade Agreements*, February. Ottawa: Status of Women Canada.

Laqueur, T. (1990) *Making Sex: Body and Gender from the Greeks to Freud*. Cambridge: Harvard University Press.

Larner, W. and Walters, W. (eds) (2004a) *Global Governmentality: Governing International Spaces*. London/New York: Routledge.

Larner, W. and Walters, W. (2004b) 'Globalization as Governmentality'. *Alternatives* 29(5): 495–514.

Latham, R. (1999) 'Politics in a Floating World: Toward a Critique of Global Governance'. In M. Hewson and T. J. Sinclair (eds) *Global Governance Theory*. New York: State University of New York Press.

Lee, R. S. (2002) 'An Assessment of the ICC Statute'. *Fordham International Law Journal* 25: 750–766.

Leibfried, S. and Pierson, P. (eds) (2005) *European Social Policy: Between Fragmentation and Integration*. Washington, DC: Brookings Institution.

Lemeke, (2000) Paper presented in the *Rethinking Marxism* Conference, University of Amherst (MA), 21–24 September.

Lemke, T. (1997) *Eine Kritik der politischen Vernunft. Foucaults Analyse der modernen Gouvernementalität*. Hamburg.

Lemke, T. (2000a), 'Foucault, Governmentality, and Critique', http://www.thomaslemkeweb.de/publikationen/Foucault,%20Governmentality,%20and%20Critique%20IV-2.pdf.

Lemke, T. (2000b) 'Neoliberalismus, Staat und Selbsttechnologien. Ein kritischer Überblick über die governmentality studies'. *Politische Vierteljahresschrift* 41(1): 31–47.

Lever, A. G. (2006) 'Women Leaders' Network of APEC: From Call to Action to Our Second Decade'. Presentation at the 11th Women Leaders' Network Meeting, Hanoi, Vietnam.

Levine, P. (2003) *Prostitution, Race, and Politics: Policing Venereal Disease in the British Empire*. New York: Routledge.

Lewis, J. (1992) 'Gender and the Development of Welfare Regimes'. *Journal of European Social Policy* 2(3): 159–173.

Liebowitz, D. J. (2001) 'Constructing Cooperation: Feminist Activism and the North American Free Trade Agreement'. In M. DeKoven (ed.) *Feminist Locations: Global and Local, Theory and Practice*. New Brunswick, NJ: Rutgers University Press.

Liebowitz, D. J. (2002) 'Gendering (Trans)National Advocacy: Tracking the Lollapalooza at "Home"'. *International Feminist Journal of Politics* 4(2): 173–196.

Lifesite (1998) 'International Criminal Court Approved. Lifesite Special report 19 July'. http://www.lifesite.net.ldn/1998/jul/98071b.html. Accessed 10 October 2003.

Lind, A. (2004) 'Engendering Andean Politics: The Paradoxes of Women's Movements in Neoliberal Ecuador and Bolivia'. In J. Burt and P. Mauceri (eds) *Politics in the Andes: Identity, Conflict, Reform*. Pittsburgh: University of Pittsburgh Press, pp. 58–78.

Lisbon European Council (2000) 'Presidency Conclusions'. 23/24 March. Lisbon.

Long, C. (2003) *The Advocate's Guide to Promoting Gender Equality at the World Bank*. Washington DC: Women's Edge.

Long, C. (2006) 'An Assessment of Efforts to Promote Gender Equality at the World Bank'. In E. Kuiper and D. Barker (eds) *Feminist Economics and the World Bank: History, Theory and Policy*. London: Routledge.

MacDonald, L. (2002) 'Globalization and Social Movements: Comparing Women's Movements' Responses to NAFTA in Mexico, the USA and Canada'. *International Feminist Journal of Politics* 4(2): 151–172.

MacKinnon, C. (1994) 'Rape, Genocide, and Women's Human Rights'. *Harvard Women's Law Journal* 17: 5–16.

Mallaby, S. (2004) *The World's Banker: A Story of Failed States, Financial Crises, and the Wealth and Poverty of Nations*. New York: Penguin Press.

Maquieira, C. (2003) 'Discoursodel Representante Alterno de Chile, 'Mujer, Paz y Seguridad' http://www.peacewomen.org/un/SCOpenDebate2003/Chile2003 es.pdf.

March, J. G. and Olsen, J. P. (1989) *Rediscovering Institutions: The Organizational Basis of Politics*. New York: The Free Press.

Marchand, M. H. and Runyan, A. S. (2000) 'Introduction: Feminist Sightings of Global Restructuring: Conceptualizations and Reconceptualizations'. In M. H. Marchand and A. S. Runyan (eds) *Gender and Global Restructuring: Sightings, Sites and Resistances*. New York: Routledge, pp. 1–22.

Marchand, M. H., Boas, M. and Shaw, T. (1999) 'The Political Economy of New Regionalisms'. *Third World Quarterly* 20(5): 897–910.

Martinez, O. (1994) *Border People: Life and Society in the U.S.–Mexico Borderlands*. Tucson: University of Arizona Press.

McBride Stetson, D. (2003) 'The Women's Movement and Welfare Reform in the United States'. Paper presented to panel: Restructuring the State 2nd ECPR Conference, Marburg, Germany, September.

McBride Stetson, D. and Mazur, A. G. (eds) (1995) *Comparative State Feminism*. Thousand Oaks, CA: Sage.

McGrew, A. (2002) 'Liberal Internationalism: Between Realism and Cosmopolitanism'. In D. Held and A. McGrew (eds) *Governing Globalisation: Power Authority and Global Governance*. Cambridge: Cambridge University Press.

McMichael, P. (2000) *Development and Social Change: A Global Perspective* (2nd edition). Thousand Oaks, CA: Pine Force Press.

McMichael, P. (2003) 'Food Security and Social Reproduction: Issues and Contradictions'. In I. Bakker and S. Gill (eds) *Power, Reproduction and Social Reproduction*. Houndsmill: Palgrave Macmillan, pp. 169–189.

Meier, P., Lombardo, E., Bustelo, M. and Maloutas, M. P. (2004) 'Women in Political Decision-making and Gender Mainstreaming: Obvious Partners?'. Paper presented at 2nd Pan-European Conference on EU Politics of the ECPR Standing Group on the EU, Bologna, June.

Meisch, L. (2002) *Andean Entrepreneurs: Otavalo Merchants and Musicians in the Global Arena*. Austin: University of Texas Press.

Melhaus, M. and Stolen K. A. (eds) (1996) *Machos, Mistresses, Madonnas: Contesting the Power of Latin American Gender Imagery*. London: Verso.

Mertus, J. (2004) 'Shouting from the Bottom of the Well: The Impact of International Trials for Wartime Rape on Women's Agency'. *International Feminist Journal of Politics* 6(1): 110–128.

Meyer, M. K. and Prügl, E. (1999) 'Gender Politics in Global Governance'. In M. K. Meyer and E. Prügl (eds) *Gender Politics in Global Governance*. Lanham, MD: Rowman & Littlefield, pp. 1–15.

Meyer, M. K. (1999) 'Negotiating International Norms: The Inter-American Commission of Women and the Convention on Violence against Women'. In M. K. Meyer and E. Prügl (eds) *Gender Politics in Global Governance*. Lanham, MD: Rowman & Littlefield, pp. 58–71.

Mies, M. (1986) *Patriarchy and Accumulation on a World Scale: Women in the International Division of Labour*. London: Zed Books.

Mink, G. (1998) *Welfare's End*. Ithaca, NY: Cornell UP.

Mitter, S. (ed.) (1992) *Computer-Aided Manufacturing and Women's Employment: The Clothing Industry in Four EC Countries*. London: Springer Verlag.

Moghadam, V. (2005) *Globalizing Women: Transnational Feminist Networks*. Baltimore: Johns Hopkins University Press.

Mohan, G. (1996) 'Globalization and Governance: The Paradoxes of Adjustment in Sub-Saharan Africa'. In E. Kofman and G. Youngs (eds) *Globalization: Theory and Practice*. New York: Pinter, pp. 289–303.

Mohanty, C. T. (2003) ' "Under Western Eyes" Revisited: Feminist Solidarity through Anticapitalist Struggles'. *Signs: Journal of Women in Culture and Society* 28: 499–536.

Molyneux M. and Razavi, S. (2005) 'Beijing Plus 10: An Ambivalent Record on Gender Justice'. *Development and Change* 36: 6.

Monarrez Fragoso, J. (2002) 'Feminicidio sexual serial en Ciudad Juarez: 1993–2001'. *Debate Feminista*. 13 April.

Moreno-Ocampo, L. (2004) Address by Prosecutor Luis Moreno-Ocampo to Third Session of the Assembly of State Parties to the Rome Statute of the International Criminal Court, The Hague, September.

Morfin, G. (2004) Comision para Prevenir and Erradicar la Violencia contra las Mujeres en Ciudad Juarez (2004). *Informe de gestion*. Mexico, DF: Secretaria de Gobernacion.

Moser, C. (1993) *Gender Planning and Development: Theory, Practice and Training*. New York: Routledge.

Moser, C. (1996) *Confronting Crisis: A Summary of Household Responses to Poverty and Vulnerability in Four Poor Urban Communities*. Washington DC: Environmentally Sustainable Development Studies and Monographs Series No. 7, World Bank.

Moser, C. (1997) *Household Responses to Poverty and Vulnerability Volume 1: Confronting Crisis in Cisne Dos, Guayaquil, Ecuador*. Urban Management Program Policy Paper 21. Washington DC: World Bank.

Moser, C. (2005) 'Has Gender Mainstreaming Failed?' *International Feminist Journal of Politics* 7(4): 576–590.

Moser, C. and Moser, A. (2005) 'Gender Mainstreaming Beijing + 10: A Desk Review of Successes and Limitations in International Institutions'. *Gender and Development* 13(2): 11–22.

Moshan, B. S. (1998) 'Women, War, and Words: The Gender Component in the Permanent International Criminal Court's Definition of Crimes Against Humanity'. *Fordham International Law Journal* 22: 154–184.

Mosse, D. and Lewis, D. (eds) (2005) *The Aid Effect: Giving and Governing in International Development*. Ann Arbor, MI: Pluto Press.

Murphy, C. (1994) *International Organization and Industrial Change: Global Governance Since 1850*. Cambridge: Polity Press.

Murphy, C. (2000) 'Global Governance: Poorly Done and Poorly Understood'. *International Affairs* 76(4): 789–804.

Nahapetian, K. (1999) 'Selective Justice: Prosecuting Rape in the International Criminal Tribunals for the Former Yugoslavia and Rwanda', *Berkley Women's Law Journal*. 14: 126–135.

Nayyar, D. and Court, J. (2002) *Governing Globalization: Issues and Institutions*. Helsinki: UNU/WIDER.

Negroponte, J. D. (2003) 'On the Implementation of Security Council Resolution 1325 on Women, Peace and Security http://www.peacewomen.org/un/SCOpenDebate2003/USA2003.html.

Newman, C. (2001) *Gender, Time Use, and Change: Impacts of Agricultural Export Employment in Ecuador*. Washington, DC: World Bank.

O'Brien, R., Goetz, A. M., Scholtle, J. A. and Williams, M. (eds) (2000) *Contesting Global Governance: Multilateral Economic Institutions and Global Social Movements*. Cambridge: Cambridge University Press.

Ortiz, A. (2003) 'Urban Development'. In V. Fretes-Cibils, M. M. Giugale and J. R. López-Cálix (eds) *Ecuador: An Economic and Social Agenda in the New Millennium*. Washington, DC: World Bank, pp. 251–264.

Ortiz-Gonzalez, V. (2004) *El Paso: Local Frontier at a Global Crossroads*. Minneapolis: University of Minnesota Press.

Ostheim, T. and Zohlnhöfer, R. (2002) 'Der Einfluss des Luxemburg-Prozesses auf die deutsche Arbeitsmarktpolitik'. *Zentrum für Sozialpolitik*, Bremen, Arbeitspapiere 09.

Ostner, I. and Lewis, J. (1995) 'Geschlechterpolitik zwischen europäischer und nationalstaatlicher Regelung'. In S. Leibfreid and P. Pierson (eds) *Standort Europa. Europäische Sozialpolitik*. Frankfurt/M., pp. 196–239.

Otto, D. (1996) 'Holding Up Half the Sky, But for Whose Benefit?: A Critical Analysis of the Fourth World Conference on Women'. *The Australian Feminist Law Journal* 6: 7–28.

Oxfam (2000) *Tax Havens: Releasing the Hidden Billions for Poverty Eradication*. Oxford: Oxfam GB.

Panich, L. and Gindin, S. (2005) 'Superintending Global Capital'. *New Left Review* 35.

Parpart, J. L., Rai, S. M. and Staudt, K. (eds) (2001) *Rethinking Empowerment. Gender and Development in a Global/Local World*. London: Routledge.

Payne, R. A. and Samhat, N. H. (2004) *Democratizing Global Politics: Discourse Norms, International Regimes, and Political Community*. Albany: State University of New York Press.

Pearson, R. (2004) 'The Social is Political'. In G. Waylen and S. M. Rai, Special issue on Gender, Governance and Globalization, *International Feminist Journal of Politics* 6(4): 603–622.

Peebles, D. (1999) *Women Leader's Network: Future Directions*. Toronto.

Perrons, D. (2003) 'Gender Mainstreaming in European Union Policy. Why Now?' Paper presented to ESRC Gender Mainstreaming Seminar, Leeds, October.

Peterson, V. S. (ed.) (1992) *Gendered States – Feminist (Re)Visions of International Relations Theory*. Boulder and London: Lynne Riener.

Peterson, V. S. (2003) *A Critical Rewriting of Global Political economy: Integrating Reproductive, Productive and Virtual Economies*. New York: Routledge.

Pheko, M. (2002) 'A Commentary on the WSSD from South Africa. *International Gender and Trade Network: Monthly Bulletin* 2 (July) http://www.genderandtrade. net.Accessed 13 January 2003.

Picchio, A. (1992) *Social Reproduction: The Political Economy of the Labour Market*. London: Cambridge University Press.

Picciotto, S. (2003) 'EU Company Taxation: Competition, Coordination, Harmonisation, Integration'. Paper Presented at the Arena Seminar, Oslo University, May.

Pierson, R., Griffin, M., Bourne, P. and Masters, P. (eds) (1993) *Canadian Women's Issues: Volume I—Strong Voices*. Toronto: James Lorimer.

Pietilä, H. (1999) *Engendering the Global Agenda: A Success Story of Women and the United Nations*. INSTRAW Occasional Paper. 1. INSTRAW.

Pincus, J. R. and Winters, J. (eds) (2002) *Reinventing the World Bank*. Ithaca: Cornell UP.

Piper, N. and Uhlin, A. (2003) *Transnational Activism in Asia: Problems of Power and Democracy*. New York: Routledge.

Polanyi, K. (1944) *The Great Transformation: The Political and Economic Origins of Our Time*. Boston: Beacon Press.

Polanyi, K. (1957) *The Great Transformation*. Boston, MA: Beacon Press.

Pollack, M. A. and Hafner-Burton, E. (2000) 'Mainstreaming Gender in the European Union'. *Journal of European Public Policy* 7(3): 432–456.

Pollack, M. A. and Hafner-Burton, E. (2002) 'Mainstreaming Gender in Global Governance'. *European Journal of International Relations* 8(3): 339–373.

Porte, C. d. l. and Pochet, P. (eds) (2002) *Building Social Europe through the Open Method of Co-ordination*. Brussels: Peter Lang.

Portillo, Lourdes. (2001) *Seniorita Extraviada*. http://www.lourdesportillo.com.

Povinelli, E. (2002) *The Cunning of Recognition: Indigenous Alterities and the Making of Australian Multiculturalism*. Durham: Duke University Press.

Prieto, M. *et al.* (2005) *Las mujeres indígenas y la búsqueda del respeto*. In *Mujeres ecuatorianas: Entre las crisis y las oportunidades 1990–2004*. CONAMU/UNIFEM/FLACSO-Ecuador/UNFPA: Quito, pp. 155–196.

Pringle, R. and S. Watson (1990) 'Fathers, Brothers, Mates: The Fraternal State in Australia'. In S. Watson (ed.) *Playing the State, Australian Feminist Interventions*. London, Verso.

P.R.O.D.E.P.I.N.E. (2001) *Documento Básico Y Orientador Sobre El Tema de Género* Quito: P.R.O.D.E.P.I.N.E.

P.R.O.D.E.P.I.N.E. (n.d.) *Sistematización del Primer Congreso de Las Mujeres de la OSG COCIP: Tema: Género y Equidad*. Quito: P.R.O.D.E.P.I.N.E.

Prügl, E. (1999) *The Global Construction of Gender: Home-based Work in the Political Economy of the 20th Century*. New York: Columbia University Press.

Prügl, E. (2004a) 'Gender Orders in German Agriculture: From the Patriarchal Welfare State to Liberal Environmentalism'. *Sociologia Ruralis* 44(4) (October): 349–372.

Prügl, E. (2004b) 'International Institutions and Feminist Politics'. *The Brown Journal of World Affairs* 2: 69–84.

Prügl, E. (2004c) 'From Equal Rights to Gender Mainstreaming: Feminist Politics in German Agriculture'. Paper presented at the 45th Annual Convention of the International Studies Association, Montreal, Canada, March.

Prügl, E. and Lustgarten, A. (2005) 'The Institutional Road Towards Equality: Mainstreaming Gender in International Organizations'. In J. Jaquette and G. Summerfield (eds) *Institutions, Resources and Mobilization: Women and Gender Equity in Development Theory and Practice*. Durham: Duke University Press, pp. 53–70.

Prügl, E and Meyer, M. K. (1999) 'Gender Politics in Global Governance'. In M. K. Meyer and E. Prügl (eds) *Gender Politics in Global Governance*. Lanham, MD: Rowman & Littlefield, pp. 1–15.

Pühl, K. (2001) 'Geschlechterverhältnisse und die Veränderung von Staatlichkeit in Europa. Ansätze eines theoretischen Perspektivenwechsels'. In E. Kreisky, S. Lang and B. Sauer (eds) *EU, Geschlecht, Staat*. Vienna: Facultas Verlags- und Buchhandels AG, WUV/Universitätsverlag, pp. 33–53.

Pühl, K. and Wöhl, S. (2003) 'Model "Doris": A Critique of Neoliberal Gender Politics from a Foucauldian Perspective'. Paper presented at the conference 'Governmentality: Prospects of Michel Foucault'. 2–3 November. Frankfurt/M., Germany. Available at http://www.copyriot.com/gouvernementalitaet.

Rahier, J. M. (2003) 'Racist Stereotypes and the Embodiment of Blackness: Some Narratives of Female Sexuality in Quito'. In N. Whitten, Jr (ed.) *Millennial Ecuador: Critical essays on Cultural Transformations and Social Dynamics*. Iowa City: University of Iowa Press.

Rahmani, L. (2005) 'International Human Rights Law: Gender Mainstreaming in the United Nations Human Rights Treaty Bodies'. PhD Dissertation in Economics. Sydney: University of Sydney.

Rai, S. (1996) 'Women and the State: Issues for Debate'. In S. Rai and G. Lievesley (eds) *Women and the State: International Perspectives*. London: Taylor & Francis.

Rai, S. M. (ed.) (2000) *International Perspectives on Gender and Democratisation*. Basingstoke: Palgrave Macmillan.

Rai, S. M. (2002) *Gender and the Political Economy of Development*. Cambridge: Polity Press.

Rai, S. (ed.) (2003) *Mainstreaming Gender, Democratizing the State? Institutional Mechanisms for the Advancement of Women*. Manchester: Manchester University Press.

Rai, S. (2004) 'Gendering Global Governance'. *International Feminist Journal of Politics* 6(4): 579–601.

Randall, V. and Waylen, G. (eds) (1998) *Gender, Politics, and the State*. London and New York: Routledge.

Ravenhill, J. (2001) *APEC and the Construction of Pacific Rim Regionalism*. Cambridge: Cambridge University Press.

Razavi, S. and Miller, C. (1995) 'Gender Mainstreaming in the World Bank, UNDP and ILO'. Geneva: UNRISD.

REAL Women of Canada (1998) 'The International Criminal Court – World Nightmare'. http://www.realwomenca.com/newsletter/1998_May_Jun/article_9.html. Accessed July 7, 2004.

Rebick, J. (2002) 'Anti-Globalization/Anti-Fundamentalism'. ZNet Commentary (March) http://www.wicej.addr.com/readings/rebick.pdf. Accessed January 13, 2003.

Rees, T. (1998) *Mainstreaming Equality in the European Union*. New York: Routledge.

Rees, T. (2004) 'Reflections on the Uneven Development of Gender Mainstreaming'. Paper presented at ESRC seminar, Gender Mainstreaming: Comparative Analysis, Leeds, May.

Regionales Entwicklungskonzept der LAG '"Landkreis Freyung-Grafenau" – Kurzfassung'. Website of the Landkreis: http://www.freyung-grafenau.de/media/custom/404_392_1.pdf. Accessed March 10, 2006.

Riddell-Dixon, E. (1999) 'Mainstreaming Women's Rights: Problems and Prospects with the Centre for Human Rights'. *Global Governance* 5(2): 149–171.

Riddle, D. (2004) *Supporting APEC SME Service Exporters: A Handbook of Best Practices*. APEC Business Advisory Council (ABAC).

Rieger, E. (1995) *Bauernopfer: Das Elend der Europäischen Agrarpolitik*. Frankfurt: Campus Verlag.

Riley, M. (2001) 'Women's Economic Agenda in the 21st Century'. Occasional Paper Series on Gender, Trade and Development. Center of Concern—Global Women's Project and the International Gender and Trade Network—Secretariat.

Rippberger, S. and Staudt, K. (2003) *Pledging Allegiance: Learning Nationalism in El Paso-Juarez*. New York: Routledge/Falmer.

Robertson, G. (2000) *Crimes Against Humanity: The Struggle for Global Justice*. Melbourne: Penguin.

Rodrigues, M. J. (ed.) (2002) *The New Knowledge Economy in Europe*. Chaltenham: Northhampton.

Rodriguez, V. (2003) *Women in Contemporary Mexican Politics*. Austin: University of Texas Press.

Rome Statute for the International Criminal Court (1998) Un Doc. A/Conf. 183/9.

Romero, M. and Yellen, T. (2004) *El Paso Portraits: Women's Lives, Potential & Opportunities: A Report on the State of Women in El Paso, Texas*. El Paso: YWCA.

Rose, N. (1999) *Powers of Freedom: Reframing Political Thought.* New York: Cambridge University Press.

Rose, N. (2000) *Powers of Freedom: Reframing Political Thought.* Cambridge: Cambridge University Press.

Rosenau, J. (1992) *Governance Without Government: Order and Change in World Politics.* In J. Rosenau and E-O. Czempial (eds) Cambridge: Cambridge University Press, pp. 3–6.

Rosenau, J. N. (1995) 'Governance in the Twenty-First Century'. *Global Governance* 1: 13–43.

Rosenau, J. N. (2003) *Distant Proximities: Dynamics beyond Globalization.* Princeton, NJ: Princeton University Press.

Rosenau, J. N. and Czempiel, E. O. (eds) (2000) *Governance without Government: Order and Change in World Politics.* Cambridge: Cambridge University Press.

Ross, A. (ed.) (1997) *No Sweat: Fashion, Free Trade and the Rights of Garment Workers.* London: Verso.

Rossilli, M. (ed.) (2000) *Gender Policies in the European Union.* New York: Peter Lang.

Roth, B. (2006) 'Gender Inequality and Feminist Activism in Institutions: Challenges of Marginalization and Feminist "Fading"'. In L. Chappell and L. Hill (eds) *The Politics of Women's Interests: New Feminist Perspectives.* Routledge: UK.

Rubery, J. (2002) 'Gender Mainstreaming and Gender Equality in the EU: The Impact of the EU Employment Strategy'. *Industrial Relations Journal* 33(5): 500–522.

Rubery, J. (2004). 'Gender Mainstreaming and Women's Employability in EU Countries'. Paper presented to ECE regional seminar, January.

Rubery, J. (2005). 'Reflections on Gender Mainstreaming: An Example of Feminist Economics in Action?'. *Feminist Economics* 11(3): 1–26.

Rubery, J. *et al.* (1998) *Women and European Employment.* London/New York: Routledge.

Rueschemeyer, D., Huber, E. and Stephens, J. D. (1992) *Capitalist Development and Democracy.* Cambridge: Polity Press.

Ruggie, J. (1982) 'International Regimes, Transactions and Change: Embedded Liberalism in the Post-war Economic Order'. *International Organization* 36(2): 379–416.

Ruggie, J. G. (ed.) (1993) *Multilateralism Matters: The Theory and Praxis of an Institutional Form.* New York: Columbia University Press.

Ruggie, J. G. (1998) *Constructing the World Polity: Essays on International Institutionalization.* New York: Routledge.

Runyan, A. S. (1996) 'The Places of Women in Trading Places: Gendered Global/Regional Regimes and Inter-nationalized Feminist Resistance'. In E. Kofman and G. Youngs (eds) *Globalization: Theory and Practice.* New York: Pinter.

Runyan, A. S. (1999) 'Women in the Neoliberal "Frame"'. In E. Prügl and M. K. Meyer (eds) *Gender Politics in Global Governance.* Lanham, MD: Rowman & Littlefield, pp. 210–220.

Runyan, A. S. (2002) 'Stop Trading Away Women's Lives: A Conversation with Marceline White, Senior Policy Associate, Women's Edge, Washington, DC'. *International Feminist Journal of Politics* 4(2): 261–267.

Rupp, L. J. (1997) *Worlds of Women: The Making of an International Women's Movement.* Princeton, NJ: Princeton University Press.

Ruppert, M. (2000) *Ideologies of Globalisation. Contending Visions of a New World Order*. London: New York.

Sainsbury, D. (ed.) (1999) *Gender and Welfare State Regimes*. Oxford: Oxford University Press.

Sargent, L. (ed.) (1979) *Women and Revolution: A Discussion of the Unhappy Marriage of Marxism and Feminism*. Boston: South End Press.

Sargent, L. (1981) *Women and Revolution: A Discussion of the Unhappy Marriage of Marxism and Feminism*. Boston: South End Press.

Schense, J. (2004) 'Prosecutor's Office Gears Up for Investigations'. *The International Criminal Court Monitor* February.

Schild, V. (2003) 'Die Freiheit der Frauen und gesellschaftlicher Fortschritt: Feministinnen, der Staat und die Armen bei der Schaffung neoliberaler Gouvernementalität'. *Peripherie* 23(19): 481–506.

Scholte, J. A. (2000) *Globalisation: A Critical Introduction*. Basingstoke: Palgrave Macmillan.

Scholte, J. A. (2002) 'Civil Society and Democracy in Global Governance'. *Global Governance* 8(3): 281–304.

Schunter-Kleemann, S. (1992) 'Wohlfahrtsstaat und Patriarchat – Ein Vergleich europaeischer Laender'. In S. Schunter-Kleemann (ed.) *Herrenhaus Europa – Geschlechterverhaeltnisse im Wohlfahrsstaat*. Berlin: Ed. Sigma, pp. 141–327.

Schunter-Kleemann, S. (1995) ' "Bei der Bäuerin wird gespart". Aspekte der Lebenssituation von Landfrauen in vier europäischen Ländern'. *Berliner Journal für Soziologie* 5(2): 191–206.

Schunter-Kleemann, S. (2003) 'Was ist neoliberal am Gender Mainstreaming?' *Widerspruch (Hg.): Feminismus, Gender, Geschlecht* 23(44): 19–34.

Seager, J. (1997) *The State of Women in the World Atlas*. 2nd revised edition. Harmondsworth, UK: Penguin Books.

Sen, A. (1990) 'Gender and Cooperative Conflicts'. In I. Tinker (ed.) *Persistent Inequalities: Women and World Development*. New York: Oxford University Press, pp. 123–161.

Shaw, M. (1997) 'The State of Globalization: Towards a Theory of State Transformation'. *Review of International Political Economy* 4(3): 497–513.

Shaw, J. (2001) 'European Union Governance and the Question of Gender: A Critical Comment'. http://www.jeanmonnetprogramme.org.papers.

Shiva, V. (1999) *Stolen Harvest: The Hijacking of the Global Food Supply*. Cambridge, MA: South End Press.

Siaroff, A. (1994) 'Work, Welfare and Gender Equality: A New Typology'. In D. Sainsbury (ed.) *Gendering Welfare States*. London: Sage, pp. 82–100.

Sikka, P. (2003) 'How about Responsible Taxes?' *Guardian 17 November*.

Sinclair, T. J. (2004) *Global Governance: Critical Concepts in Political Science*, Volumes I—IV. London: Routledge.

Slatter, C. (2003) 'Beyond the Theory–Practice–Activism Divide'. Paper presented at workshop on Gender and Globalization in Asia and the Pacific: Feminist Revisions of the International. January 13.

Slaughter, A. (2004) *A New World Order*. Princeton: Princeton University Press.

Smith, A. M. (2001) 'The Politicization of Marriage in Contemporary American Public Policy: The Defense of Marriage Act and the Personal Responsibility Act'. *Citizenship Studies* 5(3): 303–320.

Smith, J., Chatfield, C. and Pagnucco, R. (eds) (1997) *Transnational Social Movements and Global Politics: Solidarity Beyond the State*. Syracuse, NY: Syracuse University Press.

Soesastro, H. (1998) 'Open Regionalism'. In H. Maull, G. Segal and J. Wanandi (eds) *Europe and the Asia Pacific*. London: Routledge, pp. 84–96.

Soesastro, H. (2003) 'APEC's Overall Goals and Objectives, Evolution, and Current Status'. In R. E. Feinberg (ed.) *APEC as an institution*. Singapore: Institute of Southeast Asian Studies, pp. 29–45.

Spatafora, M. 'Women, Peace and Security, Statement to the Security Council of the United Nations'. Permanent Representative of Italy, to the UN, on behalf of the European Union. http://www.peacewomen.org/un/SCOpenDebate2003/EU2003.pdf.

Spener, D. and Staudt K. (eds) (1998) *The U.S.–Mexico Border: Transcending Divisions, Contesting Identities*. Boulder, CO: Lynne Rienner Press.

Squires, J. (2005) 'Is Mainstreaming Transformative? Theorizing Mainstreaming in the Context of Diversity and Deliberation'. *Social Politics* Fall: 366–388.

Stallabrass, J. (2006) 'Spectacle and Terror'. *New Left Review* 37 (January–February).

Standing, G. (1989) 'Global Feminization through Flexible Labor'. *World Development* 17(7): 1077–1095.

Staudt, K. (1998) *Free Trade? Informal Economies at the U.S.–Mexico Border*. Philadelphia: Temple University Press.

Staudt, K. (2002) 'Dismantling the Master's House with the Master's Tools? Gender Work in and with Powerful Bureaucracies'. In K. Saunders (ed.) *Feminist Post Development Thought: Rethinking Modernity, Post Colonialism and Representation*. London: Zed Press, pp. 57–68.

Staudt, K. (2003) 'Gender Mainstreaming: Conceptual Links to Institutional Machineries'. In S. M. Rai (ed.) *Mainstreaming Gender, Democratizing the State? Institutional Mechanisms for the Advancement of Women*. Manchester: Manchester University Press.

Staudt, K. and Beatriz, V. (2005) 'Women, Public Policy, and Politics: The Global Crossroads of Juarez-El Paso'. *Region y Sociedad*.

Staudt, K. and Coronado, I. (2002) *Fronteras No Mas: Toward Social Justice at the U.S.–Mexico Border*. New York: Palgrave USA.

Staudt, K. and Coronado, I. (2005a) 'Civic Action for Accountability: Anti-Violence Organizing in Juarez-El Paso'. In D. Shirk (ed.) *Reforming the Administration of Justice in Mexico*. El Colegio de Mexico: Notre Dame University Press (in Spanish).

Staudt, K. and Coronado, I. (2005b) 'Resistance and *Compromiso* at the Global Frontlines: Gender Wars at the U.S.–Mexico Border'. In C. Eschle and B. Maiguashca (eds) *Critical Theories, World Politics, and the Anti-Globalisation Movement*. London: Routledge.

Staudt, K. and Spener, D. (1998) 'The View from the Frontier: Theoretical Perspectives Undisciplined'. In D. Spener and K. Staudt (eds) *The U.S.–Mexico Border: Transcending Divisions, Contesting Identities*. Boulder, CO: Lynne Rienner Press, pp. 3–34.

Staudt, K. and Vera, B. (2006) 'Mujeres, politics públicas y política: los caminos globales de Juárez-El Paso'. *Región y Sociedad*, XVIII, 37, 127–172.

Sternbach, N. S., Navarro-Aranguren, M., Chuchryk, P. and Alvarez, S. E. (1992) 'Feminisms in Latin America: From Bogotá to San Bernardo'. In A. Escobar and

S. E. Alvarez (eds) *The Making of Social Movements in Latin America: Identity, Strategy, and Democracy*. Boulder, CO: Westview Press, pp. 207–239.

Stienstra, D. (1994) *Women's Movements and International Organizations*. New York: St Martin's Press.

Strange, S. (1995) 'The Defective State'. *Daedalus, Journal of the American Academy of Arts and Sciences* Spring.

Stratigaki, M. (2005) 'Gender Mainstreaming versus Positive Action: An On-going Conflict in the EU Gender Equality Policy'. *European Journal of Women's Studies* 12(2): 165–186.

Symington, A. (2002) 'Globalization on Our Terms: A Time for Radical Action'. In *Re-Inventing Globalization: Highlights of AWID's 9th International Forum on Women's Rights in Development*. Guadalajara, Mexico 3–6 October 2002, pp. 10–11. Toronto, Canada: Association for Women's Rights in Development.

Symington, A. (2003) E-mail communication, November.

Tambiah, Y. (ed.) (2002) *Women and Governance in South Asia: Re-Imagining State*. Colombo: International Centre for Ethnic Studies.

Tarrow, S. (1998) *Power in Movement: Social Movements and Contentious Politics*. 2nd edition. Cambridge: Cambridge University Press.

Tarrow, S. (2005) *The New Transnational Activism*. Cambridge: Cambridge University Press.

Tax Justice Network (2005). *Tax Us If You Can: The True Story of a Global Failure*. London: Tax Justice Network.

Taylor, V. (2000) 'Marketisation of Governance: Critical Feminist Perspectives from the South'. DAWN. http://www.DAWN.org/publications.

Teague, P. (1989) *The European Community: The Social Dimension*. London: Kogan Page.

Teightsoonian, K. (2004) 'Neoliberalism and Gender Analysis Mainstreaming in Aotearoa/New Zealand'. *Australian Journal of Political Science* 39(2): 267–284.

Teipel, B. (1996) *Der landwirtschaftliche Betrieb im Güterrecht des BGB*. Frankfurt/Main: Peter Lang.

Terry, J. (1999) *An American Obsession: Science, Medicine, and Homosexuality in Modern Society*. Chicago: University of Chicago Press.

Terraviva (editorial) (1998) 'Who's Obstructionist? Arabs Ask'. *Terraviva. The Conference Daily Newspaper*. http://www.ips.org.iss/tv020703.htm. Accessed November 2, 2003.

Threlfall, M. (2002). 'The European Employment Strategy and Guidelines: Towards an All-Working Society?' Paper presented to workshop, Loughborough University, April.

Thomas, L. (2002) 'Interview with Naomi Klein'. *Feminist Review* 70: 46–56.

Tiano, S. (1994) *Patriarchy on the Line: Labor, Gender and Ideology in the Mexican Maquila Industry*. Philadelphia: Temple University Press.

Tidow, S. (1999) 'Benchmarking als Leitidee: Zum Verlust des Politischen in der europäischen Perspektive'. *Blätter für Deutsche und Internationale Politik* 3: 301–309.

Tong, R. P. (1998) *Feminist Thought: A More Comprehensive Introduction*. Boulder, CO: Westview.

Trubek, D. M. and Mosher, J. S. (2003) 'New Governance, Employment Policy and the European Social Model'. In J. Zeitlin and D. M. Trubek (eds) *Governing Work and Welfare in a New Economy*. Oxford: Oxford University Press.

True, J. (2003) 'Mainstreaming Gender in Global Public Policy'. *International Feminist Journal of Politics* 5(3): 465–490.

True, J and Mintrom, M. (2001) 'Transnational Networks and Policy Diffusion: The Case of Gender Mainstreaming'. *International Studies Quarterly* 45(1): 27–57.

Truong, T.-D. (2000) 'A Feminist Perspective on the Asian Miracle and Crisis: Enlarging the Conceptual Map of Human Development'. *Journal of Human Development* 1(1): 159–164.

Tzannatos, Z. (2006) 'The World Bank, Development, Adjustment and Gender Equality'. In E. Kuiper and D. Barker (eds) *Feminist Economics and the World Bank: History, Theory and Policy*. London: Routledge.

UNCTAD Secretariat and United Nations (2004) *China's Accession to the WTO: Challenges for Women*. New York: United Nations Development Programme.

United Nations (2000) *Press Release, GA/9725*. 10 June 2000.

United Nations (2002) 'A/CONF.199/20*'. In *Report of the World Summit on Sustainable Development*, Johannesburg, South Africa, August 26–September 4.

United Nations Commission on Global Governance (1995) *Our Global Neighbourhood*, The Commission on Global Governance. Oxford University Press.

United Nations Development Fund for Women (UNIFEM) (2000) *Progress of the World's Women 2000*. New York: UNIFEM.

United Nations Development Programme (1995) *Human Development Report*. New York: Oxford University Press.

United Nations Development Programme (1996) *Human Development Report*. New York: Oxford University Press.

United Nations General Assembly (2000) *Report of the Ad Hoc Committee of the Whole of the Twenty-Third Special Session of the General Assembly*. In *A/S-23/10/Rev.1* Supplement No. 3. Twenty-Third Special Session.

United Nations General Assembly Security Council (2001) 'Report of the Secretary-General on the Work of the Organization: Prevention of Armed Conflict' (S/2001/574) 7 June. http://daccessdds.un.org/doc/UNDOC/GEN/N01/404/64/PDF/N0140464.pdf?OpenElement. Accessed September 12, 2007.

United Nations Inter-Agency Network on Women and Gender Equality Task Force on Gender and Trade. *Trade and Gender: Opportunities, Challenges and the Policy Dimension*. New York and Geneva.

United Nations Millennium Development Goals. 'Goal 8: Develop a Global Partnership for Development'. http://www.un.org/millenniumgoals/.

United Nations SC/6816, Anwarul, C. (2000) 'Peace Inextricably Linked with Equality between Women and Men says Security Council, in International Women's Day Statement'. Security Council press release 8 March. http://www.un.org/womenwatch/news/articles/chowdhuryiwd00.htm.

United Nations Security Council (2000) 'Resolution 1325' (S/2000/1325). 31 October.

United States Senate (1993) 'Congressional Record: 103rd Congress, Debate on the Steven's Amendment to the NAFTA Implementing Legislation'. November 19.

Uzendoski, M. (2003) 'Purgatory, Protestantism, and Peonage: Napo Runa Evangelicals and the Domestication of the Masculine Will'. In N. Whitten (ed.) *Millennial Ecuador: Critical Essays on Cultural Transformations and Social Dynamics*. Iowa City: University of Iowa Press, pp. 129–153.

Valverde, M. (1998) *Diseases of the Will: Alcohol and the Dilemmas of Freedom*. New York: Cambridge University Press.

Van Staveren, I. (2001) 'Global Finance and Gender'. In J. A. Scholte (ed.) *Civil Society and Global Finance*. New York: Routledge.

Van Staveren, I. (2007) 'Gender Indicators for Monitoring Trade Agreements'. WIDE Briefing Paper. Brussels.

Velasquez, C. (2000) *Memoria Del Taller De Políticas Públicas Y Equidad Entre Hombres Y Mujeres, Peguche*. Quito: P.R.O.D.E.P.I.N.E.

Verloo, M. (2002) 'The Development of Gender Mainstreaming as a Political Concept for Europe'. Paper presented at the Conference on Gender Learning, Leipzig, September 6–8.

Vila, P. (ed.) (2003) *Ethnography at the Border*. Minneapolis: University of Minnesota Press.

Walby, S. (2005a) 'Comparative Gender Mainstreaming in a Global Era'. *International Feminist Journal of Politics* 7(4): 453–470.

Walby, S. (2005b) 'Gender Mainstreaming: Productive Tensions in Theory and Practice'. *Social Politics* Fall: 321–343.

Warbrick, C. and McGoldrick, D. (2001) 'The Preparatory Commission for the International Criminal Court' Current Developments: Public International Law'. *International and Comparative Law Quarterly* 50: 420–435.

Ward, K. (ed.) (1990) *Women Workers and Global Restructuring*. Ithaca, NY: ILR Press.

Ward, N. and Almås, R. (1997) 'Explaining Change in the International Agro-Food System'. *Review of International Political Economy* 4(Winter): 611–629.

Waring, M. (1988). *If Women Counted: A New Feminist Economics*. San Francisco: Harper and Row.

Washington Valdez, D. (2002) 'Death Stalks the Border'. June (also in Spanish). http://www.elpasotimes.com/borderdeath.

Waylen, G. (2004) 'Putting Governance into the Gendered Political Economy of Globalization'. *International Feminist Journal of Politics* 6(4): 557–578.

Waylen, G. (2006a) ' "You Still Don't Understand": Why Troubled Engagements Continue between Feminists and (Critical) IPE'. *Review of International Studies* 32(1): 145–164.

Waylen, G. (2006b) 'Constitutional Engineering: What prospects for the Enhancement of Gender Rights?' *Third World Quarterly* 27: 7.

Waylen, G. (2007) *Engendering Transitions*. Oxford: Oxford University Press.

Waylen, G. and Rai, S. M. (2004) ' "Preface" to special issue on Gender, Governance and Globalization'. *International Feminist Journal of Politics* 6(4): 1–7.

WEDO. (1999) 'WEDO Primer: Women and Trade'. Women's Environment and Development Organization. http://www.wedo.org/global/wedo_primer.htm.

Weiss, T. G. (2005) 'Governance, Good Governance, and Global Governance: Conceptual and Actual Challenges'. In R. Wilkinson (ed.) *The Global Governance Reader*. New York: Routledge, pp. 68–88.

Weldon, S. (2006) 'Inclusion, Solidarity and Social Movements: The Global Movement against Gender Violence'. *Perspectives on Politics* 4(1): 55–74.

West, L. A. (1999) 'The United Nations Women's Conferences and Feminist Politics'. In M. K. Meyer and E. Prügl (eds) *Gender Politics in Global Governance*. Lanham, MD: Rowman & Littlefield, pp. 177–193.

Whatmore, S. (1991) *Farming Women: Gender, Work and Family Enterprise*. Houndmills, UK: Macmillan Academic and Professional Ltd.

White, M. (n.d.) 'Making Trade Work for Women: Opportunities and Obstacles', reference material. Available at http://www.womensedge.org/pages/referencematerials/reference_material.jsp?id=169.

White, M. (2000) Senior Policy Associate, Women's EDGE. Interview. Washington, DC, January 13.

Whitworth, S. (1994) *Feminism and International Relations: Towards a Political Economy of Gender in Interstate and Non-Governmental Institutions*. New York: St. Martin's Press.

Wichterich, C. (2000) *The Globalized Woman: Reports from a Future of Inequality*. London.

Wilkinson, R. (2005) 'Introduction: Concepts and Issues in Global Governance'. In R. Wilkinson (ed.) *Global Governance Reader*. London: Routledge.

Williams, M. (2003) *Gender Mainstreaming in the Multilateral Trading System*. London: Commonwealth Secretariat.

Wilson, A. (2004) *The Intimate Economies of Bangkok: Tomboys, Tycoons, and Avon Ladies in the Global City*. Berkeley: University of California Press.

Winkler, N. (1990) 'Die Frau in der bayerischen Landwirtschaft'. *Bayern in Zahlen* 44(2): 60–64.

Wöhl, S. (2003) 'Individualisierende Verantwortungszuschreibungen in der Sozialpolitik. Perspektiven des Gouvernementalitätsansatzes von Michel Foucault'. In Institut für Sozialforschung (ed.) *Mitteilungen*. Frankfurt/M.: Heft 14, pp. 120–146.

Women's Caucus for Gender Justice (WCGJ) (1999) 'Excluding Crimes against Women from the ICC is not an Option'. http//www:iccwomen.addr.com/reports.marpaneleng.htm. Accessed June 16, 2004.

Women's Caucus for Gender Justice (WCGJ) (2000) *Recommendations and Commentary to the Elements Annex and Rules of Procedure and Evidence*. Submitted to the Preparatory Commission for the International Criminal Court 12–30 June 2000. http:www.iccwomen.org/icc/iccpc062000pc/elementsannex.html. Accessed October 2, 2002.

Women's Environment and Development Organization (WEDO) (1999) 'WEDO Primer: Women and Trade'. http://www.wedo.org/global/wedo_primer.htm.

Women's Initiatives for Gender Justice (2006) 'Three Women Elected to the Bench of the ICC'. http://www.iccwomen.org/.Accessed March 13, 2006.

Women's International Coalition for Economic Justice (2000) 'North Shares Responsibility for Slow Progress in Beijing+5!' http://www.whrnet.org/beijing/responsability.htm. Accessed June 28, 2000.

Women's Rights Action Network Australia (2005) Australian NGO Shadow Report on the Implementation of the Convention on the Elimination of All forms of Discrimination Against Women (CEDAW). October (with the endorsement of 103 organisations).

Wong, R. (2001) *History of the Women Leader's Network*. CIDA and Kartini International.

Wood, C. A. (2003) 'Adjustment with a Woman's Face: Gender and Macroeconomic Policy at the World Bank'. In S. E. Eckstein and T. Wickham-Crowley (eds) *Struggles for Social Rights in Latin America*. New York: Routledge, pp. 209–230.

Woods, N. (2002) 'Global Governance and the Role of Institutions'. In D. Held and A. McGrew (eds) *Governing Globalization: Power, Authority and Global Governance*. Cambridge: Polity Press.

World Bank (1992) *Governance and Development*. Washington, DC: World Bank.

World Bank (1994) *Enhancing Women's Participation in Economic Development: A World Bank Policy Paper*. Washington, DC: World Bank.

World Bank (1996) *Ecuador Poverty Report: A World Bank Country Study*. Washington, DC: World Bank.

World Bank (2000a) *Advancing Gender Equality: World Bank Action since Beijing*. Washington, DC: World Bank.

World Bank (2000b) *Précis: Evaluating Gender and Development at the World Bank*. Operations Evaluation Department. Washington, DC: World Bank.

World Bank (2001) *Engendering Development through Gender Equality in Rights, Resources, and Voice*. Washington, DC: World Bank/Oxford University Press.

World Bank (2002a) 'Building Institutions for Markets'. http://econ.worldbank.org/wdr/WDR2002.

World Bank (2002b) *Integrating Gender into the World Bank's Work: A Strategy for Action*. Washington, DC: World Bank.

World Bank (2006a) *World Bank Group: Working Toward a World Free of Poverty*. Washington, DC: World Bank.

World Bank (2006b) 'Gender Equality as Smart Economics, World Bank Gender Action Plan, Sept'. http://siteresources.worldbank.org/INTGENDER/Resources/GAPNov2.pdf.

World Commission on the Social Dimension of Globalization (2004) *A Fair Globalization: Creating Opportunities for All*. Geneva, Switzerland: International Labour Organization.

World Economic Forum. n/d 'About us'. http://www.weforum.org/site/ home public.nsf/Content/About+the+Forum+Subhome. Accessed June 2, 2004.

Worth, J. R. (2004) 'Globalization and the Myth of Absolute Sovereignty: Reconsidering the "Un-signing" of the Rome Statute and the Legacy of Senator Bricker'. *Indiana Law Journal* 79: 245–265.

Xinhua News Agency (2003) ' "Black list" of Anti-globalization Activists Denounced before Cancun Meeting'. August 27.

Yanz, L. (1996) 'Mujer a Mujer, Canada and Maquila Solidarity Network'. Toronto, October 9.

Yeoh, B. S. A., Teo, P. and Huang, S. (eds) (2002) *Gender Politics in the Asia-Pacific Region: Women's Agencies and Activisms*. New York: Routledge.

Young, B. (2001a) 'Geschlechterpolitik und disziplinierender Neoliberalismus in der Europäischen Union'. In H.-J. Bieling and J. Steinhilber (eds) *Die Konfiguration Europas. Dimensionen einer kritischen Integrationstheorie*, Münster, pp. 131–161.

Young, B. (2001b) 'Globalization and Gender: A European Perspective'. In R. M. Kelly, J. Bates, M. E. Hawkesworth and B. Young (eds) *Gender, Globalization, and Democratization*. Lanham, MD: Rowman & Littlefield, pp. 27–47.

Young, B. (2003a) 'Financial Crises and Social Reproduction: Asia, Argentina and Brazil'. In I. Bakker and S. Gill (eds) *Power, Production, and Social Reproduction: Human In/security in the Global Political Economy*. New York: Palgrave, pp. 103–123.

Young, B. (2003b) 'Economic and Monetary Union, Employment and Gender Politics: A Feminist Constructivist Analysis of Neo-liberal Labour-Market Restructuring in Europe'. In H. Overbeek (ed.) *The Political Economy of European Employment. European Integration and the Transnationalization of the (Un)employment Question.* London/New York: Routledge, pp. 99–112.

Young, B. and Hoppe, H. (2003). *The Doha Development Round, Gender and Social Reproduction.* Berlin: Friedrich Ebert Stiftung.

Yunus, M. (1994) 'Preface: Redefining Development'. In K. Danaher (ed.) *50 Years Is Enough.* Boston: South End Press.

Zein-Elabdin, E. (2003) 'The Difficulty of a Feminist Economics'. In D. K. Barker and E. Kuiper (eds) *Toward a Feminist Philosophy of Economics.* New York: Routledge.

Zhang, Y. (2003) 'Whither APEC after Cancun and Bangkok? Regionalism on Trial'. Paper prepared for a joint international conference by the Shanghai Institute of International Studies and the New Zealand Asia Institute, Shanghai, December.

Ziche, J. and Wörl, A. (1991) 'Situation der Bäuerin in Bayern'. *Landwirtschaftliches Jahrbuch* 68(6): 659–728.

Zuckerman, E. and Qing, W. (2003) *Reforming the World Bank: Will the New Gender Strategy Make a Difference? A Study With China Case Examples.* Washington, DC: Heinrich Boll Foundation/Gender Action.

Zuckerman, E. and Qing, W. (2005) *Reforming the World Bank? Will the Gender Strategy Make a Difference A Study With Chinese Examples*, 2nd edition. Washington, DC: Heinrich Boll Foundation/Gender Action.

Index

In this index appendices and notes are indicated in italics, enclosed in parenthesis, following the page number. E.g. Arria Formula, 204(n.8)

Notes are indicated by n. Appendices by app. Works (books, documents, plays etc.) are entered in italics.